Z 116 .A2 G27 1972
Gaskell, Philip.
A new introduction to
  bibliography

7-13-89

D0207604

A New Introduction to Bibliography

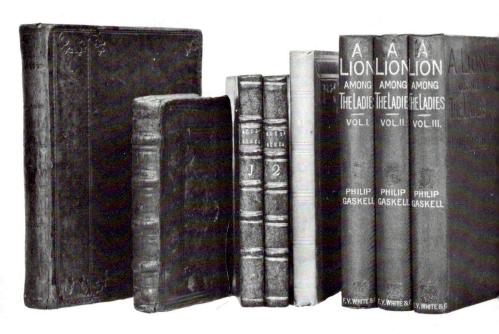

Books as material objects: English trade bindings of *c.* 1580 (front left, S.T.C. 21574), of *c.* 1670 (back left, Wing W818, etc.), and of *c.* 1760 (the third edition of *Rasselas*); with Tennyson's *Maud*, 1855, and a three-decker of 1888 in publishers' cloth.

A New Introduction to Bibliography

PHILIP GASKELL

1972

OXFORD UNIVERSITY PRESS

NEW YORK & OXFORD

D. HIDEN RAMSEY LIBRARY
U.N.C. AT ASHEVILLE
ASHEVILLE, N. C. 28804

98

COPYRIGHT © 1972 BY OXFORD UNIVERSITY PRESS, INC.
LIBRARY OF CONGRESS CATALOGUE CARD NUMBER: 72-90032
PRINTED IN THE UNITED STATES OF AMERICA

To Don McKenzie
in friendship and admiration

Preface

FOR more than forty years R. B. McKerrow's *An introduction to bibliography for literary students* has been the only adequate exposition of its subject. McKerrow's purpose was to show how the transmission of texts —especially the literary texts of Elizabethan and Jacobean England— might be affected by the processes of printing, and he succeeded brilliantly in doing so. His style was lucid and engaging, and his experience both as an amateur printer and as an editor of sixteenth- and seventeenth-century literature fitted him exactly for the task. The result is a classic of scholarship.

In the years since 1928 (when McKerrow's book took its final form) new generations of scholars have discovered many details of printing history that were then unknown, so that McKerrow is to this extent out of date. Furthermore, an increasing majority of investigators are concerned today with the textual problems of the eighteenth, nineteenth, and twentieth centuries and, although McKerrow remains a fair guide up to about 1800, he did not attempt to describe the technology of the machine-press period.

This *New introduction*, therefore, follows McKerrow in aiming to elucidate the transmission of texts by explaining the processes of book production, but in addition it incorporates work done since McKerrow's day on the history of the printing technology of the hand-press period, and it attempts for the first time to give a general description of the printing practice of the machine-press period. It is a new book, not a revision of McKerrow, and it necessarily breaks a good deal of new ground. Little has yet been published about the techniques and routines of nineteenth- and twentieth-century book-production, and there are bound to be both errors and gaps in a first survey. But someone has to make a start, and I hope that what I have done will encourage others to correct the errors and fill the gaps.

Many friends have generously given help already. Before starting I discussed the plan of the book with Fredson Bowers, Harry Carter, the late Herbert Davis, David Foxon, Charlton Hinman, D. F. McKenzie, and Desmond Neill. Then Giles Barber, David Foxon, D. F. McKenzie, James Mosley, Howard Nixon, Jacques Rychner, the late Allan Stevenson, G. Thomas Tanselle, and Michael Turner read certain sections of the book as they were written and supplied me with many valuable comments and corrections for which I am deeply grateful; similarly Harry Carter read the whole work in its near-final form, and made a number of important suggestions for its improvement. And there are those whom I have pestered from time to time over the past four years, and who have patiently answered my importunity: all those I have mentioned already, and in addition L. A. Beaurline, W. H. Bond (who let me see the late W. A. Jackson's bibliographical notebook), Pat Bradford, Nina Burgis, Jackson Burke, John Carter, Matthew Carter, David Fleeman, Elizabeth Harris, André Jammes, R. A. Leigh, A. N. L. Munby, Simon Nowell-Smith, W. G. Rawlings, Richard Sayce, W. B. Todd, H. D. L. Vervliet, Jeanne Veyrin-Forrer, and Leon Voet (who showed me the manuscript of part of volume 2 of *The golden compasses*).

All this may suggest that the book was written by a committee. It was not; and those who helped me are not responsible for its faults. Nevertheless my debts are real, and I particularly want to thank David Foxon for his illuminating commentary on the final sections, and D. F. McKenzie for his encouragement throughout. Don McKenzie's enthusiasm and scholarship, though projected half way round the world, have been my constant support; and I am proud to dedicate this book to him, who was once my pupil.

PHILIP GASKELL

Trinity College, Cambridge
1967–1972

Preface to the Second Impression

MOST of the additions and corrections which are incorporated in this second impression have been given me by generous correspondents. They are Iain Bain, Nicolas Barker, Warner Barnes, Terry Belanger, Peter Blayney, R. H. Carnie, John Carter, John R. Hetherington, John Joliffe, James Moran, J. S. G. Simmons, G. Thomas Tanselle, Geoffrey Wakeman, Franklin B. Williams Jr., and W. P. Williams. I do thank them all most warmly.

There are numerous minor alterations, corrections of misprints, and additions to the bibliography; together with the following more substantial changes: p. 9, fig. 1(*b*), caption. P. 14, nn. 8a, 10, leading and the bourgeois size (Dr. Belanger). P. 15, modern use of old type-size names (Dr. Belanger). Pp. 16–33, section on type faces, corrections of detail (Mr. Barker). P. 35, n. 23a, upper and lower case (Mr. Hetherington). P. 39, n. 36a, equipment

(Mr. Joliffe). P. 40, n. 3a, layout. P. 45, justification of short lines (Mr. Moran). P. 51, n. 33a, signature conventions (Mr. Blayney). P. 52, colophons (Mr. Hetherington). P. 58, fig. 26, caption, one deckle, not two. Pp. 82–3, 106, quiring, especially in quarto (Mr. Hetherington). P. 115, n. 30a, author's proofs. P. 117, page-for-page reprints (Mr. Hetherington). P. 131, order of printing the reiteration (Professor Tanselle). P. 142, purchase of paper (Mr. Barker, Dr. Belanger). P. 148, wooden boards (Mr. Hetherington); n. 5a, cutting (Mr. Barker). P. 152, longitudinal labels (Mr. Carter). P. 156, n. 6, rolling press (Mr. Barker). P. 168, shared printing (Mr. Blayney). P. 173, n. 8, file copies (Professor Carnie). P. 180, n. 38a, sixteenth-century provincial presses. P. 181, printing for the author. P. 183, advertisements (Dr. Belanger). P. 184, authorship and copyright (Dr. Belanger). P. 196, signatures in Newton. P. 204, n. 8, dry flong (Mr. Hetherington); n. 10, stereo corrections (Mr. Barker). P. 234, stabbing (Mr. Barker). P. 235, n. 9a, gold blocking (Mr. Carter). P. 237, collating marks (Mr. F. B. Williams). P. 245, n. 16a, canvas bindings (Mr. Hetherington). P. 249, non-woven covering materials (Mr. Moran). P. 260, folding machines and sheet-work (Mr. Barker). P. 267, steeling copperplates (Mr. Bain, Mr. Wakeman). P. 279, n. 12a, kernless Monotype founts (Mr. Barker). P. 314, n. 1a, interchangeable Monotype founts. P. 318, old- and new-style dating. P. 339, author's expectations; n. 5, author's punctuation.

Some reviewers argued that I concentrated too much on the technical processes of printing, while dealing inadequately with bibliographical applications. I accept this, and I hope to be able to put the balance right in a major revision (especially of the last section) in a few years' time. I am unrepentant of my fondness for writing A1^a, f. 23^b, etc., rather than A1^r, f. 23^v, etc., if only because this has been the common usage of incunabulists for the past 150 years; but there is much to be said for the more usual superior ^{r} and ^{v}, and those who prefer this form will doubtless continue to use it.

PHILIP GASKELL

Trinity College, Cambridge
1 June 1973

Acknowledgements

GRATEFUL acknowledgement is made for permission to reproduce copyright material and photographs belonging to the Bodleian Library (figs. 137-8), the British Museum (fig. 140), Cambridge University Library (figs. 22-3, 84-109), the Clarendon Press (figs. 17(b), 20; Appendix A), Edward Towgood & Son (fig. 79), the Pennsylvania Historical Society (fig. 66), Joh. Enschedé en Zonen (figs. 3(b), 6, 15(a)), the Plantin-Moretus Museum (figs. 9(a), 65), the St. Bride Library (fig. 21), the Victoria and Albert Museum (figs. 134-6, 139, 141), Mr. C. C. Dickens (figs. 133-5); and to the Bibliographical Society and to the authors of the extracts in Appendix B.

Contents

Contents

Contents

B

Contents

List of Figures

List of Figures

Note on Production

THE format of this book is metric royal 8vo. It has been set in
Monophoto Ehrhardt: 11 on 12½ pt. for the text, 10 on 11 pt.
for small type in the text and for appendixes, and 8 on 9 pt. for
the footnotes. The keyboard operator worked from the author's
unedited typescript. Dyeline slip proofs, followed by dyeline
page proofs, were corrected successively by the reading department and by the author. The English 'edition' of the book was
printed by offset-litho on a Mann Perfector, in a sheet size of
1272 × 960 mm., on Crusade Coated Cartridge 100 g/m² paper,
from Ozasol P3 positive process presensitized plates. It was
folded on a Camco S.C.3 for B.F.M.P. imposition E. The sewing was done in 16-page sections on a Smyth No. 12. The cases
were made from Winterbottom Winchester Buckram 135 J Plain
and 0·080 in. Dutch grey board, blocked in gold foil. The
rounding-and-backing, double-lining, casing-in, and pressing
were carried out on a Smyth continuous line. A set of duplicate
negatives was sent to New York for the American 'edition'.

The American 'edition' of the book was printed from negative working
presensitized plates by photo offset lithography on a Harris Single, in a
sheet size of 49 x 74 in., on basis 50 lb. Warren Decision Opaque paper. It
was folded on a Dexter N Quad. The sewing was done in 32-page
signatures on a Smyth No. 12. The cases were made from Holliston
Payko and .088 Binders board, stamped in anodized aluminum foil. The
rounding-and-backing, single-lining, casing-in, and building-in were
carried out on a Kolbus continuous line.

A New Introduction to Bibliography

Introduction

To students of literature and history, bibliography means primarily the study of books as material objects. To this Sir Walter Greg appended a further definition, calling bibliography the science of the transmission of literary documents; and by transmission he meant not only the genealogy and relationship of variant texts, but also the evolution of particular texts in the processes of their production and reproduction.[1]

This implies, as Greg himself insisted, that the chief purpose of bibliography is to serve the production and distribution of accurate texts. Book lists can be useful, the study of early book production is a contribution to history, but bibliography's overriding responsibility must be to determine a text in its most accurate form.

There is no reason to confine bibliography to literary documents. All documents, manuscript and printed, are the bibliographer's province; and it may be added that the aims and procedures of bibliography apply not only to written and printed books but also to any document, disc, tape, or film where reproduction is involved and variant versions may result.

Here we shall be chiefly concerned with the transmission of documents as printed books. Bibliography can help us to identify printed books and to describe them; to judge the relationship between variant texts and to assess their relative authority; and, where the text is defective, to guess at what the author meant us to read. Plainly it is a basic tool for editors, whose aim is to provide modern readers with accurate and comprehensible versions of what their authors wrote. But librarians, too, aim to hand on texts, by caring for the books in their keeping and making them available; and to do this effectively—to know what they have got—they too must use the techniques of bibliography.

Bibliographers, like other scholars, have to be able to think logically, to judge critically, and to persevere in tediously repetitive tasks; but in addition they must understand the history of book production. The study of printed books as material objects and the right interpretation of the printed documents of the past will be based primarily on a knowledge of how authors' manuscripts were transcribed in type, printed, distributed, and sold; and it is with the history of book production that the greater part of this manual is concerned.

[1] Greg, W. W., *Collected papers*, Oxford 1966, pp. 75-88, 207-25, 239-66.

The historical account is arranged in two main parts, dealing with book production before and after 1800 respectively; and within these parts are sections concerning particular aspects of printing technology and procedure, arranged so that subdivisions of the subject may be referred to separately. There is then a third main part which explains how an understanding of the history of book production may be used in approaching problems of identification, description, and the establishment of the text.

THE MAIN PERIODS OF BOOK PRODUCTION

Broadly speaking the history of printing technology may be divided into two periods, the hand-press period and the machine-press period, separated by developments which took place soon after the beginning of the nineteenth century. Throughout both these main periods printing was based on the technique of pressing sheets of paper on to movable metal types which had been inked, and the chief differences between them derived from the fact that the productivity of powered printing machinery, and later of powered composing machinery, was vastly greater than that of the earlier hand processes.

It is likely that for some years after the invention of printing in the mid fifteenth century the techniques of the new craft underwent experiment and at least minor change. Little is known, however, about the methods of Gutenberg and his immediate successors, and we cannot be sure when their techniques settled into the forms that were to be maintained with remarkably little change for the rest of the hand-press period. Nevertheless it is clear that experiment was over by the year 1500, and it will be convenient to take the hand-press period as referring here to the sixteenth, seventeenth, and eighteenth centuries, a time of such technical stability in European printing that it may be described all together. The machine-press period can then be said to encompass the whole of the nineteenth century, and the first half of the twentieth up to about 1950, since when Gutenberg's central invention, movable alphabetic metal type, has begun to be superseded by new methods which dispense with metal altogether.

For the whole of both periods, from 1500 to 1950, the process of printing has consisted essentially of assembling metal types of letters of the alphabet into words, lines, and pages; arranging groups of pages of type into patterns and fixing them into portable metal frames; inking the surface of the type pages (or sometimes, in the later hand-press and in the machine-press period, of replicas of the type pages); pressing sheets of paper on to them, one group of pages for each side of the sheet; and finally ordering the printed sheets ready for folding and sewing into books.

BOOK PRODUCTION
THE HAND-PRESS PERIOD
1500-1800

The Hand-printed Book

PRINTING types are representations in reverse of letters of the alphabet, cast in relief on the ends of rectangular lead-alloy stalks about 24 mm. high. In a printing house of the hand-press period alphabets of type were kept in cases, wooden trays divided into many separate compartments with a supply of letters of the same sort in each compartment. The workman who assembled the type for a book, the compositor, set up his manuscript (or printed) copy on his case and picked up the letters he wanted one by one with his right hand. He set them up in a small tray called a composing-stick held in his left hand, and he separated each word with spaces, short pieces of blank type. Each line, as it was completed, was made to come to an even margin by the alteration of the amount of space between the words, a process known as justification. When the composing-stick, which could accommodate several lines of type, was full he transferred its contents on to another tray called a galley, large enough to hold a whole page of type; and when he had set enough for a page he tied it round with string and put it aside, and proceeded to set the next one.

Books were not printed leaf by leaf, but on large sheets of paper with a number of pages on each side, which were later folded and cut at the edges to make a group, or section, of leaves; books usually consisted of several such sections sewn together at the back. So the compositor set enough pages for a whole sheet, and arranged those that were to go on each side of it in a special order, and fixed them in a pair of iron frames (chases), one for each side; this process was known as imposition, and the two chases with their pages of type locked in and ready for printing were called formes.

Trial prints (proofs) of the formes were then made, and compared with the copy from which they had been set. Errors were marked on the proof by a corrector (and sometimes by the author as well) and the marked proofs were used by the compositor as a guide in correcting the type.

Next the formes were placed in turn on the printing press, the hand-powered machine which was used to press sheets of paper on to the inked surface of the type-pages. It consisted of a wooden frame; a screw which, worked by a handle, forced a flat impression surface (the platen) down towards the type; and a movable carriage upon which type and paper were run in under the platen for printing, and then out again so that the type could be re-inked and a fresh piece of paper inserted. It was normally worked by two pressmen. One fitted a sheet of paper into a frame hinged to the back of the carriage, folded it down on to the type, ran the carriage under the platen with a small windlass, and pulled the bar which turned the screw and pressed the paper on to the type; then reversed these operations and changed the paper. Meanwhile the other man got the ink ready—it was simply a black oil paint—and dabbed it over the face of the type when the press was open. Having worked through their heap of paper and probably printed as many sheets on one side as there were to be books in the edition, the pressmen turned it over, changed the forme, and printed the other side in the same way.

So the setting and printing went on, sheet by sheet, until all were finished. Then the warehouseman arranged all the heaps of printed sheets in order on a bench, and took one sheet from each heap in turn, until at the end he had collected a copy of the whole book in sheets; and so on, copy by copy, until all the sheets were used up. Later the books were delivered to the binder, who folded up each sheet, sewed them together into individual volumes, and covered the volumes with paper or leather.

Printing houses of this period were of various sizes. A few were great establishments with ten or more presses, run by masters of discrimination and learning, but many were poky little shops with one, two, or three presses (and eight or ten workmen in all) with masters lacking all but the most rudimentary skills. Balzac, who had been a printer himself, describes at the beginning of *Illusions perdues* a provincial French printing house of a type common enough in eighteenth-century Europe: 'The whole of the ground floor was one large room, lit by an old-fashioned window looking onto the street and by a large sash-window giving onto an enclosed yard. It was in fact possible to get to the master's office by a passage at the side, but in the country the processes of printing always provoke such lively curiosity that the customers preferred to go in by a glazed door set in the shop-front and giving onto the street, even though this meant going down some steps, the floor of the workshop being below road-level. These gaping sightseers never took account of the difficulties of going through the shop. If they stared up at the arbour of sheets of paper hanging from the cords attached to the ceiling, they bumped into composing frames or knocked their hats off on the iron bars which braced the presses. If they were watching the nimble movements of a compositor as he gathered the types from the hundred and fifty-two boxes of his case, reading his copy, rereading the line in his stick as he slipped in a lead, they would run into a ream of wetted paper weighted down with paving stones, or knock their hips against the corner of a bench; all this to the great amusement of the 'monkeys' and 'bears' [compositors and pressmen]. No one ever arrived without some mishap at the two large cages at the far end of that gloomy room (which projected like a pair of wretched pavilions in the courtyard), the foreman being ensconced in one of them and the master-printer in the other.' This master, with his three creaking presses and his 2,100 kg. of worn type, was an ex-pressman who, although illiterate, could 'estimate the price of a page or a sheet at a glance for any size of type. He would persuade his ignorant customers that large type cost more to pick up than small; or, if it was small they wanted, that small type was more awkward to handle.'[1]

Inspection of a book printed during the hand-press period demonstrates the result of these methods. A typical opening of the book shows two pages of text, the type somewhat old-fashioned in design and with the unfamiliar long ſ, often heavily impressed into a rough-looking paper. At the top of each page there is usually a headline, sometimes with a running (i.e. re-curring) title reading across from the left-hand page of the opening (the verso) to the right-hand page (the recto), sometimes with a separate heading or title on each page; and at the outer ends of the headlines are the page numbers. Other layouts were occasionally used, but the arrangement de-scribed here was much the most common. In the sixteenth century many printers numbered the leaves (foliation) rather than the pages (pagination).

At the bottom of each page there is an extra line below the text, mostly blank but with the catchword (the first word of the next page) at its end; it is called the direction line. The top and bottom of the book are known as the head and tail respectively, and the front (away from the back, or spine) is the fore-edge;[1a] similarly the margins round the type on each page are called the head, tail, outer (at the fore-edge), and inner margins.

A closer inspection of the folds at the inner margins of successive open-ings (which should be carried out delicately so as to avoid damage to the binding) will reveal the sewing; and it may be seen that one or more pairs of leaves, joined to each other at the back, are held in place by a double stitch of thread running up the fold. The groups of leaves thus sewn to-gether are known as gatherings, and each gathering will consist of one or more pairs of leaves joined at the back (they are called conjugate pairs), and will have been made from one folded sheet, or a fraction of a sheet, or from several folded sheets tucked one inside another (quired). Each gathering is identified by means of a signature—it is generally a letter or letters of the alphabet—placed in the direction line of its first recto and often repeated on subsequent rectos, the order of the gatherings being indicated by the alphabetical order of the signatures. As a rule the main signature series begins at the start of the text of the book, but in front of this are certain preliminary leaves or gatherings, such as the title-page (which may be preceded by a half-title), dedication, preface, table of

[1] Balzac, H. de, *La comédie humaine*, Pleiade ed. vol. iv, Paris 1952, pp. 469–70, 466, translated.
[1a] Binders rhyme fore-edge with porridge.

contents, etc. (The preliminaries were not included in the main signature series of new books because it was usual to print them last; reprints, however, sometimes began the main signature series at the beginning of the preliminaries.) The printer may identify himself, and record the place and date of printing, on the title-page by means of an imprint, or at the end of the book in a colophon.

Next the paper should be considered. It will be hand-made, rough-surfaced compared with modern book papers, and off-white in colour. If it is held up to the light it will show as watermarks a pattern of broad-spaced lines (chain lines) crossed by lines that are close together (wire lines), and some of the leaves may also contain a watermarked picture or legend. The edges of the leaves may have been trimmed smooth by the binder, or left rough (uncut); it may even be that they are still joined together at the folded edges (unopened).

Finally, the binding. Working from the inside outwards, there will probably be one or two leaves of blank paper at each end of the book, which are of a different colour or texture from the printed leaves; these are the endpapers, which were added by the binder. There may also be strips of printed waste, or even of vellum cut from manuscripts, used by the binder in securing the spine of the volume. Next come the boards, the stiff upper and lower covers that were made in early days of wood, then of pasteboard and finally of millboard, with a paper paste-down inside, and covered on the outside with leather or rough paper. Various skins were used for leather bindings—calf, goat, and sheep were the commonest —and the surface was often decorated with heated brass tools, either using gold leaf (gilt) or plain (blind). In bindings of the later hand-press period the title of the book was tooled on the spine, though an early book may also have the title written on the fore-edge in ink—a relic of the time when it was placed on the shelf the other way round.

Next we consider the making of the hand-printed book in detail; and begin with Gutenberg's central invention: printing type.

Printing type

MANUFACTURE[1]

Printing types, three-dimensional representations of letters of the alphabet reversed left to right, were cast in an alloy of lead, antimony, and tin called type-metal; it was hard enough to wear well yet had a low melting point, and it neither shrank nor expanded when it cooled. The over-all height of each piece of type, called its height to paper, varied in the sixteenth century from printer to printer and even from fount to fount, being at first in the range 24·0–27·5 mm.;[2] thereafter standardization gradually took place. National standard heights began to emerge during the eighteenth century

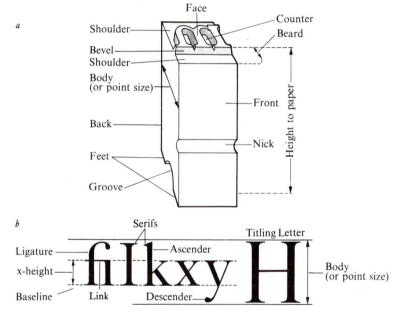

FIG. 1 (*a*). A piece of type and the names of its parts. The chief purpose of the nick, which could take various forms and could even (in France) be placed on the back of the letter, was to indicate the orientation of the face; it also helped to identify the fount to which a piece of type belonged (based on B.S. 2961: 1958).

1 (*b*). The names of the parts of impressions from type (based on B.S. 2961: 1958); the serifs in this example are bracketed. The first British Standard calls the ligature a 'logotype' and the link a 'ligature', but there are objections to the use of logotype (which has other meanings) in this sense.

[1] The best modern account is in Carter, H., *A view of early typography*, Oxford 1969, ch. 1.
[2] Audin, M., *Les types lyonnais primitifs*, Paris 1955.

but it was not until the end of the nineteenth century that any international type standards were established.

In order to accommodate alphabets of different sizes, types were made in different bodies; and, because letters of the same alphabet varied in width, types of the same body varied likewise. A group of type-cast alphabets and other symbols such as points and figures all of one body and design was called a fount, each variety (or sort) of type being supplied in approximate proportion to its frequency of use.

From the early days of printing, founts of type were cast in a wide variety of bodies and designs (or faces). Outsize faces, requiring bodies of up to 80 mm. were either cut individually in wood or metal, or were cast in sand from wooden or metal patterns, but most faces were intended to be cast in hand moulds on bodies in the range 3-15 mm.; and all, gothics and romans alike, were made in the same way. First a relief pattern of each letter was cut by hand on the end of a steel punch some 45 mm. long. The punches were then hammered into small blocks of copper (matrices); and each matrix was carefully trimmed so that the bottom of the impression of the punch was square to the sides and bottom of the block and was set at the right depth from its top surface. (This trimming of the matrices was called justification, a term also used for an entirely different process in typesetting.)

When a fount of type was to be cast, each matrix in turn was fixed in the mould, a steel box made in two parts, clad in wood for insulation and ease of handling. The type-caster put the two halves of the mould together, complete with the first matrix, and held them thus in his left hand, while with his right he lifted a ladle-full of molten type-metal. He then dropped the metal suddenly into the mouth of the mould, and at the same instant gave it a jerk or toss to force the metal into the recesses of the matrix (the precise form of the jerk varying with the different letters); the rest of the metal from the ladle filled the rectangular shaft between the two parts of the mould, and all of it solidified almost immediately. Next the caster laid down his ladle, removed the spring which held the matrix in place, touched the matrix with his thumb in order to loosen the type, opened the mould, and with one of the two iron picks attached to the upper part of it ejected the new letter on to the casting table. Visitors would laugh at the workman's jerking and whirling with the mould, but that was where the skill lay; a hand caster could turn out some 4,000 types a day (which is one every 10-12 seconds), but only the best men could avoid a high proportion of imperfections in that number.

When enough letters of a sort had been cast, the breaks—the jets of metal from the mouth of the mould—were snapped off by another workman, the flat surfaces of the shank were rubbed smooth, and the feet of the types

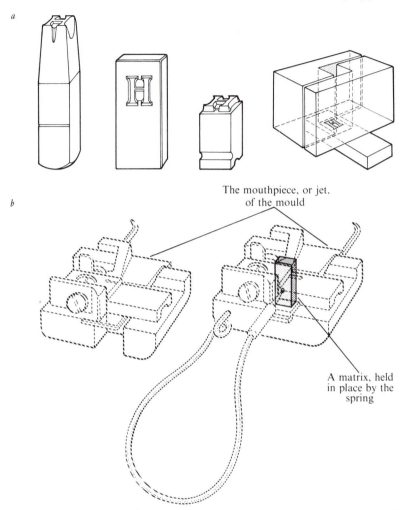

The mouthpiece, or jet,
of the mould

A matrix, held
in place by the
spring

FIG. 2 (*a*). Punch, matrix, and type; and the principle of the hand mould shown schematically.

2 (*b*). The two halves of the hand mould.

were planed to remove traces of the jet; finally, the type faces were inspected for defects, and the sort was wrapped up in a packet for delivery. The caster meanwhile had substituted another matrix for the first and carried on, the mould being self-adjusting for the widths of the various letters of the fount.

There were never more than a handful of punch-cutters at work at a time during the hand-press period. Very few engravers commanded the necessary artistry, and in any case the trade did not require endless sets of closely similar punches, for each set of punches could make many sets of matrices.

In the earliest days of printing one or two printers may have cut their own punches, but even then most punch-cutters appear to have been specialist engravers such as die-sinkers or goldsmiths; and by the later fifteenth century punch-cutters were independent professionals, cutting sets of punches to order for particular printers or, increasingly, striking matrices from punches which remained their own property and selling justified matrices (or unjustified 'strikes') to the printers. From then until the later sixteenth century there was much trade in matrices, though not yet in cast type. The printer would own several sets of matrices and moulds of various sizes, and would employ specialist casters to make type for him with them, using his own metal. Printers thus financed and organized the production of type by independent craftsmen, but did not actually make it themselves.[3]

During the 1560s and 1570s type-founding began to evolve as a separate trade offering a finished product—cast type—to the printers, who would generally have found it more economical than the earlier system. The cost of the equipment for a fairly small type foundry was about three times the cost of the equipment for a printing house of average size; and printers were chronically short of capital. During this period three great specialist foundries were begun which set the trade on the course it was to follow until the end of the eighteenth century: they were the Guyot-Plantin foundry in Antwerp; the Egenolff-Sabon-Berner-Luther foundry in Frankfurt, hub of the European book trade; and the Le Bé foundry in Paris. These foundries bought up the best available materials and employed the finest punch-cutters; and by the early seventeenth century a growing majority of printers throughout Europe were buying type ready made, rather than having it cast from their own materials.[4]

TYPE SIZES; AND DESCRIPTION

There was from an early stage a tendency towards the standardization of type sizes. This may have arisen originally from the difficulty of altering the gauge of the mould, which could be used for casting different sets of matrices to the same body, but there was also an obvious convenience to the printer in being able to set different founts (of gothic and roman, for instance) alongside each other, and of using the same spacing material for several founts. At all events, when printers owned matrices they often had different founts cast on to the same body, very likely in the same mould, and at the same time punch-cutters produced faces that fitted comfortably on particular bodies. Later, when specialist type-foundries were casting

[3] Carter, H., op. cit., chs. 1, 5.   [4] Carter, H., op. cit., ch. 5.

founts for sale, it was to everybody's convenience that standard type sizes should be evolved and identified by name, and this is what happened during the early and middle sixteenth century.

Not that the standardization of type-sizes ever became complete or invariable during the hand-press period. Individual printing communities developed their own series of sizes, and the international trade in matrices and type led to a proliferation of standards. Thus in England three or four sizes of type were identified by name in the mid sixteenth century; by the later seventeenth century, English printers were naming ten or eleven different sizes; by the end of the eighteenth century the number had risen to about eighteen.[5] Body-sizes were no more than approximately constant: founders or printers might want to bring one body into line with another, or to cast a face on to a body other than the one for which it had been intended; and every one of ten supposedly standard bodies measured by Moxon in 1683 had changed slightly in size when they were remeasured by Smith for his *Printer's grammar* of 1755.[6] As to face sizes, the punch cutter could vary the proportions of his design, especially in the relationship of x-height to ascenders and descenders, so that a face cut by one man for a particular body might appear larger or smaller than a similar face cut by someone else for the same body, if indeed it did not actually differ in its over-all dimensions.

Nevertheless there were approximate standards in type-sizes, and they should be referred to in descriptions of early type. The full description of a type of the hand-press period will if possible include both its original designation (e.g. 'Pica roman. Caslon No. 2') and measurements made from its printed image of the apparent sizes of its body and face.

To take the measurements first, the apparent sizes of body and face will not be exactly the same as were the actual sizes of the original metal type. Type was thrust deep into roughish paper which had been softened by damping; the impression blurred at the edges as the type sank in, and then changed in size as the paper dried and shrank. (Paper shrinkage, which was more pronounced across the chain-lines than along them, generally reduced its dimensions by about 1 per cent, and occasionally by as much as $2\frac{1}{2}$ per cent.)[7] The apparent body-size is taken by measuring twenty lines of the type vertically, several times over on different pages if possible, and the answer is given to the nearest millimetre.[8] The distance is measured

[5] Gray, G. K., and Palmer, W. M., *Abstracts from the wills . . . of printers . . . of Cambridge from 1504 to 1699*, London 1915, pp. 70-1; Moxon, J., *Mechanick exercises*, eds. Davis, H., and Carter, H., 2nd ed., Oxford 1962, pp. 19-21; Smith, J., *The printer's grammar*, London 1755, p. 19.

[6] Moxon, J., op. cit., p. 21; Smith, J., op. cit., p. 26.

[7] This is from my own observation; I do not know that any systematic investigation of paper-shrinkage has been made.

[8] It would be possible to use typographical points, which are small units of linear measure, rather

from a given point in a line to the corresponding point in the twenty-first line above or below; if less than twenty lines are available for measurement, a smaller number is used and the answer is converted to the twenty-line standard. It is important to make sure that the lines measured are set solid, that is to say without interlinear leads, the thin strips of typemetal, wood, or card that could be slipped in between each line of type.[8a] This can usually be established by finding a place where the descender from a letter such as g or p comes down immediately above an ascender rising from the line below; provided that the gap between them is 0·5 mm. or less (up to 1 mm. in the case of very large type) the lines are probably set solid, but if it is wider they are either leaded or printed from a fount cast on an oversize body. (It may be mentioned in this connection that titling capitals were generally cast full on the body, with no room for a matching set of small letters with descenders; see fig. 1 (b).)

The apparent body-size having been dealt with, the apparent size of the face is measured directly with a finely graduated scale and a magnifying glass. The vertical distance in millimetres is taken between the top of an ascender and the bottom of a neighbouring descender and is multiplied by 20: this gives the approximate 20-line measurement of the *minimum* body on which the face could be cast, not allowing for overhangs; it is often slightly less than the apparent body-size of a fount. Then the x-height and the capital height are measured in millimetres and the result is presented in the form: '[face height × 20] × [x-height]: [capital height]'. The measurements of the apparent size of a typical pica roman might then read: 'Body 82. Face 80 × 1·7: 2·5'.[9]

Once the apparent size of a fount is known it should be possible to discover its intended standard size by reference to the following table of the nine bodies most commonly used during the hand-press period. It gives the actual sizes as cast in Plantin's shop in Antwerp in the later sixteenth century, the sizes as measured by Moxon in 1683 and Smith in 1755, and the range of apparent sizes found in European and American printing of the seventeenth and eighteenth centuries, together with their names in English,[10] French, and Dutch.

The final stage in the description of an early type involves the identifica-

than millimetres, for measuring the apparent sizes of early type; but it is better to keep points for the measurement of type in the metal.

[8a] If none of the type being measured appears to be set solid one has to be content with measuring the apparent size of the face alone.

[9] Adapted from a system introduced by H. D. L. Vervliet in his edition of *The type specimen of the Vatican Press 1628*, Amsterdam 1967.

[10] Pica rhymes with Leica, primer with trimmer, and brevier with revere; nonpareil is pronounced 'nónprul'. Bourgeois, a body size between brevier and long primer introduced in the eighteenth century, is pronounced to rhyme with rejoice.

TABLE 1: *Names and Body-sizes of Text Types in the Hand-press Period*

English name	Dutch name	French name	20-line measurements in mm.			Range of apparent sizes, 1600–1800
			Plantin, late 16th century	Moxon 1683	Smith 1755	
double pica	ascendonica	gros parangon	140	160	147	139–60
great primer	text	gros romain	117	122	119	116–22
english	Augustyn	St. Augustin	94	92	95	91–5
pica	mediaan	cicéro	79	81	85	79–85
small pica	descendiaan	philosophie	72	—	74	70–4
long primer	garamond	petit romain	66	66	68	65–9
brevier	brevier	petit texte	53	54·5	54	52–6
nonpareil	nonpareil	nonpareille	40	41	43	40–3
pearl	peerl	perle	—	33	34	33–4

The term pica is still used occasionally for the Anglo-American 12-pt. body, and *cicéro* for the Didot 12-pt. body, although they are only approximately equal. There are similar parallels for the other bodies: great primer (etc.) for 18-pt.; english for 14-pt.; long primer for 10-pt.; brevier for 8-pt., and so on.

SOURCES: *Inventory of the Plantin–Moretus Museum punches and matrices*, Antwerp 1960; Voet, L., *The golden compasses*, ii; Moxon, J., *Mechanick exercises*, London 1683; Smith, J., *The printer's grammar*, London 1755; Hart, H., *Notes on a century of typography*, Oxford 1900; Gaskell, P., 'Type sizes in the eighteenth century', *Studies in bibliography*, v, 1952–3, pp. 147–51; type-founders' specimens.

tion of its face, a task that is often difficult and sometimes impossible. A brief guide to the general development of type design follows in the next section, but for the identification of particular faces it will be necessary to refer to early founders' and printers' type-specimens (see the reference bibliography, pp. 396–7). Even when the relevant specimens are available, difficulty may be caused by the facts that sets of punches might be revised, touched up, or added to during their long lives (a surprising amount of early-sixteenth-century type-founding material survives in working order today), and that the appearance of a face could be altered by differences in the width[11] of the bodies on which it was cast; two founts cast at different times from different sets of matrices may not be obviously of the same face even though both derive from the same basic set of punches. But only too often the right specimen cannot be found, and it is better to admit ignorance or uncertainty than to make a mis-identification.

TYPE FACES

If the body-sizes of early types were numerous, the faces cast on them were legion. It is not practicable to offer more than a general guide to them here, but even the broad classification of type faces has its problems, both because there is no generally agreed scheme for arranging the various letter forms found in type, and because the forms have to be classified in several ways

TABLE 2: *The Classification of Type Faces*

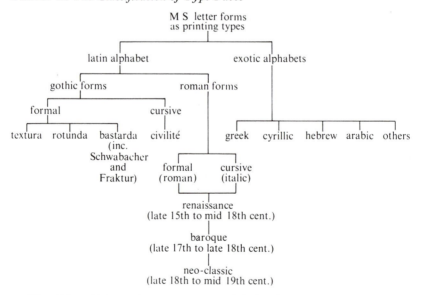

----

[11] The width, or thickness, of type is also known confusingly as its 'set'.

at once. Thus the table which follows is linguistic in dividing the Latin alphabet from the Greek and from the other exotic alphabets; morphological in distinguishing the Latin gothics from the Latin romans; and historical in its treatment of the successive forms of roman and italic.

This scheme, while much influenced by the draft and final versions of the official German standard for type classification (DIN 16 518, 1959 and 1964), does not follow either of them exactly. The chief differences are that the gothic Schwabacher and Fraktur forms are included here in the bastarda group; and that the roman traditions of Jenson and Aldus are both dealt with in the renaissance group of romans.

GOTHIC TYPE[12]

The main groups of gothic type faces were based (like nearly all the type of the early period) on hand-written forms which had been developed before the invention of printing. Textura, the type of the first printed books, was derived from a formal book hand written with a minimum of curves; the letters are upright, narrow, and angular, standing on crooked feet, and the ascenders are usually decorated with barbs or thorns; f and ſ do not normally descend below the base line.[13] There were three main traditions of textura design: the early German form, seldom seen after the fifteenth century; a late-fifteenth-century French form which, although it did not survive in France itself, was used by English printers throughout the

a   liũ hominis.Ut ois qui credit in ip= ſum non pereat:ſed habeat vitã eter= nam.Offr.Benedictus ſit deus pater,

b   bibii: in illa enim finis cunctozum admonetur hominum/et bibens cogitat quid futurum ſit. Melior eſt ira riſu: quia per triſtitiam vultus/ cozigitur animus delinquentis. Cor ſapien=

FIG. 3 (*a*). Late-fifteenth-century French texturas used in London (*Missale Saresberiense*, London (Pynson) 1500, Duff 329; Trin. Coll. Cam. VI. 18. 21, f. 122ᵃ).

3 (*b*). Mid-seventeenth-century Dutch textura, the *Augustijn Duyts* of Christoffel van Dijck, with bastarda form of f and ſ, recast from original materials at Haarlem (Enschedé en Zonen, J., *The House of Enschedé 1703–1953*, Haarlem 1953, p. 18).

[12] For an introduction to gothic type see Vervliet, H. D. L., *Sixteenth-century printing types of the Low Countries*, Amsterdam 1968, ch. 3; for further references, see pp. 396–7.
[13] Some sixteenth-century Dutch texturas were provided with alternative forms of f and ſ with pointed 'bastarda' descenders; see fig. 3 (b).

hand-press period as their normal 'black letter'; and the Dutch form, also late fifteenth-century, and also destined for long life in the Low Countries.

Less condensed as a rule than the texturas, the rotundas are distinguished, as their name suggests, by curved letters c d e, etc. They are true black letters in their great contrast between thick and thin strokes; they have mere thickenings for serifs, and f and ſ do not have descenders. Some of the smaller and less formal varieties (especially the 'fere-humanisticas') resemble thickened romans, though even these forms were used with obviously gothic capitals. Rotundas were widely used for all but the most formal texts in the fifteenth century, but fell out of fashion during the sixteenth century, surviving longest in Spain.

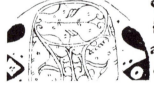

a ſua tam reprobis ꝗ electis. qui omnes cū ſuis,pprijs reſurgēt corporibus:que nunc geſtāt: ut recipiant ſecūdū opera ſua ſiue

zis opa fūgit.ff.ð bis qui no.ifa.ob hec vba.nec id excuſat boiem : ꝗ cōſilio alterius fecit:qz debuit ꝶ potuit explorare apud ſe

b Ciceronem filiū ſuū. Officioꝛ liber mcipit. Prefatio generalis in libros omnes.

Van ꝗ te marce fili·annum iam audietem cratippū·idqz athemis·abundare oportet·p= ceptis·inſtituaſꝗ phie·ꝛꝓt

FIG. 4 (*a*). Formal rotundas from Venice (Gregorius IX, *Decretales*, Venice (Jenson) 1475, Goff G-449; Trin. Coll. Cam., Gr. 2. 191, f. 3ᵃ).

4 (*b*). Formal and fere-humanistica rotundas used by Gutenberg's successors; the initial letter is hand-drawn (Cicero, M. T., *De officiis*, Mainz (Fust and Schoeffer) 1466, Goff C-576; Trin. Coll. Cam. VI. 14. 24, f. 1ᵃ).

The bastardas were based on a variety of quickly written but not fully cursive book hands, and differ considerably in their degree of formality. The least formal of them, the frequently crude bastardas of England, France, and the Low Countries, generally have rounded letters of small x-height, often with a tendency to forward slope, sprinkled with a number of cursive forms such as single-decker a, d with a flourished ascender, open-tailed g and (most characteristic of the whole group) f and ſ with pointed descenders. The German bastardas quickly became more sophisticated; chief amongst them were the Schwabacher group (*c.* 1485-1540), which tended towards the rotundas, and Fraktur (from *c.* 1512), closer in spirit to textura. The English, French, and Dutch bastardas went out of use by the mid sixteenth century, but Fraktur, cut with a contrived formality that belied its cursive origins, became the most successful of all the gothic types, surviving as a book face in Germany until the mid twentieth century.

a

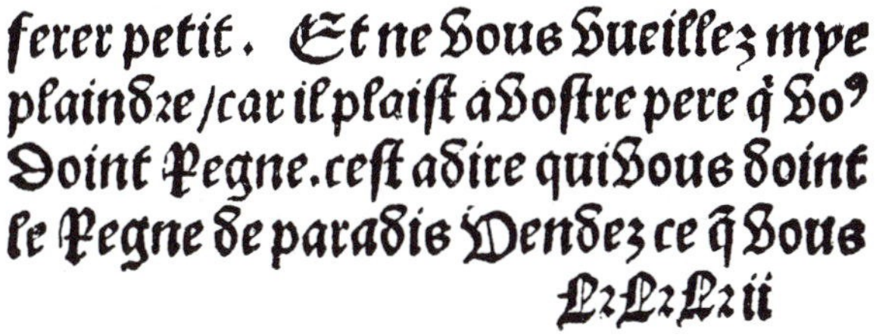

ferer petit. Et ne Sous Sueillez mye plaindze/car il plaist aSostre pere q̃ So⁹ Doint Pegne.cest adire quiSous doint le Pegne de paradis Dendez ce q̃ Sous Lr Lr Lr ii

b

Js ist das Buch von der Geburt Jhesu Christi/ der da ist ein Sohn Dauids/ des Sohns Abraham. ABraham zeugete Jsaac. Jsaac zeugete Jacob.

FIG. 5 (*a*). French bastardà; note the use of Lr for K in the signature (*Biblia*, French, Paris (Vérard) *c.* 1498, Goff B-623; Trin. Coll. Cam. VI. 17. 23, 3K2ᵃ).

5 (*b*). German Frakturs (*Biblia*, German, Franckfurt am Mayn (Zephelium et al.) 1560, Adams B1179; Trin. Coll. Cam. A. 11. 7, f. ²243ᵃ).

Civilité is the name that became attached to a group of gothic cursive types, the earliest and best of which were cut in the mid sixteenth century by the French punch-cutter Robert Granjon and by his imitators. They were based on a relatively informal hand, closely related to the English 'secretary', and were fairly popular for a while in spite of their poor legibility and extravagant use of space. The civilités never approached the typographic importance of italic, the roman cursive, but they were used occasionally in France and the Low Countries until the nineteenth century.

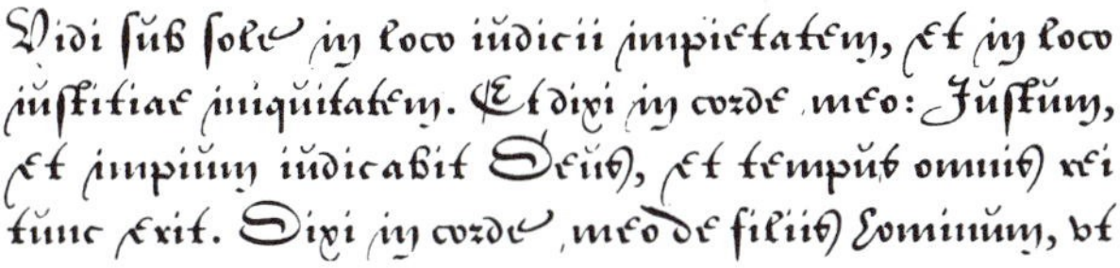

Vidi sub sole/ in loco iudicii impietatem, et in loco iustitiae iniquitatem. Et dixi in corde meo: Justum, et impium iudicabit Deus, et tempus omnis rei tunc erit. Dixi in corde meo de filiis hominum, vt

FIG. 6. Civilité; Granjon's *St. Augustin* of 1566, Carter and Vervliet A4, recast from original materials at Haarlem (Enschedé en Zonen, J., *The house of Enschedé 1703-1953*, Haarlem 1953, p. 12).

ROMAN AND ITALIC TYPE[14]

Like the early gothics, the first roman type faces were based on a formal
book hand, in this case one which had been perfected in Italy by humanistic
scribes during the first half of the fifteenth century. Following their model,
they were used at first chiefly for editions of classical authors, gothic types
being preferred for printing religious and vernacular works. But the superior
legibility of roman encouraged its use in all sorts of books. In Italy a few
vernacular books had been set in roman from the beginning, and during
the early sixteenth century rotunda gradually gave way to roman in Italian
printing. Roman prevailed at Paris and at Antwerp around 1540, and in
other French printing centres a few years later. Books in English began to
be set in roman from the late 1550s, although the Bible survived in 'black
letter' until 1640. In the Low Countries the Bible continued to be printed
in gothic type for even longer, but ordinary books in Dutch went into roman
during the second quarter of the seventeenth century. Only in Germany,
German-speaking Switzerland, and Scandinavia did ordinary vernacular
books continue to be printed in gothic types throughout the hand-press
period.

A cursive version of roman, *italic*, was cut as type at the beginning of
the sixteenth century and was at first used by itself as a text type; but again
it was less legible than roman, and it quickly slipped into subservience to
the parent form. Later still the subordination of italic was expressed by
type designs that were sloped romans, often lacking in individual character.

Renaissance romans and italics. A good many different typographical interpretations of the roman book hand appeared in the fifteenth century,
ranging from faces that had so many gothic characteristics as scarcely to be
roman at all, to others which pointed the way to a purely roman typography,
and which have been followed more or less ever since. We can see with
hindsight that two early romans in particular set the pattern for the later
development of the face which was to become the standard roman for most
of the sixteenth, seventeenth, and eighteenth centuries, and which is still
the fundamental influence upon twentieth-century typography. These
were the 114–15 mm. romans introduced by the Venetian printers Jenson
(in 1470) and Aldus Manutius (in 1495). Much has been made of the dif-

---

[14] There is no good general introduction to the development of roman and italic type-forms, but on
Jenson, Aldus, and Garamont, see Carter, H., *A view of early typography*, Oxford 1969, ch. 4; on van
den Keere, Vervliet, H. D. L., *Sixteenth-century printing types of the Low Countries*, Amsterdam 1968,
pp. 30-2 and *passim*; on Caslon, Mosley, J., 'The early career of William Caslon', *Journal of the Printing
Historical Society*, iii, 1967, pp. 66-81; on Kis, Carter, H., and Buday, G., 'Nicholas Kis and the Janson
types', *Gutenberg Jahrbuch*, 1957, pp. 207-12; and on *romain du roi*, Jammes, A., 'Académisme et
typographie', *Journal of the Printing Historical Society*, i, 1965, pp. 71-95. See also the further references
on pp. 396-7.

a aut inania & furda fimulacra malefici dæ
partes mundi quæ confpiciuntur:aut mc
aut quæcunq; animalium nocentiffima:f
uatoris fola doctrina cuncti fimul græci a
uerbum Chrifti audiuerunt ad tantum pl
uerum deum regem ac dominum cæli: et

b mus; quas adolefcentes, non poffumus :
quo in confilio nobis diutius permanen
dum effe non puto: nam ut interdum nó
loqui moderati hominis eft; fic femper
filere cum eo , quem diligas, perignaui:
neq; Hercule; fi in officio permanfimus

FIG. 7 (*a*). Jenson's 115 mm. roman (Eusebius Caesariensis, *De evangelica praeparatione*, Venice (Jenson) 1470, Goff E-118; Trin. Coll. Cam. Gr. 2. 111, f. 4ᵇ).

7 (*b*). Aldus's 114 mm. roman (Bembus, P., *De Aetna dialogus*, Venice (Aldus Manutius) 1495/6, Goff B-304; Trin. Coll. Cam. Gr. 11. 232, A1ᵇ).

ferences between these magnificent types, and indeed Jenson's version is perhaps nearer to calligraphy than the Aldine roman, which is cut with a brillance and regularity that is purely typographic; nevertheless, comparison of good, early impressions of the two shows close similarities between them. Aldus's type is slightly more condensed than Jenson's, with greater x-height and a little less weight; and there are a few unimportant differences of detail—notably the cross-bar of e, which Jenson slopes and Aldus makes horizontal. But the design of individual lower-case letters is remarkably similar, and it may be that Aldus's contemporaries (and perhaps his punch-cutter Francesco Griffo as well) looked upon the type of 1495 as a development or refinement of Jenson's roman of 1470, rather than as something radically new.

At all events the development was approved, and it was Aldus's roman, not Jenson's that was taken as a model by the supremely accomplished French punch-cutters of the 1530s and 1540s, of whom the greatest was Claude Garamont.[15] But these designers did more than copy the Aldine original: they developed it in a whole range of new sizes, and produced a

[15] The spelling 'Garamont' is used here for the punch-cutter, 'Garamond' for his type.

series (as we should say today) of romans hitherto unparalleled for elegance and utility. The quality of these Parisian romans was recognized immediately; matrices, cast type, and even sets of punches were traded all over Europe; Garamond and a few close imitations[16] dominated roman typography for the next hundred years, and remained in production for a hundred years more.

a quæ Græci fcriptores inanis arrogantiæ caufa fibi affump
)arum multa fciffe viderentur, ea conquifiuerunt, quæ nih
: ars difficilior cognitu putaretur: nos autem ea,quæ videl
ertinere, fumpfimus. Non enim fpe quæftus aut gloria c
lum, quemadmodum cæteri, fed vt induftria noftra tuæ n

b alias interim cauffas prętendentes,bellum fufcepiffe.ac tu
fium res,& contra Megarenfes fcitum,& fiqua alia volui
Fines autem pluribus erroribus fcatent. quamuis enim
interfuiffe, & fe omnia polliceatur effe narraturum: tar
lium Athenienfium & Peloponnefiorum, quod prope (

Fɪɢ. 8 (*a*). Garamont's first *gros romain* roman, *c*. 1530 (Cicero, M. T., *Opera*, Paris (R. Estienne) 1538-9, Adams C1640; Trin. Coll. Cam. Z. 6. 18, p. 3).

8 (*b*). Garamont's second *gros romain* roman, mid 1540s with later revisions; this type remained in production until the mid eighteenth century (Dionysius Halicarnaseus, *Scripta omnia*, Francofurdi (heirs of A. Wechel) 1586, Adams D625; Trin. Coll. Cam. II. 3. 1³, p. 234).

As early as the 1570s, however, a new and powerful version of the renaissance roman was cut for Plantin by Hendrik van den Keere, a Belgian punchcutter of great skill and originality. It had increased contrast and x-height in the lower case and a hefty set of capitals; and, although its distribution was limited at first, it was eventually to have a decisive influence on the development of renaissance roman. For by the early seventeenth century the centre of type production was moving from Paris to the Lower Rhine, and the roman model taken by the most successful Dutch punch-cutters (such as Cristoffel van Dijck of Amsterdam) was that of van den Keere. The Low Countries romans of the seventeenth century followed his lead in contrast and x-height, but they were cruder faces, provincial for all

---

[16] Not to be confused with several twentieth-century types of the same name, which are based on different designs.

^a❡ Nolite diligere mundum, neque ea quę
in mundo funt. Si quis diligit mundum,
non eft charitas patris in eo: quoniam om

^bftro, tanti Principis, lumine perfundi fpei
ego illum ederem, fuafit, tum ipfius Vi
ritas, tum Muneris quo fungor ratio.

FIG. 9 (*a*). Van den Keere's *ascendonica* roman lower case of 1576 with Granjon's capitals, Vervliet R18 (Vervliet, H. D. L., *Sixteenth-century printing types of the Low Countries*, Amsterdam 1968, p. 251).

9 (*b*). Anglo-Dutch double pica roman cut at Oxford, *c.* 1682 (Morison, S., *John Fell*, Oxford 1967, p. 155).

their vigour. They suited the taste of the time, nevertheless, English printers preferring to buy type from the Dutch foundries although the Garamond romans were still available in France; and when the Oxford and Cambridge University Presses were re-equipped with the best available typographic materials late in the century, type and type-founding apparatus were obtained from the Low Countries; Oxford also employed a German-Dutch punch-cutter, Peter de Walpergen.

Yet another reinterpretation of the renaissance roman face was made in the eighteenth century, in England, where William Caslon began his urbane imitations from the Dutch in the 1720s. Caslon rejected the brash contrast of the later Dutch founts, and produced types that were without serious blemish, but also without much life; they were tasteful, subdued, and rather dull. Nevertheless they were so much better than anything else that

ce, by which they were inabled to difcover the po-
the heavens, with vaftly more eafe, than we could
it could have been imagined more, than that they
/ided with fome fitter aftronomical inftrument for
ɔfe than we? That any ftone fhould have fo amaz-

FIG. 10. Caslon's great primer roman of 1728, leaded (Pemberton, H., *A view of Sir Isaac Newton's philosophy*, London (Palmer) 1728; Trin. Coll. Cam. T. 10. 116, p. 13).

was readily available (imported type was necessarily harder to get and more expensive than the local product) that British printers rapidly re-equipped with Caslon. These types were imitated in their turn (notably by the Scottish founder Alexander Wilson in the 1740s and 1750s, and by Isaac Moore of Bristol in the 1760s), but most English books of the middle and late eighteenth century were printed in type from the Caslon foundry. After a period of disuse at the beginning of the nineteenth century, Caslon roman was revived, and has been available ever since from Caslon's successors.

The first italic type was an 80 mm. fount cut for Aldus by Griffo (the punch-cutter who, probably, had produced the influential Aldine roman of 1495), and it was used initially for the text of a series of octavo classics that began to appear in 1501. Its x-height was notably small, and the fount was equipped with many ligatures (tied letters) and with upright capitals; it was quickly and widely imitated.

Next came a group of 'calligraphic' italics based on the *cancellaresca* hand and initiated in 1524 by the writing master Lodovico degli Arrighi (called Vicentino). They too had upright capitals, but were distinguished by the curved ends of their long ascenders and descenders. They were used, almost exclusively for text settings, until the early seventeenth century.

a

  Matre pulchra filia pulchrior,
 o Quem criminosis cunque uoles modum
     Pones iambis, siue flamma,
  Siue mari libet Adriano.
 N on Dindymene, non adytis quatit
   Mentem sacerdotum incola Pythius
   Non liber æque, non acuta
   Sic geminant corybantes æra

Fig. 11 (*a*). Aldus's 80 mm. italic of 1501 (Horatius Flaccus, Q., *Opera*, Venice (Aldus Manutius) 1501, Adams H854; Trin. Coll. Cam. Gr. 11. 3, b2ª).

b S e' fosse' sparso in far salubri effetti
 A l'infelice' Grecia, ch'ognihor langue'
 I n servitù, sarebbe' fuor d'affanni .
 E 'l tempo, che' s'è speso in nostri danni,
 S arebbe' andato in mille' belle' ludi;

11 (*b*). The Arrighi-Lautizio *cancelleresca corsiva* italic of 1524, with added epsilon and omega (Trissino, G. G., *Canzone*, Rome (Arrighi and Perugino) *c.* 1524, Adams T948; Trin. Coll. Cam. Gr. 10. 45, A3ª).

Both the Aldine and the Vicentine italics were gradually superseded in the mid sixteenth century by a more practical form of the face emanating from Paris, which had sloped capitals, fewer ligatures, and a relatively large x-height. The finest and most influential of these French italics were the work of Robert Granjon, an artist of the stature of his countryman and

near-contemporary Garamont and one of the greatest all-round type designers of any period. Appearing from the 1540s to the 1560s, Granjon's italics
were a perfect complement to the Parisian romans; they could be used alone,
as at first they generally were, or they could be combined with roman for
picking out particular words or passages. Like the romans, the French italics
set the pattern for the standard renaissance founts of the later hand-press
period. Van den Keere did not cut an italic, but van Dijck's widely-used
italics of the mid seventeenth century were slightly coarsened versions of
Granjon's types, and Caslon based his spidery italic on the van Dijck design.

a

Q v i s *neget inuentum Germanorum ingeniofum*
C *artula quo recipit tot monumenta typis?*
Q *uo quicquid factum eft vnquā, fcripfitq̃, vetuftas*
Afferitur, cupidè pofteritas ve legit.
Q *uot regum hiftoriæ latuiffent, dicta fophorum,*
T *euthonicus rectè ni reparaffet honos!*

b

D v m *latitans domiporta vagor, menfasq̃ paratu*
O *rno, vel in venerem luxuriofa vocor:*
O *mnes certatim redimunt, me colligit vfus,*
D *elitijs nequeo tum exaturare famem.*
D *epofui quando concham, (quæ grata voluntas)*
P *roteror, aut rifu fæpe reuoluor humi.*

c *Graeco, reftituere me & emendare poffe confiderem ; fed*
quod is omnium veterum maxime vel merito fuo vel genio
quodam & placendi forte in manibus hominum pectoribufque
haereret. Formam vero & inftitutum operis fic mihi definiui

d

now explained, *viz. That all Men are not ca-*
pable, or fufficient Judges of the Truth and Di-
vinity of the Gofpel, for want of that previous
Difpofition which is requifite (at leaft in fome

Fig. 12 (*a, b*). Two influential italics by Granjon: (*a*) the *mediane cursive pendante*, 1562, and (*b*)
the *mediane cursive droite à l'allemande*, 1565 (Sambucus, J., *Emblemata*, Antwerp (Plantin) 1566,
Adams S219; Trin. Coll. Cam. Gr. 3. 96, Q4ᵃ, C1ᵃ).

12 (*c*) The *augustijn cursijf* of Christoffel van Dijck, *c.* 1655, in use at Cambridge (Horatius Flaccus,
Q., *Opera*, ed. Bentley, R., Cambridge Univ. Press 1711, McKenzie 97; Trin. Coll. Cam.
Z 2. 39, c2ᵃ).

12 (*d*). Caslon's english italic of 1727 (Sharp, T., *An enquiry into the causes of infidelity*, London
[Bowyer] 1730; Trin. Coll. Cam. X. 36. 13³, p. 27).

Baroque romans and italics. Although all the early types were copied from existing book hands, the medium of the steel punch both eliminated the random irregularities of hand-written letters, and encouraged the regularization of the letter forms by the repetition of stock elements of design in different letters; efforts were made to retain the effect of irregularity by providing ligatures and alternative forms of some of the letters, but were only partly successful. The next stage, which first became important in the seventeenth century, was to develop new designs, specifically for type, which made a feature of the mechanical element in type production. A variety of influences helped to direct the form that these developments took: intellectual analyses of letter-forms in the sixteenth and seventeenth centuries, the new calligraphy of the seventeenth-century writing masters with its brilliant contrast and near-vertical stress,[17] the economic advantages of narrow letters, and the increase of legibility with x-height.

There were two main trends in the new type-designs of the seventeenth and eighteenth centuries: one was towards an increase of contrast, combined with a movement of stress from oblique to vertical; the other was towards narrower types of large x-height. These trends are to be found both separately and combined in the very various seventeenth and eighteenth century types now called baroque. Their history is complex, but the following developments were especially important.

Part of the new approach—increased contrast and large x-height—had been foreshadowed by van den Keere's romans of the 1570s; and some remarkable 'modern' titling capitals with almost vertical stress and virtually unbracketed serifs which appeared in Rome in 1613–14 were produced in association with roman founts that were undoubtedly influenced by van den Keere.[18] Very similar capitals were made in Germany during the later seventeenth century, this time in association with a new style of roman lower case, a very narrow letter, still with oblique stress but of great x-height; the finest example, probably cut by the Hungarian Nicolas Kis in the 1680s, is better known by the names of the Leipzig foundries of Janson and Ehrhardt which owned the matrices. This new roman spread during the remainder of the century to other German foundries, and appeared in even more exaggerated forms, with the beginning of a tendency towards vertical stress. The German italics which generally accompanied these romans were also condensed letters of great x-height, but in this they were more like their renaissance predecessors than were the romans, the italic

---

[17] *Contrast*: the difference in weight between the thick and the thin strokes. *Stress*: the alignment of the thick and thin strokes; in vertical stress the vertical strokes are thick, the horizontal strokes thin.

[18] Vervliet, H. D. L., ed., *The type specimen of the Vatican Press 1628*, Amsterdam 1967, facsimile pp. 27, 50, 53.

triginta annos tyrannidem tenuit. Ad hunc mc
Hafnia anno 1593 Cragius, fimiliter edidit Tc
ma Leidenfi idem retinente, quod utique ind
nis. Sic quum præmiffum effet ab Lacedæmonii
bus fumma fit in republicâ poteftas ; additur `
nem *Nulli enim affurgunt Lacedæmonii, præte*

FIG. 13. *Text* roman and italic in the Janson-Ehrhardt style, perhaps by Nicholas Kis, *c.* 1685 (Gronovius, J., *Thesaurus Graecarum antiquitatum*, vol. vi, Lugd. Bat. (van der Aa) 1699; Trin. Coll. Cam. W. 3. 18, a2ᵇ).

retaining calligraphic forms and showing a general similarity to the Dutch italics of the mid seventeenth century.

Another influential new type of the later seventeenth century was the *romain du roi* designed for the Imprimerie Royale by a team of Academicians under the Abbé Jaugeon, and cut with some modification during the 1690s by Philippe Grandjean. The proportions of the roman letters were deliberately taken from Garamont's romans, but otherwise the design was entirely original. For the first time the stress was uncompromisingly vertical, while the italic was intended to be a mechanically sloped roman, quite unconnected with calligraphy. (There were also some minor peculiarities of the design that were not imitated elsewhere: ascenders with serifs on both sides, spurred 'l', etc.)

ette médaille, où l'on voit Aftrée qui defcend du
its de la Paix, de la Juftice & de l'Abondance. La
, SPES FELICITATIS ORBIS. PAX ULTRAJECTEN-
ᴵCCXIII. fignifient que *le monde efpéra un bonheur*

FIG. 14. The *caractères du roi* of Jaugeon and Grandjean, 1690s, *petit parangon* roman and italic (Louis XIV, *Médailles sur les principaux événements du règne entier de Louis le Grand*, Paris (Imp. Roy.) 1723; Trin. Coll. Cam. Y. 16. 11, p. 313).

The various new features of roman type design first seen in the seventeeth century—increased contrast, vertical stress, condensation, large x-height, sloped romans—were combined in various ways by a number of eighteenth-century punch-cutters who, like the French Academicians, were conscious innovators. Prominent amongst them were J. M. Fleischman, a Bavarian working in Holland in the 1740s; Louis Luce and P. S. Fournier, Parisian contemporaries of Fleischman; John Baskerville of

ut curiofe intelligerem: Sunt iufti atque fa-
pientes, et opera eorum in manu Dei: et
tamen nefcit homo utrum amore, an odio
dignus fit: fed omnia in futurum fervantur
incerta, eo quod univerfa æque eveniant
iufto et impio, bono et malo, mundo et im-

quantité de bien & de	*parce qu'elle nous eft*
mal, qui rend en un	*moins connue. Elle ref-*
fens toutes les condi-	*femble à ces figures*
tions égales.Si les Rois	*d'Optique, qui de loin*
ont plus d'agrémens	*repréfentent une belle*

Gratum opus agricolis: at nunc horrentia Martis

ARMA, virumque cano, Trojæ qui primus ab ori
Italiam, fato profugus, Lavinaque venit
Litora: multum ille et terris jactatus et alto,

cenatis non folum fervatus, fed e-
tiam in amicitiam receptus eft.
Quapropter Maecenati et Augufto
in omnibus Scriptis fuis venerabi-
liter adfurgit. Scripfit Carminum

FIG. 15 (*a*). Fleischman's *Augustyn* roman, 1740s, recast from original materials at Haarlem (Enschedé en Zonen, J., *The house of Enschedé 1703-1953*, Haarlem 1953, p. 24).

15 (*b*). The *St Augustin* roman and italic of P. S. Fournier, *c.* 1740 (*Encyclopédie*, ii, Paris 1751; Trin. Coll. Cam. 301. a. 1. 2, p. 663).

15 (*c*). Baskerville's great primer roman and italic of 1754-7, leaded (Vergilius Maro, P., *Opera*, Birmingham (Baskerville) 1757, Gaskell 1; Trin. Coll. Cam. Z. 11. 98, O1ª).

15 (*d*). The third english roman, leaded, of the Wilson foundry, 1760 (Horatius Flaccus, Q., *Opera*, Glasgow (Foulis) 1760, Gaskell 383; Trin. Coll. Cam. Roth. C. 1. 6, p. xi).

Birmingham, printer and type-founder from the 1750s; and Alexander Wilson, a Scot who was both a type-founder and a professor of astronomy, and whose most original typographical work was done in the 1750s and 1760s. Most of the italics which accompanied the mid-eighteenth-century baroque romans followed traditional renaissance patterns, but Fournier paid little attention to the old calligraphic forms; while Baskerville's italic was a lean, elegant letter, the most radical departure from tradition since the French academic italic of the 1690s, with its roots in the calligraphic innovations of the late-seventeenth- and early-eighteenth-century writing masters.

Neo-classic romans and italics. Most of the individual features of the fully neo-classic (or 'modern') face were included in the baroque romans which became increasingly popular during the second half of the eighteenth century, especially in England. But one further development remained to be made, and this last, logical step was taken by F. A. Didot (one of a talented family of Parisian printer-founders) in the early 1780s. The baroque designers, although they favoured strong contrast and had experimented with vertical stress, nevertheless retained the sloped and bracketed serifs that derived from obliquely-stressed pen forms; even the unusual two-sided flat serifs of the *romain du roi* had been bracketed. Didot's new roman of 1784, however, at last fulfilled the logic of vertical stress; the ascender serifs of the lower case were thin horizontal lines without brackets.

Israëlitae manna colligunt; die sexto duplum colligunt.
Lex de manna asservando in urna coram Domino collo-
canda.

1. Profectique sunt de Elim, et venit omnis multitudo filiorum Israel in desertum Sin, quod est inter Elim et Sinaï, quintodecimo die mensis secundi, postquam egressi sunt de terra AEgypti.
2. Et murmuravit omnis congregatio filiorum Israel contra Moysen et Aaron in solitudine.

Fig. 16. F. A. Didot's corps dix (81 mm.) roman of 1784, with corps sept italic (*Biblia*, Latin, vol. i, Paris (Didot) 1785; Trin. Coll. Cam. Gr. 22. 1, p. 168).

Didot's first neo-classic type did not show marked contrast, but later developments of the form, by Didot himself and by Bodoni in Italy, resulted by 1800 in faces of great contrast combined with vertical stress and un-bracketed, hair-line serifs. The italics that accompanied all these faces were sloped romans, varying in contrast in the same way as their parent forms, and seldom showing any trace of renaissance broad-pen calligraphy. The later development of these types is discussed on pp. 209–13.

GREEK TYPE[19]

Only one exotic alphabet, namely greek, was of major importance in western European typography, for the hebrew, arabic, and other near-eastern alphabets cut as type during the hand-press period for works of biblical exegesis were narrowly confined to specialist printers. But printing in the classical languages was widespread, and most printers kept a fount or two of greek, even if it was no more than a small one used for setting a few words of Greek within a Latin text.

Greek typography in the fifteenth century was largely experimental. One style, associated with Jenson, was based on a latinized hand, in which the letters were generally square, upright, and separated from each other, but it need not concern us here since it was superseded late in the fifteenth century by a more cursive style and was not revived until recent times. The cursive style of greek type, however, was an immediate success; introduced by Aldus in the 1490s and perfected by Garamont and Granjon in the mid sixteenth century, it dominated greek typography for nearly 300 years.

The Aldine greek was based on a form of humanistic cursive hand which relied for its good looks on a multiplicity of alternative letters, ligatures, and contractions. It was an unfortunate model for type, not because it was ugly or difficult to read—we find it difficult because its abbreviations are unfamiliar nowadays, but scholars of the sixteenth and seventeenth centuries preferred it to the latinized hand—but because it was unsuited to typography: founts of cursive greek required 450 or more sorts of type, three times as many as a fount of roman. But the influence of the awkward Aldine originals of the 1490s, and then of the superb interpretations of Garamont (1540s) and Granjon (1560s), was irresistible.

It was possible to make a fount of cursive greek with fewer punches than there were to be sorts; vowel punches and accent punches were cut separately and then tied together in different combinations for striking the matrices (a device also used occasionally in making accented sorts for roman founts). Alternatively vowels could be cast without accents as kerned letters, with bodies only half as wide as usual, part of the face being cast on the overhang, or kern. Accents were cast separately on narrow bodies which were then combined with the kerned vowels to make accented sorts. Both methods were in use by the early sixteenth century, although printers pre-

---

[19] Scholderer, V., *Greek printing types 1465–1927*, London 1927.

a

ΣΑ Δὴ δὲ δηῖμαι πῶ ἐ
μαυτοῦ καρδίαν·
Ἠθηνῇ βασά·πάνυ δὲ
βασά·τίπαρα·

αὐτηδὴ μενῖση δωματα ἠλεῖ
πειν ἠκαπὰ πςοθεσις·
χ̄τλωὲμαυτω καρδίαν·
ὁ καὶ βέλπον,ὅτι μεταφί
ρ̄ ἀπὸ τω βιουω̃ντλὼ κ̄

b

Θειόζατι Αὐζοκράζορες Σεῆρς, καὶ Ἀντωνεῖνος τῖς Σ
Κλαύδιῳ Ρχφῖνῳ ὁ πολείτης ὑμῶν, ὁ διὰ τλὺ ωεθα
-ιωεσιν ἐπὶ παιδεία κ̣ τὸν ἐν λόγοις σωνεχῆ βίον, τλὺ
ἐγχειρξμὴν τῖς Σοφίταις κ̄ τὰς Θείας τῆ ωε·γόνων

Fig. 17 (*a*). Aldus's 146 mm. and 114 mm. greeks of 1495-6 (Aristophanes, *Comoedia novem*, Venice (Aldus) 1498, Goff A-958; Trin. Coll. Cam. N. 4. 2, χ2ᵃ).

17 (*b*). Granjon's *gros parangon* greek, 1565, after Garamont, recast from original materials at Oxford (Morison, S., *John Fell*, Oxford 1967, p. 99).

ferred to use unkerned sorts, keeping the kerned vowels for emergencies.[20]

Aldus himself reduced the number of ligatures and contractions in one of his later greek founts (the 80 mm. greek of 1502), but it was his earlier, multi-ligatured founts that were followed; and, from the middle of the sixteenth century until the middle of the eighteenth, printers used the best copies they could get of Garamont's interpretation of the humanistic cursive. During the same period there was a tendency to reduce the number of sorts in a fount of greek by deleting some of the least-used ligatures and contractions; by the 1740s

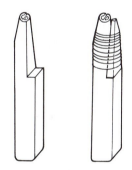

Fig. 18 (*a*). Stepped vowel punch, with separate accent punch.

the Scottish founder Alexander Wilson was producing greek types that were avowedly based on Garamont's designs, but which had only some eight alternative sorts and eighteen ligatures and contractions.

It was the same Wilson who made the first deliberate break with the Aldine tradition in the 1750s with a fine double pica greek which, although its letter-forms were closely related to those of Granjon's design,

[20] Vervliet, H. D. L., *Sixteenth-century printing types of the Low Countries*, Amsterdam 1968, p. 11 shows a 'stepped' punch; for kerned accents see Morison, S., *John Fell*, Oxford 1967, pp. 98, 257.

Fig. 18 (*b*). A piece of greek type—the vowel alpha—kerned for use with separate accents, shown here in combination with a smooth breathing.

was intended for use with no more than a few ligatures, and with none of the old contractions.

Πάν⌐ϊες ἅμα, Ζεὺς δ' ἦρχε· Θέτις δ' ϔ λήθε⌐ ἐφε⌐μ

Παιδὸς ἐϔ, ἀλλ' ἤγ' ἀνεδύσα⌐ο κῦμα θαλάσσης,

Ἠερίη δ' ἀνέβη μέγαν ϔρανὸν, Οὔλυμπόν τε·

FIG. 19. Alexander Wilson's double pica greek, second version, 1756 (Homer, *Works*, Glasgow (Foulis) 1756-8, Gaskell 319; Trin. Coll. Cam. II. 11. 17, i, p. 21).

But the ligatures and contractions were going out of use in any case; from the middle of the century printers all over Europe used them less and less, even with founts of Aldine character. At the same time further experiments in designing greek without ligatures were made by Baskerville, Bodoni, and others, and new, simpler forms were becoming commercially available at the end of the hand-press period.

FOUNTS, CASES, AND TYPE-STOCK

A fount of type was a set of letters and other symbols in which each sort was supplied in approximate proportion to its frequency of use, all being of one body-size and design. A fount of roman type consisted of CAPITAL LETTERS, SMALL CAPITALS, small ('lower case') letters, accented letters, ligatures (tied letters such as ffl, made from a single punch and matrix), punctuation marks, figures, and a few special symbols such as &, *, ℞, etc.; this usually added up to about 150 sorts, and there were in addition spaces to go between words (short pieces of type of various thicknesses without letters cast on them) and quads (very wide spaces) for filling out blank lines, which were specific to the body but not to the design. Italic founts, which lacked small capitals, generally had about the same total number of sorts as roman because of the addition of extra ligatures and decorated (or 'swash') capitals.

A special form of tied letter appears to have been made in the fifteenth and sixteenth centuries by placing the matrices for several letters side by side in the mould, and casting them all together as a single type. Like the matrices for music type (in which the lines of the stave have to run right across the face of the type to join the lines of the types on either side), matrices were specially justified for this purpose without the usual margin on either side of the impression of the punch. Tied letters made in this way may be difficult to distinguish from true ligatures made from a single

a ABCDEFGHIJKLMNOPQRSTUVWXYZÆQu℣℟Çͧ& (3

ABCDEFGHIKLMNOPQRSTUVWXYZÆ (26)

abcdefghijklmnopqrstuvwxyz æ œ ſſ ſi ſh ſt ſſi ſl ſt ff fi fl ffi ffl ç

âãáà éèèëēẹ íìîī úùûüū óòôõñ q q́ (68)

. . ˙ , ’ ; : ? ! - - [ ) * * § † (17)

1 2 3 4 5 6 7 8 9 0 (10)

| | | | ▮ ▮ ▬ ▬

b ABCDEFGHIKLMNOP QRSTUVWXYZ Z̨Æ [27]

abcdefghijklmnopqrsſtuvw xyz æ œ ÿ ÿ ll ct ſt as is us ff fi fl fr ffi ffl ſi ſl ſp ſſ ß ſt [49

áàâéèêëíìîī óòôô úùûü āēīōū ς ꝓ ꝑ ꝓ̃ q̃₃ q̃₃ q̃ q̃̃ ẃ ỳ [35]

, ; : ! ?) [6]

1 2 3 4 5 6 7 8 9 0 [10]

Fig. 20. Synopses of founts of sixteenth-century roman and italic type, cast from original materials at Oxford: a pica roman of mixed origin, perhaps partly by Garamont; and Granjon's *mediane cursive droite à l'allemande* (cf. Fig. 12 (*b*)). They total 153 and 127 sorts respectively. The italic lacks an ampersand and alternative swash capitals other than *V* and *Z*. Spaces and quads, printed high between the synopses, show as black rectangles (Morison, S., *John Fell*, Oxford 1967, pp. 133, 139).

matrix.[21] Another device was to make matrices for accented sorts with the punches already used for unaccented sorts: the letter punch was stepped on its shank so that one of several accent punches could be bound on to the step to make a combined punch (fig. 18 (a)).[22]

Type was stored for use systematically in cases, large wooden trays that were divided into little compartments (boxes), one for each sort. The 'lay' of the case—that is, the conventional order in which the sorts were arranged in the boxes—followed one of two traditional patterns which were certainly established by the mid seventeenth century and probably long before.[23] The earlier of the two, the single lay, employed one large, squarish case for a fount of type, and it held about 34 kg. (75 lb.) of type when it was full. The capital letters were arranged in rows of equal-sized boxes along the top of the case, with the small letters in boxes of various size beneath them. The single lay appears to have been the normal form everywhere until the mid sixteenth century, and it remained in use in the German-speaking countries throughout the hand-press period.

The other traditional pattern, the divided lay, employed two cases to a

[21] Carter, H., *A view of early typography*, Oxford 1969, pp. 20–1.
[22] Vervliet, H. D. L., *Sixteenth-century printing types of the Low Countries*, Amsterdam 1968, p. 11.
[23] Gaskell, P., 'The lay of the case', *Studies in bibliography*, xxii, 1969, pp. 125–42.

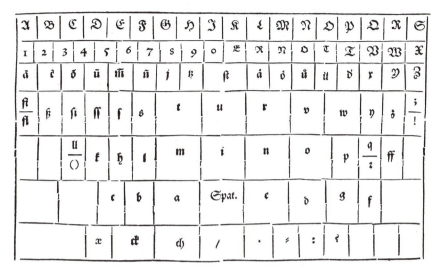

F IG. 21. Seventeenth-century German single lay for gothic type (Wolffger, G., *New-auffgesetztes Format-büchlein*, Graz 1672; St. Bride 20958, facing f. 1)

fount, each of them being smaller and more oblong than the single-lay case; deep ones could take 18–20 kg. (40–5 lb.) of type each, but pairs were usually filled with about 27 kg. (60 lb.) in all. Capitals, small capitals, and (sometimes) figures were placed in the boxes of the upper case, which were all of a size, while the small letters, punctuation marks, and spaces went in the variously-sized boxes of the lower case.[23a] Plantin had cases of both the single and the divided lay made for him in 1563–7, and English printers were referring to 'pairs' of cases by 1588; the divided lay was used in France by 1723 and probably before.[24] There were national variants of the divided lay. In one form of the lower case, found in Holland and France (and also at the Oxford University Press, where French compositors were employed in the later seventeenth century), the letters h and y were kept in small, peripheral boxes. In the English national variant of the lower case, however, h and y, more used in English than in French, were kept in larger boxes near the middle of the case. A divided lay something like the French version was known in Spain; while American printers adopted the English pattern. Details of early Italian lays are lacking, but there is some evidence that a divided lay was used by the later hand-press period.

[23a] 'Upper' and 'lower' cases because they were placed one above the other on the compositor's frame. Type set in capitals is sometimes said to be in upper case, and type in small letters to be in lower case.

[24] Voet, L., *The golden compasses*, ii (there are no page references in the present work to *The golden compasses*, vol. ii, which was still in manuscript when Dr. Voet kindly allowed me to see it); Gaskell, P., op. cit., pp. 128–9.

A	B	C	D	E	F	G	A	B	C	D	E	F	G
H	I	K	L	M	N	O	H	I	K	L	M	N	O
P	Q	R	S	T	V	X	P	Q	R	S	T	V	X
â	ê	î	ô	û	Y	Z	ffl	ffl	J	U	Y	Z	!
á	é	í	ó	ú	J	U	fl	fl	Æ	æ	W	w	?
à	è	ì	ò	ù	Apost.	ſt	ſſ	ff	ë	ï	ü	j	-division

ç	ç	k	w		1	2	3	4	5	6	7	8
&	b	c	d	e	s	ſ	f	g	h	9 / æ	0 / œ	
& z	l	m	n	i	o	p	q	ffi fi	ffi fi	; demi cadra tine	: Cadra tine	
y x	v	u	t	Espaces	a	r	•	,	Cadrats			

Fig. 22. Divided lay, French pattern, early eighteenth century (Fertel, M. D., *La science pratique de l'imprimerie*, Saint-Omer 1723; U.L.C. 7850. c. 46, f. p. 12).

Lays for exotic founts were usually adaptations of those used for the latin alphabet. Thus English learned printers would lay their hebrew or arabic founts in pairs of ordinary cases; while Russian printers laid cyrillic type in a single case, following a transliteration of the German arrangement. The greek cursives were a necessary exception, and a French manual of 1723 shows a fount of cursive greek similar to Garamont's laid in three pairs of special cases, in a total of 750 boxes.[25]

Printers ordered founts of particular sizes either by specifying the total number of letters required, or by weight; and founders charged for the cost of the metal plus the cost of casting or, in the eighteenth century, by weight

[25] Fertel, M. D., *La science pratique de l'imprimerie*, Saint-Omer 1723, f. pp. 13, 14.

A	B	C	D	E	F	G	A	B	C	D	E	F	G
II	I	K	L	M	N	O	H	I	K	L	M	N	O
P	Q	R	S	T	V	W	P	Q	R	S	T	V	W
X	Y	Z	Æ	J	U	Œ	X	Y	Z	Æ	J	U	
1	2	3	4	5	6	7	â	ê	î	ô	û	¶	§
8	9	0	fb	fk	ffi	ffi	à	è	ì	ò	ù	†	‡
ä	ë	ï	ô	ü	ft	k	á	é	í	ó	ú	‖	*

						s	()	?	!	;	fl	ff
ct	[]	æ	œ	ç	'						ff	ff
&	b	c	d	e		i	f	f	g	fh	fi	fi
ffl												
j	l	m	n	h		o	y	p	q	w	n	m
H.S.												
z	v	u	t	*Spaces*		a	r		, .	: -		Qu.
x												

FIG. 23. Divided lay, English pattern, eighteenth century (Smith, J., *The printer's grammar*, London 1755; U.L.C. 860. d. 44, pp. 186-7).

alone, the small bodies costing more per unit of weight than the large. Founts were supplied in quantities approximately proportional to the frequency of use of the various sorts, the fount schemes or 'bills of letter' being worked out by the founders. In the eighteenth century a 'full bill' was based on a quantity of 3,000 lower-case letters m, and included 7,000 a, 12,000 e, 400 x, 800 A, and so on, plus spacing material and italic; a full bill of roman plus half a bill of italic weighed 365 kg.[26] Large types for display were supplied in smaller numbers, and might be charged for by the piece; thus a printer might order a 20-m fount of canon roman, and get 40 a, 60 e, 20 m, 8 x, 14 A, etc.

Full bills of text types were bulky as well as heavy—a full bill of pica occupied about 16 pairs of cases—and type that was not in use was stored in baskets or paper wrappers. Eighteenth-century printers used fount cases

[26] Figures (which varied a good deal) from Smith, J., *The printer's grammar*, London 1755, pp. 38-48. See also Voet, L., op. cit., ii, and Moxon, J., op. cit., p. 19 n.

for storage, which were arranged like ordinary cases but were some three times deeper than usual.

But few printers of the earlier hand-press period kept type in these eighteenth-century quantities. French printers of the seventeenth century were accustomed to buy founts of around 100,000 pieces of pica (about 180 kg.), and other sizes in proportion;[27] while Jaggard printed the whole of the Shakespeare First Folio with a worn fount of pica which can have weighed no more than about 90 kg. (200 lb.).[28] Many printers' inventories have survived, which show that total stocks of type were characteristically between 225 and 900 kg. of type per press in the sixteenth and early seventeenth centuries (often including a considerable proportion of worn type waiting to be melted down), and between 450 and 2,250 kg. per press in the later seventeenth and in the eighteenth century.[29] Plantin of Antwerp was exceptional in the later sixteenth century in possessing nearly 21,000 kg. of cast type; this worked out at 3,500 kg. for each of the six presses he usually operated (though at one time he was working sixteen presses at 1,300 kg. of type for each).[30] In 1588 Thomas Thomas, Cambridge University printer, had one press and 1,400 kg. of type, but 40 per cent of the type was old metal waiting to be melted down; of the rest, 22 per cent was standing in pages, 22 per cent was in cases, and 16 per cent was in store. Cantrell Legge, another Cambridge University printer, also had a single press in 1625, but only 550 kg. of type.[31] After its reorganization at the end of the seventeenth century, the Cambridge University Press normally operated two presses, and had about 1,000 kg. of type for each.[32] The large book-printing house of Schipper in Amsterdam owned eleven presses in 1755 and 1,150 kg. of type for each,[33] while a small provincial office bought by the Société Typographique de Neuchâtel in 1769 had three presses and 625 kg. of type for each of them.[34] In 1800, finally, Strahan the King's Printer in London owned nine presses and 2,000 kg. of type for each.[35]

No two printers of the hand-press period possessed stocks of exactly similar founts of type and of ornaments; a printer's typographical equipment was unique, and identifiably so. In the fifteenth and early sixteenth

[27] Martin, H. J., *Livre, pouvoirs et société à Paris au XVIIe siècle*, Genève 1969, i, p. 369 and n. 19.

[28] Calculated from Hinman, C., *The printing and proof-reading of the first folio of Shakespeare*, Oxford 1963, i, pp. 49–50, 73–4, etc.

[29] List in Gaskell, P., *The decline of the common press*, Cambridge University Ph.D. thesis 2902, 1956, p. 217; and further inventories collected since 1956.

[30] Voet, L., 'The making of books in the renaissance', *Printing and graphic arts*, x, 1966, p. 59 (44,000 Antwerp pounds).

[31] Gray, G. J., and Palmer, W. M., *Abstracts from the wills . . . of printers . . . of Cambridge from 1504 to 1699*, London 1915, pp. 70–1, 83.

[32] McKenzie, D. F., *The Cambridge University Press 1696–1712*, Cambridge 1966, i, ch. 3.

[33] *Catalogus der letteren . . . boekdrukkery . . . weleer behoort hebbende aan de weduwe van Jan Jacobsz. Schipper*, Amsterdam 1755.   [34] S.T.N. MS. 1236, f. 58.   [35] B.M. Add. MS. 48910.

centuries, when printers usually had founts cast up from their own matrices in their own moulds, there would be minor differences of thickness, of body size, and of individual variant sorts, even between founts that derived ultimately from the same basic set of punches. Thus in the period 1485–1501 at least fifty printers in Germany and Switzerland acquired founts of Schwabacher in body sizes around 90 mm. to 20 lines which can be distinguished from each other by their variant letters, etc., but which derived from no more than about eight sets of punches.[36] (Incunabulists, indeed, work on the assumption that a fount belonging to a fifteenth-century printer was unique to him, which is likely to be true enough of the fount as cast, but is not necessarily true of its punches.)

From the later sixteenth century until the end of the period, when printers increasingly bought complete founts of cast type from the type-foundries, the similarities between founts became greater, but even then slight differences are nearly always observable. The founders were constantly revising their stock; punches would be touched up, matrices would be lost and replaced, new sorts would be added and old ones withdrawn, so that even founts of the same variety from the same founder could differ in minor detail. Besides this printers sometimes specified an abnormal body size or set for a particular face.

But above all it is the combination of different founts of type in a printer's stock, each one in a particular state of revision (or mixture of various states of revision) and wear, that identifies him. Add to this his stock of unique woodcut ornaments and initials (see pp. 154–6), and his finger-print is plain, a typographical equipment that belonged to him alone.[36a]

Only the largest printers of the sixteenth and seventeenth centuries were in a position to choose between one type design and another, the great majority of smaller printers being limited by shortage of capital to the output of one or perhaps two local foundries. By the eighteenth century alternative designs were becoming more widely available, but there is little evidence that ordinary printers cared much about the niceties of type design: what they wanted was a type that would not offend the conservatism of their customers, and one that was made of good hard-wearing metal. English printers enthusiastically exchanged their debased yet costly Dutch types for Caslon's urbane founts when they became available at very reasonable prices in the 1730s and 1740s; but when, a few years later, the typefounder Fry offered founts in Baskerville's eccentric design (which was well known to be bad for the eyes) he found few takers.[37]

---

[36]   Carter, H., *A view of early typography*, Oxford 1969, pp. 57–8.

[36a]   But not for all time; a printer's type, initials, ornaments, etc., might (like the rest of his equipment) be lent, pledged, sold, or seized.

[37]   Reed, T. B., *A history of the old English letter foundries*, rev. Johnson, A. F., London 1952, pp. 300–1.

Composition

Type was set up from copy, manuscript in the case of a new work, probably printed if it was for a new edition.[1] In the very early days copy was often an old manuscript book, and even when copy was specially written for the printer it was common until well into the seventeenth century for authors to write on quires of folded sheets. From the later seventeenth century copy was more usually written on loose leaves of paper, which were more convenient for the printer.

Manuscript copy, as printers often complained, might be an ill-written author's draft much blotted and corrected, but it seems that a good many manuscripts intended for the printer were fair-copied, either by the author or by a professional scribe. Hornschuch, in his correctors' manual of 1608, implied that it was normal for vernacular manuscripts to be fair-copied for the printer, adding that the scribes who did it cared more for calligraphic elegance than for the accuracy of the text.[2]

The copy having been delivered to the printing house, various decisions had to be taken about the size and form of the printed book that was to be set from it. These were necessarily the responsibility of the master or his deputy, who had to get in the paper that would be needed and to fit the book's production into the work pattern of the shop. The master might also interest himself in the detailed typographic design—Plantin insisted on seeing a specimen page before composition began[3]—but much of it was left to the compositor to decide on the basis of 'house style' and the precedents of similar books.[3a] At the same time the copy might be 'prepared'—read through, corrected, and annotated—probably by the corrector if the house was large enough to employ one. Copy-preparation by the corrector was apparently common in continental Europe in the seventeenth and eighteenth centuries, and the practice was recommended to English printers by Smith in his manual of 1755.[4]

[1] On copy of the hand-press period see Simpson, P., *Proof-reading in the sixteenth, seventeenth and eighteenth centuries*, Oxford 1935 (repr. 1970); and Hellinga, W. Gs., *Copy and print in the Netherlands*, Amsterdam 1962. I have also referred to an unpublished paper by R. L. Beare on continental proofs and copy of the seventeenth century.

[2] Hornschuch, H., ’Ορθοτυπογραφία, Lipsiae 1608, p. 22.

[3] Voet, L., *The golden compasses*, ii.

[3a] Some authors gave clear instructions for the layout of their books; see Greg, W. W., *Collected papers*, Oxford 1966, pp. 99-100, for an example of 1591; and U.L.C., Add. MS. 7913, f. 1ᵇ, for one of 1692.

[4] Beare, R. L., op. cit.; Moxon, J., *Mechanick exercises*, eds. Davis and Carter, 2nd ed., Oxford 1962, p. 192 and n.; Smith, J., *The printer's grammar*, London 1755, p. 273.

Many examples of printers' copy have survived from the hand-press period, some of them annotated with instructions concerning layout, italicization, capitalization, etc. Copy, manuscript or printed, can generally be recognized even in the absence of such notes by the marks—sometimes very faint—with which the compositors indicated the endings of the type-pages (see p. 50), and by such signs as set-off from fresh-made proofs, inky thumb-marks, and a general air of dog-eared grubbiness.

Although a rough estimate of the length of the book had to be made at the very beginning in order to come to a decision about format, it was then necessary to know its length more precisely, chiefly so that the right amount of paper for the edition could be ordered.[4a] To this end the compositor—or sometimes the master or overseer—'cast off' the copy by counting words and by computation according to the sizes of type and page that had been decided on.[5] Casting off also helped the overseer to allot work on the book, and enabled informed final decisions to be made about its typographical details so that, for instance, the text would not overrun the last whole sheet by a page or two.

Printed copy, or the manuscript of a poem or verse play, could easily be cast off with such accuracy that the exact contents of each type page could be predicted, and even a prose manuscript could be cast off with fair accuracy by a skilled man, although this was much more difficult. With the copy accurately cast off, setting could begin anywhere in the book, and more than one part of it could be set in type at a time.

Casting off made it possible to set sheets 'by formes', when the compositor set all the pages for one side of the sheet and sent them to be printed before the pages for the other side of the sheet were set, instead of setting all the pages for the sheet one after the other in their proper order. In spite of its awkwardness—for the two series of pages for the two sides of a sheet were not consecutive but had to interlock with each other—setting by formes appears to have been a common practice in English and in some continental printing up to the mid seventeenth century. Several books set from prose manuscripts in sixteenth-century London have pages of regular length on one side of the sheet (that is, in one forme), and pages of irregular length on the other (four octavos printed by Thomas Marshe in the 1560s, for instance, and the first edition of Sidney's *Defence of poesie*, printed by Thomas Creede in 1595);[6] probably these books were cast off with less than perfect accuracy and then set by formes, a forme with regular pages preceding one with irregular pages which had to be made to fit with what had already been set

---

[4a] Format was (and is) often decided by convention; see pp. 300-4 below.

[5] Moxon, J., op. cit., pp. 239-44.

[6] Bond, W. H., 'Casting off copy by Elizabethan printers', *Papers of the Bibliographical Society of America*, xlii, 1948, pp. 281-91.

and printed. Again, study of recurring types in London-printed verse plays of the later sixteenth and early seventeenth century proves that a high proportion of them were set by formes, individual pieces of type being found in both formes of a pair; the first folio of Shakespeare (London 1623) is only the most celebrated example.[7] Setting by formes was also practised in Madrid at this period, a late occurrence being Calderón's *Tercera parte* (a verse quarto, Madrid 1664).[8]

The reason for setting by formes is not entirely obvious. The practice certainly makes a limited stock of type go further, and some of the London printers who set by formes around 1600 were chronically short of type. But other printers who were not short of type also set by formes, Plantin for instance who had books set by formes up to about 1565 and then changed to continuous setting.[9] The method of 'half-sheet imposition', moreover (see p. 83), which was known before 1500, saves just as much type as setting by formes in foldings other than folio, and is much easier to manage. It may be that setting by formes was an early trade practice (deriving perhaps from the normal method of copying manuscript books by the side of the sheet rather than by consecutive pages) which was later abandoned on account of its inconvenience, soonest in countries with an advanced printing technology. Plantin, as we saw, gave it up in the 1560s, and it has not been recognized in Dutch, French, or German printing after 1600;[10] it persisted in England until the second, and in Spain until the third, quarter of the seventeenth century; Moxon mentioned it in 1683 only to dismiss it as undesirable;[11] and it does not appear to have been used at the Cambridge University Press around 1700, or at the Bowyer or S.T.N. offices in the eighteenth century.[12]

Preparation and casting off completed, the copy was given out to individual compositors for setting in type. How it was divided was influenced by the size of the shop. Where there were no more than two or three compositors there appears to have been a tendency for individual workmen to concentrate on particular books (often several books at a time), and to set at least whole sheets or whole formes. Where there were a larger number of compositors in the complex work-flow of concurrent production, small divisions of copy ('takings' or 'takes') were handed out to whoever was ready for them, so that the setting of sheets, formes, and even individual pages were on occasion shared between different compositors. Shared setting

[7] Hinman, C., *The printing and proof-reading of the first folio of Shakespeare*, Oxford 1963, *passim*.

[8] Cruickshank, D. W., 'The printing of Calderón's *Tercera parte*', *Studies in bibliography*, xxiii, 1970, pp. 230–51. Current work by R. M. Flores suggests that the first edition of *Don Quixote* (prose, Madrid 1604–5) was also set by formes.

[9] Voet, L., op. cit.   [10] Beare, R. L., op. cit.

[11] Moxon, J., op. cit., pp. 210–11.   [12] See the bibliography, pp. 393–4.

seems to have been uncommon in the small English printing houses of the seventeenth century,[13] but it is referred to in the sixteenth-century records of the Plantin–Moretus house, and in Bowyer's records of the 1730s;[14] and the compositors' marks on surviving continental copy of the seventeenth century often imply shared setting.[15] Eventually—by the mid eighteenth century in France—compositors formed 'companionships' for the efficient and equitable distribution of work for shared setting (see p. 192). When setting was shared the compositors involved might work either simultaneously or consecutively; simultaneous shared setting (especially if it took place in two or more different printing houses, as was not uncommon in London around 1600)[16] might result in pages or sections of irregular length.

SETTING TYPE[17]

The compositor's apparatus was in three main parts. There were the type cases, which have already been described (pp. 34-6), and which were propped up for use on a timber frame at a convenient working height; a composing stick, which was a hand-held tray in which pieces of type from the case were assembled; and galleys, larger trays on to which lines of type were transferred when the composing stick was full.

The earliest frames seem to have been no more than a pair of trestles on which the large case of the single lay was placed, but later on more elaborate structures were used, with a double slope on top for the two cases of the divided lay, and often incorporating racks for storing cases; double frames were also made, so that cases of another fount could be put up, or italic alongside the roman. Until the mid seventeenth century compositors generally sat to their work, but from then on it became more usual to compose standing up, an easier position for fast work.[18]

Sheets of copy were put up on the case, either folded into a special clip called a 'visorium'—the normal continental method up to the nineteenth century—or held against the right-hand side of the upper case by an arrangement of weights and string, as was usual in England in the later hand-press period and probably before.[19] The compositor then took his stick in his

[13] It was not normal in dramatic printing *c.* 1600, and Moxon assumed that one compositor would set at least a whole sheet.

[14] Voet, L., op. cit.; McKenzie, D. F., 'Printers of the mind', *Studies in bibliography*, xxii, 1969, pp. 64-74.   [15] Beare, R. L., op. cit.

[16] Greg noted several examples in *A bibliography of the English printed drama to the Restoration*, e.g. no. 202.

[17] The classic early description of the compositor's trade is Moxon, J., op. cit., pp. 193-246.

[18] The early illustrations (up to Saenredam, 1628, for instance) generally show seated compositors; Moxon (1683, p. 33) specifies the standing position.

[19] Moxon, J., op. cit., p. 204; Hansard, T. C., *Typographia*, London 1825, pp. 408-9.

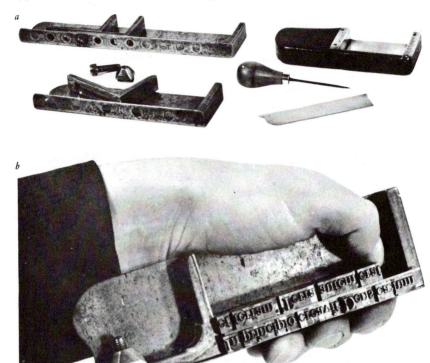

FIG. 24 (*a*, *b*). Nineteenth-century English compositors' equipment. (*a*) A stick with two slides for setting text and marginal notes in parallel, a fixed wooden stick for newspaper columns and an ordinary stick in parts, together with a bodkin and a setting rule; the design of the two iron sticks was established by the mid seventeenth century. (*b*) Setting the bible in double pica. The first line contains an error due to foul case, the second has a turned letter; there is a setting rule between the lines.

left hand, read the first few words of his text, and began to pick up the type with his right hand.

The adjustable slide of the stick had first to be set to the 'measure', the length of the line of type required and thus the width of the column of type in the book. This measure was generally a multiple of the body size of the type being used, and was obtained by laying the right number of letters 'm' on their sides in the stick, pushing the slide up to them and screwing it up tight.[20] Alternatively the stick could be set with a gauge made of a strip of wood or metal, or simply by measuring the position of the slide against a printed page or a line of set type.[21]

Having set the stick the compositor placed a setting rule (a strip of brass

[20] Smith, J., *The printer's grammar*, London 1755, pp. 196–7.
[21] Moxon, J., op. cit., pp. 203–4.

rule of the right length) against its back plate and started to pick up the letters of the first word in the copy. Each piece of type was 'sighted' in the case before it was taken up to see which end had the letter cast on it and to locate its nick,[22] but the compositor did not look at it again as he carried it towards the stick, his eyes being engaged in sighting the next letter. He felt its shank, however, between the thumb and first two fingers of his right hand, to ensure that it was not obviously thicker or thinner than it ought to be, and placed it under his left thumb in the left-hand corner of the stick, face up and with the nick away from the back plate. The subsequent letters of the word followed one by one, the stick in the compositor's left hand following his right as it moved about the case from box to box; and when the word was finished he put in a space and proceeded to the next.

In due course the compositor came towards the end of his measure, and his stick contained a line of type which read (from his point of view) from left to right but of which the letters were upside down and mirror-fashion. At this point he found, nine times out of ten, that the last word would not fill his measure precisely, so he either drove the line out (if he had too much room) or got it in (if he had too little) by altering the amount of space between some or all of the words in the line. First, probably, he read the line in the stick and corrected any mistakes, which could be mended much more quickly now than later, though not all compositors did so in spite of the fact that they had to correct their errors in their own time.[23] Then he changed the spaces between the words one by one until the line was a tight sliding fit in the stick, picking out rejected spaces and choosing additions or replacements from his central box of mixed spaces. This process, which gave a straight right-hand margin on the printed page, was called justification. Short lines were justified with spaces and quads so that they would lock up tight in the forme with the rest.

Moxon in the seventeenth century specified two sorts of spaces: thick spaces measuring four to the 'em' (the body size of the type concerned),[24] which is the same as the modern printer's middle space; and thin spaces, which measured seven to the em, considerably thinner than the modern thin space and in fact what would now be called a hair space.[25] By the middle of the eighteenth century, however, English printers were using thick spaces of three to the em, middle spaces of four to the em, and thin spaces of five to the em, which is the system still in use; and a similar development appears to have taken place in France during the second quarter of

---

[22] See fig. 1, p. 9; the nick established the orientation of the letter.

[23] Fertel (1723, p. 45) urges the compositor to correct line by line in the stick, whereas Moxon says nothing about it; practice probably differed from compositor to compositor.

[24] Used thus the em is not a particular measurement but varies with the body. The term could also mean specifically the pica em, or about 4·2 mm.   [25] Moxon, J., op. cit., p. 103 n.

the eighteenth century.[26] But nowhere during the hand-press period were spaces of different widths kept apart in separate boxes of the case, a practice dating from the early nineteenth century.

It was sometimes necessary (or at least helpful) to justify by splitting a word at the end of the line, adding a hyphen and carrying the remainder over to the next line although, since the position of the break in the word was governed by convention, the spacing usually had to be altered as well. Until the later seventeenth century it was also permissible to simplify justification by varying the spelling of some words and by employing contractions; see pp. 344–6 for more about this.

Before proceeding to set the second line, the compositor removed the setting rule from the back of the stick and placed it in front of the line which had just been set; its purpose was to increase the stability of each new line as it was assembled, and to enable its individual types to slide sideways during justification, unimpeded by any slight roughness of the line beneath. The second line was then set, and was followed by another, and so on until the stick was full. The number of lines that the stick could take depended of course both on its size and on that of the type, but in England was typically from three to six. The compositor emptied the lines from an English stick of this sort on to a wooden tray called a galley, which lay on the right-hand side of his upper case. To do this he put the stick down on the lower case and, using his setting rule and a similar strip of wood (reglet) as supports, he applied pressure evenly round the block of type with the fingers and thumbs of both hands for the transfer. Set type can behave like a fluid, and any clumsiness at this point could cause new-set type to collapse into 'pie' (muddled type).

At all periods, but uncommonly before the eighteenth century, the lines of type might be 'leaded', thin strips of typemetal, reglet, or card being slipped in between each one in order to spread the lines out vertically. The leading might be done either in the stick (in which case quads were often set at the ends of the lines in order to prevent thin pieces of type from slipping up and down beside the ends of short leads), or after the lines had been transferred to the galley and were being made up into a page.

Moxon's deep, adjustable composing stick, which remained the normal English pattern and was also used apparently in Holland, Germany, and Scandinavia,[27] was not the only sort of stick used in the hand-press period. Wooden composing sticks without slides were used for bookwork in the

---

[26] Smith, J., *The printer's grammar*, London 1755, p. 111; Fertel, M. D., *La science pratique de l'imprimerie*, Saint-Omer 1723, pp. 16–17; *Encyclopédie*, v. Paris 1755, s.v. 'espace'.

[27] Moxon himself was following Dutch practice; German sticks were illustrated in the eighteenth-century manuals, and Scandinavian sticks in Bengtsson, B., *Äldre typografisk teknik*, Stockholm 1946, p. 41.

sixteenth century, and for jobs in narrow columns (encyclopedias, newspapers, etc.) until the end of the nineteenth century (fig. 24).[28] Although wooden sticks were not in themselves adjustable, they could be used for measures narrower than their fixed settings by starting or ending each line with a particular amount of spacing material, which was removed when the stick was emptied.

French adjustable sticks were not so deep as English ones, and were emptied as each line was set. Setting rules were not used, and the compositor emptied the justified line by holding the stick in his left hand, placing a strip of wooden reglet on the front of the line and picking it out with his right hand alone (fig. 25). This was quickly done and probably took no more time over-all than the English method of emptying the stick with both hands every four or five lines.

Long lines of type—more than about 20 cm.—which were common in display work such as the title-pages of large books, might be set straight on to the galley or the imposing stone. In the nineteenth century, and perhaps before, adjustable broadside sticks were made, usually of wood and measuring as much as 100 cm. in length.

It may be as well to emphasize at this stage that real (as opposed to theoretical) printing was a complex craft carried out by fallible and inconsistent human beings of widely different capabilities. It was usual to set type in the way that has just been described, but the old printers were men, not abstractions, who had good days and bad ones; who got on each other's nerves and lost their tempers; who had moments of disastrous clumsiness; and who improvised and botched without hesitation whenever their tools or materials did not precisely meet the needs of the moment. For every generalization that is made about the history of printing technology, for every rule supposedly observed by hand printers, there may have been an exception; or—for there was no rule about this either— there may not.

Even the ablest compositors made mistakes, as is shown by Benjamin Franklin's account of setting up Willem Sewel's *History of the Quakers* in Philadelphia in 1728: 'It was a folio, pro patria size [i.e. foolscap], in pica, with long primer notes. I compos'd of it a sheet a day, and Meredith worked it off at press; it was often eleven at night, and sometimes later, before I had finished my distribution for the next day's work, for the little jobbs sent in by our other friends now and then put us back. But so determin'd I was to continue doing a sheet a day of the folio, that one night, when, having impos'd my forms, I thought my day's work over, one of them by accident was broken, and two pages reduced to pi, I immediately distributed

---

[28] [Plantin, C.], *Dialogues*, Anvers 1567, pp. 242–3; illustrated in Bengtsson, op. cit., p. 41.

and compos'd it over again before I went to bed.'[29] One wonders whether the two pages of the broken forme were as well set the second time as the first.

Then there was the continual drunkenness at work of the journeyman Hans van Leuven *alias* Elzevier (who was the father of the founder of the famous Elzevier Press). Plantin of Antwerp sacked him in 1573, but hired him again a few days later. And there was the curious behaviour of Plantin's compositor Michel Mayer, who in June 1564 spent Sunday, Monday, Tuesday, and Wednesday in a brothel, then went to sleep on a box in his room on Thursday morning, and finally packed his things and left the establishment without saying a word to anyone; Mayer too was hired again later by Plantin.[30]

Disruptive behaviour was not confined to the workmen. The following account of a quarrel which took place in about 1540 between Thomas Platter and Balthasar Ruch, partners in a printing business in Basel, comes from Platter's autobiography. Platter had offended Ruch, who was looking for a chance to get his own back: 'On one occasion, while it was still Fair time and we could not finish printing the works we had been given, we were also printing on our days off, and we had been printing all that Sunday; then the journeymen had to be fed and paid overtime. That night I was correcting a proof at about eleven o'clock when Balthasar began needling me, and finally swearing and saying "I don't know what you're on about, you from the Valais—whatever we do, it's wrong!" . . . I answered his nastiness back. He says nothing, but taking hold of a heavy pine board he gets behind me while I am working on the proof and is on the point of bringing it down on my head with both hands. Then I look round and see the blow coming, I jump up and ward it off with my arm. Then we were hitting each other and struggling; he scratched my face badly and tried to gouge my eye out with his fingers. When I saw what he was up to, I drew back for a punch and hit him so hard on the nose that he fell on his back and lay there for some time, so that his wife stood over him and cried out "Mercy! You've done my husband in!" Meanwhile the journeymen, who had just gone to bed, hearing the row quickly got up again and came downstairs. He was still lying there, my scratched face was still bleeding. Soon afterwards he got up and wanted to attack me again. "Let him come," I said, 'I'll give it him, and better!' Then the journeymen shoved me out of the door. . . . Next day our partners came in. They were displeased, as were the men, that we should be the masters, and should behave towards each

[29] Franklin, B., *The life of Benjamin Franklin written by himself*, ed. Bigelow, J., 3 vols., London 1879, i, pp. 189–90. The edition of Sewel referred to by Franklin is Sabin 79604.
[30] *Gedenkboek der Plantin-dagen, 1555–1955*, Antwerp 1956, p. 245, nn. 2, 3.

other in this way.'[31] Again, one wonders whether that proof was ever properly read.

Before going on to consider what the compositor did next, we should consider the possibility that type was occasionally set from dictation. This can never have been a common practice: however fast a compositor picks up type, he has time to read his copy while his hands are at work, and dictation could not significantly increase his output; dictation, moreover, is inherently less accurate than ocular copying as a method of transcription. Nevertheless there is an account of a sixteenth-century Swiss scholar, Heinrich Pantaleon, who was employed in the 1540s in the Basel printing house of Michael Isengrinius, a firm which specialized in learned printing, as a *lector*; and it is clearly stated that he dictated copy to the compositors.[32] There is no other evidence for the practice, however, and it is possible that Pantaleon's eighteenth-century biographer had misunderstood a description of the method of proof-correction normal in the hand-press period whereby a reader (or *lector*) read the copy aloud to the corrector (see p. 112). A few actual errors in printed texts do appear to have resulted from mis-hearing, rather than mis-reading, the copy (p. 352), but they are not necessarily evidence of setting from dictation; they are more likely to have been introduced into the text during dictation for manuscript fair-copying, or during proof-correction by reading aloud.

PAGE AND GALLEY

Galleys are two- or three-sided trays, nowadays made of metal and three or four times as long as they are wide. Until almost the end of the hand-press period, however, long galleys were unknown, and the compositor emptied his stick on to a wooden tray not much larger than the page he was setting. For composition was always by pages, not (as it was later) by galleys. Galleys were therefore made in various sizes to suit different pages—they were sometimes known as octavo, quarto, or folio galleys—and the larger ones

---

[31] Platter, T. and F., *Zwei Autobiographieen*, ed. Fechter, D. A., Basel 1840, pp. 91–2, translated.

[32] Zeltner, J. K., *C.D. correctorum in typographijs eruditorum centuria speciminis loco collecta*, Nürnberg 1716, pp. 408–9. The Latin text is quoted by McKerrow (pp. 243–4), and may be translated: 'After this he [Heinrich Pantaleon] was handed over to Johannes Bebelius, printer of Basel, and for a time acted as reader in the house of Isengrinius. For at one time, as distinct from today's practice, one person was picked out from amongst the others in order to read aloud from the manuscript in a clear voice to the typesetters what was to be printed. As a result, those who set up the words they heard from the reader's mouth made short work of it; and it was read out from three or four sheets to a like number of compositors. But in our time, as everyone knows, he whose task it is to do the initial setting up is accustomed to have the copy in front of his eyes for him to see. This method, which was doubtless changed because of the ignorance of the printers, appeals to me most since it takes time into account and is less subject to daydreaming.' The last sentence is equally obscure in the original: 'Qui modus haud dubie propter ignorantiam Typographorum mutatus, cum temporis rationem habeat, & hallucinationibus minus est [*sic*] obnoxius, maxime mihi arridet.'

Fig. 25. A French composing room of the mid eighteenth century. A visorium and page galleys can be seen on the upper cases, and a compositor is emptying his stick one-handed in the French way. Two empty chases stand by the imposing stone, where a third compositor is planing down a forme; between them are the quoin- and furniture-drawers. Perfected sheets are hung up on cords to dry the paper, having been lifted by means of the peel which stands by the wall on the left. The far end of the room serves as a warehouse. (*Encyclopédie*, planches vii, Paris 1769, 'Imprimerie en caractères', pl. 1.)

generally had a false bottom called a 'slice' which could be withdrawn with the type on it when a page was finished.

When the compositor had set the right number of lines for his page and put them on to the galley, he marked the place in the copy where the new type page ended, and added a marginal note giving the number of the next page both in the book and in the sheet; this was chiefly in order to correlate copy and printed page for the corrector, but it might also help the compositor to impose the pages in the right order and give them their page numbers. A typical annotation of this sort (actually written in the margin of the printed copy for a book printed at Basel in 1563)[33] was $\frac{601}{9DD}$ meaning that the *next* page to be set would be numbered 601, and that it would be the ninth page—not the ninth leaf—of signature 2D. Annotations in the same or in a closely similar form were made in English printing houses from the later sixteenth century until after the end of the hand-press period.

The compositor next added the headline, with running title and page number; and the direction line at the bottom of the page, containing the catchword (the first word of the next page) and, on certain pages, the signa-

[33] B.N. Rés. m. z. 13, sig. C4ᵃ.

ture (see the next section). Finally he tied the whole page round with string (page cord) to keep it together, transferred it from the galley to a paper wrapper and put it on to some convenient surface for storage until he was ready to assemble it with other pages for printing. After the first sheet or two of a book, the compositor took headlines and direction lines from the pages of a sheet that had already been printed (see p. 109).

SIGNATURES

Books were printed, as we have seen, not leaf by leaf but on large sheets of paper with a number of pages on each side, which were later folded up to make groups of leaves. It was necessary, when assembling the sheets of a book, to get them the right way up and in the right order; and to this end each sheet was signed on the first page with a letter of the alphabet so that they could readily be arranged in alphabetical order; similar signatures were also placed on the rectos of a few leaves after the first of each sheet in order to help the binder with his folding.

Overwhelmingly the commonest signatures were the 23 letters of the Latin alphabet (A to Z, omitting I or J, U or V, and W), a convention deriving from the manuscript period.[33a] The twenty-fourth sheet was then signed Aa (etc.), the forty-seventh Aaa, and so on. It was usual for dupli-cated signature-letters to be set out in full, but English printers in the eighteenth century preferred to set 3A for Aaa, 6A for Aaaaaa, etc. Signa-tures on rectos after the first of each sheet were distinguished by numerical suffixes; the second signed recto of sheet Aa, for instance, would be signed Aa2 (or in England, perhaps, 2A2). Thus Bb3 would be found on the third recto of the twenty-fifth sheet, and 5C4 on the fourth recto of the ninety-fifth sheet.

The precise form of the signatures varied from time to time and from place to place.[34] It was common in the sixteenth century to begin the series of signatures for the text with a lower-case alphabet, a–z, and to continue with A– or aa– (or less commonly with Aa– or AA–). A characteristically English habit was to begin the main signature alphabet with B, rather than A, to allow for a sheet of preliminaries signed A, and following up as usual with Aa– (or 2A–). Roman rather than arabic numerals for suffixes (e.g. Aij rather than A2) were widely used until the end of the sixteenth century, but later were a French peculiarity.

[33a] A rare variant used at the Jaggard house in early seventeenth-century London was a 20-letter signature alphabet, omitting X, Y, and Z.

[34] Sayce, R. A., 'Compositorial practices and the localisation of printed books, 1530–1800', *The Library*, xxi, 1966, pp. 1–45.

The signing of preliminary leaves varied even more widely; the sensible practice of signing the main series A– and the preliminaries a– was always quite common, and English printers who began the main series with B would often sign the preliminaries A a b c (etc.). But it was even commoner to use symbols in forms such as * ** ***, or even (without logical order) * † ¶ § (etc.). During the fifteenth and sixteenth centuries printers got over the resulting difficulties by adding (usually adjacent to the colophon) a summary of the signatures called the register.

PRELIMINARIES, PAGINATION, CATCHWORDS, ETC.

The preliminary leaves or sections (which were nearly always printed after the text of a book except in reprints, and sometimes even then) consisted essentially of the title-page, the author's or publisher's prefatory matter and, sometimes, a table of contents. Fifteenth-century books generally had no preliminaries, but were signed by the printer in a colophon at the end. After the general adoption of title-pages around 1500, colophons lost their former importance, but they remained relatively common until well into the seventeenth century, and they never disappeared entirely.

It was common practice from early times to protect a book by leaving the first leaf blank, and it was this leaf that was made to serve the useful purpose of carrying a short-title of the book printed on it; which then developed into the full title-page announcing the title and author of the book, and soon giving the name of the printer and the place and date of publication as well. By the seventeenth century it was becoming common to protect the title-page with an initial blank leaf; which in turn, by the eighteenth century, often had a short-title printed on it (the half-title);[35] and in lavishly-printed books the half-title itself would occasionally be protected by a preliminary blank leaf.

Like the text, the title-page was set from copy, which might indicate roughly how it was to be set out. Details of the layout, however, and choice of type were commonly left to the compositor.[36]

Most books had headlines, an extra line of type and quads above the text of each page, which included the running title and the numerals of the foliation or pagination. The numbering of leaves gave way to the numbering of pages late in the sixteenth century, although there were isolated survivals of the earlier practice until the mid eighteenth century.

[35] Nineteenth-century printers called the half-title the 'bastard title', and used the term 'half-title' for the book title used as a heading for the first chapter of a volume.

[36] Hellinga, W. Gs., *Copy and print in the Netherlands*, Amsterdam 1962, pl. 147 shows a manuscript layout for a title-page of 1682; but the choice of type for titles was commonly left to 'the taste and judgment of the compositor' until the end of the nineteenth century (Gould, J., *The letter-press printer*, 6th ed., London [*c*. 1892], p. 26).

It became usual in the mid sixteenth century to complete each page with the first word of the following page set as a catchword at the end of the direction line. The practice was intended to help the compositor to get the pages in the right order for printing,[37] but, although the full use of catchwords was general in English and in most continental printing until the later eighteenth century, they were not always considered necessary. Special forms, such as catchwords on verso pages only, or only on pages without signatures, are found from time to time in French and German books, while Parisian printers normally set catchwords only on the last page of each gathering.

DISTRIBUTION

The distribution of set type back into the cases took place alternately with setting in order to keep both type and compositors occupied. When his case was getting low—it would begin to run out of individual lower-case sorts when it was down to between a quarter and a third of its full weight— the compositor stopped setting and turned to pages of type from a forme (probably of the same book) that had already been printed off, and which were waiting on the stone or on a special galley, stripped of their headlines and direction lines (see p. 109). He lifted about five lines from the top of the nearest page on a setting rule and balanced it on his left hand, with the face of the letter towards him and the last line uppermost. Then he picked up about 2 cm. of type from the right-hand end of the uppermost line (i.e. the last word or two of the last line) with the thumb and forefinger of his right hand, read it, and dropped the pieces of type one by one into their proper boxes; and so on, inch by inch and line by line, until the case was replenished.

A full pair of cases of the divided lay contained about 27 kg. of type, of which about 20 kg. was available for setting; the remaining 7 kg. consisted of capitals and rarely-used sorts which remained in the case when the common sorts ran out. Set type weighed about 0·0175 kg./cm.², so that a full pair of cases sufficed for something like 1150 cm.² of matter; that is $5\frac{1}{2}$ pages the size of this one, or just over two pages of the Shakespeare first folio.

It appears that Jaggard's fount of pica roman would run to no more than about eight pages of the First Folio, but that his compositors probably worked most of the time from two pairs of cases, not four, at least half the fount being set up at any one time. There is also some evidence that, in Jaggard's small shop, particular compositors tended to work from particular

[37] Moxon, J., op. cit., 237–8.

cases.[38] In the nineteenth century, when there was plenty of type, a man would work at his own frame, carrying cases to it from the general stock.

OUTPUT

In the earlier hand-press period, compositors' output was measured, rather roughly, by the page or by the sheet; later a more accurate measurement by ens was adopted, which it will be convenient to use here. One en is half an em of any size of type, and the number of ens in a setting of type is proportional to the number of pieces of type in it. This line is $29\frac{1}{2}$ 11-pt. ems long (59 11-pt. ens); while this whole page contains 2,794 11-pt. ens and would contain about 3,055 individual pieces of type, including spaces.

From 1785, when a scale of prices for piece-work composition was laid down in London, right up to the present century, a 'normal' rate of 1,000 ens per compositor per hour was postulated in England, this rate including the distribution of an equivalent quantity of set type and the correction of the compositor's own mistakes.[39] Distribution (which took from a quarter to a third as long as setting) and correction both took time, so that this rate actually involved setting at 1,500 ens per hour or more.

Competent workmen could certainly achieve this output. Piece-work hands at the Cambridge University Press at the end of the nineteenth century had to demonstrate their ability to keep it up for a succession of 54-hour weeks before they might be promoted to become time hands (who were paid by the hour, and dealt with such things as make-up and authors' corrections).[40] Good compositors at the Harper Establishment in New York in the 1850s could set from 2,000 to 3,000 ens per hour;[41] and in type-setting competitions in America in the 1880s the remarkable rate of 4,000 ens per hour (corrected, but not including distribution) was regularly achieved.[42]

But, although a net rate of 1,000 ens per hour may have been a convenient and even a practicable norm in the nineteenth century, evidence from the hand-press period shows that we must abandon any idea of an earlier normal rate. Even at the Cambridge University Press around 1900, where the 1,000-en norm was supposed to prevail, elderly piece-work compositors were earning only one-third of the wages earned by colleagues still in the

---

[38] Hinman, C., *The printing and proof-reading of the first folio of Shakespeare*, Oxford 1963, i, pp. 39 ff.

[39] Howe, E., *The London compositor*, London 1947, p. 59.

[40] Scurfield, G., *A stickful of nonpareil*, privately printed, Cambridge 1956, p. 21. But Southward wrote in 1900: 'There are many compositors who can set more than 2,000 ens per hour, but we know also that the average performance of an office of 50 men, on book or jobbing work, is less than 1,000 ens an hour' (*Modern printing*, iv, London 1900, p. 87).

[41] Abbott, J., *The Harper establishment*, New York 1855 (repr. Hamden 1956), p. 60.

[42] Barnes, W. C., McCann, J. W., and Duguid, A., *A collection of facts relative to fast typesetting*, New York 1887, *passim*.

prime of life.[43] And in the eighteenth century and before, when the full working week was not 54 hours long but a soul-destroying 72 hours— 12 hours a day, Monday to Saturday—we find both that actual output varied enormously from time to time and from compositor to compositor, and that it was generally far less, seldom more than a half, of the later theoretical norm of 1,000 ens per hour.

In 1683 Moxon, writing of journeymen's piece-work contracts, indicated that compositors' daily rates, and therefore their output, could vary by factors of up to two;[44] and Charles Manby Smith, writing of his work as a compositor in Paris in the 1820s, mentioned a good compositor in his shop who regularly worked four times as fast as his less competent neighbour.[45] Details of the actual weekly output of the compositors at the Cambridge University Press at the beginning of the eighteenth century show fluctuations, both collective and individual, by factors of up to three, spread over periods of months as well as of weeks. The average weekly output of the fastest compositor over the year 1701–2 was 38,000 ens, but he was also capable of setting 64,000 ens per week for five weeks; another compositor set an average of 27,000 ens per week for a period of 80 weeks, then 20,000 per week for a further period of 59 weeks, yet on one occasion he set 60,000 ens per week for a fortnight.[46]

The highest of these actual rates (64,000 ens per week) fell short of the later norm (which would have required 72,000 ens per 72-hour week) by more than 10 per cent, possibly because the Cambridge compositors included make-up and imposition amongst their tasks, jobs which were often done by clickers (p. 192) or by time hands in the nineteenth century; and there is indeed no evidence that 1,000 ens per hour was regularly achieved anywhere in the hand-press period. But the grosser discrepancies—such as the Cambridge compositor who for months on end turned out only a third of what he could do at top speed—require another explanation; and it is to be found in the labour conditions of craft printing.

The most important factor, perhaps, was the variable flow of jobs, which could keep journeymen short of work for long periods, and even force them into part-time employment either with another printer or outside the trade altogether. There was also a widespread tendency amongst pieceworkers, who sold their labour as a commodity, to work for no longer and earn no more than they required for their immediate needs; and their response to the grinding monotony of repetitive labour and over-long hours was frequent

---

[43] Scurfield, G., op. cit., p. 25.
[44] Moxon, J., op. cit., p. 327; and see p. 173.
[45] Smith, C. M., *The working man's way in the world*, London 1853 (repr. London 1968), p. 62.
[46] McKenzie, D. F., *The Cambridge University Press 1696–1712*, Cambridge 1966, i, chs. 3, 4; idem, 'Printers of the mind', *Studies in bibliography*, xxii, 1969, pp. 7–22.

absenteeism. The great fluctuations in output found at Cambridge in the early eighteenth century were in fact normal for the hand-press period; the records of the Plantinian business in the sixteenth and seventeenth centuries, and of a variety of eighteenth-century houses all show comparable variations.

The next stage of the compositor's work was to impose the pages he had set into formes. In order that this process may be fully understood, we must first consider the paper on which books were printed, the nature of which partly determined their shapes and sizes.

Paper

MANUFACTURE[1]

The manufacture of paper, which reached Europe from the East early in the twelfth century, expanded rapidly with the invention and spread of printing, and by the beginning of the sixteenth century large quantities of paper were being made and traded all over the continent. Like printing, paper-making was a stable technology throughout the hand-press period; a few minor improvements in equipment were introduced, and there were general fluctuations in paper quality connected with changing local trade conditions; but the methods of the paper-maker, and the nature of his product, were practically the same in 1800 as they had been in 1500—and indeed long before.

The raw material of white paper was undyed linen—or in very early days hempen—rags, which the paper-maker bought in bulk, sorted and washed, and then put by in a damp heap for four or five days to rot. The 'sweated' rags were next cut up into small pieces and placed in wooden mortars where they were pounded to a pulp (or stuff) by water-powered hammers, impurities being carried off through filters by running water. The pounding took place in two or three stages, separated by pauses for further rotting. A rotary machine invented in Holland in the late seventeenth century did not pound but minced the rags into pulp with revolving knives. Hollanders, as they came to be called, not only required less power but also made stuff several times faster than stamping mills; and, although it was believed that stuff made in hollanders resulted in a weaker paper than did pounded stuff, their economic advantages were so great that they replaced most of the stamping mills in Holland, France, and England during the eighteenth century.

The final stuff was transferred to the vat, a large open tub measuring about 1·6 m. by 0·8 m., with a capacity of some 1,500 litres (330 gallons). It was diluted there with water to the appearance and consistency of liquid porridge; it was kept tepid with a small charcoal furnace let in to the side of the vat, and it was stirred up occasionally with a paddle.

The team at the vat consisted of the maker (or vatman) and the coucher (pronounced koocher), assisted by the layer. Their tools, apart from the vat itself, were a pair of moulds and a deckle, a heap of rectangular pieces of felt slightly larger than the moulds, and a standing press. The two moulds, which were twins, were oblong rectangular wire sieves mounted on wooden

---

[1] A generalized account assembled from the sources detailed on pp. 397–8, and from observation at Balston's and Barcham Green's hand-vats in the early 1950s.

FIG. 26. A royal paper-mould and the deckle which was shared with its twin, made for Springfield Mill, Kent, and dated 1932. The size is indicated by the watermark, a Strasbourg bend, on the left; in the hand-press period the watermark was more usually placed on the right. The tranchefiles can just be seen at each end of the mould; the moiré effect is caused by the fact that it is double-faced (pp. 65–6).

frames, and the deckle was a removable wooden rim which could be fitted to either mould to make it into a tray-like sieve with a raised edge. The maker fitted the deckle to a mould, and taking mould and deckle together by the shorter sides, dipped the long edge that was towards him into the stuff in the vat. When about a third of the mould was under the surface, he lifted it out and turned it flat so that stuff flowed over its whole area. Then, as the water was draining away between the wires of the sieve, he gave the mould a sideways shake, first in one direction and then in the other, locking the fibres together and 'shutting' the sheet; this was the point at which great skill was required to produce sheets of uniform texture and strength throughout the making. The maker then lifted the deckle and slid this first mould along a board to the coucher, from whom he received the second mould of the pair in return. The coucher carefully turned the first mould over on to a piece of felt, on which the new and still friable piece of paper was deposited, and then pushed the empty mould back to the maker, who had meanwhile fitted the deckle to the second mould and made another sheet. So they made on with each mould in turn, laying new-made paper and felts alternately in a heap until they had completed a 'post' of so many sheets, the number varying with the size of the paper;[2] and from time to time the vat was replenished with stuff.

When the post of paper and felts was complete the layer took it to the standing press where the water was pressed out of it, as many as five or six men gathering to pull at the bar. Now the paper was strong enough to handle, and the layer separated it from the felts, pressed it again, and hung it up to dry. At this stage the paper was called waterleaf, and was absorbent like blotting-paper. The next operation, therefore, was to give it a relatively impermeable surface by sizing, whereby the sheets were dipped by handfuls into hot size, a solution of animal gelatine made from vellum or leather shavings boiled in water, with the addition in the later part of the period of alum. Finally the sized paper was pressed, dried, pressed again and, if it was intended for writing on, smoothed by rubbing or hammering (there was no point in smoothing printing paper, which would lose its surface when it was damped by the pressmen). The finished paper was sorted for imperfections and told out into quires and reams for sale.

The paper-maker's ream consisted of 20 quires of 24 or 25 sheets each, the smaller ream (480 sheets) being normal in England and Holland, while the larger ream (500 sheets) became standard in most but not all French and Italian mills.[3] Each quire was folded in half for packing and storage across its longer side, and the two outer quires (the ones most likely to be damaged as a result of the inadequate wrapping that was usual) were made up of more or less imperfect sheets, not all of which could be used for printing; they were known as cassie or cording quires. Thus the 480-sheet ream contained 432 perfect sheets plus a few more that were imperfect but usable.

Throughout the hand-press period the majority of paper mills had only one vat and eight or ten workmen; a substantial minority had two vats, but larger mills (Whatman's Turkey Mill in late-eighteenth-century Maidstone had five vats)[4] were exceptional. Output per vat varied with the size of the paper being made, and also to some extent with the number of hands available in the vat room; with full vat crews a large size of paper (royal) could be made at the rate of just under 3,000 sheets per vat per day, while for a

[2] The number of sheets per post varied at Springfield Mill, Kent, in the early years of the present century from 130 sheets of single medium (of which 20 posts, $4\frac{1}{4}$ reams, were made at one vat in one day) to 44 sheets of Imperial 300 lb. (12 posts, 1 ream, per vat per day).

[3] 28 out of 61 lots of imported paper offered to Fell in 1674 were in 480-sheet reams, the other 33 lots being in 500-sheet reams (*The Library*, vii, 1927, pp. 404–8); the Dutch reams were all 480s, the French mostly 500s except in the smaller sizes.

[4] Balston, T., *James Whatman father & son*, London 1957, p. 120.

small size (foolscap) the rate could approach 5,000 sheets per day.[5] There was a considerable wastage from accidents that occurred during making and sizing, however, and the final output might be 20 per cent less than the output at the vat.

PAPER IN ENGLISH PRINTING[6]

Practically all the white paper used by English printers up to 1670 came from foreign mills, and much the greatest part of it from France, especially Normandy. There were indeed a good many mills working in England from the later sixteenth century, but they suffered from the lack both of skilled workmen and of a regular supply of linen rags (English people wore wool, not linen) and, with few and unimportant exceptions, they made brown paper, not white. Foreign paper continued to supply the greater part of the English market during the last quarter of the seventeenth century and the first quarter of the eighteenth, but now it came chiefly from Holland, either from Dutch mills, or from French mills trading through Dutch ports. During the same period, however, an English white paper industry was developed (and soon protected by a discriminatory tariff), which supplied an increasing proportion of the paper used by English printers, even though the finest qualities had still to be imported from abroad. Soon afterwards the output of the English mills began to increase rapidly, supported by a parallel increase in the import of rags, until by the last quarter of the eighteenth century English white paper was available in such quantity and such quality that the import of foreign paper had almost ceased.

MOULDS AND WATERMARKS

Every piece of hand-made paper bears in its substance the pattern of the mould in which it was formed, a pattern which can be seen when the paper is held up to the light. The rectangular grid of the brass-wire sieve appears as chains running at intervals of about 25 mm. parallel to the shorter edges of the sheet, and wires, a millimetre or slightly less apart, crossing the chains parallel to the longer edges; the wooden bars of the mould-frame, on to which the chains were fastened, show up as shadows on either side of the chains. These effects are due to disturbances of the fibres of the stuff caused by the parts of the mould, and especially to the small indentations made by the brass wires in the underside (or mould side) of the sheet. Indeed it is

[5] *Encyclopédie méthodique, arts et métiers mécaniques*, v, Paris 1788, p. 511; Johnson, R., *New duty on paper. The paper-maker and stationer's assistant*, London 1794, A4b–A6a.
[6] From notes communicated by the late Allan Stevenson; and Coleman, D. C., *The British paper industry 1495–1860*, Oxford 1958, pt. 1.

normally possible (provided that the paper has not been too vigorously polished) to see with a raking light which was the mould side of the sheet, for it shows a pattern of both chain and wire indentations, while the other side (the felt side) is more or less flat, or shows wire humps only.

The outer edges of the sheet—the deckle edges—are rough and uneven where the stuff seeped between the deckle and the mould; and half a chain's width in from the shorter edges there is usually an extra chain on each side without bar shadows, called tranchefiles.[6a] There may be pale drip marks in the neighbourhood of the tranchefiles, where drops of water fell from the deckle or from the maker's hand on to the new-made sheet. Often, too, there are knots of badly-beaten fibre visible in the substance of the sheet.

Watermarks,[7] which were pictures or letters fashioned in wire and sewn with knots of fine wire to the surface of the mould so that their images appeared in the paper along with the chain and wire marks, had first appeared in the thirteenth century as the personal or trade marks of individual paper-makers and mills, and by the beginning of the hand-press period they were very widely used, taking a great variety of pictorial and armorial forms. Not all paper was watermarked, especially during the later hand-press period when much poor-quality printing paper was made without any marks, but most medium-quality paper, and nearly all the fine, had watermarks of some sort. In the early days of paper-making the marks had been placed almost anywhere on the surface of the mould, but by the fifteenth century they were normally put in the centre of one half of the oblong, so that when a sheet of paper was folded in half (as in a folio) the watermark appeared in the centre of one of the two leaves. As a rule the mark was supposed to be seen from the mould side of the sheet and the design was therefore made in wire as a mirror image of what was intended to appear in the paper.

By 1500, although watermarks were still mainly mill—or at least district—marks, there was a tendency to give them a conventional significance of another sort. The marks of some mills or districts could already indicate paper quality, and by the early sixteenth century a correlation between the design of the mark and the size of the sheet was beginning to appear in some of the chief paper-making districts.[8] Watermarking did not become more than locally systematic during the sixteenth century, however, and many marks indicating the mill or district of origin of the paper continued to be used without reference to its size or quality. It was during the seventeenth

---

[6a] There is no generally accepted English name for tranchefiles, but some authorities say 'edge wires', or 'water bar wires'.

[7] For watermarks to 1600 see Briquet, C. M., *Les filigranes*, ed. Stevenson, A. H., 4 vols., Amsterdam 1968.

[8] Plantin, for instance, was ordering paper by the watermark/size name in the 1560s (Voet, L., *The golden compasses*, ii).

century that international watermark conventions, indicating either quality or size, or both, began to be adopted; and during the eighteenth that size and quality marks completely replaced the trade marks.[9]

During the sixteenth and seventeenth centuries, when watermark designs were losing their trade significance, individual mills added initials or other symbols to them as private trade marks, at first to the main design, and then additionally as an extra mark known as the countermark in the middle of the other half of the mould. French countermarks, which first appeared sporadically in the mid sixteenth century, continued to indicate the maker's name (and in the eighteenth century the quality of the paper) until the end of the hand-press period; Dutch and English countermarks of the seventeenth and eighteenth centuries, however, soon lost their trade significance, and became mere appendages of the main marks.

No two paper moulds of the hand-press period were ever precisely identical, and individual moulds can be identified by their paper images; even the two moulds of a pair, which were deliberately made to look alike, can be told apart by the paper made in them. Often the differences between the moulds of a pair are gross and obvious—chain-lines differently spaced, new elements in the watermark design, etc.—but if not, tiny details of the individual wires will be different. It is only necessary as a rule to make a careful and systematic study of the watermarks, and especially of their relationship to the chains and wires of the mould, to find characteristics that are unique to each particular mould. Watermarks of the fifteenth and sixteenth centuries are particularly easy to tell apart, for the knots of wire with which the designs were sewn on to the moulds show up as 'dots' on the lines of the pattern in relative positions that were not in practice repeated exactly in different examples. Later the watermarks were tacked on with a running stitch, which makes them more difficult to identify; but, as James Whatman the younger pointed out in a forgery case in 1771, 'they will differ in a wire or something'.[10]

Not only can individual moulds be identified by the paper made in them, but they can be followed in the same way through their working lives. Each mould of a pair might make 2,000 or more sheets of paper in a day and, although in practice particular pairs of moulds would be laid up from time to time, when in use they were subject to severe wear which resulted in noticeable deterioration of the mould surface: wires of the sieve were gradually bent or broken, watermarks were distorted and lost elements of

---

[9] There is no comprehensive work on watermarks of the later hand-press period; see the references on pp. 397–8 and, for a short summary, Gaskell, P., 'Notes on eighteenth-century British paper', *The Library*, xii, 1957, pp. 34–42.

[10] Balston, T., *James Whatman father & son*, London 1957, p. 148.

the design, the knots worked loose and were resewn, and (owing to the repeated stresses of making) the marks tended to drift along the wires towards the right-hand end of the mould.[11] So heavy was this wear that a pair of moulds in continuous use could be worn out and due for replacement in less than twelve months.[12] Watermarks had an even shorter life, and might drop off the mould in about six months, when they would be repaired or replaced, or simply left off altogether.

It is not always possible to examine a mould pattern or a watermark in as much detail as one would like. Sometimes the interesting part is lost in the binding of a book, sometimes it is so heavily printed over that it is virtually hidden by the ink on the surface of the paper. Books can seldom be disbound for the benefit of bibliographers (although it is worth remembering that they sometimes have to be rebound, when they are completely dismembered), but we can now see through printing ink by means of beta-radiography. The paper that is to be examined is simply sandwiched between a sheet of Perspex impregnated with carbon-14 and an unexposed photographic film, and left in the dark for a few hours. More or less of the beta radiation is transmitted to the film by the thinner and thicker parts of the paper in much the same way as is visible light, but unlike light it is not stopped by the carbon particles of printing ink; the film therefore takes a perfect image of the mould pattern and watermark in the paper but does not register the printing on the surface.[13]

Productivity at the vat could be increased by the use of two-sheet moulds for the smaller sizes of paper. Each mould of such a pair was twice the normal size and the deckle had a central cross bar. Two sheets were made each time it was dipped by the maker, and they were turned out together on to a single felt by the coucher. Two-sheet moulds, which appear to have been a Dutch invention of the late seventeenth century, were constructed so that the two sheets were made either end to end or side by side (fig. 28).[14] Paper made in side-by-side two-sheet moulds can easily be identified by the fact that in a whole sheet (i.e. one that has deckle edges all round) the chain lines are parallel to the longer edges. Such paper was certainly made from the 1690s, probably in Holland. Paper made in end-to-end two-sheet moulds, on the other hand, cannot readily be distinguished from paper made in

[11] The deterioration of moulds is fully discussed in Stevenson, A. H., *The problem of the Missale speciale*, London 1967.

[12] Whatman bought an average of 10 new pairs of moulds a year for the six vats of Turkey and Loose Mills in 1780-7, giving an average life per pair of moulds of just over seven months; Balston, T., op. cit., pp. 60, 120.

[13] Beta-radiography was developed during the 1950s in the U.S.S.R.; see Simmons, J. S. G., 'The Leningrad method of watermark reproduction', *The book collector*, x, 1961, pp. 329-30 and plates, for an account of the technique and its origin.

[14] Povey, K., and Foster, I. J. C., 'Turned chain lines', *The Library*, v, 1950-1, pp. 184-200.

a    *b*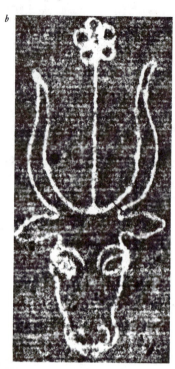

FIG. 27 (*a*, *b*). A photograph (*a*) and a beta-radiograph (*b*) of the same watermark in a leaf of a fifteenth-century printed bible. The dots showing where the mark was sewn on to the cover of the mould can be discerned in the bull's horns. (*Biblia latina*, Nuremberg (Koberger) 1477, Goff B-552, Trin. Coll. Cam. VI. 17. 14, f. [451].)

ordinary single moulds, since the chain lines run in the usual way; nevertheless, paper from pairs of such moulds will show combinations of four different examples of the watermark, not two, and it is also likely that only one of the shorter edges of each sheet will have the tranchefile and drip marks. Two-sheet moulds were in use in England at the Whatman mill by 1768,[15] probably though not certainly of the end-to-end variety; and end-to-end two-sheet moulds were used in France by 1788.[16]

Eighteenth-century printers sometimes made use of half sheets of double-sized paper in place of single sheets of the ordinary size, occasionally in books and commonly in English newspapers (a practice which enabled newspaper publishers to avoid half the stamp duty payable between 1712 and 1794).[17]

[15] Balston, T., op. cit., p. 23.

[16] *Encyclopédie méthodique, arts et métiers mécaniques*, v, Paris 1788, p. 512.

[17] Povey and Foster, op. cit., p. 185. Cases are also known of fifteenth-century printers cutting large sheets (approximately royal in size) in half and using them in place of small ones (approximately foolscap); Bühler, C. F., 'Chainlines versus imposition in incunabula', *Studies in bibliography*, xxiii, 1970, pp. 141–5.

FIG. 28 (*a*, *b*). Diagrams of end-to-end (*a*) and side-by-side (*b*) two-sheet moulds. The tranche-files, chain-lines, and marks are not drawn to scale.

Such paper was usually of inferior quality and unwatermarked; but, although its chain lines appear to run the 'wrong' way, it can be told from paper made in two-sheet side-by-side moulds by the fact that one of its long edges is always cut, not deckled.

Until the middle of the eighteenth century all moulds were of the laid (chain and wire) pattern, with the wire mesh fastened directly to the bars of the mould frame. In about 1755, however, James Whatman the elder made some paper for Baskerville of Birmingham with moulds of which the mesh was woven like cloth, the brass wires being spaced closely and evenly across each other.[18] This earliest wove paper was only partially successful, since the mesh was fastened as usual to the bars of the frame, and the shadows of the bars showed clearly in the paper. By 1759, however, Whatman had produced a wove paper without shadows, probably (as was normal later) by making the moulds with two wire meshes to each one,

[18] Balston, T., op. cit., pp. 14–15 and *passim*.

fastened one on top of the other with a small space in between. Such moulds were called double-faced to distinguish them from the ordinary single-faced moulds which continued to be used for making laid paper, complete with bar shadows, for the rest of the eighteenth century.[19] Wove paper, which was slightly more difficult to make than laid, was very slow to be taken up by the trade; the Whatmans made little of it until the 1780s, and it was not until the last decade of the century that it was used in any quantity by printers. *Papier vélin* was first made in France by the Montgolfiers at Annonay in 1777–9.[20]

SORTS OF PAPER: QUALITY, WEIGHT, AND SIZE

Printing papers of the hand-press period—that is to say the white papers made for writing, printing, and copper-plate printing, and not including the wide variety of coarser papers that were made for wrapping and for industrial purposes—were produced in a confusing variety of qualities, weights, and sizes.[21] The quality of paper was chiefly determined by the selection of rags for its making, pure white linens making the finest paper, while coloured linens, canvas, old rope, and even a proportion of woollens went into the poorer qualities. When a paper-maker offered his customers a choice of two or three qualities of paper they were called fine, second, and ordinary (*fin*, *moyen*, and *bulle* in France). These qualities depended of course on the makers' standards, one man's fine not necessarily being better than the next man's second. Paper of the same quality might then be classed as good, retree, or broke according to its imperfections, the retree and broke sheets going into the cassie quires.

The weight of a paper (which was roughly proportional to its thickness, white papers of the hand-press period not differing much in their final density) was more or less independent of quality, so that a good-quality writing paper and a poor-quality printing paper might both be light in weight. Weight differed with the proportion of fibre to water in the stuff, a thicker or denser stuff, used with a coarser mould, making a thicker and heavier paper; and the price of a paper of a given quality and size varied approximately with its weight. Nowadays the weight of a paper can be conveniently expressed in terms of grammes per square metre of a sheet, but in the hand-press period it was given in pounds (or *livres*, etc.) per ream. Since the size of the sheet and the number of sheets in the ream could vary, the earlier method can be misleading. Thus, while it is clear that sheets of 'demy 25' weigh a quarter as much again as those of 'demy 20',

---

[19] The terms 'single-faced' and 'double-faced' were used at Barcham Green's in the 1950s; the lower mesh is also known as the 'backing wire'.

[20] Audin, M., 'De l'origine du papier vélin', *Gutenberg Jahrbuch*, 1928, pp. 69–86.

[21] See for instance Table V in Gaskell, P., 'Notes on eighteenth-century British paper', *The Library*, xii, 1957, p. 41.

it is far from obvious that sheets of 'double demy 50' (measured in lb. per 500-sheet ream), of 'crown 15' (lb. per 480-sheet ream), and of *carré 20* (*livres* per 500-sheet ream) all weighed exactly 73 gr./m.[2]

Paper sizes have always been subject to gradual change and much minor variation—there were eventually some 300 English names and combinations of names for paper sizes[22]—but in fact there were normally no more than about half a dozen main groups of sizes in use at any given time by hand-press printers. In the fourteenth century four standard sizes were laid down for Bolognese paper-makers: they were *imperialle*, 74 × 50 cm.; *realle*, 61·5 × 44·5 cm.; *meçane*, 51·5 × 34·5 cm.; and *reçute*, 45 × 31·5 cm.[23] The same four sizes, more or less, were still those most commonly made in Europe during the fifteenth century. Haebler noted that most fifteenth-century folios were printed either in *forma regalis* on paper measuring about 70 × 50 cm., or in *forma mediana* on paper measuring about 50 × 30 (or perhaps 35) cm.;[24] these correspond approximately to the Bolognese *imperialle* and *meçane*. Briquet found that the commonest sizes of French fifteenth-century paper measured about 60 × 41·5 cm. and 43 × 30·5 cm., similar to the earlier *realle* and *reçute*.[25]

These four ancient sizes did not disappear but, joined by three more main sizes, formed the basis of the system of paper sizes that developed during the hand-press period. There were nevertheless various gradual changes in paper sizes, which are suggested by the collections of dimensions analysed in the following table. In considering them the following points should be borne in mind.[26]

First, and most important, the dimensions given here are approximate, not absolute. Mould sizes varied slightly; intermediate sizes were occasionally made; the dimensions of some of the main sizes tended to increase during the period and to be replaced by sizes which had new names attached to the old dimensions; and the eighteenth-century dimensions come from official tables of sizes which were not followed precisely by all makers.

Secondly, proportion: much medieval paper was made with sides in the ratio $1:\sqrt{2}$ (which is approximately $1:1\cdot4$) and thus had the property of remaining the same shape when it was folded in half one or more times. From the sixteenth century onwards, however, paper was increasingly made with side-ratios tending towards $1:1\cdot25$, which with alternate folds became about $1:1\cdot6$, making tall, narrow folios and squarish quartos.

[22] Labarre, E. J., *Dictionary and encyclopaedia of paper and paper-making*, Oxford 1952 (repr. Amsterdam 1969), pp. 253–67.

[23] Briquet, C. M., *Les filigranes*, ed. Stevenson, A. H., Amsterdam 1968, i, pp. 2–3.

[24] Haebler, K., *The study of incunabula*, New York 1933 (repr. New York 1967), p. 49.

[25] Briquet, C. M., op. cit., p. 4.

[26] These five considerations derive from discussions with the late A. H. Stevenson.

Thirdly, most of the printing paper of the sixteenth century was in the foolscap size range, which was considered the ordinary size, the shapes and sizes of books printed on it being determined by the folding. The ordinary size then increased gradually, and by the eighteenth century it was in the demy range.

Fourthly, certain main sizes of British paper were made in the eighteenth century in printing and writing varieties, the printings in each case being both larger and of poorer quality than the writings.

Fifthly, watermarks: the marks given here were not used exclusively for particular sizes, especially during the sixteenth century; even in the eighteenth century the fine varieties of several large sizes might all have the same watermark. There was a tendency at seventeenth-century French mills for the fine variety of a particular size of paper to cheapen and for its conventional watermark then to replace the mark for ordinary; thus some once-common ordinary marks—crown, foolscap, hand, etc.—disappeared. A good deal of paper, moreover, was made without any watermark at all; it was usually but not always of ordinary quality.

FIG. 29. Strasbourg lily (Heawood 1809, ? England, 18th cent.). The symbols below the shield might take other forms, or might be omitted. LVG (standing originally for Lucius van Gerrevink) was also in common use as a counter-mark.

FIG. 30. Strasbourg bend (Heawood 73, Madrid, 1748). This is a bend sinister; the true bend was equally common. Also shown is the counter-mark IV (originally for Jean Villedary).

FIG. 31. Fleur de lys (Heawood 1479, Amsterdam, 1658).

FIG. 32. Grapes (Heawood 2269, Paris, 1680). Found in many variant shapes, often with other symbols.

FIG. 33. Horn (Heawood 2686, England, 1683). The horn, which might be hung either way round, was also displayed in a crowned shield like the Strasbourg lily, fig. 29.

FIG. 34. Arms of Amsterdam (Heawood 417, place unknown, 1720). There were many variants; see Heawood 342–438.

FIG. 35. Arms of England (U.K.) (Heawood 448, London, 1736). The crowned GR was a common countermark in paper used in eighteenth-century England, but was known as early as 1674.

FIG. 36. Foolscap (Heawood 2020, Amsterdam, 1688).
The symbols below the collar might take other forms or be
omitted; the head might face in either direction.

FIG. 37. Propatria (Churchill 142, England, 1772).
Also shown is the JW countermark of the
Whatman mill.

FIG. 38. Vryheyt (Churchill 81, place unknown, 1704).

FIG. 39 Britannia (Churchill 225, England, 1764).

FIG. 40. Pots (Heawood 3561, London, 1660; Churchill 463, ? France, 1650). There were many varieties, with handles facing either way.

FIG. 41. Arms of Genoa over two circles (? 'les trois O') (Heawood 759, Palermo, 1726). There were many variants.

FIG. 42. Arms of London (Heawood 461, England, 1713).

TABLE 3: *Paper Sizes and Watermarks*

For notes on the interpretation of this table, see pp. 67–8. Figures 29–42 show typical forms of common watermarks, but the range of variant forms was enormous, and reference should be made to the collections of watermarks mentioned below.

SOURCES

14th–16th cents.:	Briquet, C. M., *Les filigranes*, ed. Stevenson, A., 4 vols., Amsterdam 1968.
17th–18th cents.:	Churchill, W. A., *Watermarks in paper*, Amsterdam 1935 (repr. 1967); Heawood, E., *Watermarks*, Hilversum 1950 (repr. Amsterdam 1970).
1674:	Chapman, R. W., 'An inventory of paper', *The Library*, vii, 1926–7, pp. 402–8.
1713:	*Instructions to be observed by the officers employ'd in the duties on paper*, London 1713.
1741:	*Encyclopédie méthodique, arts et métiers mécaniques*, v, Paris 1788, pp. 536–8, 555–92; the figures are converted to metric measure in Briquet, C. M., op. cit., i, p. 6.
1781:	Tables attached to the Act of 21 Geo. III, c. 24 (1781).

TABLE 3

Group	Date	Country of Origin	Dimensions (cm.)	Dimensions (in.)	Watermark Type and Fig. Ref.	Name
Super royal (with *imperial*)	14th cent.	Italy	74 × 50			Bolognese imperialle
	1674	Holland	68·5 × 47	27 × 18½	Strasbourg lily (29)	super royal
	1741	France	70·5 × 53			super royal
	1741	France	86 × 57·5			impérial
	1781	England	70 × 49	27½ × 19¼		super royal
Royal (with *lombard*)	14th cent.	Italy	61·5 × 44·5			Bolognese realle
	16th cent.	France	57 × 43·5		grapes (32)	
	16th cent.	France	60 × 44		grapes (32)	
	16th cent.	Italy	58 × 42		anchor	
	1674	France	61 × 44·5	24 × 17½	grapes (32)	royal
	1674	France	57 × 44	22½ × 17¼	fleur-de-lys (31), grapes (32)	lombard
	1674	Holland	59·5 × 46	23½ × 18	Strasbourg bend (30)	royal
	1713	England	59·5 × 47	23½ × 18½	Strasbourg bend (30)	printing royal
	1741	France	59·5 × 43·5			royal
	1741	France	57·5 × 48·5			lombard
	1781	England	66 × 51	26 × 20	Strasbourg bend (30)	printing royal
	1781	England	61 × 49	24 × 19¼		writing royal
Medium (with *carré*)	1674	Holland	52 × 42·5	20½ × 16¾	Strasbourg lily (29)	medium
	1674	(?)France	51 × 42	20 × 16½	Horn in crowned shield	medium
	1741	France	54 × 42			carré
	1781	England	58·5 × 45·5	23 × 18		printing medium
	1781	England	57 × 44·5	22½ × 17½		writing medium
Demy (with *écu*)	14th cent.	Italy	51·5 × 34·5		grapes (32)	Bolognese meçane
	16th cent.	France	50 × 35		Strasbourg lily (29)	
	1674	Holland	49·5 × 38	19½ × 15		fine demy

TABLE 3 (*cont.*)

Group	Date	Country of Origin	Dimensions (cm.)	Dimensions (in.)	Watermark Type and Fig. Ref.	Name
Demy, cont.	1674	France	52 × 39·5	$20\frac{1}{2} \times 15\frac{1}{2}$	grapes (32)	large demy
	1674	France	51 × 37·5	$20 \times 14\frac{3}{4}$	grapes (32)	small demy
	1713	England	50 × 40	$19\frac{1}{4} \times 15\frac{1}{4}$	fleur-de-lys (31)	printing demy
	1713	England	48·5 × 38·5	$19 \times 15\frac{1}{4}$	Strasbourg lily (29)	writing demy
	1741	France	51·5 × 38·5			écu
	1781	England	56 × 44·5	$22 \times 17\frac{1}{2}$	fleur-de-lys (31)	printing demy
	1781	England	51 × 39·5	$20 \times 15\frac{1}{2}$	Strasbourg lily (29)	writing demy
	1781	England	98 × 61	$38\frac{1}{2} \times 26$		double demy
Crown (with *post*, *bastard*)	16th cent.	France	45 × 35		grapes (32), crown	
	1674	France	48·5 × 35	$19 \times 13\frac{3}{4}$	grapes (32)	Rouen crown
	1674	France	45·5 × 35	$18 \times 13\frac{3}{4}$	fleur-de-lys (31), small horn (33)	Morlaix crown
	1674	France	48·5 × 37	$19 \times 14\frac{1}{2}$	arms of France	crown
	1713	England	48·5 × 37·5	$19 \times 14\frac{3}{4}$	horn (33)	large post
	1713	England	46·5 × 37	$18\frac{1}{4} \times 14\frac{1}{2}$	fleur-de-lys (31)	crown
	1741	France	48 × 36·5			grand cornet
	1741	France	46 × 35			couronne
	1741	France	46 × 35·5			bastard
	1781	England	49·5 × 39	$19\frac{1}{2} \times 15\frac{1}{4}$	horn (33)	post
	1781	England	51 × 38	20 × 15	fleur-de-lys (31)	crown
Foolscap	14th cent.	Italy	45 × 31·5			Bolognese reçute
	16th cent.	France	42 × 32		Strasbourg lily (29), pot (40), grapes (32)	
	1674	Holland	43 × 33	17 × 13	Amsterdam (34)	foolscap
	1674	France	43 × 33·5	$17 \times 13\frac{1}{4}$	Foolscap (36), Amsterdam (34), England (35)	foolscap, arms, pantalon

1674	(?)Italy	43×31	17×12¼	arms (?Genoa)	Venice, Genoa
1713	England	44·5×34·5	17½×13½		printing foolscap
1713	England	40·5×33	16×13		writing foolscap
1741	France	43×34			pantalon
1741	France	43×33		Turgot's arms	teillère
1741	France	42×32·5		Amsterdam (34), propatria (37), vryheit (38)	propatria
1781	England	42·5×34·5	16¾×13½	propatria (37), vryheit (38), Britannia (39)	foolscap
Pot					
16th cent.	France	42×29		catharine wheel	
16th cent.	France	40×29		serpent	
16th cent.	France	38×28		pot (40), Strasbourg lily (29), hand, eagle, bell	
1674	France	40·5×31	16×12¼	pot (40)	Caen pot
1674	France	40·5×31	16×12¼	horn (33)	arms, Rochel horn
1674	France	40·5×31	16×12¼	Genoa (41)	Morlaix pot
1674	France	38×29	15×11½	arms of Spain	Morlaix
1713	England	39·5×31	15½×12¼	England (35), London (42)	pot
1741	France	39×31			pot
1741	France	37×29			petit à la main
1781	England	39·5×31·5	15½×12½	England (35), London (42)	pot

DESCRIPTION

A sheet of hand-made paper is identified by its major dimensions, by the patterns of the mould wire and the watermark, and by its weight and quality. No two sheets of hand-made paper are precisely alike, however, and the lots of paper on which books were printed might be made up of batches of paper from different pairs of moulds or even from different mills. Therefore the description of the paper in a single copy of a book—or even in several copies—is not a description of all the paper used for the book, for which we should have to examine every copy of the impression. We have to be content in practice with the examination and description of a small sample of the paper used for the whole impression, and the larger the number of copies examined the more likely the sample is to be representative of the whole.

The length and breadth of the sheet are taken if possible from an uncut copy of the book, multiplied by the factors appropriate to the folding (see p. 86). If an uncut copy cannot be found, the approximate dimensions of the paper may be obtained by adding 0·5–1·0 cm. each way to the length and breadth of the leaf of a small book, or 1·0–2·0 cm. each way to those of a large book, before multiplying by the required factors. Thus a lightly cut octavo measuring 18·5 × 12·25 cm. might count as measuring 19·0 × 12·75 cm., which multiplied by 2 and 4 respectively give a sheet size of 51·0 × 38·0 cm., or demy.

The pattern of the laid mould is described by giving the spacing in millimetres of the chain-lines and wire-lines in the vicinity of the watermark; the distance between adjacent chains may be measured directly, but for the wires it is easier to measure the distance across a particular number of marks and to divide the result by that number. In the case of a wove mould the mesh of the wire pattern is measured in wires per cm.

The watermark is named or described, with a reference if possible to a similar design in one of the great collections of watermark patterns such as Briquet or Heawood (see p. 72). Its dimensions are given, together with a note of its relationship to the chain-lines of the mould (marks were usually centred on or between chains). A similar description is given of any counter-mark. If more details are needed it is best to supply a photograph or beta-radiograph.

The quality and weight of hand-made papers are not easily measured, and are usually assessed in the light of a general knowledge of the printing paper of the period. A guide may be had by taking a number of micrometer readings of the thickness of individual leaves, but thickness could differ within a batch of paper, and even at either end of a single sheet. Some authorities measure the bulk or thickness of the whole book, but this can be misleading since the result can be greatly affected by the degree to which the book is pressed down when the measurement is made, and also to some extent by its humidity.

Imposition

The compositor imposed the pages for each side of a sheet by arranging them on a flat surface, surrounding them with wooden spacing pieces of less than type height, and locking them into an iron frame with long and short wedges; the order of the pages in each forme (as the pages imposed in this way for each side of the sheet were called) being such that, when a sheet of paper printed from them was folded to make a section of a book, the pages followed each other in the proper sequence. The following description of how this was done refers to a sheet of which the pages had been set consecutively and were thus all available together for imposition, and to an imposing surface (or stone) which would accommodate only one forme at a time. Some stones were big enough to take both formes of a sheet side by side, in which case they might be imposed together rather than one after the other. Alternatively the sheet might have been set by formes, when the pages for one forme would be ready for imposition well before those for the other, and the compositor would have to take special care to get them in the right order.

We left the compositor some time ago with the pages for the first sheet of a book stored on a convenient surface, tied round with string and complete with their headlines and direction-lines. He now slid the pages for one of the formes on to the imposing stone, a flat slab of marble or limestone raised to table height on a frame. Using the catchwords (or 'directions' as they were sometimes called) to tell which page followed which, he arranged them in their proper order, and he used the catchwords rather than the page numbers for this purpose because, as we shall see, the headlines for all but the first few sheets of a book were added after the pages had been laid out on the stone, not before.[1] Next the chase was set down on the stone around the pages. This was a rectangular frame of square-section iron bars, usually with removable cross-bars inside. Chases were made in pairs, and for most of the hand-press period they were of a standard size that fitted comfortably in the bed of the wooden press, namely about 56×46 cm. over all, 52×42 cm. inside;[2] it was not until the later eighteenth century that chases were regularly supplied in various sizes to suit different jobs.

The spaces between the type pages and the bars of the chase were filled

---

[1] Not all books had catchwords, however; Parisian printers (for instance) must have used some other way of getting their pages in the right order on the stone.

[2] Moxon, J., *Mechanick exercises*, eds. Davis and Carter, 2nd ed., Oxford 1962, p. 43.

Fig. 43. An octavo forme on the imposing stone, locked up with wooden furniture and quoins. Beside it are the compositor's mallet, planer, and shooting-stick.

up with wooden furniture, and long wedges were fitted round the edges. Short wedges, or quoins, were then put in between the long wedges and the inside of the chase, loosely at first so that the string with which the pages were tied up could be unwound and removed, and so that any pieces of type that were sticking up above the rest could be knocked down with a wooden planer. Finally the quoins were driven home with a mallet and 'shooting stick' to lock the forme up tightly.

Sixteenth-century chases might be made of wood, as some of Plantin's were.[3] Chases with thumb-screws in two of the sides for locking up the forme without the use of quoins were used in France and Germany until the seventeenth century and in Italy until the eighteenth century, but there is no evidence of their use in Holland or England (except by Baskerville, whose methods were peculiar to him).[4]

If the job had been done properly—if all the lines of type were correctly justified and the pieces of furniture were not binding against each other— the forme was now virtually a solid slab of wood and metal and, although it did not have a bottom like a tray, it could be moved about or lifted without the type falling out. The compositor therefore pushed it to one side (or stood it on its edge on the floor, leaning against his frame) and proceeded to impose the second forme of the sheet in the same way.

FORMAT

In bibliographical usage the format of a book of the hand-press period means the arrangement of its formes and the subsequent folding of the printed sheets as indicated by the number and conjugacy of the leaves and the orientation of the paper in the gatherings, and is expressed in the terms folio, quarto, octavo, etc. A book made up of sheets printed from pairs of four-page formes folded twice to make four-leaf, eight-page, gatherings with horizontal chain lines is called a quarto; and it is still called a quarto, not a folio, if the eight-page sheets were cut in half before folding to make gatherings of pairs of leaves with four pages each. If the size of the paper can be established by measuring the leaves or identifying the watermark it is added to the format statement, thus indicating the size and shape of the book in the terminology of the trade: foolscap quarto, demy octavo, etc.

We shall see later that books of the machine-press period were commonly printed from multiple impositions on large sheets of paper which were then cut up for folding into ordinary gatherings. For such books a

---

[3] Information from Professor J. Gerritsen.

[4] Zonca, V., *Nova teatro di machine et edificii*, Padoua 1607, p. 64; Hornschuch, H., 'Ορθοτυπογραφία, Lipsiae 1608, A8ᵇ; Fertel, M. D., *La science pratique de l'imprimerie*, Saint-Omer 1723, p. 181; *The Library*, x, 1955, pp. 41–2; *Signature*, xii, 1951, p. 51; Gaskell, P., *John Baskerville, a bibliography*, Cambridge 1959, p. xix.

format statement such as 'crown octavo' does not necessarily indicate either the imposition scheme or the size of the large sheets; what it does indicate —properly used—is that the size of the sub-units of the sheets used for the gatherings was crown, and that the sub-units were folded octavo-fashion into gatherings of eight leaves.

Paper sizes have already been considered; now we must examine the impositions and foldings that printers used. The usual terminology is folio (abbreviated 2º) for sheets folded once across the longer side, giving two leaves or four pages to the sheet; quarto (4º), when a second fold is made across the first, making four leaves, eight pages; octavo (8º), with a third fold across the second, making eight leaves, sixteen pages; duodecimo (12º), folded twice across the longer dimension and three times across the shorter, making twelve leaves, twenty-four pages; long twelves (long 12º), when the sheet is folded once across the shorter side and five times across the longer, again making twelve leaves, twenty-four pages; and sixteenmo (etc.) for the more complex foldings (16º (etc.) up to 128º). Large books of plates were sometimes made up of broadsheets, not folded at all (1º), while a handbill might be in the form of a half-sheet or quarter-sheet ($\frac{1}{2}$º, $\frac{1}{4}$º).

The compositor laid out his type pages on the stone in the mirror image of the order in which they were to appear on the printed sheet. To take the simple case of a sheet of folio, which is folded once across its longer dimension, pages 1 and 4 appear on the outside of the folded sheet and pages 2 and 3 on the inside. If the sheet is laid out flat with pages 1 and 4 upwards, page 1 is on the right and page 4 on the left. The forme from which

OUTER FORME   INNER FORME

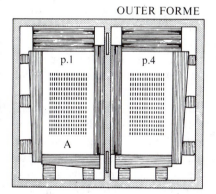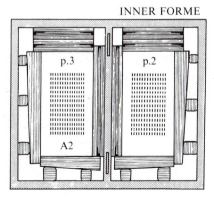

FIG. 44. The two formes for a sheet of folio, showing the disposition of the pages (cf. fig. 46). The furniture is so arranged that the head-, side-, foot-, and gutter-sticks will not bind on each other when the quoins are driven up tight. The cross of the chase has slots in it to protect the points of the press when the tympan is folded down.

this outer side of the sheet was printed therefore had type-page 1 on the left and type-page 4 on the right; and it was called the outer forme. The forme from which the inner side of the same sheet was printed, containing pages 2 and 3, was called the inner forme. Similarly for other formats; the formes were laid out as mirror images of the printed sheets, and the outer forme always contained page 1, the inner forme page 2.

It will also be obvious that a sheet of paper folded in folio had the chain lines in the paper running up and down the leaves (vertically), not across (horizontally); and that the watermark was in the middle of one of the leaves (it could be in either leaf) with the countermark, if any, in the middle of the other. Each format, in fact, had its own characteristics of chain-line direction, watermark position, etc.

The following diagrams (figs. 46–63), which represent printed sheets, not formes, are intended both to explain how the various impositions and foldings worked, and to make them easier to identify in early books. By no means all the possible formats are included—Savage's manual of 1841 illustrated more than 150 impositions[5]—but all the really common ones are here. By using the diagrams in conjunction with the notes which follow it will usually be easy enough to see how a particular hand-printed book was made; in difficult cases it will be found helpful to make a model of the sheet with a piece of 'quarto' paper. But it is well to remember that throughout the period nearly all books were printed in one of the four normal formats, folio, quarto, octavo, or duodecimo, or in half-sheet versions of quarto, octavo, or duodecimo; and that other formats were used only for special cases, such as very small books, or books with pages of unusual shape.

Preliminary mention must be made of quiring, of impositions for gathering by half sheets, and of anomalous chain-lines and watermarks in paper. It was normal in the early days of printing to impose for gatherings of several sheets tucked, or quired, inside each other. Thus a folio gathering might consist of three folio sheets, the outermost of which contained pages 1 and 12 (printed from the outer forme) and pages 2 and 11 (from the inner forme); the middle sheet had pages 3 and 10, 4 and 9; and the innermost sheet had pages 5 and 8, 6 and 7. All three sheets were signed with the same letter (A1 on page 1, A2 on page 3, and A3 on page 5), and the folding is designated '2° in 6s'. In the fifteenth century folio gatherings consisted of up to five sheets; quarto (and occasionally octavo) gatherings might consist of two sheets. Patterns of quiring changed in later periods. Folios were generally gathered in 6s during the sixteenth and seventeenth centuries, but most eighteenth-century folios were gathered by single sheets (i.e. in 2s) despite

5 Savage, W., *A dictionary of the art of printing*, London 1841, pp. 335–400.

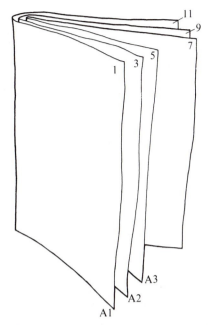

FIG. 45. A gathering, or section, of three sheets of folio, quired (2^6 in 6s).

the extra sewing that this entailed. Quarto in 8s remained common in English printing until the seventeenth century, and was continued in Bible printing until 1800. Octavo gatherings were rarely quired after the fifteenth century.

Impositions for gathering by half sheets in formats other than folio were used occasionally from early times, but did not become really common until the eighteenth century; they too required extra sewing. Two methods were used which produced closely similar results. In one, called half-sheet imposition,[6] all the pages for a half sheet were imposed in one forme (see figs. 49, 53, 59); this forme was first printed on one side of the whole sheet, then the heap of paper was turned (end over end in quarto and octavo, side over side in duodecimo) and printed from the same forme on the other side. Each printed sheet was then slit in half to yield two copies of the same half sheet. In the other method, the pages for two successive half sheets were imposed in two formes (see figs. 48, 52, 58) and printed in the normal way; again the printed sheets were cut in half, but this time each one yielded copies of the two successive half sheets which were different from each other, but which were sometimes indistinguishable from similar half sheets printed by half-sheet imposition. It is seldom possible to tell which method has been used in printing particular half sheets in quarto or octavo.

[6] Or 'work and turn'. See Povey, K., 'On the diagnosis of half-sheet imposition', *The Library*, xi, 1956, pp. 268–72.

Turned chain-lines—that is, chain-lines in the paper that appear to run the wrong way for a particular format—are occasionally found, mostly in late-seventeenth-century and in eighteenth-century books. They resulted from the use either of double-sized sheets of paper cut in half before printing (when one of the long sides has a cut, not a deckle edge), or of sheets made in side-by-side two-sheet moulds (when there will be deckle edges all round); both varieties are likely to have tranchefiles along one of the long edges only.[7] Confusion may also be caused by paper in which the watermark is located elsewhere than in the normal position; such paper was rarely made, but may now and again be found with the watermark in the middle, or next to an edge, of the sheet.

THE IDENTIFICATION OF FORMAT

The following procedure may be used to identify the format of a particular book.

1. Make notes of:
    a. The dimensions of the uncut leaf (making allowance for cut edges by adding 1·0–2·0 cm. each way for large books, or 0·5–1·0 cm. each way for small books).
    b. The direction of the chain-lines.
    c. The position of the watermark.
    d. The number of leaves per gathering.

2. Refer to Key I to see if the book appears to be in one of the normal formats (2°, 4°, 8°, or 12°) or in long 12°; if it does, check the relevant diagram and note; finally, using Key III, multiply the dimensions of the leaf by the factors appropriate to the format to obtain the size of the uncut whole sheet, and find its name in the tables of paper sizes, pp. 73–5.

3. If the book does not appear to be in one of the normal formats or in long 12° (remembering that it may have been heavily cut down, and that chain-lines and watermarks are not quite always reliable guides), and if it is not more than 15 cm. tall, refer to Key II, and check the possibilities with Key III.

4. If there is still no clear answer, either because the format appears to be abnormal or because there are several alternatives, consult one of the early printers' manuals (pp. 87, 393) and make reversed paper models of possible imposition schemes, paying attention as far as possible to deckle, cut and conjoint edges, tranchefiles, and point-holes.

[7] See pp. 63–5.

KEY I: *Large and Medium Formats*

1. *uncut height*   30 cm. or more
   chain-lines   vertical
   watermark   in the middle of the leaf
   leaves per gathering   2, 4, 6, 8, or 10
   } 2° (see fig. 46 and note A)

2. *uncut height*   19 cm. or more
   chain-lines   horizontal
   watermark   in the middle of the
   spine fold
   leaves per gathering   4 or 2
   } 4° (see figs. 47–9 and note B)

3. *uncut height*   15 cm. or more
   chain-lines   vertical
   watermark   at the head of the spine
   fold
   leaves per gathering   8 or 4
   } 8° (see figs. 50–3 and note C)

4. *uncut height*   15 cm. or more
   chain-lines   vertical
   watermark   at the head of the leaf
   leaves per gathering   12
   } long 12° (see fig. 54 and note D)

5. *uncut height*   12·5 cm. or more
   chain-lines   horizontal
   watermark   at the fore-edge of the
   leaf
   leaves per gathering   12, 6, or 8 and 4
   } 12° (see figs. 55–9 and note E)

KEY II: *Small Formats*

(see figs. 60–3 and note F)

NOTE: Books in formats from 16° down to 128° were usually printed on the smaller sizes of paper, especially pot and foolscap, so that their cut heights are seldom much more than the minimum uncut heights given in this key. See also the table of typical leaf sizes in Key III.

6. *chain-lines*   vertical
   leaves per gathering   8 or 16
   minimum uncut height   10·0 cm.   long 24°
             7·5 cm.   32°
             5·0 cm.   96°
             3·75 cm.   128°

Key II: *Small Formats* (*cont.*)

7. *chain-lines*   horizontal
   leaves per gathering   8 or 16
   minimum uncut height   9·5 cm.   16°; 24° (the 16 way)
                              6·3 cm.   48°
                              4·75 cm.   64°

8. *chain-lines*   vertical
   leaves per gathering   6 or 12
   minimum uncut height   10·0 cm.   18°; long 24°
                              5·0 cm.   72°

9. *chain-lines*   horizontal
   leaves per gathering   6 or 12
   minimum uncut heigh   9·5 cm.   24° (the 16 way)
                              6·3 cm.   36°; 48°

Key III: *Sheet Sizes*

format	to find sheet size, multiply		dimensions of uncut leaves from three representative sizes of paper in cm. (height × width)		
	height of leaf by	width of leaf by	pot	demy	royal
1°	1	1	39·0 × 31·0	51·0 × 38·0	60·0 × 46·0
2°	1	2	31·0 × 19·5	38·0 × 25·5	46·0 × 30·0
4°	2	2	19·5 × 15·5	25·5 × 19·0	30·0 × 23·0
8°	2	4	15·5 × 9·75	19·0 × 12·75	23·0 × 15·0
long 12°	2	6	15·5 × 6·5	19·0 × 8·5	23·0 × 10·0
12°	3	4	13·0 × 7·75	17·0 × 9·5	20·0 × 11·5
16°	4	4	9·75 × 7·75	12·75 × 9·5	15·0 × 11·5
18°	3	6	10·3 × 6·5	12·6 × 8·5	15·3 × 10·0
long 24°	3	8	10·3 × 4·9	12·6 × 6·4	15·3 × 7·5
24° the 16 way	4	6	9·75 × 5·2	12·75 × 6·3	15·0 × 7·7
32°	4	8	7·75 × 4·9	9·5 × 6·4	11·5 × 7·5
36°	6	6	6·5 × 5·2	8·5 × 6·3	10·0 × 7·7
48°	6	8	6·5 × 3·9	8·5 × 4·75	10·0 × 5·75
64°	8	8	4·9 × 3·9	6·4 × 4·75	7·5 × 5·75
72°	6	12	5·2 × 3·25	6·3 × 4·25	7·7 × 5·0
96°	6	16	5·2 × 2·4	6·3 × 3·2	7·7 × 3·75
128°	8	16	3·9 × 2·4	4·75 × 3·2	5·75 × 3·75

Notes on the format diagrams

The diagrams are based primarily on impositions shown in the following four manuals: Wolffger, G., *Neu-auffgesetztes Format-Büchlein*, Graz 1673; Moxon, J., *Mechanick exercises*, London 1683; Fertel, M. D., *La science pratique de l'imprimerie*, Saint-Omer 1723; and Smith, J., *The printer's grammar*, London 1755.

The wavy sheet margins indicate deckle edges, and the grids of vertical lines represent the chain-lines and the tranchefiles (though not all paper had tranchefiles). Watermarks are shown in particular halves of the sheets, but they could as easily be in the opposite halves. (It will be remembered that not all paper was watermarked; and that countermarks, which are also shown, were rare before the mid seventeenth century.)

The layouts of the pages are shown in the orientation they had as a printed sheet lying on the open tympan of the press as seen by the pressman (these details are explained in the section on presswork).[8] The figure at the top of each page is the page number; and the signature letter and leaf number is given at the foot of every page in order to make the features of each leaf readily apparent (although in fact no more than the first few recto pages of each sheet were so signed). Point-hole positions are shown at o o (with alternative positions at x x in figs. 51, 56).

The cuts whereby sections of the printed sheet were removed before folding are indicated by plain lines with pairs of shears drawn at the ends. Folds are shown by dashed lines. Spine folds (marked S) connected conjugate pairs of leaves; but the other folds, although they made some of the edges conjoint when the sheet was first folded, were normally opened later by the binder's plough, or with a paper knife.

[8] In France and Germany quarto sheets were oriented the other way round; see p. 127.

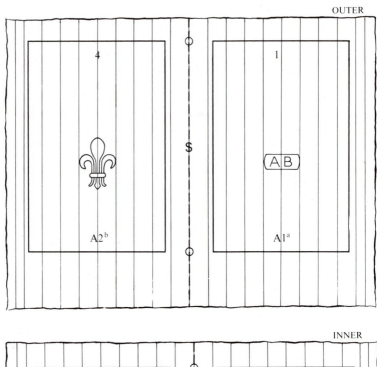

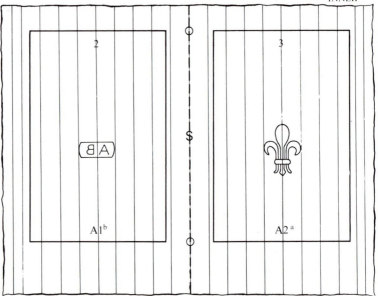

Fig. 46. Sheet of folio (2°); see note A, p. 106.

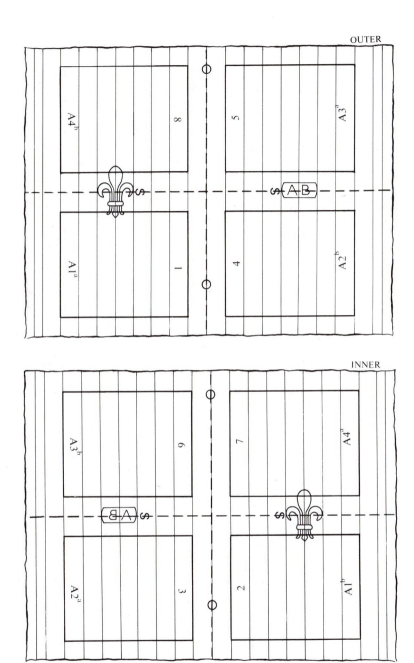

FIG. 47. Sheet of quarto (4°); see note B, p. 106.

H

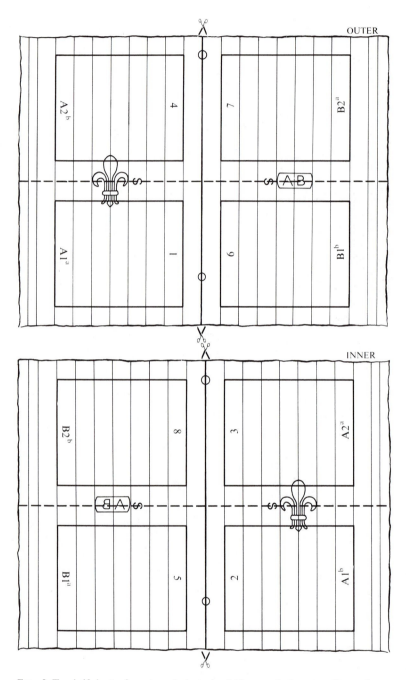

FIG. 48. Two half-sheets of quarto worked together (4° in 2s, 2 sigs.); see note B, p. 106.

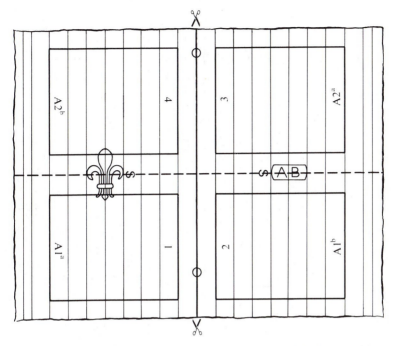

FIG. 49. Half-sheet of quarto imposed for work and turn (4° in 2s, half-sheet imposition); see note B, p. 106.

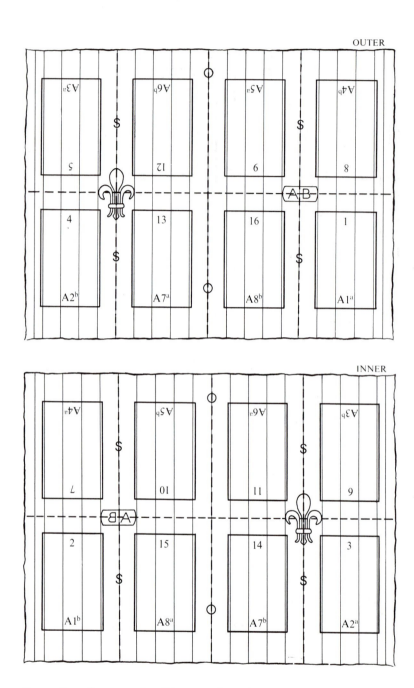

FIG. 50. Sheet of common octavo (8°); see note C, p. 106.

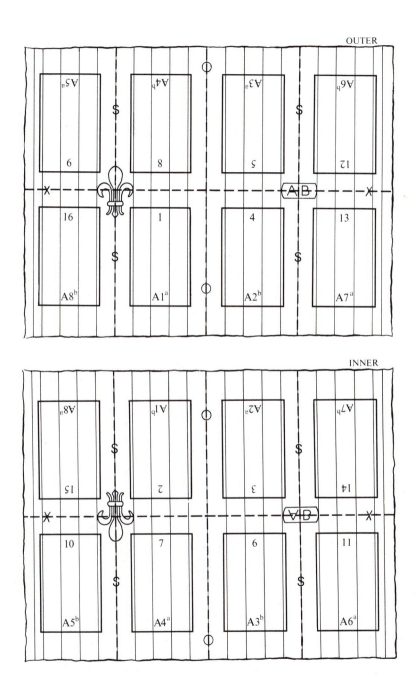

Fig. 51. Sheet of 'inverted' octavo (inverted 8°); see note C, p. 106.

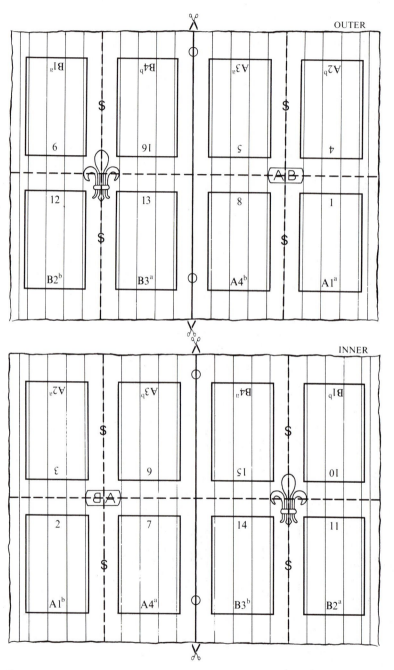

FIG. 52. Two half-sheets of octavo worked together (8° in 4s, 2 sigs.); see note C, p. 106.

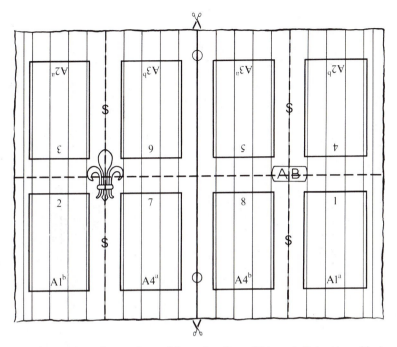

Fig. 53. Half-sheet of octavo imposed for work and turn (8° in 4s, half-sheet imposition); see note C, p. 106.

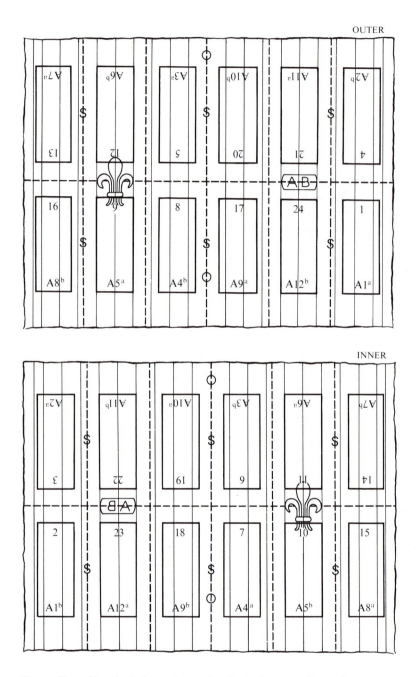

FIG. 54. Sheet of long duodecimo, or long twelves (long 12°); see note D, p. 106.

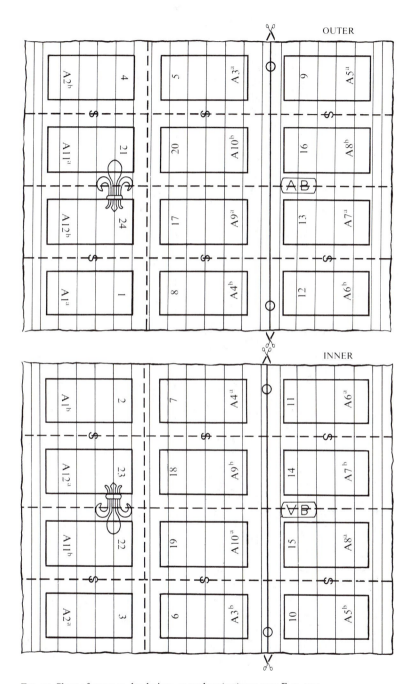

FIG. 55. Sheet of common duodecimo, or twelves (12°); see note E, p. 107.

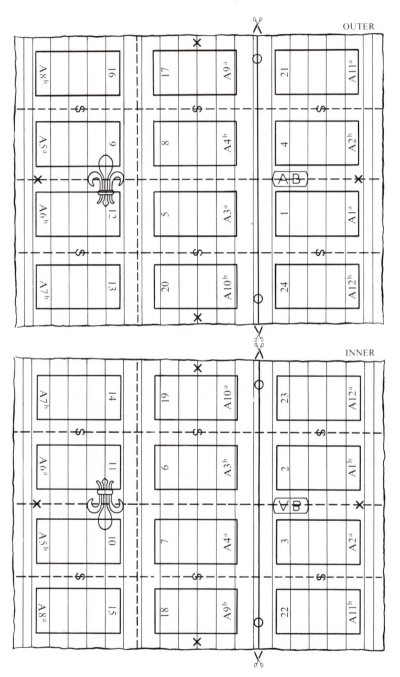

FIG. 56. Sheet of 'inverted' duodecimo, or twelves (inverted 12°); see note E, p. 107.

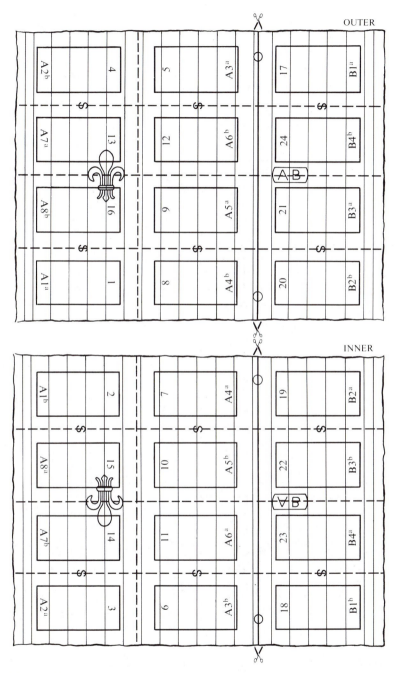

FIG. 57. Sheet of duodecimo, or twelves, with two signatures, 16 pages and 8 pages (12° in 8s and 4s, 2 sigs.); see note E, p. 107.

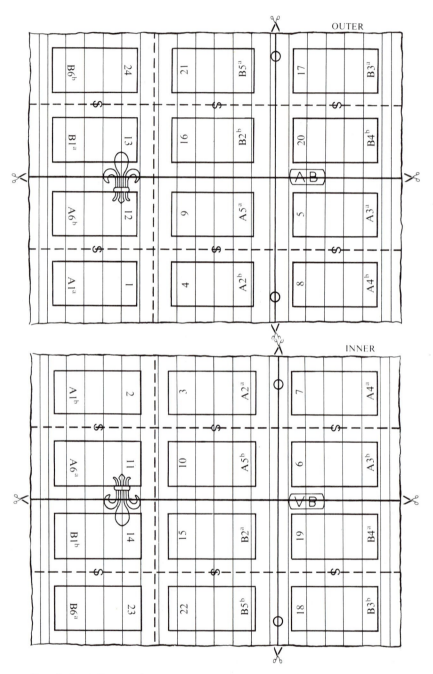

FIG. 58. Two half-sheets of duodecimo, or twelves, worked together (12° in 6s, 2 sigs.); see note E, p. 107.

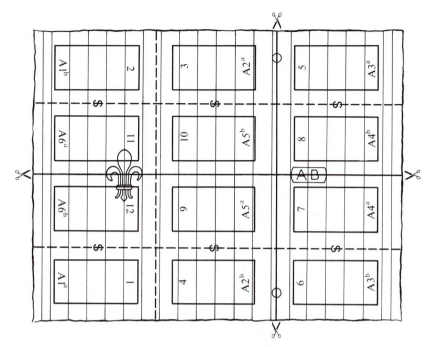

FIG. 59. Half-sheet of duodecimo, or twelves, imposed for work and turn (12° in 6s, half-sheet imposition); see note E, p. 107.

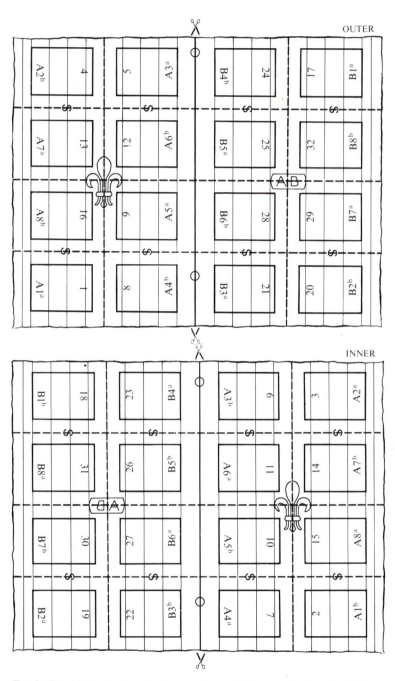

FIG. 60. Two half-sheets of sextodecimo, usually called sixteens, worked together (16° in 8s, 2 sigs.); see note F, p. 107.

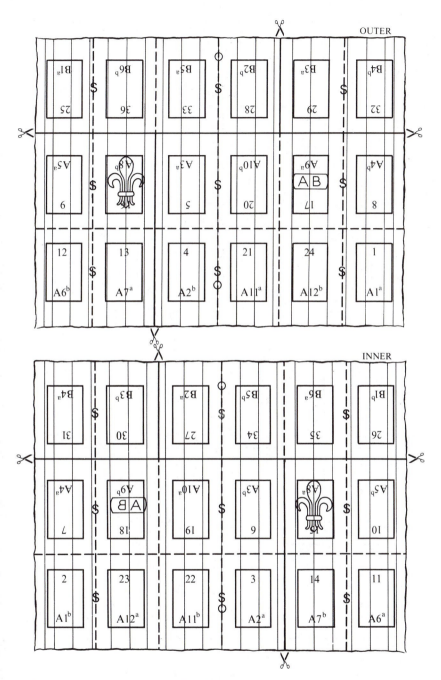

F IG. 61. Sheet of octodecimo, usually called eighteens, with two signatures, 24 pages and 12 pages (18° in 12s and 6s, 2 sigs.); see note F, p. 107.

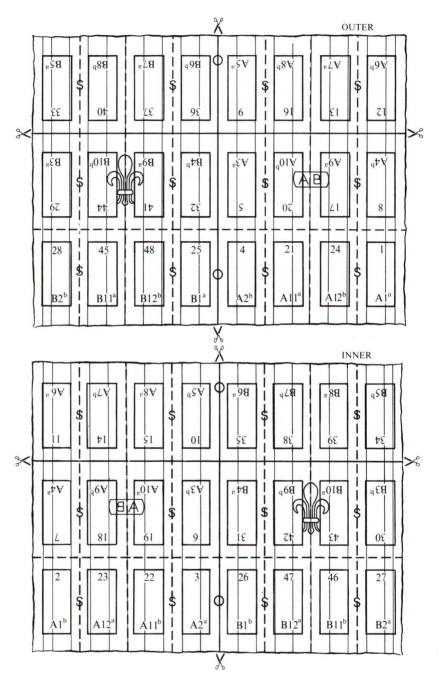

FIG. 62. Two half-sheets of long twenty-fours—the form vicesimoquarto is no longer used—worked together (long 24° in 12s, 2 sigs.); see note F, p. 107.

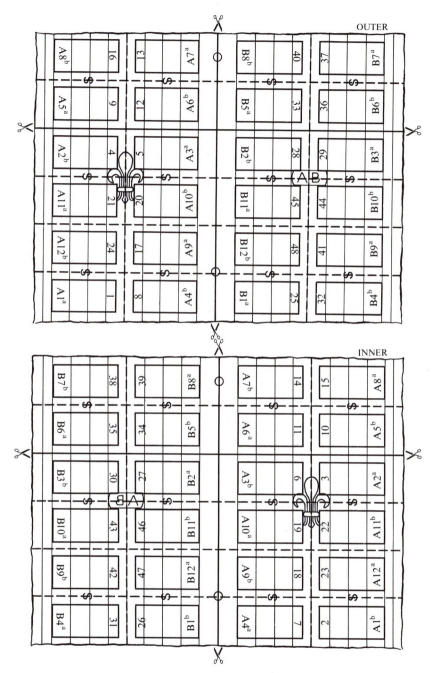

FIG. 63. Two half-sheets of twenty-fours—the form vicesimoquarto is no longer used—imposed the sixteen way and worked together (24° in 12s the 16 way, 2 sigs.); see note F, p. 107.

NOTE A: *Impositions in 2°* (figs. 44–6)

Watermark: in the middle of leaf 1 or of leaf 2.

Each sheet of quired folio (2° in 4s, 6s, 8s, or 10s) was signed A1, B1 (etc.) on the first page of the first sheet of the quire, A2, B2 (etc.) on the first page of the second sheet, and so on.

Very large books with horizontal chain-lines may have been printed on half double-sized sheets (common in English newspapers of the eighteenth century), or they may be collections of broadsheets (1°). Broadsheets, if they were very wide, might alternatively be imposed sideways; a collection of such 1° sheets would have vertical chain-lines, but the watermark would be offset from the middle of the leaf.

NOTE B: *Impositions in 4°* (figs. 47–9)

Watermark: (1) whole sheets: in the middle of the spine fold of leaves 1 and 4, or of leaves 2 and 3; (2) 4° in 2s: in the middle of the spine fold, or no mark.

4° was often quired in 8s until the seventeenth century; and in the fifteenth century it was occasionally quired in 6s, 10s, or 12s.[8a]

In France and Germany it was usual to lay 4° formes on the press the other way round (so that page 1 printed at the frisket end of the tympan).

It is normally impossible to tell whether 4° in 2s was printed by whole sheets with two signatures, or by half-sheet imposition.

NOTE C: *Impositions in 8°* (figs. 50–3)

Watermark: (1) whole sheets: at the head of the spine fold of leaves 1, 4, 5, and 8, or of leaves 2, 3, 6, and 7; (2) 8° in 4s: at the head of the spine fold of the four leaves, or no mark.

As with 4° in 2s, it is normally impossible to tell whether 8° in 4s was printed by whole sheets with two signatures or by half-sheet imposition.

Inverted 8° (fig. 51) can be told from common octavo by the different arrangement of deckle edges and tranchefiles. It was especially characteristic of sixteenth- and seventeenth-century Italian books, where it was used in association with the alternative point-holes x x; but inverted 8° was also illustrated as a common German imposition by Hornschuch of Leipzig in 1608; its purpose may have been to get the first page of the sheet away from the edge of the paper.[9] There were half-sheet versions of inverted 8°.

NOTE D: *Impositions in long 12°* (fig. 54)

Watermark: at the head of leaves 5 and 6, or of leaves 11 and 12.

Long 12° was commonly used for small devotional books in France, Germany, the Low Countries, Spain, and England during the first half of the sixteenth century, and it continued to be used in Spain for the rest of the sixteenth century and in Germany until the eighteenth century; elsewhere it disappeared, and the folding was not shown in any manual until 1770.[10]

[8a] *GW* 4645, 4217, 4245.

[9] Cook, D. F., 'Inverted imposition', *The Library*, xii, 1957, pp. 193–6; Hornschuch, H., op. cit., p. 12.

[10] Foxon, D. F., 'Some notes on agenda format', *The Library*, viii, 1953, pp. 168–70; Luckombe, P., *A concise history of . . . printing*, London 1770, p. 414.

An alternative Spanish version has the watermark at the head of leaves 1 and 2, or of leaves 7 and 8.[11] The layouts shown in the late-eighteenth-century manuals were different again, but they are not known to have been used.

NOTE E: *Impositions in 12°* (figs. 55–9)

Watermark: (1) common 12° whole sheets: at the upper fore-edge of leaves 7 and 8, or of leaves 11 and 12; (2) common 12° in 6s (two signatures): half the mark in the upper fore-edge of leaf 1, or 3, or 4, or 6; (3) common 12° in 6s (half-sheet imposition) half the mark in the upper fore-edge of leaf 4, or 6; (4) inverted 12° whole sheets: in the upper fore-edge of leaves 1 and 2, or of leaves 5 and 6; (5) 12° in 8s and 4s: in the upper fore-edge of leaves 7 and 8 of the 8-leaf section, or of leaves 3 and 4 of the 4-leaf section.

Duodecimos were folded by removing the offcut along the line indicated which was then folded up separately and quired inside (in 8s and 4s, alongside) the remainder of the folded sheet. Although it seldom happened in practice, it was possible to shuffle copies of the main sections and offcuts of 12° sheets or half-sheets and thus produce aberrant watermark patterns. Rules were occasionally printed as guidelines for making the offcuts.

Various alternative layouts were less commonly used. Inverted 12° (fig. 56) was, like inverted 8° (q.v.), especially characteristic of sixteenth- and seventeenth-century Italian printing, where it was similarly used with the alternative point-holes x x in the *middle* of either the long or the short edges of the sheet (common 12° always had offset point-holes);[12] but inverted 12° does not appear to have been used in Germany. Two alternative English layouts are known: one (STC 23633, *c.* 1586) has the watermark on the upper fore-edges of leaves 9 and 10, or of leaves 11 and 12;[13] the other (Moxon, 1683) has the watermark in the upper fore-edges of leaves 7 and 8, or of leaves 9 and 12;[14] neither appears to have been common. There seems to be no clear evidence that the nineteenth-century imposition of 12° without cutting (see pp. 196–7) was ever used in the hand-press period.

NOTE F: *Impositions for small formats* (figs. 60–3)

Only a few common impositions are shown here; and for each folding there were numerous alternative layouts. A variety of unusual impositions, with a commentary, is given in Savage, W., *A dictionary of the art of printing*, London 1841, repr. 1968.

The commonest of the small formats were 18° in 12s and 6s (or in 6s), and the two varieties of 24°, gathered in 8s or 12s; English printers normally imposed 24° for gathering in 12s, but many continental printers imposed 24° for gathering in 8s. Miniature books of the eighteenth century were sometimes in 32°; and Plantin in the sixteenth century employed what is perhaps the ultimate small folding: 128° in 8s.[15]

[11] e.g. Mares's *Floreta española*, Alcalá 1598 (Trin. Coll., Camb., G. 26. 28, uncut).

[12] Cook, D. F., op. cit., but the 12° imposition on p. 194 is wrongly illustrated, the four leaves in the middle being reversed.

[13] T., W., *A godlie & comfortable letter* [*c.* 1586], fragments as endpapers in U.L.C. D*. 16. 32E.

[14] Moxon, J., op. cit., p. 225.   [15] *Kalendarium* [*etc.*], Plantin, Antwerp 1570.

IMPOSITION IN PRACTICE

Books were normally imposed as a series of regular sheets of the chosen format, the preliminaries being printed last, perhaps (if they were not extensive) filling up the last sheet of text and then being detached so that they could be placed at the front. Occasionally preliminaries were printed in a format different from that of the text, or even as part of an entirely different book that was under way at the same time and which happened to have an odd half or quarter sheet unused. Again, the preliminaries of pamphlets were sometimes arranged as an outset conjugate with the final leaves of the text, and wrapped round the rest of the gatherings.

Small sizes of paper (pot, foolscap, and demy) were always more commonly used than large (medium and royal); and scarcely any books were printed on paper larger than royal in the sixteenth or seventeenth centuries. Books in miniature formats were attempted from time to time, although they may always have been more curious than useful. Unfolded sheets have survived of a *Kalendarium* printed by Plantin in 1570, which is a foolscap 128° in 8s, imposed as a single whole sheet with 16 signatures; its uncut leaves would measure only $4\cdot3 \times 2\cdot6$ cm.[16] There was a considerable vogue in the mid seventeenth century for miniature editions of the classics which the Elzeviers exploited for economic reasons (see p. 177), using the two 24° impositions, but spectacles were then neither common nor efficient and pocket editions soon returned to a larger format.

Errors in imposition—pages printed in wrong positions in the forme—were rare; they were immediately obvious in proof, and indeed it is in surviving proof sheets that most of the known mistakes of this kind are found. A blemish which looks like wrong imposition, but is not, occurred when the second forme of a sheet was laid on the press the wrong way round, so that all the pages of the forme were wrongly backed up, with the result in an octavo of a page order running 1 6 7 4 5 2 3 8 9 14 15 12 13 10 11 16. Alternatively, a forme might be backed up, not with its own second forme, but with a forme belonging to another sheet. (Sheets wrongly printed should be distinguished from sheets correctly printed but wrongly folded: for instance, one of the various wrong ways of folding an octavo sheet gives the page-order 1 2 7 8 5 6 3 4 13 14 11 12 9 10 15 16.)

The normal placing of the points (see p. 128, and the format diagrams, figs. 46–63) made it practically impossible to print the second side of the sheet with the paper, rather than the forme, turned end to end. Similarly, the eccentric placing of the points prevented sheets from being turned the

---

[16] Hellinga, W. Gs., *Copy and print in the Netherlands*, Amsterdam 1962, p. 178 and pl. 51.

wrong way round in half-sheet imposition, an error that was virtually unknown in the hand-press period.

STRIPPING, AND SKELETONS

When a forme had been printed off it was returned to a compositor for stripping, generally to the compositor who had set and imposed it, although this was not always possible. First he cleaned the ink off the forme, laying it on a wooden letter board, loosening the quoins and scrubbing the face of the letter with lye (an alkaline solution of potash in water), and finally rinsing it thoroughly in water. The forme was then laid on the stone, or on a special distributing frame if there was one, and the quoins and outer furniture were lifted out and laid round the chase.

Every forme of a book was arranged in essentially the same way. The number and pattern of the pages were regularly and exactly repeated, and it saved labour to re-use the chase, quoins, furniture, headlines, and regularly repeated rules or ornaments from a forme that had been printed off, rather than to find or set them afresh for each new forme. All these re-usable parts, the typographical parts which left their mark upon the paper, and the chase, quoins, and furniture which did not, are known collectively today as the 'skeleton forme'.

For the first sheet or two of a book there were no skeletons available, so the compositor set his headlines, etc., for each page as he went along, then found chase, quoins, and furniture when he was ready to impose them. When a forme was returned for distribution, however, its quoins and furniture were carefully laid out in order round the chase, so that they could go back into the same relative positions as before. Then the typographical part of the skeleton was transferred to the new pages (with the necessary alterations of page numbers) either directly so that they were placed in the same relative positions as before, or by way of a galley, in which case their relative positions might be changed; and the forme was imposed with new pages in an old skeleton.[17] It appears from mistakes in signatures (and occasionally in catchwords) that direction lines were sometimes transferred with the skeleton.

It was possible to print a whole book using only one skeleton, a new forme not being imposed until the last one had been printed off and stripped. The recurrence of a single set of headlines, etc., on both sides of successive sheets indicates that this did sometimes happen, although it must be borne in mind that the fact that the typographical part of a skeleton forme is found

---

[17] Moxon, J., op. cit., pp. 229–30, describes the transfer of furniture etc. from an old to a new forme, but says nothing about transferring the typographical parts of the skeleton; nevertheless we know from the re-use of headlines that this was the normal practice in English printing at least until the mid eighteenth century.

to be transferred from sheet to sheet does not prove that the chase, quoins, and furniture were similarly transferred. The reason for single-skeleton working may have been shortage of type, not because the skeleton itself was especially costly or uneconomical of type, but because the printer could not keep more than a few pages standing at a time and thus had no need of more than one skeleton; or it may have been some casual shortage of any of the constituent parts of the skeleton.

Commonly, however, two or more skeletons were made for a book. The pattern of their occurrence is usually easy to establish, but it is unwise to read too much significance into it. Comparison of the skeleton pattern and the actual printing arrangements of the second edition of Newton's *Principia* (Cambridge University Press 1713) shows both a major change in the skeleton pattern that accompanied a minor interruption of printing, and a minor change in the skeleton pattern that reflected major delay and change in the printing arrangements.[18]

An economical arrangement for foldings other than folio, much used in the eighteenth century when setting by formes was no longer usual, was half-sheet imposition with one skeleton, which again required only enough pages for a single forme to be set in type at a time. Indeed, this method was so convenient—both sides of the sheet could be printed one after the other without changing formes—that it appears to have been used by many printers of the later hand-press period for its own sake, not because of any shortage of materials.

The compositor would probably distribute the type from a forme as he stripped it; but if it was not immediately required for resetting—say at the end of a book—he might tie the pages round with cord and wrap them in paper for storage until that fount of type was needed again.

PROOFS AND CORRECTION[19]

Proofs—trial prints—of newly-imposed formes were made so that any errors that had crept into the text in the process of setting the copy in type (and there were always some) might be discovered and rectified before the sheet was printed. This is not to say that there were not supposed to be any differences between the copy and the type, for it had been the compositor's duty to correct or normalize the spelling, punctuation, and capitalization (known nowadays as the 'accidentals') of the manuscript. The function of proof-correction was to ensure that the words of the

---

[18] McKenzie, D. F., 'Printers of the mind', *Studies in bibliography*, xxii, 1969, pp. 29–31.

[19] See Moxon, J., op. cit., 233–9, 246–50, and Simpson, P., *Proof-reading in the sixteenth, seventeenth and eighteenth centuries*, Oxford 1935, repr. 1970.

copy—the 'substantives'—were reproduced as faithfully as possible in an acceptable orthographic style.

Two people were chiefly involved in the correction of a forme: the compositor who had set it, and who was now required to make good his own mistakes, and a corrector who both acted as a check upon the compositor and was able to add a second and perhaps more learned opinion in cases of difficulty. The larger businesses employed professional correctors, either full- or part-time,[20] but in the smaller houses (such as those of seventeenth-century London) correction was normally carried out by the master or a senior journeyman; less commonly the corrector was the author or the author's representative. Correction can seldom have been left to the compositor alone, for he was usually a piece-worker who had to correct his own mistakes in his own time, and who would have been tempted to overlook such errors as would take long to mend; and Moxon makes it clear that a professional corrector's loyalty was to the master, not to the journeymen.[21]

Having imposed a forme, the compositor carried it to the press room, where a press crew was required to pause in its work and pull a proof for him, often on an old press kept for the purpose. It was usual to take formes singly for the first proofs, not in pairs, and first proofs were pulled on one side only of a piece of defective or spoiled paper. One of the pressmen then carried forme and proof back to the compositor and, laying the forme on the imposing stone, brushed it over with lye to clean it ready for correcting in the metal. It must be emphasized that in the hand-press period it was always normal to take proofs for the first time after the pages had been imposed as a forme, not before. Pages may occasionally have been proofed in galleys—in 1563 Plantin bought some galleys for pulling (*à tirer*) folio pages[22]—but the practice was never common, and there is no evidence that type was normally proofed in long galleys before the early nineteenth century (see pp. 194–5).

The compositor may have read the first proof himself for 'literals'— mistakes in individual letters, which always occurred in some numbers however skilled the compositor—but he is more likely to have handed it straight over, together with the relevant section of the copy, to the corrector. The corrector then settled down with his 'reader'[23] to check the proof for errors, using the marks that the compositor had made on the copy (p. 50) to find the place where each type page began.

---

[20] There might be several correctors; Plantin normally employed one corrector for each 2 to 3 presses at work (Voet, L., *The golden compasses*, ii).

[21] Moxon, J., op. cit., p. 327.   [22] Information from Professor J. Gerritsen.

[23] By the mid nineteenth century the corrector had come to be called the 'reader' and the reader had become the 'reading boy' or 'copyholder'. The printer's reader should not be confused with the publisher's reader, who was an editorial adviser.

Nowadays, when copy and proof are usually supposed to agree in detail, proofs are best corrected by ocular comparison with the copy, but in the hand-press period, when the printed text was not a literal reproduction of the manuscript but a normalized version with much alteration of detail, the corrector preferred to have the copy read aloud to him by his reader while he followed the proof and marked the mistakes. In this way he could both check that the substantives of the text were correct and approve the revised accidentals without being distracted by the orthographic vagaries of the manuscript. (An alternative procedure was sometimes used for dealing with difficult manuscripts in the nineteenth century: the boy read aloud from a proof, while the corrector followed the copy and marked up a second proof.)[24]

The reading aloud was performed in a conventionalized sing-song. The following example recorded in the 1840s may represent the practice of the later hand-press period. It will be observed that the accidentals are largely ignored. Here is the copy, from the first epistle of Pope's *Moral essays*:

> "Odious! in woollen! 'twould a saint provoke,"
> Were the last words that poor Narcissa spoke;
> "No, let a charming chintz and Brussels lace
> Wrap my cold limbs, and shade my lifeless face:
> One would not, sure, be frightful when one's dead—
> And—Betty—give this cheek a little red."
> . . . "I give and I devise" (old Euclio said,
> And sigh'd) "my lands and tenements to Ned."
> "Your money, Sir?" "My money, Sir! what, all?
> Why,—if I must—(then wept) I give it Paul."
> "The Manor, Sir?" "The Manor! hold," he cried,
> "Not that,—I cannot part with that"—and died.[25]

And this, complete with mistakes, is the reading boy's version: '. . . turns odious in woollen 'twould a saint provoke close were the last words that poor narcissa spoke turns no let a charming chintz and Brussels lace wrap my cold limbs and shade my lifeless face one need not sure be frightful though one's dead and Betty. . . . Give my cheek a little red close turns again I give and I devise close old Euclio said and sighed turns my lands and tenements to Ned close turns again your money sir close turns again my money sir what all why if I must close then wept turns again I give it Paul close turns again the manor sir close turns again the manor hold close he cried turns again not that I cannot part with that close and died . . .'[26]

It was still normal at the end of the nineteenth century for the reading

[24] Southward, J., and Powell, A., *Practical printing*, 5th ed., London [1900], i, pp. 539–40.
[25] Pope, A., *Works*, ed. Roscoe, W., London 1847, iv, p. 200.
[26] Smith, C. M., *The working man's way in the world*, London 1853 (repr. London 1967), pp. 288–9.

boy not to specify the accidentals unless the copy was 'of a more than ordinary complexity'.[27]

When the work being corrected was in a foreign language the reading aloud was even more formalized, often to the extent of spelling out every word letter by letter. The proofs of the folio *Iliad* printed in Greek at the Foulis Press in Glasgow in 1756 were read not only by the corrector James Tweedie, but also by Andrew Foulis, one of the partners in the firm (and incidentally a graduate), and by the two editors, Professors Moor and Muirhead, there being six readings in all. Amongst Tweedie's notes on one set of proofs (which has been preserved) is the acid comment: 'N.B. I keep, or endeavour to keep, strictly to my Copy, right or wrong: According to orders. A⟨nd⟩ leave it to my Betters to correct both *it & me*: *neither* of whom, I plainly see, are without our faults. J.T.'[28]

A few cases are known in printed texts of the hand-press period of errors which appear to have been caused by a mishearing rather than by a misreading of the copy (see p. 352). Some of them could have been caused by the corrector misunderstanding the reader (who was not concerned to convey the full meaning of the words he mouthed) and so supplying a missing word wrongly. Like the compositor, the corrector worked more or less automatically, and did not necessarily take in the general sense of what he was reading. Charles Manby Smith has a story of a man who spent all day checking every word of a newspaper for the printer, but who still called for the same paper in the evening to read it for the sake of its contents.[29]

Having checked the text, the corrector considered the order of the pages to make sure that the imposition was right (even though the first proof was printed on one side only it still showed the order of the pages when it was folded, the pages of the other forme simply being blank). Likewise he looked over the signatures, running titles, and page numbers; and finally handed the marked proof—but not the copy—back to the compositor for correcting in the metal, by which time the proof of the second forme of the sheet was probably ready for him.

The conventional signs used by correctors to mark errors in the margins of proofs were of early origin—the most important of them were in use by the early sixteenth century—and they remain essentially unchanged today.[30] It is pleasant to be able to interpret a corrected proof of the sixteenth century (of which a good many have survived) with almost as much ease as one

---

[27] Southward, J., *Modern printing*, ii, London 1899, p. 180.

[28] Gaskell, P., *A bibliography of the Foulis Press*, London 1964, p. 209.

[29] Smith, C. M., op. cit., pp. 292–3.

[30] The English correctors' marks (also used in the Low Countries) are shown in Moxon, J., op. cit., pp. 247–9; the German in Hornschuch, H., op. cit., pp. 16–17 (reproduced in Simpson, P., op. cit., p. 127); and the French in Momoro, A. F., *Traité élémentaire de l'imprimerie*, Paris 1793, plate [27].

marked up last week. Three marks, which were common to printers of the hand-press period everywhere, did not refer to particular sorts of type, but were of general application. They were: a stroke through a word or letter that was to be deleted, with ꝰ in the margin; a caret mark (∧) placed where a word or letter was to be inserted, the addition being noted in the margin; and a stroke through a word or letter that was to be changed, the substitution being written in the margin. Two symbols for particular sorts were in general use: # for a space and ⊙ for a full point. There was also a widespread tendency to write a cross in the margin (which nowadays means a broken letter) to draw attention to a variety of errors. Then there were certain marks which varied in different places: English correctors used the space symbol and a caret to separate words that were run together, but in Germany the symbol ⌐ was used; 9 was used to indicate a turned letter in England, ⁄ in Germany; and although dots placed under words or letters wrongly struck out by the corrector were generally used, the additional use of 'stet' was confined to England. But it cannot be said that there were different national systems of correction marks; there was one international system, and some minor national variants.

The corrected proof was returned to the compositor, who gathered the type he would need for the correction into his stick. Then he unlocked the forme on the stone and, with a bodkin in the palm of his right hand, he lifted out the wrong letters and put the right ones in their place. If it was necessary to rejustify a line with a correction in it, it was done on the stone, not in the stick, the length of the line being tested against the others with the fingertips. Correcting in the metal was not difficult when it was merely a matter of changing one letter or word for another; but should a passage have been wrongly omitted, or set twice, several lines or even pages would have to be 'over-run', words being moved on from line to line and every line needing rejustification (which in this case was often done in the stick). New errors might be introduced during this process, especially if pages had to be interchanged in the forme to correct the imposition, when their edges could fall into pie (muddled type) and need resetting. Surviving proofs show that compositors of the hand-press period did not tick off completed corrections on the proof, as is often done now, but they did use the type collected in the stick for making corrections as a check on what had been done.

The first proof was, from the printer's point of view, the most important one and, to judge from the extreme rarity of books marred by the characteristic errors of the first proof—especially the considerable number of foul-case and turned letters which a compositor working at normal speed cannot well avoid—it was a process in the production of a book that was practically never omitted.

The first proof might be followed up with a 'revise' (or 'review'), a further proof intended not primarily for correction but as a demonstration that the corrections marked on the first proof had been properly carried out. The revise was read not against the copy, but against the corrected first proof.

The first proof, and any revises pulled to check it, constituted the first stage of proof correction, and it might be the only stage. Frequently, however, this was followed by a second and a third stage. Stage two was to pull a clean proof for the author, after the first-proof corrections had been made, printed on both sides of the sheet; no doubt a first-proof revise was sometimes re-used for this purpose. During the earlier hand-press period authors commonly attended at the printing house to correct proofs, but by the eighteenth century authors' proofs were often sent out to them.[30a] Whether the author referred to copy in reading proofs is likely to have depended on the type of book, as it does today; an author may feel the need to check the proofs of a detailed technical manual against his copy, but not those of a novel. By the eighteenth century authors were in the habit of calling for revises of their proofs if much correction was to be done.

The third and final stage of proof correction was the press proof, when a forme or sheet was read for residual blemishes, and as a final check on the imposition, headlines, pagination, etc., just before the actual printing run was about to begin—or, in English printing around 1600, while the run was in progress, so that any resulting corrections had to be made stop-press. Once again, a revise might be called for if corrections to the press proof were substantial.

Numerous surviving proofs, and the early descriptions of Le Roy and Ashley (1579, 1594) and Jaggard (1622)[31] indicate that these three main stages of proofing, with their attendant revises, were well known by the later sixteenth century; first proofs and press proofs have survived, and Jaggard discusses authors' proofs. There is also much evidence that similar routines were followed during the rest of the hand-press period and afterwards, and indeed the proofing procedures of modern book printers are still essentially the same.[32]

This is not to say that every book was proofed in three definable stages, for some books were less well proofed than others. Authors did not always read proofs; revises might be omitted and routines conflated. But we may

---

[30a] James Yonge, writing to his printer in 1692, did not expect proofs to be sent to him, but asked for a copy of each sheet as it was 'drawn off', so that 'befor the whole be finished I may send up a correction of the errata' (U.L.C. Add. MS. 7913, f. 1ᵇ).

[31] Quoted in *The Library*, x, 1955, pp. 41-2, and McKerrow, R. B., *An introduction to bibliography*, Oxford 1928, pp. 206-7.

[32] A similar three-stage system of proofing is described in Southward, J., *Modern printing*, i, London 1899, pp. 211-12.

say with some confidence, first that it was very rare for a book to escape proof-correction altogether;[33] and secondly that copy was normally consulted by the printer (if he consulted it at all when proofing) only at the first-proof stage, not afterwards.

The compositor's mistakes, then, were pointed out by the corrector and he made them good at his own expense, that is in his own time. But if the corrector called for any alterations which could not reasonably be blamed on the compositor they were charged to the house;[34] and if the corrector failed to notice any of the compositor's errors they became the corrector's responsibility, and he was charged if a sheet was spoiled as a result and had to be reprinted.[35] Similarly, mistakes marked by the author were mended free of charge by the compositor; but if the author made more than a modest number of alterations and additions to the text (as opposed to corrections), it was customary for him to pay the compositor privately for the extra work.[36]

Serious errors discovered after the sheet had been printed off were corrected in various ways, which are described in the section on presswork, pp. 134–6.

STANDING TYPE

Printers of the hand-press period could not afford to keep much type standing for long. About 50 kg. of type in cases was needed to set an average sheet, so that what Moxon called a 'very large' fount of pica (450 kg., including a considerable quantity of italic)[37] provided for no more than about eight sheets of whatever books were being printed in it. As a rule then the text type of substantial books had to be distributed for re-use soon after a sheet was printed off. Indeed there were occasions when Plantin (who had more type than most printers) found it worth while to interrupt the printing of a lengthy book, distribute and re-use the type on something more urgent, and finally re-set what had been distributed and go on with the earlier book.[38]

Nevertheless type in relatively small quantities was sometimes kept standing, even for years. Special settings, such as title-pages, which used little type, or settings of unusual founts which were seldom needed, were most often kept for re-use. Short books of up to three or four sheets were occasionally kept for reprinting from the sixteenth century onwards; the formes were usually stripped as if for distribution (except that the headlines and direction-lines were likely to be retained) and the pages were tied round with cord and wrapped in paper for storage. A new impression

---

[33] See also McKenzie, D. F., 'Printers of the mind', *Studies in bibliography*, xxii, 1969, pp. 42–9.

[34] In the nineteenth century 'house' corrections were often circled on the proof to distinguish them from corrections for which the compositor was responsible (Southward, J., op. cit., p. 208).

[35] Moxon, J., op. cit., p. 250.   [36] Ibid., p. 251 n.   [37] Ibid., p. 25.

[38] Voet, L., 'The making of books in the renaissance', *Printing and graphic arts*, x, 1966, p. 46.

printed from such pages may often be identified on a collating machine as a result of small disturbances to the type caused by re-imposition in new furniture. From 1587 to 1637 editions in England were supposedly limited by decree to 1,500 copies from one setting of type (or 3,000 copies of certain small books),[39] but there is evidence that the regulation was often ignored. Four pages of type for the *Genealogies of the scriptures* printed by Dr. John Speed in London were kept and used in nine separate impressions during the period 1631-40.[40]

Parts of longer books were sometimes printed from standing type during the earlier hand-press period. If a reprint was going to be needed immediately, the last sheet, or the last few sheets, would be reprinted (or printed in larger numbers) straight away, the earlier sheets then being reset.[41] More than this was rare before the second half of the eighteenth century, when books of medium length—up to about 20 sheets—of marked popularity might be kept in type (and usually in formes) for several impressions after the first, which were often described on their title-pages as new editions;[42] the impressions can sometimes be told apart by differences in their press figures (see pp. 133-4; 'editions', 'impressions', etc., are defined on pp. 313-16. There were also long runs of page-for-page reprints of the English Bible, the Prayer Book, etc., from the late sixteenth to the eighteenth century, but these were resettings, not reprints from standing type.)[40a]

Standing type-pages could of course be re-imposed for a reprint in a format different from the original, as if for a special issue (see pp. 136-7). Less commonly the measure as well as the format was changed. The type used for a four-page folio tract, which had been set to a measure of 148 mm. and published in London early in 1733, was over-run through the stick and rejustified to a measure of 75 mm. (each long line making two short ones), and issued a few months later as an eight-page octavo.[43] Similarly John Taylor's Greek and Latin *Demosthenes* was put out by the Cambridge University Press in quarto and octavo issues, and the type of the quarto was over-run to a shorter measure for printing the octavo; this occurred over a considerable period of time (1757-69), but it was a special case, involving ligatured greek type that would have been especially difficult to reset.[44]

[39] Greg, W. W., *A companion to Arber*, Oxford 1967, pp. 43, 95.

[40] Willoughby, E. E., 'A long use of a setting of type', *Studies in bibliography*, ii, 1949-50, pp. 173-5.

[40a] Work in progress by Mr. John R. Hetherington.

[41] Bowers, F. T., 'Notes on standing type in Elizabethan printing', *Papers of the Bibliographical Society of America*, xl, 1946, pp. 205-24.

[42] Todd, W. B., 'Recurrent printing', *Studies in bibliography*, xii, 1959, pp. 189-98; and see pp. 314-15, 317.

[43] Steele, O. L., '*The case of the planters of tobacco in Virginia, 1733*', *Studies in bibliography*, v, 1952-3, pp. 184-6.

[44] Demosthenes, [*Works*], vol. ii, 4°, Cambridge 1757; and ibid., 2 vols., 8°, Cambridge 1769. There is a similar relationship between vol. 'iii' of the same quarto edition, Cambridge 1748, and Taylor's octavo Demosthenes and Lycurgus, *Orationes duae*, Cambridge 1743. The procedure is described in Fertel, M. D., *La science pratique de l'imprimerie*, Saint-Omer 1723, pp. 190-1.

Presswork

All printers used what was substantially the same sort of printing press throughout the hand-press period, a hand-powered screw press built in a wooden frame. Wooden hand-presses were constructed and used in ways that varied slightly from country to country and from time to time, but the differences were neither considerable nor mechanically important. The description which follows of the English printing press of the seventeenth and eighteenth centuries applies, with but few changes, to presses elsewhere in Europe and, so far as we can tell, to presses of the sixteenth century as well.[1]

The common press—so called to differentiate it originally from the copperplate printer's rolling press, and later from the iron hand-press—consisted of a wooden frame which contained two groups of moving parts. These moving parts were the carriage assembly, which carried the type and paper in and out of the press so that the type could be inked and the paper changed after each impression; and the impression assembly, by means of which the paper was pressed down on to the inked type. The chief members of the frame were two upright cheeks about 2 m. high and placed 60–65 cm. apart, carrying between them the winter and, above it, the head, two massive cross timbers mortised into the cheeks which contained the vertical thrust of the impression; and the cheeks were braced from their tops to the ceiling, to prevent the press from twisting or shifting about in use.

The carriage assembly ran horizontally fore and aft between the cheeks, about 75 cm. from the ground. Two ribs, or rails, ran across the winter to supports at their ends, and on them slid the moving parts of the carriage: a plank on which was mounted the coffin, a shallow box containing the press stone. This stone was a block of marble or limestone with a top measuring about 62×47 cm. The plank was hauled in and out between the cheeks by girths at each end which were wound round a small windlass underneath the ribs.

When a forme was in place on the press stone, paper was lowered on to it by means of a tympan and frisket. The tympan consisted of a parchment-

---

[1] Based on the research for Gaskell, P., *The decline of the common press*, Cambridge University Ph.D. thesis 2902, 1956; for a detailed census of surviving wooden presses, with measurements and illustrations, see Gaskell, P., 'A census of wooden presses', *Journal of the Printing Historical Society*, vi, 1970, pp. 1–32.

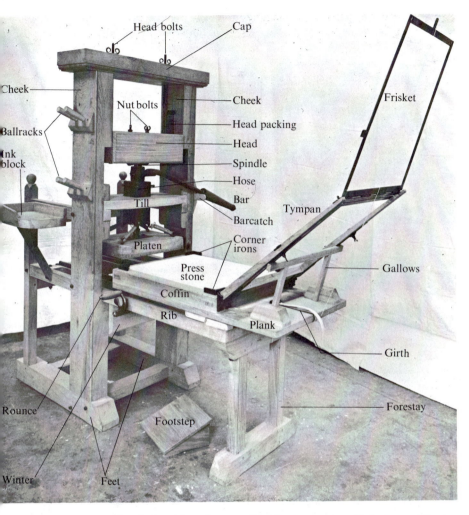

FIG. 64. A modern replica of a late-eighteenth-century English common press, with the names of its parts. The tympan and frisket would normally be covered, and there would be wooden braces from the cap to the roof.

covered frame of wood and iron hinged to the front end of the coffin; measuring about 66–72 × 51–59 cm. over-all, it was packed with sheets of cloth or paper held behind the parchment with an inner frame (the inner tympan). The printing paper was laid upon the parchment of the open tympan, where it was pierced by two points, adjustable pins bolted to the frame of the tympan; it was then held in place on the points by the frisket, a further iron frame hinged to the top of the tympan, and covered with parchment or paper cut with holes to let the inked type print through when paper, tympan, and frisket were folded down together on to the forme.

Fig. 65. A Low Countries common press (probably eighteenth-century, Gaskell B3) in the Plantin-Moretus shop at Antwerp. A forme is laid but not fixed on the stone, and an ink-ball hangs on the cheek. On the right is the paper bank, and a rolling press can just be seen on the left.

The impression assembly hung from the head of the press between the cheeks and above the winter. The winter was not adjustable for height within its mortises, but the head was tenoned into long mortises in which it could be raised and lowered to adjust the height of the impression assembly. In English, Dutch, and some French presses the head was slung on two bolts from the cap, a smaller timber that joined the tops of the cheeks, and it was drawn up tight against packing in the tops of the mortises; the height of the head was adjusted by altering the amount of packing above the head tenons. German, Scandinavian, and probably Italian presses, on the other hand, had no cap, and the head was adjusted by the insertion of packing both above and below the head tenons.

Embedded in the head was a brass nut, and in the nut worked the spindle, a steel bar 60 cm. long, of which the top 13 cm. were cut as a screw. Immediately below the screw the spindle was squared and pierced to take the bar, a crooked iron rod with a wooden handle. Further down still the shank of the spindle, rounded again, entered the hose, which was an oblong rectangular wooden box, 25 cm. long by 12·5 cm. square, bored with a hole to take the spindle down its long axis. When the bar was pulled through about 90° and then returned to its former position, the spindle moved down about 15 mm. in the nut and then up again. The hose, which had an internal collar slotted into the spindle, moved down and up too, but it was prevented from rotating with the spindle by the till, a plank fixed between the cheeks beneath the head which was pierced with a rectangular hole to take the hose. The bottom, or toe, of the spindle rested in a metal cup on the back of the platen, the flat-bottomed block which was pressed by it on to the back of the tympan, and so pushed the paper on to the inked type. The platen was lashed up tight to the toe of the spindle by cords which connected hooks at its four corners to another set of hooks at the four lower corners of the hose. Thus the platen was held in permanent contact with the toe of the spindle, moving up and down with it as it was turned, but being unable to turn with it.

An alternative form of hose, probably invented in Holland in the earlier seventeenth century, took the form of an iron yoke on either side of the spindle in place of the wooden box. The mechanical difference between the two forms was slight, and iron hoses, though widely known, remained rare outside the Netherlands.

The platen (generally made of hardwood, but occasionally cast or faced in metal) measured 45–49 × 29–32 cm. at the face, its longer dimension running from side to side of the press. It thus covered half of the back of the tympan, so that the press had to be worked twice, with the carriage in different positions, for the whole of the tympan to be pressed by the platen.

The size of the type area that could be worked on the common press was limited in theory by the dimensions of the platen and of the press stone. A small platen could in two pulls cover a type area of 58 × 45 cm., a large one 64 × 49 cm. (although they would not print well at the very edge); while the press stone generally measured about 62 × 47 cm. In practice, however, printers were limited by the inside dimensions of the standard chase (about 52 × 42 cm.) less a minimum of about 3 cm. each way for furniture and quoins. Thus in normal working the type area was limited to about 49 × 39 cm. (19 × 15½ in.), but with a large press and a large chase it could be pushed up to about 62 × 47 cm. (24½ × 18½ in.).[2]

The size of the paper that the press could take was limited by the length

[2] The larger press could thus work a type area 50 per cent greater than that worked by the smaller one. Moxon's mid-seventeenth-century Dutch press was small, Stower's late-eighteenth-century English press was large (Moxon, J., op. cit., § 10; Stower, C., *The printer's grammar*, London 1808, ch. xii).

FIG. 66. The impression assembly of a press by Ouram of Philadelphia, *c.* 1804, seen from behind. The open box-hose and large-diameter screw were characteristic of early-nineteenth-century American presses. The unadjustable metal links between hose and platen are probably not original but replace an earlier lashing of cord. Lying on the till are a pair of dividers and a metal shooting-stick (Pennsylvania Historical Society, Ephrata; Gaskell USA 11).

of the tympan, for the sheet could not be longer than the distance between the hinges at its ends, and tympans were made wide enough to take paper of this maximum length. The length of Moxon's tympan (1683) was 66 cm., so that the largest standard paper size that it could accommodate was royal (*c.* 60×46 cm.). The tympans of surviving eighteenth-century common presses are around 70 cm. long, and could therefore just take super royal paper (*c.* 70×50 cm.).

We cannot be certain of the details of the printing presses of the sixteenth century, since they were never closely described and none appear to have survived. Nevertheless they probably did not differ much from the later common presses, for the sixteenth-century illustrations of printing presses (mostly poor and repetitive woodcuts used as printers' devices) suggest only one substantial peculiarity: this was a spindle and screw which appears in a few early cuts to have been made of wood (though other cuts, equally early, show presses with metal spindles and screws).[3]

FIG. 67. A French press-room of the mid eighteenth century. The presses, which are braced to the ceiling, have windlasses in the gallows for tightening the girths but, unlike Fertel's press of 1723, they have no head-bolts, the head tenons simply being packed in the mortises. The puller on the left is changing the paper as his beater inks a folio forme. The puller on the right is pulling the first half of his forme, while the beater distributes the ink on the balls, stepping back at the same time to overlook the heap. (*Encyclopédie*, planches vii, Paris 1769, 'Imprimerie en caractères', pl. 14.)

[3] The principal illustrations are collected in Enschedé, J. W., 'Houten handpersen in de zestiende eeuw', *Tijdschrift voor boek- en bibliotheekswesen*, iv, 1906, pp. 196-215.

The difference between a press with a wooden screw and one with a metal screw was important because the former was able to develop little more than half the power developed by the latter from an equal pull on the bar; this was because of the greater diameter and greater frictional losses of the wooden screw.[4] However it is not necessary to suppose that wooden press screws preceded steel ones. Steel press spindles, with brass nuts cast on the screws, were within the technological capacity of (for instance) mid-fifteenth-century Mainz, and a press with a wooden screw may have been built in a place that lacked an advanced metal technology rather than at a particularly early date.

PREPARING THE PAPER[5]

The heap of printing paper was first set out for the pressmen by the warehouse-keeper, who normally took it from a batch of paper that had been bought for the particular book that was being printed (see p. 142). He removed the cording quires from the paper-maker's reams (the quires made up of more or less imperfect sheets, which he would later sort for usable paper) and arranged the good quires, still folded in half, into tokens of 250+ sheets up to the total number of tokens required for a sheet of the edition (or, if the edition were very large, up to the number required for a day's work). These tokens were to be the pressmen's units of work, and there was a strong tendency for edition sizes to be exact multiples of 250. The additional sheets over 250 were put into the heap for use as proof-, tympan-, and register-sheets, and to cover accidents at press. The allowance of extra sheets for these purposes was very small—it varied slightly with the edition size, but was typically about 3 per cent—which helps to explain why so many imperfect sheets, and even lightly-corrected press proofs, were included in completed books.

The warehouse-keeper would put slightly imperfect paper, such as the better sheets culled from the cording quires, into the heaps for the middle sheets of the book, where it would be less obtrusive than at the ends (the grossly imperfect sheets were put by and sold). Remnants of paper from batches bought for other books, if they were of the right size and quality, might be put in anywhere.

The heap was given to the pressmen the day before it was to be used,

---

[4] A common press with a steel screw and a brass nut, mean diameter x and coefficient of friction y, develops about 1·8 times as much thrust at the toe of the spindle from a given pull at the bar as a similar press with a wooden screw and nut, mean diameter $2x$ and coefficient of friction $2y$. (Thrust $\simeq \dfrac{E(\frac{R}{r})}{\tan\theta + \mu}$, where E is the pull on the bar, R the length of the bar, r the mean radius of the screw, θ the angle of incidence of the thread, and μ the coefficient of friction.)

[5] Moxon, J., op. cit., pp. 320–2, 278–81.

so that they might wet it and leave it to stand overnight under a heavy weight. The quires were drawn one by one through a pan of water, unfolded, and laid out flat on a board one on top of another, a sheet being folded down to mark each token. Paper had to be wetted in order to secure a good colour on the printed sheet, for there was not enough power available in the common press—only about 2·25 kg./cm² over the area of the platen even though it covered only half the forme at a time[6]—to force the fibres of dry rag paper to take ink evenly and fully.

Next morning the heap, now damp right through, was set up on one end of the horse (later called the bank), a bench long enough to take two piles of paper end to end, and about as high as the coffin of the press. In the sixteenth century the horse was placed on the far side of the press, parallel to the ribs, but in the seventeenth and eighteenth centuries the more usual position was on the near side, set out at slightly less than a right angle from the fore-end of the ribs.

INK[7]

Printing ink was constituted of two parts, varnish and colour, which were manufactured separately and then combined to make ink. The varnish was the liquid vehicle, or medium, in which the colour was conveyed to the surface of the type and thence to the paper. There the varnish 'dried'— it was really a complex process of oxidation and solidification rather than simple evaporation—and bound the colour to the paper.

Varnish was made of old nut or linseed oil, reduced by boiling, with the addition of a small quantity of resinous material to prevent it from spreading sideways into the paper and causing unsightly stains. The colour for the black ink was a lampblack obtained by condensing the smoke of burning resin, which was then calcified by heating to remove residual tars which might also have been a cause of staining and discoloration, and finally ground to an extremely fine powder. For red ink the usual colour was ground vermilion (i.e. red mercuric sulphide).

The earliest printers, and especially Gutenberg and Schoeffer, made superb black inks, rich and pure in colour and free of any tendency to stain, which have proved to be entirely stable. From then on there was a decline in quality and, although there was always a considerable difference between the best inks in use and the worst, no printer managed to make or acquire an ink as fine as Schoeffer's until after the end of the hand-press period. There can be little doubt that the decline was caused by the fact

---

[6] A common press gave a thrust of about 3,160 kg. at the toe of the spindle from a pull on the bar of 68 kg.; see p. 124 n. 4 for the formula.

[7] Bloy, C. H., *A history of printing ink, balls and rollers, 1440–1850*, London 1967.

that good ink cost three or four times as much to make as bad. Printers of the hand-press period were chronically short of work, and competed by cutting costs; with no market for a really fine ink, the art of making it was forgotten. Baskerville tried very hard to find a notably good ink in the mid eighteenth century, but he failed.

Ink was being manufactured and sold by specialist firms in France in the earlier sixteenth century, and Plantin of Antwerp, who bought his ink ready-made by the ton, sold a consignment of ink to an Edinburgh printer in 1581.[8] But, while much printing ink was made and traded by specialist ink-makers throughout the hand-press period, some printers continued to make their own ink—or at least some of its constituents—until well into the nineteenth century.

Ink was worked up for use on the ink-block of the press (a small table mounted behind the near-side cheek) and transferred to the surface of the type by one of the pressmen using a pair of ink balls.[9] These were leather pads 15 cm. in diameter, mounted in wooden cups and handles and stuffed with wool or horsehair. The ball pelts, which were usually sheepskin, were fixed to the handles with nails which were only lightly knocked in, and were removed after the day's work (and often during the midday break as well). This was so that the stuffing could be teased out and cleared of lumps, and so that the pelts could be softened by currying and soaking them in urine; the smell is said to have been revolting. The amount of stuffing in the balls was varied to suit the nature of the work; large, soft balls with weak ink were used for low-grade work; small, hard balls and strong ink for work of better quality.[10]

Rollers for inking were not developed until after the end of the hand-press period, but they would have made little difference to the operation of the common press. A forme could be inked with balls as fast as the press could be worked, and the ordinary journeyman printer could wield them skilfully enough: bad inking, unlike bad ink, was never common. When balls were compared with rollers in the nineteenth century, their chief disadvantage was seen to be their cost: they were relatively uneconomical of ink, and they involved a considerable regular outlay on the materials of their construction, especially pelts.

MAKING READY[11]

While one of the pressmen was busy with ink and balls, the other received one or both formes for a sheet from the compositor, together with the final

8 Bloy, C. H., op. cit., p. 66; Voet, L., *The golden compasses*, ii.
9 Moxon, J., op. cit., pp. 282–91.
10 Savage, W., *Practical hints on decorative printing*, London 1822, p. 24.
11 Moxon, J., op. cit., pp. 263–77.

proof, and prepared the press for printing the first forme. Which forme this was could depend either on the compositor (if only one forme was delivered at a time) or on the pressmen (if both were delivered). In England there was a strong tendency to print the inner forme first, although it was not an invariable rule. In a representative sample of 200 English books of the seventeenth and eighteenth centuries, 73 per cent of the sheets (which numbered over 2,500 in all) were found to have been printed inner forme first, the periods of greatest regularity in the respect being 1641-1700 (90 per cent printed inner forme first) and 1701-50 (86 per cent).[12] Foreign practice has not been investigated in similar detail, but the early manuals suggest that German printers preferred to start with the outer forme;[13] and that French printers may also originally have preferred to print the outer forme first but that by the mid eighteenth century they were normally printing the inner forme first.[14]

A reason for printing the inner forme first may have been that it could be imposed before the last page of the outer forme was set. Alternatively the reason may have been that it prevented page 1 from being marred by a deep impression of page 2 showing through from behind, for it ensured that page 1 was printed last. (Perhaps it was also for reasons of appearance that there was a similar though less marked tendency in England to print the outer forme on the felt side of the paper, which was not so obviously ribbed as the mould side, and made a better show of page 1.)[15]

The orientation of the formes on the bed of the press in England was with page 3 (or, in the outer forme, page 1) next to the platen in folios and octavos, and with the same pages away from the platen in quartos and duodecimos.[16] In France and Germany, quarto formes were oriented like folios and octavos with pages 3 or 1 towards the platen, and only duodecimos had pages 3 or 1 away from the platen.[17] It was necessary to have rules so that the second forme should not be laid on the wrong way round, although it may be wondered why all impositions were not treated in the same way as duodecimo, of which the orientation was fixed by the placing of the points for the offcut. (The format diagrams, pp. 88-105, show the printed sheet on the open tympan, not the forme; the pages next to the platen during printing are on the right, those away from the platen on the left.)

[12] Povey, K., 'Working to rule, 1600-1800: a study of pressmen's practice', *The Library*, xx, 1965, pp. 13-54.

[13] From Hornschuch, H., op. cit. (1608), onwards.

[14] Fertel, M. D., op. cit. (1723), gives the inner forme as the *retiration* in his imposition diagrams, but the *Encyclopédie* (viii, 'Neufchastel' 1765, p. 617) says that the inner forme (*le côté de deux et trois*) was normally printed first.

[15] Povey, K., op. cit.   [16] Moxon, J., op. cit., p. 239.

[17] According to the imposition diagrams in the manuals; Fertel, for instance (op. cit., pp. 140 ff.), clearly indicates the orientation with a pair of 'fists'.

The pressman's first task with a new book was to make register, which meant laying on the first forme relative to the bed of the press and the press points so that, when the paper was printed on one side, turned over, and replaced on the points, the pages of the second forme would fall square on the backs of those of the first. Since the two formes were (or should have been) closely similar to each other, it was only necessary to find the right position for one of them. In a process which need not be described in detail,[18] the pressman established the positions of the (probably standard) furniture and quoins against which his standard chases would be locked up, and adjusted the press points on the tympan.

The pressman chose long-shanked points for small paper, short-shanked points for large; and in impositions other than duodecimo they were fixed at each side of the tympan half way between its ends. The near-side point was placed further in towards the middle of the tympan (and of the sheet) than the off-side point. This guarded the pressmen against the accident of the sheet being turned over from side to side rather than from end to end, for in that case the point holes would locate it in an obviously wrong position on the tympan.

In duodecimo impositions the points could not be placed half way between the ends of the tympan because there were pages in the way. They were therefore placed one third of the way from the frisket end of the tympan, and formes were oriented so that the division for the offcuts came under the points. With the points away from the centre of the sheet, it had to be turned over from side to side, and they were therefore placed an equal distance in from the edge; it was of course impossible in this case to turn the sheet over mistakenly from end to end and still use the same point holes.

The proper positions for the formes and the points being fixed, a sheet of paper from the heap was pasted to the face of the tympan where it served as a guide to positioning the sheets on the tympan during the printing of the first forme; this was the tympan sheet.

The tympan parchment was thoroughly wetted for work, and a woollen blanket, folded in two, was placed as packing between the outer and the inner tympan. This ensured that the type would dig well into the damp paper, so that there was no need for the make-ready of the machine-press period, whereby tissue overlays were pasted on to the tympan to compensate for worn type. Blocks, which tended to be less than type-high, were commonly underlaid with paper or card.

Next came the frisket. If the frisket frame was newly covered, an impression of the forme was pulled on it, and the printed areas were cut out with a knife. The grid that remained (corresponding to the furniture of the

[18] Moxon, J., op. cit., pp. 264–8.

forme) would both hold the printing paper against the tympan when it was folded down on to the type, and protect it from being dirtied by anything on the bed of the press beyond the margins of the pages. Each press was equipped with several frisket frames, and a frisket cut for any standard format would be kept for re-use; hence the practice of making them with parchment, rather than—as later—with brown paper. Standard friskets could then be modified for use with particular formes, patches being pasted or sewn on where there were blank pages, and thin pieces of wood attached to the patches to act as bearers, preventing the platen from dipping into the blanks.

Finally the forme was checked for odd pieces of type lying on it, in danger of being picked up by the balls and deposited on a page; the stays for tympan and frisket, the bar-catch, footstep, etc., were adjusted to the pressman's liking; the heap was positioned on the horse; and everything was ready to begin printing.

Make-ready sounds a lengthy process, but with a press in going order and ordinary impositions it could be carried out very quickly; press crews could change formes, and even books, in a matter of minutes.

PULLING AND BEATING[19]

The two pressmen took it in turns to pull on the bar and beat the forme, the senior man generally making the press ready and taking the first turn as puller, while the other knocked up the balls and prepared the ink. The length of the turn was so many tokens of 250 sheets printed on one side, the number in the seventeenth century being commonly three or six. Each token so printed was conventionally supposed to represent one hour's work but, as we shall see, not all formes could be printed at the same rate.

The beater moved his balls over the forme with a rocking motion while the press was open. The rest of the time he distributed the ink over the surface of the balls by turning and rolling them against each other, taking up a dab of ink every two or three sheets, and simultaneously looking over the last-printed sheet as it lay on the horse to see that it had no obvious blemishes and that he was maintaining a good colour with his inking (fig. 67).

Meanwhile the puller lifted a sheet of clean paper from the heap and laid it on the tympan in line with the edges of the tympan sheet. Then he lowered the frisket on to it (which pressed it on to the points) and folded tympan, paper, and frisket together down on to the forme. Next, taking the handle of the windlass (the rounce) in his left hand he gave it one full turn anti-clockwise, thus running the rear half of the forme back under

[19] Moxon, J., op. cit., pp. 289–99.

the platen. Keeping his left hand on or near the rounce, he grasped the crooked bow of the bar with his right hand, drew it towards him while slipping his hand along to its end, and ended with one strong straight pull.

The movement of the bar turned the spindle through about ninety degrees, and the screw working in the nut caused it to descend about 15 mm. Taking the hose with it, the spindle forced the platen down on to the back of the rear half of the tympan, which in turn pressed the paper on to the rear half of the inked forme, pressure being achieved between the nut in the head of the press, which could not rise, and the carriage supported by the winter, which could not descend. The packing between the tops of the head tenons and their mortises had some elasticity and this, combined with the elasticity of the tympan blanket and of the whole wooden frame of the press, then forced the screw to move back into the nut, turning the bar back to the off-side cheek after the pull and raising the spindle to its original position; and, since the hose moved up and down with the spindle, and the platen was lashed to the hose, the platen was lifted clear of the tympan. Visitors would be surprised by the loud creaking and groaning of the presses as the timbers gave and rubbed against each other.[20]

The amount of elasticity in the mechanism of the press could be much reduced. A printer who wanted to achieve a sharp impression from unworn type of even height-to-paper would put hard rather than soft packing in the tympan, and he would use incompressible packing in the head mortises to intensify the effect of the pressman's pull by bringing it up with a jolt. Plantin described the pressmen pushing the bar back on to its catch after the pull, rather than allowing it to spring back;[21] and Baskerville took particular care to use hard packing in his tympans.[22]

The puller then gave the rounce another half turn anti-clockwise to bring the second half of the forme under the platen, and pulled again. Finally, resting the bar on its catch on the off-side cheek, he gave the rounce one and a half turns clockwise to run the carriage right out again. He raised tympan and frisket in one flowing movement, lifted the new-printed sheet off the points, and laid it on the horse at the end of the unprinted heap; then turned immediately to laying on the next sheet. At 250 sheets an hour, the whole cycle was repeated every 14–15 seconds.

If a forme contained type in one half only—as did, for instance, a folio forme with one page blank—the bar was only pulled once for each impression, which eased the puller's task slightly. In the eighteenth and early nineteenth centuries small formes with type areas smaller than the platen

[20] Hansard, T. C., *Typographia*, London 1825, p. 416 n.

[21] [Plantin, C.], *Dialogues*, Anvers 1567, pp. 246–7.

[22] *Signature*, xii, 1951, p. 45.

were occasionally imposed sideways across the bed of the press, and the paper (which might theoretically be as large as demy, but was probably smaller) was laid sideways across the tympan; in this way the whole forme was printed at one pull. The use of this method is indicated by point holes at the ends, rather than at the sides, of the sheet.[23]

Presses were sometimes worked by a single pressman, who beat the forme and pulled alternately. In this case, which was called working at half press, his rate of work was rather less than half that of the normal crew of two. Pressmen sometimes employed boys (called devils or flies) privately by the week to take printed sheets off the tympan, and thus speed up their rate of work.[24] Such aid would have been especially valuable to a man working at half press, and indeed it probably explains how one of the pressmen at Cambridge, working alone in 1700, achieved an output considerably greater than half the maximum rate achieved in the same printing house by crews of two pressmen (p. 140).

PRINTING THE REITERATION (OR PERFECTING)[25]

Having printed the sheets of the heap on one side, the pressmen turned it over (from side to side for duodecimo, otherwise from end to end), and changed the first forme for the second. The register was tested, and any necessary adjustment was made by shifting the second forme slightly on the bed of the press. The reiteration was then printed off in much the same way as the white paper, the sheets going through the press in the same order as before. The chief difference was that the puller located the paper on the tympan by fitting the point holes over the points.

The tympan sheet, no longer needed as a guide to the alignment of the sheets, was replaced by a linen cloth, which was less likely than paper to take set-off (ink marks) from the impressions of the first forme; but if set-off did occur and threatened to set back and spoil subsequent impressions of the first forme, the tympan cloth could be rubbed over with lye to clean it. Protective set-off sheets of waste paper were inserted by hand printers of the nineteenth century between sheets of the reiteration and their dry, hard-packed tympans, and were changed as often as necessary; and a few printers of the hand-press period preferred this device to the use of a soggy tympan cloth.[26]

[23] Foxon, D. F., 'On printing "at one pull", and distinguishing impressions by point-holes', *The Library*, xi, 1956, pp. 284–5; the method may also have been used in the fifteenth century (*Studies in bibliography*, xxiii, 1970, p. 144). Not to be confused with the 'inverted' impositions described on pp. 106–7, which may also show point-holes at the ends of the sheet.

[24] Moxon, J., op. cit., p. 338.

[25] Moxon, J., op. cit., pp. 297–8.

[26] Early-seventeenth-century set-off sheets are used as endpapers in two bindings in Trinity College Library, Cambridge (D. 5. 25 and D. 11. 38).

The early accounts agree that the heap was turned over, and the reiteration printed, immediately after the printing of the white paper. Indeed the printer would be unwilling to leave the heap for long with only one side printed, for the paper would begin to dry and shrink—or would be liable to change shape differentially if it had to be redamped—so that it became impossible to fit the point holes over the points and make register. Exactly how long is uncertain, but experiment with a damp cloth over a heap suggests that it could be kept for no more than two or three days without distortion.

The sixteenth-century account of Le Roy suggests that the heap was normally printed as white paper in the morning, turned at the midday break, and perfected in the afternoon.[27] If this was indeed the usual practice it may be supposed that, if the whole edition of a sheet could not be printed and perfected in one day (either because it exceeded the normal day's work, defined in the same account as 1,250–1,300 perfected sheets, or because work on a smaller number of sheets was begun late in the day), part of it would have been printed and perfected on one day, and the remainder on the following day; and that this would result in the second forme of the first day's work being left on the bed of the press to become the first forme of the second day's work. Such a procedure offers to explain some puzzles in early books, as when some copies of a particular sheet are found to have been printed inner forme first, while other copies of the same sheet were printed outer forme first; or as when patterns of progressive stop-press corrections to both formes of a sheet are found in several copies in combinations that are incompatible with it having been printed in a simple, consecutive way.[28] (It has been supposed that such situations resulted from 'concurrent perfecting', on the hypothesis that two presses started work simultaneously on the same sheet, one printing the inner forme and the other the outer, and that they exchanged heaps—or would it have been formes?—half way through.[29] But there is no early evidence for any such practice; concurrent perfecting would always have been difficult to fit into the normal complexity of work flow in a printing house with two or more presses, and if it happened at all it is unlikely to have been more than an exceptional resort in cases of urgency when the speed of two-press operation was necessary.)

Although the sixteenth- and seventeenth-century accounts of printing suggest that it was usual to print both formes of a sheet at a single press—

---

[27] *The Library*, x, 1955, p. 41.

[28] McKenzie, D. F., *The Cambridge University Press 1696–1712*, Cambridge 1966, i, p. 128; *The Library*, iv, 1949–50, p. 247.

[29] The hypothesis is discussed by K. Povey in *The Library*, x, 1955, pp. 43–8.

and this was certainly the normal practice at the Cambridge University Press at the end of the seventeenth century—it ceased to be normal in English printing of the eighteenth century. The detailed records of Bowyer's business show a clear preference for printing the two formes of a sheet consecutively at two different presses in the 1730s,[30] and the evidence of press figures confirms that Bowyer's practice was the normal one from the 1720s until the end of the century.

PRESS FIGURES[31]

From the late seventeenth until the end of the eighteenth century, British pressmen sometimes set an arabic figure or other symbol at the bottom of a page of the forme they were about to work off; they would put it in any page that did not already have a signature in it. The earliest known examples of press figures date from the 1680s, but at first the practice was relatively uncommon. Some 10 per cent of English books were figured in the 1690s, and 25 per cent from 1700 to 1720; up to this time the figures were more often symbols, such as asterisks, than numbers. Then from 1720 until 1800, a majority—some 60 per cent—of English books were figured, now usually with numbers; a few books were figured in Scotland and Ireland, and in America,[32] but the practice was unknown elsewhere.

Press figures appear to have been used for two very different purposes. One, which may have been the earlier and may have been connected with the use of symbols or letters rather than numbers, was to enable pressmen to identify their own work, probably so that they could keep a check on their wages. The other, for which the evidence is later in date (it appears to coincide with the practice of consecutive perfecting at different presses), and which may have been connected with the use of numbers as figures, was to enable the master to identify the pressmen's work so that he could penalize individuals in cases of bad workmanship. In the first case the pressman voluntarily put his mark on the sheets he printed; in the second the master compelled his pressmen to mark their work with the number by which their press was known, fining them if they failed to do so.

It is clear from the correlation of the figures in particular eighteenth-century books with the relevant printers' records that press figures of both sorts were used with considerable irregularity. The pressman who marked his own work for his own purposes at Cambridge in 1701–3 did not figure all the formes he worked, and he used sometimes one symbol, sometimes

---

[30] McKenzie, D. F., 'Printers of the mind', *Studies in bibliography*, xxii, 1969, p. 20.

[31] The best general account (from which the percentages in this paragraph are taken) is Povey, K., 'A century of press figures', *The Library*, xiv, 1959, pp. 251-73; it includes references to earlier papers.

[32] Tanselle, G. T., 'Press figures in America', *Studies in bibliography*, xix, 1966, pp. 123-60.

another.[33] In Bowyer's printing house in the 1730s pressmen sometimes failed to figure a forme, and sometimes they figured it with a wrong press-number.[34] When the Cambridge pressman printed both formes of a sheet, he only figured one of them; but when Bowyer's men printed both formes of a sheet they generally figured both, and an unfigured forme might have been printed at any press. Finally, the highest press number in a series does not necessarily indicate the number of presses actually in use; often there were fewer presses at work than the number suggest, and there is also the possibility (though there is little evidence for it) that very high numbers —the figure '22' has been recorded[35]—may have referred to pressmen, not presses.

CANCELS, ETC.[36]

Errors discovered after a sheet had been printed could be corrected (if it was thought worth it) in various ways. Of these the simplest was to print a list of errata at the end of the book or amongst the preliminaries; and the most radical was to destroy all the copies of the sheet, reset it and reprint it. Whole sheets were undoubtedly cancelled in this way on occasion, but they are usually difficult to identify unless an uncancelled copy of the sheet happens to survive. Differences in the paper of a cancelled whole sheet may give a clue, but the warehouseman might at any time put out small remnants of paper left over from printing other books so that paper evidence by itself seldom gives a clear indication of whole-sheet cancellation. (But the first 28 sheets of Baskerville's Virgil of 1757 were printed on an unprecedented wove paper, and the rest, plus a number of whole-sheet and single-leaf cancels, were printed on laid paper, so that whole-sheet cancels on laid paper show up in the wove part of the book.[37]) Evidence of whole-sheet cancellation may sometimes be found in the running titles of the headlines. There was generally considerable regularity in the use of skeleton formes through a hand-printed book (see pp. 109–10), and whole-sheet cancellation was very likely to interrupt the pattern, often to the extent of introducing a special set of headlines.

The cancellation and replacement of individual leaves (or occasionally of conjugate pairs of leaves) was much cheaper than whole-sheet cancellation, and it became very common, especially during the eighteenth century. The method usually employed was to reset the text of the leaf to be cancelled and to print a new leaf (together with any other cancels) on a spare

---

[33] McKenzie, D. F., 'Printers of the mind', *Studies in bibliography*, xxii, 1969, p. 51.

[34] Ibid., pp. 52, 70–4.

[35] In Piozzi, H. L., *Observations on a journey*, 2 vols., for Strahan and Cadell, 1789, ii, p. 162.

[36] Chapman, R. W., *Cancels*, London and New York 1930 (still the best general account).

[37] Gaskell, P., *John Baskerville a bibliography*, Cambridge 1959, pp. 19–22.

section of a later sheet of the book—typically a sheet of preliminaries—or even on a sheet of another book of similar format. (The leaf that was to be cancelled is nowadays called the cancellandum, plural cancellanda, and the leaf that was to replace it is called the cancellans, plural cancellantia.) After the sheet that was to contain a cancel had been folded, the cancellandum was cut out close to the inner margin and thrown away, and the cancellans was pasted on to the stub.

Most cancellantia are easy to identify. The stub of the cancellandum (not to be confused with the stubs of such things as inserted plates) is often visible; and occasionally a cancellans will have been inserted like a plate so that *two* stubs are visible. Sometimes cancellantia were marked with a symbol such as an asterisk, or they may show aberrant running titles, signatures, or press figures; again, cancellantia may have extra or missing lines of type, or they may not line up exactly with the other pages of the sheet. If none of these signs appear, the paper will usually give cancels away: even if cancellantia are printed on paper of the same thickness, quality, and colour as that of the rest of the sheet, the patterns of chain-lines, watermarks, and (if the book is uncut) edges will practically always be interrupted by cancellation. Finally, a few copies of an edition seem generally to have slipped through with their cancellanda uncancelled, so that examples of the original settings may sometimes be found (occasionally slashed by the warehouse keeper's shears or cut with a knife, deliberate defacement which escaped notice).

Comparison of cancel leaves with their uncancelled originals shows that the errors thus corrected were sometimes trivial. Baskerville's four-volume Ariosto of 1773 had a total of sixty-six cancelled leaves, most of them correcting no more than a single letter of the Italian text;[38] and on several occasions in the 1750s and 1760s Rousseau's publisher Marc-Michel Rey wrote to encourage the author to use up the blank leaves of final sheets for printing cancels.[39]

Other methods of correcting sheets after printing were overprinting by running the sheet through the press again; overprinting by stamping inked type by hand on to each copy of the sheet; printing corrections on slips of paper and pasting them over the errors; and amending the mistakes in each copy in manuscript.[40] Sometimes several sorts of correction are found in a single book: a work by Augustine Vincent printed by Jaggard in 1622

---

[38] Gaskell, P., op. cit., pp. 61-3.

[39] 'Comme il y a 4 pages de blanc a la derniere feuille voulez vous que j'y fasse des cartons?' (Rey to Rousseau, 23 Oct. 1760, concerning the printing of *La nouvelle Héloïse; Correspondance complète de Jean Jacques Rousseau*, ed. Leigh, R. A., vii, Genève and Madison 1969, p. 264).

[40] Tillotson, G. and A., 'Pen-and-ink corrections in mid-seventeenth-century books', *The Library*, xiv, 1933-4, pp. 59-72.

contained a list of sixty-one errata, seven cancelled leaves, four slips pasted in, and a line overprinted by running a sheet through the press a second time; its title (happily enough) was *A discovery of errors* (S.T.C. 24756).[41]

SPECIAL PAPER[42]

It was not uncommon throughout the hand-press period for a fraction of an edition of an important or expensive book to be produced in a way that marked it off from the ordinary copies; thus there might be an issue on large paper, thick paper, fine paper, or coloured paper, or on some other material such as vellum, linen, or silk. The special copies might be intended for presentation, or they might be sold at a higher price than the ordinary copies. Special issues were seldom embellished with typographical changes (such as additional page borders) until the nineteenth century, but the special sheets were sometimes distinguished by symbols such as asterisks; technically they may be 'states', not 'issues' (see pp. 315–16).

When the papers or other materials used for different issues of a book were of different sizes, it was necessary to adjust the margins of 8°, 12°, and small formats by altering the amount of furniture between the pages in the formes. In the later part of the period special issues were sometimes imposed for a folding other than that used for the ordinary issue; thus the same pages might be imposed in 8° for ordinary paper and (with more ample margins) in 4° for large paper. In such cases it would probably be more convenient to work with separate sets of skeletons (apart from head- and direction-lines), one set for each issue.

There appears to have been no firm rule as to whether the special-paper copies should be printed before or after the ordinary ones, both practices having been identified. Presswork is better at the end of a run than at the beginning, but on the other hand the type is least worn at the beginning.

Special issues on vellum were especially characteristic of fifteenth- and early-sixteenth-century printing, when they usually cost about three times as much as the ordinary copies on paper;[43] indeed there was a vellum issue of the very first printed book, the 42-line Bible. Coloured-paper issues became common in Italian printing of the sixteenth century, the earliest examples being three Aldine editions of 1514 with special copies printed on blue paper.[44] The special issues of the seventeenth and eighteenth

[41] Wood, E. R., 'Cancels and corrections in *A discovery of errors, 1622*', *The Library*, xiii, 1958, pp. 124–7.

[42] There is no general account of special-paper copies, but a large number of particular eighteenth-century examples are detailed in Gaskell, P., *A bibliography of the Foulis Press*, London 1964.

[43] Haebler, K., *The study of incunabula*, New York 1933, repr. New York 1967, p. 187. But Plantin's copies on vellum cost eight times as much as copies on paper (Voet, L., *The golden compasses*, ii).

[44] Weiss, W., 'Blaues Papier für Druckzwecke', *Gutenberg Jahrbuch*, 1959, p. 30.

centuries were usually on large or fine paper, sometimes folded differently from the ordinary copies. A few printers made a particular feature of their special issues: Plantin put out his great polyglot Bible (Antwerp 1569–72) on four different sorts of paper and on vellum; while a Foulis Press *Iliad* (Glasgow 1747) was issued in foolscap 8°, Greek and Latin; pot 8°, Greek and Latin; foolscap 8°, Greek only; pot 8°, Greek only; foolscap 4°, Greek only; pot 4°, Greek only; and vellum 8°, Greek only.[45]

TWO COLOURS; AND MUSIC

Printing a second colour, usually red, alongside the black is as old as printing, but it has always been considerably more expensive than printing in black alone and has remained uncommon except in Catholic service books. The earliest printers experimented with printing two (or occasionally more) colours at a single impression, which gave perfect register between the black printing and the red but which meant that both black and red ink had to be applied to the type between each impression.[46] The only really satisfactory way of doing this was to take the type that was to print red out of the forme (normally isolated initials and words), ink the red type and the black type separately, and then replace the red type, between each impression; for if both the inks were applied with all the type locked together in the forme, even with the careful use of masks, the red type inevitably became contaminated to some extent with black ink.[47]

Unlocking the forme to remove and replace the red type between each impression was inevitably very slow, and by the beginning of the sixteenth century two-colour printing was normally done by means of two impressions to each side of the sheet, which was much quicker even though the register between black and red was never quite so good. Two-impression colour printing could be done either red first or black first, and surviving colour proofs of the sixteenth century suggest that the red-first method (fully described by Fertel in 1723)[48] may have been the earlier.[49]

If the red was to be printed first, the whole forme was set up, red and black type together, and proofed, often in red ink; and the parts that were to be printed in red were underlined on the proof. A new parchment frisket was prepared and lined with paper (in order to prevent it from sagging and

[45] Voet, L., *The golden compasses*, ii; Gaskell, P., *A bibliography of the Foulis Press*, London 1964, no. 84.

[46] Masson, I., *The Mainz psalters and canon missae 1457–1459*, London 1954, pp. 25–30.

[47] Haebler, K., op. cit., pp. 127–34.

[48] Fertel, M. D., *La science pratique de l'imprimerie*, Saint-Omer 1723, pp. 277–83.

[49] L2086-1937 in the Victoria and Albert Museum Library is a red colour-proof and L2848-1937 is part of a red colour-frisket; several other early colour proofs and friskets are known. Plantin normally printed red first (Voet, L., *The golden compasses*, ii).

biting when it got damp during the run), and an impression of the forme was pulled on it in red. Guided by the marked proof, the pressman then cut rectangular holes in the frisket where the red type was to print through, and he pasted the resulting patches of parchment and paper on to the face of the tympan precisely in line with the holes in the frisket from which they were cut. Next the heap was printed off with red ink, the patches on the tympan giving extra impression to the red type, and the frisket protecting the paper from being marked by the rest of the type. The colour frisket was then discarded (several used colour friskets have been found in sixteenth-century bindings) and an ordinary frisket was fitted. The red type was removed from the forme, the holes being filled with quads and spaces, and the sheets were run through the press again, this time being printed in black from the rest of the forme. Finally the patches were cleared off the tympan, a new colour frisket was fitted and the whole process was repeated for the other side of the sheet.

The black-first method of colour printing, described by Moxon in 1683, was essentially similar.[50] The whole forme was proofed, and the colour frisket pulled, in black ink. The red type was then removed from the forme, the spaces being filled with quads, and put aside, together with the colour frisket. Using an ordinary frisket the heap was printed off in black. Next the colour frisket was cut out, but this time the patches were put into the forme as underlays for the red type, which was now put back and locked up. (It was obviously not essential to put the frisket patches under the red type; they could just as well have been stuck to the tympan as in Fertel's red-first method.) Finally the red type was printed off, using the colour frisket to protect the parts of the sheet already printed in black.

There seems to have been very little to choose between the two methods. If the black were printed first there was no need to prepare and handle red ink before the actual run; and Fertel suggested that it was quicker to paste frisket patches on to the tympan than to use them as underlays.

The whole performance of sticking the frisket patches on the tympan (or of underlaying the type with them) could be avoided if specially tall type, above standard height, were used for setting the red part of the forme. Such special type was introduced at the Plantin-Moretus house in about 1680; and French regulations of 1723 specified that tall type intended for printing in red should be marked with a special nick.[51]

Music,[52] too, was printed in the late fifteenth and early sixteenth centuries

[50] Moxon, J., op. cit., pp. 299-300.
[51] Voet, L., *The golden compasses*, ii; Veyrin-Forrer, J., 'Aperçu sur la fonderie typographique parisienne au xviie siècle', *The Library*, xxiv, 1969, pp. 209-10.
[52] For the bibliography of music printing, see p. 396.

by double impression, the staves (lines) being printed at one impression and the notes at another. Single-impression music type began to appear in the late 1520s, each piece of type bearing a note (complete with stem if it had one) and sections of the stave, made so that the stave lines joined with the lines of the adjacent pieces of type. This sort of single-impression type was limited to reproducing simple music, however, and from the 1580s the more sophisticated music that was then beginning to be written was increasingly printed from plates. Engraved copper plates were used at first; then from the early eighteenth century pewter plates, both punched and engraved, replaced copper; and finally from the second quarter of the nineteenth century there was a great outpouring of music printed from lithographic plates and stones. Music printing from movable type continued alongside plate printing, and was brought to maturity in the 1750s by J. G. I. Breitkopf, whose music type consisted of small, standard-sized type units about the size of a note head, with which a complex score—staves, notes, stems and all—could be built up piece by piece, in the same way as complex decorative designs could be built up with printers' flowers.

Special copies for presentation and the like might be embellished with a few words printed in gold, but this was done by hand, not by the normal two-colour method. Words to be printed thus were set up and locked tight in a composing stick. The face of the letters was then 'inked' with a colourless varnish, and the stick was turned over and pressed by hand on to the right place on the sheet. Gold leaf was laid down over the varnish impressions of the type, where it adhered; the varnish quickly dried, and the surplus leaf was rubbed off, leaving only the forms of the letters gilded.[53]

OUTPUT

The output of pressmen during the hand-press period, like that of compositors, did not in practice conform to any theoretical norm. The token of 250 sheets printed on one side was conventionally called an hour's work, but this figure was at best a mean: a large forme of small type took longer to print than a small forme of large type, and there were besides formes to change and make-ready (which slowed up the printing of a small edition more than that of a large one) and occasionally such extras as printing in two colours. In fact the rate of work achieved was usually less than 250 impressions per hour, or 3,000 impressions per 12-hour day, though it is impossible to generalize further. The maximum possible rate for emergencies was considerable: rates in the region of 400–450 impressions

[53] Moxon, J., op. cit., pp. 301–2.

per hour were achieved in the early nineteenth century with frequent changes of pressmen.[54]

During one week in 1700 a team of two pressmen at the Cambridge University Press pulled a total of 20,700 impressions, or an average of 3,450 impressions a day; but then later in the same year another press team (including one of the same men) produced the following successive weekly averages of impressions per day: 2,534; 2,300; 1,616; 2,116; 1,784; 2,834; 1,566; and so on. The difference between the maximum average of 3,450 impressions per day and the minimum average of 1,566 involved a factor of more than 2, and the rates fluctuated rapidly between wide limits. Similar variation characterized work 'at half press' (i.e. when a press was worked by a single journeyman). The Cambridge pressman who was the common member of the two teams mentioned above also worked by himself for several successive weeks in 1700, when his daily averages of impressions were 1,034; 1,766; 1,100; 2,034; and 1,208. Again there was a factor of about 2 in the difference between his highest and his lowest rates, and again there were abrupt fluctuations in his output from one week to the next (though it will be remembered that a pressman might employ a boy to help him, which probably explains the extraordinarily high half-press rate of 2,034 impressions a day).[55]

Records of wages paid at other printing houses during the hand-press period, both in Britain and abroad, all tell the same story: there was always a wide variation from week to week in the amount of work actually done by pressmen, just as there was in the amount done by compositors—and no doubt for the same reasons (see pp. 54–6).

During the earlier hand-press period—up to about the middle of the seventeenth century—pressmen in England, France, and the Low Countries seem generally to have contracted with their masters to print a certain number of impressions per day or per week for a fixed wage, the actual number printed fluctuating to a certain extent, and the wage varying with the difficulty of the work, and probably also with the amount of work available or the amount the journeyman wanted to do (a system similar to that of the compositors' piecework contracts, pp. 55, 173).[56] The contract number in England was usually 2,500 or 3,000 impressions a day; Plantin's pressmen contracted for 2,500 impressions; and French contracts were similarly in the range 2,500–3,350 impressions per day.[57]

---

[54] This with ink balls and (probably) Stanhope presses (which were not much faster than wooden two-pull common presses); *Notes and queries*, 4th ser., iii, 1869, p. 486.

[55] McKenzie, D. F., *The Cambridge University Press 1696–1712*, Cambridge 1966, i, chs. 3, 4; idem, 'Printers of the mind', *Studies in bibliography*, xxii, 1969, pp. 7–22.

[56] McKenzie, D. F., op. cit. (1969), p. 11 and n. 18.

[57] Moxon, J., op. cit., pp. 327–8; Hinman, C., *The printing and proof-reading of the first folio of*

By the end of the seventeenth century pressmen were contracting for a price per token—i.e. piecework payment for the number printed—heavy work being paid up to 75 per cent more per token than light work, with extra payments made for such jobs as altering the margins for large paper, or for printing in two colours.[58] During the eighteenth century a less flexible scale was adopted in England, whereby a flat rate per token was paid regardless of the difficulty of the work.[59]

Plantin's pressmen earned slightly more than his compositors up to about 1580, after which the situation was reversed. French pressmen of the sixteenth and seventeenth centuries earned as much as 40 per cent more than ordinary compositors, but in English printing houses of the later seventeenth and of the eighteenth centuries it was the other way round, the compositors earning almost half as much again as the pressmen.[60] By this later period pressmen in England were despised as mere 'horses', the 'great guzzlers of beer' who were rebuked by the young Benjamin Franklin for their mindless intemperance.[61]

Shakespeare, Oxford 1963, i, p. 42; Voet, L., 'The making of books in the renaissance', *Printing and graphic arts*, x, 1966, pp. 48–9; Febvre, L., and Martin, H. J., *L'apparition du livre*, Paris 1958, p. 199; Martin, H. J., *Livre, pouvoirs et société à Paris au XVIIe siècle*, Genève 1969, i, p. 376.

[58] McKenzie, op. cit. (1966), i, pp. 85–7. Alteration of margins, printing in two colours, etc., also affected the standard rates of charges to customers (Strahan ledgers).

[59] Philip, I. G., *William Blackstone and the reform of the Oxford University Press in the eighteenth century*, Oxford 1957, p. 30.

[60] Voet, L., *The golden compasses*, ii; Febvre, L., and Martin, H. J., op. cit., p. 200; McKenzie, D. F., op. cit. (1966), i, pp. 83, 90; idem, op. cit. (1969), pp. 67–70.

[61] Franklin, B., *The life*, ed. Bigelow, J., London 1870, i, p. 160.

The Warehouse[1]

We have already seen how the printer's warehouse-keeper dismantled the paper-makers' reams and set out the good quires in heaps for the pressmen, culling the cording quires for usable sheets and putting the rest aside for re-sale. As a rule he took paper from particular lots for particular books, not from a general stock, for it was never normal for a printer to sink capital in a stock of paper sufficient for miscellaneous book-printing. A batch of paper was specially ordered from a paper supplier for a particular book, the order generally being placed and the cost met by whoever was financially responsible for printing it, be it a bookseller or the author or the printer himself; alternatively the printer could buy the paper and charge it out with the sheets.[3] Enough paper would normally be ordered at once for the whole edition (which was one reason why casting-off was an early necessity), and as far as possible it would be supplied as a single lot, of even size and quality and with a single watermark-design throughout.[4]

Many books of the hand-press period, even very long ones, are found to have been printed on a single batch of paper throughout, but at least as many others were printed on two or more lots of paper, usually organized in runs extending over a number of consecutive sheets. It is easy to see how this could have come about. The paper supplier might have been unable to offer the whole order for a book in a particular sort of paper, and would therefore have made it up with a batch of similar but not identical paper, possibly deriving from a different mill; or the printer (etc.), unable to get the complete order from one supplier, might have gone to another paper dealer for the rest of it. Alternatively the printer might not have ordered enough paper for the whole book, either because he miscalculated (or increased the number of the edition after ordering) or because he could not afford to buy the whole lot at once, and was then obliged to take a slightly different paper when he re-ordered. In all these cases the batches of different papers would not as a rule be mixed, but would be put out consecutively by the warehouse-keeper.

[1] Moxon, J., op. cit., pp. 311-22.

[2] On paper stock see Stevenson, A. H., *The problem of the Missale speciale*, London 1967, ch. 6.

[3] Plantin, whose output of his own publications was exceptionally large and who could not obtain much locally-made paper, did keep a considerable stock; but even he ordered paper specially for his larger books; Voet, L., *The golden compasses*, ii.

[4] Not of course with a single watermark, for the most homogeneous lot of paper must have been made with at least a pair of moulds. Not all printers (etc.) bothered about uniformity of paper in a book.

Sometimes paper is found in a book which does not belong to a main run or runs, and which may even differ from copy to copy. This would normally be the result of the deliberate introduction of odd papers by the warehouse-keeper (slightly defective sheets saved for the middle of the book, for instance, or remnants of batches of similar paper originally bought for other books but not quite used up). Similarly anomalous paper may also be found when a whole sheet has been cancelled and reprinted.

Ephemeral jobs, and small books and pamphlets undertaken by the printer himself, are likely to have been printed on such odds and ends of paper—remnants and the like—as were available in the warehouse.

DRYING THE PAPER

After the heap had been printed on both sides, the warehouse-keeper hung it up in order to dry the paper (not in order to dry the ink, which set rather than evaporated). Racks for this purpose were fixed below the ceiling of the warehouse or other drying room—which was often the composing room or the pressroom, as the early illustrations show (fig. 25)—and doublings of one or two dozen sheets were lifted on to them two at a time with a wooden peel, a tool similar to the peel with which bakers used to load and unload their ovens. Each doubling overlapped its neighbour on the rack, and the chances were that, when they were taken down after drying and piled again into a heap, the sheets would be in the same order as before, although this was not certain to happen. The length of time the paper took to dry varied with the size of the doublings, and with the temperature and humidity of the drying room; it could be as little as a day or as much as a week.

Drying large numbers of sheets could have presented difficulties. Plantin, with fifteen or sixteen presses at work in the 1570s, had something like 150-200 reams (75,000-100,000 sheets) of paper to dry each week, and may have needed to use some form of artificial heating;[5] certainly the larger establishments of the early machine-press period, which produced comparable numbers of damp sheets, found it necessary to install heated drying rooms.

GATHERING THE BOOKS

When the heaps of all the sheets of a book had been dried and piled together again, they were set out in signature order on a long table, with the first recto pages upwards and to the near side. Then the gatherer, still probably the warehouseman, took off the top copy of the last sheet of the book and then walked along the line of sheets, taking off one copy of each in turn,

---

[5] Each of Plantin's presses used about 15 reams of paper a week for ordinary work, or about 6 reams a week for the smaller amount of two-colour liturgical work he undertook (Voet, L., *The golden compasses*, ii); on the number of presses, see Table 4, p. 165.

until he had gathered a complete copy of the book in sheets. This book was knocked smooth at the edges and laid down, together with any inserts such as plates and cancellantia, and the process was repeated over and over again until at last all the sheets were taken from one of the heaps; theoretically all the heaps should have run out together, but in practice some contained fewer sheets than others. The books were then collated to ensure that each was made up correctly, and they were finally folded in half (2º, 4º, and 8º across the longer side, 12º across the shorter side),[6] pressed, and baled up for delivery or storage. The unused sheets from all the heaps except the one which ran out first were kept to make good any imperfections that might later be found in the books: eventually they were used or sold as waste.

The relationship between the order of printing of the sheets and the order of their gathering into books must always have depended on the habits of individual workmen; when these habits were consistent, the order of printing may have been echoed, either directly or inversely, by the order of gathering, so that some of the complete books would tend to contain sheets printed early in their runs, and others sheets printed late.

Let us hypothesize a case of remarkable regularity, in which all the sheets of a particular book were printed inner forme first. The heaps, moreover, were not too large to be turned straight over for printing the reiteration, so that early impressions of the inner forme were backed by early impressions of the outer forme, and vice versa. Thus each heap was delivered to the warehouseman with the final impressions of both formes on the topmost sheet, and with that of the outer forme facing upwards. It is conceivable that the order of the heaps was then preserved unaltered through the drying process, and that they were eventually laid on the gathering table, still with the outer formes upwards to show the first page of each signature. Then the sheets were gathered from the top of each heap in the reverse of the printing order, so that the first book to be gathered contained the last printed sheets, and so on through the heaps until the early impressions were used for the last copies to be gathered.

If, however, a sheet of the same book was printed outer forme first, similarly regular treatment meant that it was finally delivered for gathering, again with the last-printed sheet on top, but this time with the inner forme upwards. For gathering it had to be turned over to show the first page of the signature, which brought the first-printed sheet to the top. This heap was then gathered in the printing order, so that the copies that were gathered first contained early impressions of this particular gathering, and vice versa.

---

[6] This was in order to avoid folding across a page. Long books were divided in quires of 12–24 sheets before this folding took place; hence 'books in quires' as a synonym for books in sheets.

But model regularity of this sort was of course uncharacteristic of craft printing, and shuffling the heaps, especially during the drying process, would normally have interfered with such hypothetical patterns. The most that can be expected is that early impressions of inner formes were usually, but not necessarily, backed by early impressions of outer formes, and late by late; and that there was a tendency towards some sort of order in the gathering.

Binding

Throughout the hand-press period the craft of binding books was normally separate from that of printing them. Each edition was distributed by its publisher-wholesaler (who might also have been its printer) through numerous retail booksellers, each of whom sold a few copies of it over his counter; it was generally the case that printers and publishers themselves also acted as retailers. Each retail bookseller had small batches of each edition bound up locally, and offered them for sale either in this form or unbound.

In London the retailer would have had his books bound by a specialist bookbinder, nearly all of whom were concentrated in the capital. In the English provinces, on the other hand, the binders were primarily large retail booksellers, who probably bound batches of books for their smaller neighbours as well as for themselves. Even the great eighteenth-century firm of Edwards of Halifax, which is remembered for its bindery, was concerned chiefly with bookselling and publishing. In the few cases where printers doubled not only as booksellers but also as binders (at the Foulis Press in eighteenth-century Glasgow, for instance) they did not bind up whole editions of their own books, but only such copies as they could themselves expect to sell, together with batches of books bought from other publishers for retail sale; the main stock of their own books was warehoused in sheets.[2]

Edition binding, in fact, was never normal in the hand-press period. It would of course have been possible for a publisher to have had a whole edition bound and to have distributed the bound copies like a modern publisher, but the economics of the trade were against it. The most important factor was that every book had to be bound separately by hand, and binding costs did not go down with quantity; it cost ten times as much to bind a thousand copies of a book as it cost to bind a hundred. Therefore to bind up more copies of an edition than could be sold within a short period of time tied up capital without any compensation. It was moreover to the provincial bookseller's advantage to buy books in sheets, for they were cheaper to transport than were bound copies.

A particular binder (for instance one of the specialist London firms) might cover many batches of copies of a book for a bookseller, or group of

---

[1] There is no good general account of the trade, but see Pollard, H. G., 'Changes in the style of book-binding, 1550–1830', *The Library*, xi, 1956, pp. 71–94; and pp. 398–9.

[2] Gaskell, P., *A bibliography of the Foulis Press*, London 1964, pp. 54–5, 347–8.

booksellers, in an unvarying trade style that can give the appearance of edition binding; but, unless a considerable and immediate sale in one area could be predicted, the batches would not necessarily have been large in number or closely related in time. Chapbooks may have been an exception, for in the eighteenth century, at any rate, they seem to have been distributed bound from London.

The normal trade binding for most of the hand-press period was an inexpensive covering of calf or sheep, and it appears that retailers actually stocked copies of most books in this form for sale over the counter. Certain classes of books, indeed, were normally sold bound: school books, classical texts, bibles and prayer books, devotional handbooks and standard collections of sermons, practical manuals, reference and law books. At the other end of the scale, controversial pamphlets, and such things as single poems, plays, or sermons were normally sold stitched (in wrappers from the mid seventeenth century). The more expensive works of literature and learning, too, were often sold stitched, or in sheets unbound, for the customer to take to his own binder; but even the better class of book seems generally to have been available in a trade binding if required, even (by the early eighteenth century) in more than one style.[3]

Some binders, especially those who had diverse interests in the book trade, supplied sets of plates for Bibles and other standard texts, sets which were not specific to particular editions.[4] Another service offered by binders was ruling the margins in red, which was done in pen and ink before folding.

BINDING TECHNIQUE[5]

When batches of books arrived at the bindery the sheets of each one were already gathered, and roughly folded in half into quires of one or two dozen sheets each. First the sheets had to be folded properly, according to the format, the page numbers in the headlines being used as guides; it was not practicable to fold to the edges of the sheets because of minor inaccuracies that had inevitably occurred when they were positioned on the tympan of the press. Having been folded, the sheets were collated by signatures. Leaves printed out of order, plates and, most probably, cancel leaves were all put in their right places at this stage. The folded book was then beaten

---

[3] From their beginning in 1669 *The term catalogues* list most of the middle range of books as 'bound'; and many of the numerous book advertisements of the eighteenth century give prices in different styles of binding.

[4] Many sets of plates are listed, primarily for sale to the trade, in *The term catalogues*; for instance (28 June 1669) 'The Historical part of the *Old Testament* newly Graved in 70 Copper-plates; and fitted to be bound with *Bibles* in Octavo and Twelves. Price 5s.' (Arber, E., *The term catalogues*, i, London 1903, p. 12).

[5] Middleton, B. C., *A history of English craft bookbinding technique*, New York and London 1963.

flat with a hammer and block, several gatherings at a time, in order to get it down to its proper thickness.

Next the book was placed on the sewing frame, and the folded sheets were sewn by hand with needle and thread on to four or five cords or thongs. In the best work the thread was passed along the inner fold, emerging to take a turn round each cord, and then back in the same manner along the inner fold of the next sheet, but in the seventeenth and eighteenth centuries it was usual to sew trade bindings 'two on', whereby the thread was passed from one sheet to its neighbour and back again at every other cord, so that two signatures were sewn at each passage of the needle. The cords themselves could be placed either outside the backs of the folded sheets, where they would show as raised bands across the spine of the book, or in slots sawn into the folds to give the book a flat back.

Then the endpapers were sewn on. These were folds or sections of blank paper (reinforced with vellum strips in the early days) which were supplied by the binder and did not form part of the printer's book. Their purpose was, as paste-downs, to reinforce the joints of the covers and, as flyleaves, to give additional protection to the end pages of the book.

The spine of the book was rounded and given shoulders ('backed') with a hammer to accommodate the covers or 'boards'. The boards were generally made of wood up to the later fifteenth century (until the end of the sixteenth century for some large books and for quarto Bibles); then of sheets of paper pasted together ('pasteboard'); and then, from the early eighteenth century in good-quality binding but later in cheap work, of rope-fibre millboard. They were attached to the books by means of the ends of the cords on to which the sheets had been sewn.

The three outer edges of the book (or occasionally the top edge, or the top and fore-edges, only) were next cut with the plough.[5a] This was a long vice in which the book was clamped, the edge to be cut upwards, so that a knife in a small frame could be pulled along it and moved sideways by degrees, progressively trimming the rough edge smooth; the boards were normally trimmed to the right size at the same time. The cut edges might then be sprinkled or brushed with colour or (less commonly) marbled, gilded, or painted.

Then the headbands were attached to the head and tail of the spine. In medieval bindings thick headbands were sewn in at the same time as the cords, but by the sixteenth century they were generally sewn on after the edges had been cut. Later still, from the early seventeenth century, head-

---

[5a] Cheap bindings were commonly cut 'out of boards' from the seventeenth century (i.e. before rounding and backing and the attachment of the boards); but cutting 'in boards' has always been normal for the better class of work.

bands were made up separately and stuck on to the book. Whichever method was used, its purpose was to resist the strains imposed on the volume by handling, especially when it was pulled from a shelf.

Next the book was covered, usually with leather. A strip of paper or vellum was pasted on to the spine to reinforce it, and a skin of the right size was stuck down over the spine and the outside of both boards, the over-lapping edges being turned in and secured inside the boards under a paper paste-down. Until the very end of the hand-press period the cover was always stuck down tight on to the spine; the hollow back that became the normal form in the nineteenth century did not appear until about 1770 in France and about 1800 in England.

The binding was finished with more or less decoration on the outside of the cover, which was normally applied by pressing hot metal stamps on to the surface of the leather, either blind (without gilding) or through gold leaf. These stamps could be large metal blocks, measuring 10 cm. or more across and applied to the cover with a mechanical press. More often they were smaller hand tools which could be used in combination to build up a decorative pattern. The most usual tools (which were generally made of brass, set in wooden handles like chisels) were simple design units such as short lines or little flowers; lines set on curved rockers (pallets); wheels with lines on the circumference (fillets); and wheels with elaborate designs on the circumference (rolls). There were also tools for individual letters of the alphabet and for figures, with which the binding could be lettered (either directly or on leather labels stuck on the cover).

The tools were heated for use at a small brazier, and no further prepara-tion was necessary for blind tooling. The face of the tool was simply pressed into the leather, its position in a complicated layout being aided by guide lines (paper patterns were not used until the nineteenth century). For gold tooling, impressions of the tools were first made in blind. An adhesive glair of egg white was next brushed into the blind impression, allowed to dry, and greased. Finally gold leaf was laid in place over the blind impressions, and fixed into them with further impressions of the hot tools, surplus gold being rubbed off. Sixteenth-century examples are also known of gold-blocking with wooden tools, used cold.

TRADE BINDING STYLES[6]

Superbly decorated bindings have been commissioned, and carefully preserved, from the medieval period up to the present day, not only in tooled leather, but also in wood and metal (sometimes carved or jewelled), in cloth and embroidery, and in pierced or painted vellum. Their stylistic

---

[6] There is unfortunately no illustrated survey.

a

b

FIG. 68 (*a*, *b*). Bindery work in eighteenth-century France. (*a*) Sewing and ploughing; (*b*) finishing with a roll. (*Encyclopédie*, planches viii, Paris 1771, 'Relieur', pls. 1, 5.)

development (which affected trade binding styles, made as they generally were by the same workmen in the same shops), is too complex to follow here. Such special bindings have survived in large numbers, however, and they are copiously—usually exclusively—described and illustrated in works of binding history.

Trade bindings are more difficult to investigate. The finer a binding, the better chance it had of survival, and cheap bindings of the earlier hand-press period are now relatively rare. The simultaneous execution of the trade binding of an edition by many different shops, moreover, makes generalization more than usually hazardous; and there are the further complications that individual finishers might be anachronistic in style; that books might be bound or rebound long after they were printed (possibly, though this was very rare, in a binding taken from an earlier volume); and that in seventeenth-century France binding and finishing were separate trades, carried on in different shops.

Early-sixteenth-century bindings generally have a medieval air about them. Many books were still large and solid, their blind-tooled covers secured with clasps or ties. Blocks and rolls tended to be large and deeply impressed, the cords to stand out thickly on the spine. Even smaller books were liable to be lumpishly bound, but here there was more variety.

From the later fifteenth century books were more often stored on their edges than on their sides (so that metal bosses to protect the covers were no longer used), but for most of the sixteenth century they were normally placed fore-edge outward on the shelf, the title of the book being written across the fore-edge in ink. Some institutional libraries were chained (when the books were necessarily shelved fore-edge outwards), the chains being attached to a staple riveted to an edge of one of the boards.[7]

Tanned calfskin—or tanned cowhide for large books—was the commonest covering material in the sixteenth century, followed by vellum (also frequent in trade bindings) and pigskin; tanned sheepskin was still unusual. Books were sometimes sold in paper wrappers and paper boards even at this early date. Certain Augsburg editions of the 1490s were equipped with wrappers of stiffened paper which were specially printed for them; this looks like an attempt at edition binding, but it found no imitators.[8] A number of north Italian books of the early sixteenth century were sold in printed paper boards, although in this case the covers were not specific to particular editions.[9] A good many small books of the sixteenth and seventeenth centuries had decorations or sub-titles printed on the first and last pages, and may have been intended to be retailed sewn but uncovered.[10] Finally, examples of sixteenth- and seventeenth-century plain paper wrappers have also survived.

Gold tooling, usually with sizeable blocks, became increasingly common from the mid sixteenth century, and was not confined to bespoke bindings. A good many heavily gilt retailers' bindings (such as the small English devotional books that were sold in large numbers from the 1560s until the later seventeenth century) were indeed intended to look expensive while

---

[7] Clark, J. W., *The care of books*, Cambridge 1901, *passim*.

[8] Nixon, H. M., *Broxbourne Library, styles and designs of bookbindings*, London 1956, pp. 14–17.

[9] Nixon, H. M., op. cit., pp. 27–8.

[10] Jackson, W. A., 'Printed wrappers of the fifteenth to the eighteenth centuries', *Harvard Library bulletin*, vi, 1952, pp. 313–21.

really being cheaply executed, with two-on sewing and a simplified attachment to sawn-in cords. Not all embroidered bindings were bespoke, either; there was a flourishing trade in retailers' bindings for service books made by professional embroiderers in London during the period 1600 to 1650.[11]

Ordinary trade bindings of the seventeenth and early eighteenth centuries had very little decoration on the covers, and were rarely gilt. Calf continued to be the prime covering material, but sheep was now introduced for the cheapest work. Vellum remained popular on the continent, less so in England; while goatskin (morocco), although well established by this time for fine work, was seldom used in trade binding except for prayer books. Tooling might involve no more than blind fillets beside the spine and, from the 1670s, a blind-tooled panel on each board. The covers, or parts of them, might also be sprinkled with acid to pattern the leather with black dots. Sawn-in cords, giving flat spines, were common in the mid seventeenth century, but then went out of fashion until they were reintroduced in about 1760.

Books began to be turned round on the shelf to show their spines in the later sixteenth century, apparently rather later in England than in Italy or France.[12] Tooled decoration appeared on the spines of better-class bindings, but titles were not normally lettered until the mid seventeenth century, and then chiefly on bespoke work. Ordinary trade bindings remained unlettered until the mid eighteenth century, although the volumes of sets were often numbered; trade bindings of the more expensive sort were given coloured leather lettering pieces from about 1700. The longitudinal labels printed on otherwise blank leaves of a few late-seventeenth-century English books may have been meant for use as fore-edge labels, or they may have been intended for labelling the bins or shelves that contained a stock of books—whether the printer's, the wholesaler's, or the bookseller's stock is unclear.[13]

The seventeenth century also saw the appearance of decorated papers, marbled and printed, but they were uncommon in retail work until they began to be used for covering the boards of half- and quarter-bound books[14] in the 1730s, and shortly afterwards for endpapers as well.

From the mid eighteenth century leather trade bindings became more sophisticated. Gold-tooled fillets and lettering pieces were normally added, and spines gold-tooled with pallets in imitation of the detailed tooling of

---

[11] Nixon, H. M., op. cit., pp. 143–4.   [12] Pollard, H. G., op. cit., p. 73.

[13] Pollard, H. G., op. cit., pp. 91–3; Jackson, W. A., 'English title labels', *Harvard library bulletin*, ii, Spring 1948. Manuscript longitudinal fore-edge labels are also known.

[14] Half binding: spine and corners of leather, the rest of the boards being covered with paper or cloth. Quarter binding: the same, but without the corner pieces. On the history of marbled paper, see Middleton, B. C., op. cit., pp. 33–9 and footnote references.

bespoke work were not uncommon. Blind-tooled panels on sprinkled calf were given up, acid being flowed over the covers to produce 'tree calf', sometimes polished. A greatly increased proportion of books were retailed in paper wrappers and paper boards, uncut to allow for later rebinding in leather. The wrappers of periodicals and ephemera were often printed; and from the 1780s printed labels were sometimes stuck on to the spines of boarded books, being supplied by the printer on a spare leaf.

Edition binding was approached in the 1760s by the printer-publisher Newbery of London, who supplied booksellers with thousands of copies of his juvenile books ready bound in a standard cover of quarter vellum and paper boards, labelled.[15] 'Juveniles' have always been a special case, however, and the generality of books continued to be bound by booksellers, not by printers or publishers, until well into the nineteenth century.

[15] Sadleir, M., *The evolution of publishers' binding styles 1770-1900*, London and New York 1930, pp. 10-12, plate 1 (a). Quarter vellum was a regular substitute for quarter calf in the ordinary trade bindings of the same period.

Decoration and Illustration[1]

PRINTED PICTURES

Pictures were printed both from relief woodcuts and from intaglio copper-plates before movable type was invented. Both processes continued to flourish as media for separate pictures, and both were rapidly applied to the decoration and illustration of books. During the early days, and for most of the sixteenth century, woodcuts, which could conveniently be printed in the forme along with the type, were much commoner in books than copperplates. They were used for elaborate illustrations, stylized ornaments, initial letters, and for words in large or complex letter-forms that were not available as type. By the end of the sixteenth century, however, engraved plates, which had to be printed separately from type, were replacing blocks for large illustrations and decorated title-pages. Woodcuts continued to decline in popularity and quality during the seventeenth century, and by its end were chiefly used for technical diagrams, illustrations in cheap editions, and stock ornaments. Meanwhile copperplates, their range of expression increased by various developments of technique, had become the normal medium for all but the cheapest book-illustration, and for a good deal of minor ornament as well. Despite the incompetence of most eighteenth-century block-makers,[1a] woodcuts never quite disappeared, and they returned to favour in the delicate form called 'wood-engraving' at the end of the hand-press period.

RELIEF BLOCKS

For most of the period woodcuts for letterpress printing were made of a hard, fine-grained wood (such as box or a fruit wood) cut into the side of the plank along the grain. Early woodcut initials, coats of arms, etc., were sometimes made from wood cut across the grain, but the use of end-grain blocks remained uncommon until the later eighteenth century. A few early blocks were made of metal—or at least were faced with metal—probably an alloy of copper or lead which could be cut with steel; no doubt type-metal was sometimes used for this purpose.

The thickness of the blocks intended for use in printed books was usually a little under type height, the difference being made up with underlays of paper. The tympan of the press also usually needed some overlaying to get good colour from a block, even with the spongy impression of the hand-

---

[1] See the bibliography p. 399.

[1a] The French block-makers of the eighteenth century were less incompetent than most, but there too copperplates were used for the finest work.

press period; J. M. Papillon, a French wood engraver of the eighteenth century, tried to overcome problems of impression by cutting different parts of his blocks to different heights.[2] Blocks cut on the plank could if necessary be as large as paper and presses would allow, but end-grain blocks of box, which might exceptionally measure 25 × 25 cm., were in practice seldom available with a side exceeding 15 cm.; the normal procedure was to fasten several pieces of end-grain wood together to make one large block. A special form of woodcut initial, common from the mid sixteenth to the mid eighteenth century, was the factotum, a square ornamental block with a hole through the middle into which a piece of type could be wedged, one block thus serving for any initial letter.

The design was cut by hand on the surface of the block with a knife or a graver (a pointed chisel which was pushed along the surface), the parts that were to remain white on the printed paper being cut away and those that were to print black being left standing. Two approaches were possible. One, which gave a positive result and which was much the commoner during the hand-press period, was to cut out large areas of white with a gouge and to leave the design standing as thin lines of black, like a drawing in pen and ink, tones being indicated by groups of closely-spaced lines. Very delicate results were obtained with positive side-grain blocks in the sixteenth century, the chief limitation being inadequacies of ink and presswork. The other, negative, approach was to engrave the design on the block so that it would print as a pattern of white lines on a black ground; its advantages were the greater ease with which fine lines could be cut and the possibility of indicating tones by cross-hatching or dotting. It was so difficult, however, to get good impressions of extensive areas of black with the wooden hand-press that negative wood-engravings were very rarely cut between the early sixteenth century and the Bewick revival of the 1790s; and even Bewick's blocks were badly printed until the coming of the iron hand-presses in the 1800s.

The design for a woodcut, which was probably the work of a specialist other than the block cutter,[3] was either drawn in reverse directly on to the block, or traced on to it from paper. If an existing print was to be copied it might be pasted on to the new block as a guide, although in this case the design on the new block would be in reverse. Mistakes made in cutting were mended either by altering the design to accommodate them, or by cutting or drilling out small parts of the block and replacing them with new wood. Patches of this sort could also be used to emend an old block.

---

[2] Papillon, J. M., *Traité historique et pratique de la gravure en bois*, Paris 1766, ii, pp. 26, 45–57.

[3] At least as far as illustrations were concerned. Plantin's designers were paid less than his block-cutters, however eminent they might be as artists; Voet, L., *The golden compasses*, ii.

The earliest blocks appear to have been printed with water-based inks, the paper being simply burnished on to the block by hand; and similar techniques continued to be used for proofing blocks. Blocks in books were inked and printed in just the same way as type, make-ready sometimes being limited to underlays. The life of a block depended on how often and how hard it was used, but if proper care was taken it could last a very long time; Plantin's blocks, which were replaced in the forme after printing with pieces of plain wood so that they should not be damaged at the rinsing trough,[4] are still preserved in good order at Antwerp.

Cuts in fifteenth- and early-sixteenth-century books were sometimes coloured by hand, apparently being intended for this treatment.[5] Colour printing from several blocks, another early development, was mostly confined to separate prints, and remained very rare in printed books. The earliest printers experimented with the simultaneous printing of several interlocked colour blocks, but later the individual colours were printed separately, like red type.

INTAGLIO PLATES

A design engraved on the surface of a plate of polished copper can be printed if the lines of the design are filled with ink, the rest of the surface being wiped clean, and damp paper is pressed hard on to the surface so that it lifts the ink out of the engraved lines. The technique of engraving the plate is similar to that of cutting a negative wood block, allowing the use of very fine lines and cross-hatched tones, but it gives a positive not a negative result. These advantages caused printers from the later sixteenth century to prefer plates to blocks for their better-quality bookwork, in spite of the need to print plates apart from type.

It is possible to make prints from copperplates by burnishing paper on to them by hand, and the earliest plates appear to have been printed in this way. But rubbing is laborious and slow, and the full potential of the copperplate process could not be reached in the absence of a special press. When and where the copperplate rolling-press was invented is unknown, but it was certainly in use in the Low Countries by the later sixteenth century, and there was a tradition that it was brought to England from Antwerp early in the seventeenth century.[6]

The rolling press consisted essentially of a frame in which two large

---

[4] Information from Professor J. Gerritsen.

[5] Some of Plantin's grander illustrated books were coloured by hand for individual customers; Voet, L., op. cit.

[6] Voet, L., op. cit.; Timperley, C. H., *A dictionary of printers and printing*, London 1839, p. 276. The rolling press may well have been known by the mid sixteenth century, even in England (STC 11714-18).

rollers were mounted one above the other, and were turned by means of four large spokes radiating from the axle of the upper one. The copperplate was warmed, inked with a dabber and wiped to clean the unengraved areas, and laid on a board together with the damped printing paper between a pair of thin felts. Then board, plate, and all were passed between the rollers, the pressman hauling on the spokes. As the rollers were forced apart, great pressure was exerted on the narrow strip of contact that moved across the plate—the reader may be reminded of the domestic wringer—far more pressure per square centimetre, in fact, than could be produced by the flat platen of the common press. Its effect may be seen in the 'plate mark' that surrounds an engraving, where a ridge of paper has been forced down over the edge of the plate.

FIG. 69. Copperplate printing in the mid eighteenth century. A plate (warmed, inked, and covered with damp paper) is pulled through the rolling press, while other plates are prepared for printing, probably alternately with the first one. A row of new-made prints hangs on a line to dry. (*Encyclopédie*, planches vii, Paris 1769, 'Imprimerie en taille-douce', pl. 1.)

A few letterpress printers owned rolling presses, but copperplate printers were generally specialists.[7] Plates for insertion in a book as separate leaves were added when the sheets were gathered in the warehouse, but ordinary sheets that were to be embellished with copperplates were sent out to the

---

[7] Although the Plantinian house owned a rolling press in the later sixteenth century, most plates were sent out for printing by specialist copperplate printers; Voet, L., op. cit.

plate printer, usually after the letterpress was printed but before gathering. Sometimes plates were added at a later stage: copies of Robert Masters's *History* of Corpus Christi College, Cambridge, survive in quires just as they were delivered to the College from the Cambridge University Press in 1753; they include the folding frontispiece but not the other six plates intended for insertion, or any of the thirty-five plates that were to be printed on the ordinary sheets.

The simplest—and, for books, much the commonest—method of making copperplates was *engraving*. The surface of the plate was given a thin ground (or coating) of wax, on to which a drawing was burnished or traced from paper. The lines of the design were then cut into the copper, through the wax, with a graver. The burrs ploughed up by the graver were scraped smooth, the remaining wax was removed and the plate was ready for use. Any mistakes could be scraped or burnished away, and the plate hammered flat again for re-engraving; the same method was used for emendation. Like woodcuts, copperplates were capable of giving several thousand impressions, but the lines would get gradually fainter as the surface was squeezed and worn in the rolling press; sometimes a worn plate would be touched up with a graver.

Other methods of making plates were occasionally used for book illustration, although none so commonly as engraving. *Drypoint* (from the late fifteenth century): the design was sketched directly on to the plate with a steel point, the burr being left alone. *Etching* (from about 1500): the design was cut in a wax ground so that, when the plate was immersed in acid, the furrows allowed the acid to bite into the copper, making grooves that would hold ink. *Mezzotint* (mostly English, from the mid seventeenth century): parts of the plate were toned by roughening it with a serrated rocker, the tone then being graded by burnishing. *Stipple* (from the mid eighteenth century): a method of toning which combined etched and engraved dots. *Aquatint* (from 1768): gradations of tone were produced on the plate by the progressive etching through and stopping out of a porous ground, usually made by allowing a solution of resin in spirit to dry out and craze on the surface of the plate. *Colour plates*, laboriously produced in the hand-press period by a combination of differential inking of the plate and hand-colouring of the print, rarely appeared in books.

Changes of artistic fashion in the style of prints cannot concern us here. Style may have some importance, nevertheless, in the investigation of book illustrations, and W. M. Ivins's *Prints and visual communication* (New York 1969) explains such things as the development of conventional methods of indicating tone.

Whatever process was employed, the cost of providing a book with a substantial set of illustrations was always considerable, and plates were especially expensive. The cost of making and printing the copperplates for some of the finely illustrated editions of the seventeenth and eighteenth centuries equalled all the other production costs for the rest of the book, paper included.[8]

Sets of plates for bibles and other standard texts were not necessarily specific to particular editions in the seventeenth and eighteenth centuries, but might appear over considerable periods of time, not only in the successive editions of a publishing series but also in editions of different publishing series. It is not usually clear whether such sets were supplied with the book in sheets or whether they were offered as an extra by the bookseller/binder.[9]

[8] Moretus's expenditure on illustrations in 1600–10 was equal to about 25 per cent of his printing-house wage bill; Voet, L., op. cit.

[9] See p. 147, n. 4.

Patterns of Production

VARIATION OF DEMAND

So far we have looked at the individual processes of hand printing in isolation. It is true that they varied a little from time to time and from place to place, and that they were often supplemented by local improvisation, but it may be said that from 1500 to 1800 printers everywhere handled closely similar tools and materials in closely similar ways. It also appears to be the case that they all made the same sort of arrangements for fitting the individual processes together into complete patterns of work. The full production details that have survived from the great Plantinian house in the sixteenth century and afterwards, from the small Cambridge University Press at the turn of the eighteenth century, and from Bowyer's sizeable London establishment in the mid eighteenth century, show the organization of all three to have been essentially alike; and most alike, paradoxically, in the constant shift and change in their patterns of production.

The printing trade has always had to accommodate great variation of demand, and its operations have had to be correspondingly flexible. A printer's orders varied enormously in size, from ephemeral jobbing—labels, bills and the like—to books both short and long. The work involved in setting the Shakespeare First Folio was more than thirty times that of setting one of the plays in quarto; and of course the amount of presswork in a book was determined not only by the number of formes but also by the number of copies in the edition. These huge differences of size were absorbed into an economical pattern of work by the method of concurrent production, whereby several jobs were worked simultaneously, plant and labour being switched from one to another whenever work was interrupted.

Demand also varied as a result of external pressures. Concurrent production thrived on multiple orders, but if the flow of orders altered markedly as a result of political, economic, or social changes—or simply because of a change in the average number of customers—the printer would respond by varying the productive capacity of his shop, primarily by altering the number of his employees and the terms of their piecework contracts.

EDITION QUANTITIES

In the earliest days of printing small editions of 200–300 copies were usual, and there were even smaller editions from time to time (such as the 12 copies

500 – 2,000

of a book that Plantin once printed for a private customer).[1] But small edition quantities mean large unit costs, and it was found to be both more attractive to the customer and more profitable to the printer to produce a rather larger number of copies at a lower unit cost; by the beginning of the sixteenth century books were normally printed in editions of 1,000 to 1,500 copies, a figure which did not change much for the generality of books until the later eighteenth century. Almost two-thirds of the books printed by Plantin in the 1560s and by Moretus in the 1590s were in editions of from 1,000 to 1,500 copies; and even as late as 1738–85 more than 90 per cent of the 514 books printed at Strahan's large London printing-house were in editions of less than 2,000 copies.[2]

There were powerful economic reasons for printing no more than about 2,000 copies, just as there were for printing at least 500. As the quantity increased the printer's capital investment, which was always alarmingly high, rose with it, and his profit as a percentage of investment fell. Quite a small edition of a sizeable book could take as much as two years to print, and it was usual to allow credit to customers for several months after delivery; similarly, whoever bought the paper had to put up a lot of money for a long time. If, therefore, the average edition quantity was increased without a corresponding enlargement of the printer's productive capacity, the result was higher interest charges and lower profits; and the printer could not enlarge his productive capacity beyond a certain point without increasing his plant, which again meant increased overheads.

Even this might have been attractive if large edition quantities had resulted in really low unit costs, and therefore prices, but that was impossible so long as printing presses were powered by hand. The unit of wages which bought the composition of one average sheet was approximately the same as the unit of wages which bought the printing of 1,500 copies of that sheet. If the edition quantity was under 1,500 copies, therefore, the compositors' wages made up the larger part of the labour costs, and the division of these wages between copies as the quantity rose resulted in a fall, rapid at first, of unit costs. Above 1,500 copies, however, composition was no longer the major element in labour costs, and the pressmen's wages (which were always directly proportional to the number of copies printed) then combined with interest charges on wages and overheads to impose a levelling-off of unit costs. It was almost impossible to get the real unit cost of a substantial book below 90 per cent of the unit cost for an edition of 1,500 copies, however many were printed; and unless the interest charges

[1] Haebler, K., *The study of incunabula*, New York 1933 (repr. New York 1967), pp. 171–5; Voet, L., op. cit.

[2] Voet, L., op. cit.; Hernlund, P., 'Strahan's ledgers', *Studies in bibliography*, xx, 1967, p. 104.

were very small, the real unit cost began to rise again shortly after the edition quantity exceeded 2,000 copies.

This is illustrated by a calculation made by the manager of the Société Typographique de Neuchâtel in 1774 for the production costs of an illustrated bible in 300 sheets, in editions of 2,000 and 4,000 copies. He took into account the (fixed) costs of composition and copperplate engraving; costs proportional to the two edition quantities for paper and presswork; and overheads assessed at one-third of the labour costs. It turned out that the unit cost for the edition of 4,000 copies was 95 per cent of the unit cost for the edition of 2,000 copies. At best this offered little inducement to print the larger number; and the allowance for overheads of only one-third labour costs was so small (English and French printers allowed considerably more at this period)[3] that there was no leeway to cover the increased interest charges on paper and wages which necessarily resulted from a longer production period.[4]

Printers did find it profitable, on the other hand, to secure a rapid turnover by printing large editions of small, cheap books for quick and certain sale. The London printers Dunn and Robinson produced 10,000 copies of piratical editions of *The ABC and little catechism* in 1585; almanacks were printed for the Stationers' Company in the 1660s in separate impressions of from 2,500 to 30,000 copies; while from 1733 to 1748 Charles Ackers of London printed 33 editions of Dyche's *Guide to the English tongue* (a spelling book for schools), 275,000 copies altogether in runs of from 5,000 to 20,000 copies.[5] Towards the end of the eighteenth century large edition quantities became rather more common, generally financed by publishers' syndicates.

In England from 1586 until 1637 edition quantities were limited by decree on behalf of the journeymen compositors to 1,500 copies of ordinary books, or 3,000 copies of books in small type and of small books such as catechisms. Edition quantities of this size were, of course, about as large as a printer would normally have chosen to undertake, but it is clear from the complaints of the journeymen that the masters ignored the decree and printed larger editions whenever it suited them to do so.[6]

The rate of survival of copies of early editions is not as a rule a direct indication of their original quantity. On the contrary it is precisely such things as school books, which were printed in the largest numbers but

---

[3] See p. 178.

[4] S.T.N. MS. 1056, p. 32.

[5] Greg, W. W., *A companion to Arber*, Oxford 1967, p. 37; Blagden, C., 'The distribution of almanacks in the second half of the seventeenth century', *Studies in bibliography*, xi, 1958, Table 1; McKenzie, D. F., and Ross, J. C., *A ledger of Charles Ackers*, Oxford 1968, pp. 249–52.

[6] Greg, W. W., op. cit., pp. 43, 94–5.

were used to death, which have survived least well, while small luxury editions, much prized but little used, may have survived almost complete. Many cheap books and most of the jobbing work of the earlier hand-press period have disappeared completely, but it is not always possible to find copies even of eighteenth-century books. Of 134 books printed at the Cambridge University Press in 1696–1712, 10 seem not to have survived at all, and more than three-quarters of the jobbing work of the same period has disappeared.[7] Of the 33 editions and 275,000 copies of Dyche's *Guide* printed in 1733–48 (and mentioned above), a recent world-wide search has turned up just five copies.[8]

PRODUCTIVE CAPACITY

The productive capacity of a printing shop depended on the plant, which set an upper limit on production, and on the amount of work supplied by the employees, which could be varied within the capacity of the plant. The greater part—often as much as two-thirds—of the printer's investment in plant was spent on type, the cost of the presses being no more than 5–15 per cent of the whole;[9] and in practice it was the extent of the type stock that limited production. The actual limits set by given quantities of type varied to some extent with the standards of individual printers (or of printing communities), for those who would set by formes and use worn type could make small founts go further; while any printer could on occasion utilize his stock of type more fully than was normally convenient.

Working within his stock of type, then, the printer varied his output according to demand by hiring more or less labour. Journeymen would be engaged or dismissed, or the amount of piecework offered them would be altered. (No doubt it was partly for this reason that the earnings of individual journeymen varied from time to time by such large amounts; see pp. 54–6, 139–41.) Variation of output did not necessarily involve variation of work rate, however. With reduced demand a printer might continue normally with the jobs in hand, maintaining the work rate but reducing the labour force, finishing his existing commitments at the same time as he would have done if demand had remained constant.

There was no economic need to be short of presses (although on occasion the number of presses was limited by official decree). The price of a common press was only about one-tenth of the cost of the 1,000 kg. of type that kept it occupied in a busy shop—or from one-third to one-half the annual

---

[7] McKenzie, D. F., *The Cambridge University Press 1696–1712*, Cambridge 1966, i, app. I.

[8] McKenzie, D. F., and Ross, J. C., op. cit., p. 18.

[9] Early inventories; see p. 38, n. 29.

earnings of a journeyman[10]—so that the master could afford to own more presses than he would normally need. In this way he could take on more hands, stretch his stock of type, and use the extra presses when there was a glut of orders; or alternatively lay men off and let presses stand idle when work was short.

Thus the Cambridge University Press owned four presses in the early eighteenth century but did not use more than two of them at a time, and Bowyer in the early 1730s owned seven presses but used from three to six of them at a time according to need.[11] The changes in the productive capacity of the Plantinian business in the later sixteenth century were even more marked. Plantin, who may have owned as many as 22 or 23 presses in the middle of his career, worked up to 16 of them together in the mid 1570s, and then abruptly reduced the number in use to 3 as a result of the Spanish Fury of November 1576, all the while engaging and dismissing workmen so that there were always from 3 to 5 employees per press (see Table 4).

The fact that printers of the hand-press period varied their productive capacity in this way means of course that particular shops cannot be supposed to have achieved particular and regular levels of output.

CONCURRENT PRODUCTION[12]

Books varied so much in size that a balance between composition and press-work could not have been kept if they had been printed serially—that is, if each book had been produced in turn, one being finished before another was begun—for, depending on the relative magnitude of their tasks and on accident, either pressmen or compositors would constantly have been waiting for the others to catch up. Printers therefore had several books in production at once—as many as ten or twelve at a time even in a two-press shop—so that when a man came to the end of a stage in the work, he would be in a position to take up something else, for there was generally something ready to be done.

This meant that an individual book took longer to print than it might have done if all the workmen had concentrated on it alone; but also that, by utilizing plant and labour less wastefully, all the books could be printed in less time altogether, and at less cost, than they would have been by serial production. The minor jobbing work such as labels, bills, and prospectuses, which every printer undertook, was a valuable—perhaps an essential—part of the scheme, for it filled gaps that were too short for the stages of book production.

---

[10] From figures in Gaskell, P., *The decline of the common press*, Cambridge University Ph.D. thesis 2902, 1956; Voet, L., *The golden compasses*, ii.

[11] McKenzie, D. F., op. cit. (1966), chs. 3, 5; idem, 'Printers of the mind', *Studies in bibliography*, xxii, 1969, pp. 52-7, 64-74.

[12] The best discussion is in McKenzie, D. F., op. cit. (1969).

TABLE 4. *Presses and workmen at Plantin's printing house on the first pay-day in January 1564–89*

Year	Presses in use	Total workmen	Workmen per press
1564	2	10	5·0
1565	5	24	4·8
1566	7	33	4·7
1567	5	19	3·8
1568	6	20	3·3
1569	10	31	3·1
1570	9	36	4·0
1571	11	43	3·9
1572	13	53	4·1
1573	12	44	3·7
1574	16	56	3·5
1575	15	53	3·5
1576	15	54	3·6
1577	3	11	3·7
1578	6	21	3·5
1579	5	20	4·0
1580	7	27	3·9
1581	8	27	3·4
1582	7	29	4·1
1583	10	35	3·5
1584	6	26	4·3
1585	6	18	3·0
1586	3	11	3·7
1587	6	18	3·0
1588	6	22	3·7
1589	4	16	4·0

SOURCE: De Roover, R., 'The business organisation of the Plantin Press', *Gedenkboek der Plantin-dagen 1555–1955*, Antwerp 1956, p. 239.

It follows that a book was not necessarily set by a particular compositor or printed at a particular press. Other things being equal it was more efficient that a compositor should continue to set a book which he had begun than that he should move to another merely for the sake of change, and of course specialist texts such as foreign languages in exotic type might require specialist compositors; but experienced men (who had adjustable composing sticks) could if necessary take up ordinary work at any point. Thus some books (especially short, simple ones, and books needing special skills) were set by a single compositor, but most were set by several. On the other hand, although one compositor might set a whole book, he would not normally be working on that book alone but would intersperse work on other jobs when it was called for, or when there was a temporary interruption in the supply of copy, type, or skeletons.

There was even less need to send all the sheets of a book for printing at a particular press. Chases were of a standard size, and most books were imposed in one of a few standard formats. Each press was equipped with several parchment friskets ready cut for regular impositions in folio, quarto, octavo, etc., which were readily interchangeable. Any forme could be locked in position on the bed of the press and matched up with the right frisket (temporarily patched if need be to mask blank pages) in a matter of minutes; the impression was deep and spongy, so that make-ready on this account was unnecessary, and the pressmen only needed to adjust the relative positions of forme and points to be ready to go. Formes were therefore sent for printing to any machine that was or soon would be ready to take them, and it was rare, even in a two-press shop, for all the sheets of a book to be printed at one press. As we have seen, it was probably normal in the sixteenth and seventeenth centuries for both formes of a sheet to be printed at the same press; but in the eighteenth century (at least in English printing houses) even this was found to be unnecessary, and the two formes of a sheet were commonly printed at two different presses.

The combination of a fluctuating productive capacity with the shifting patterns of concurrent production resulted in considerable complexity of working even in small shops with two presses and four or five compositors. Each compositor would normally be employed on several books at a time, and the larger books would each be set by several compositors; each press would probably print parts of most of the books that went through the shop; and it was unlikely that any two books would be precisely alike in their patterns of composition and presswork.

Work patterns in larger shops were even more complex.[13] During one fortnight in February 1732 Bowyer employed 14 compositors, whose individual piecework earnings ranged from £1. 3s. 7d. to £3. 5s. 4d., and 9 pressmen (working 4 full presses and 1 half press), earning individually from £0. 14s. 9d. to £2. 0s. 10d. The compositors worked on 26 jobs altogether during the period (5 of them minor); 1 compositor worked on 1 job, 4 on 2 jobs each, 2 on 3 jobs, 2 on 4 jobs, and 1 on 5 jobs; while 2 pairs of compositors worked on 3 and 4 jobs respectively. Most of the major jobs were divided between

---

[13] These Bowyer examples are worked out from McKenzie, D. F., op. cit. (1969), pp. 64–74.

several compositors, who mostly took a sheet or a half sheet apiece, but who might on another occasion divide a sheet unevenly between them. During the same period the pressmen were dealing with 24 jobs (5 of them minor, and 19 of them parts of jobs that were going through the composing room during the same fortnight). The 5 minor jobs were each printed at a single press, as were 3 other jobs; but 4 jobs were printed at 2 presses, 5 at 3, 6 at 4, and 1 at all 5 presses. There was a preference for sending the two formes of a sheet to two different presses.

The production histories of books printed under such circumstances were necessarily complicated. The first edition in English of Voltaire's *History of Charles XII* will serve as an example. Bowyer printed 1,000 copies of the first 12¼ sheets of this prose octavo in four weeks of January and February 1732. The setting was shared by 4 compositors, up to 3 of them during the same payment period of a fortnight. The copy was apparently cast off accurately, since sheets K and L were set first. During the middle payment period of a fortnight, 1 compositor set the whole of sheet B, 11 pages of C, half of D, 11 pages of E, half of F, half of G, 12 pages of H, and the whole of I; a second compositor set 5 pages of C, half of D, 5 pages of E, half of F, half of G, and 4 pages of H; a third compositor set sheets M and N, and 4 pages of O; and each of these 3 compositors was also engaged on other work during the same fortnight. Sheet F was reset later. During the course of the work 4 different presses were used for printing the book; single presses took both formes of 4 of the sheets and the quarter sheet, but the 2 formes of the other 8 sheets were each printed at different presses. All 24 formes of the 12 whole sheets were marked with press figures, one of them apparently with the wrong figure.

A few points remain to be made. The shifting patterns of concurrent production meant that there could be no regular correlation between particular skeleton formes and particular compositors or presses. Neither did the number of skeletons used in a book necessarily reflect the numbers of men or machines employed in its production, or the edition quantity. Type accounted for at least 85 per cent of the cost of the materials in a forme and, provided that there was no casual shortage of chases, quoins, or furniture, the number of skeletons in use was likely to be determined by the amount of type a printer could afford, or found it convenient, to keep standing.

When a book could be cast off accurately it was unnecessary to set the sheets, or even the pages, in the right order. Setting by formes (pp. 41–2), still a current practice in early-seventeenth-century London, was mentioned by Moxon in 1683 with the implication that it was uncommon, and there is no mention of it in printers' records of the eighteenth century. But the whole sheets of such things as page-for-page reprints continued to be worked out of order. In 1700 the 21 sheets of an octavo prose reprint were produced at Cambridge in the following order: *setting*: E K / H B S / C / L U D X / F $\frac{1}{2}$ G / $\frac{1}{2}$ G I R Q P / N O T / A M; *presswork*: E H / K B / S L U / C D / X F / G I R Q / P N O / T A M.[14] The purpose of such extreme disorder, if any, is hard to surmise.

Two other practices were really special forms of concurrent production. The printing—or at least the setting—of a book was sometimes shared between two or more shops. Greg pointed to a number of examples in the English printed drama around 1600, notably the first two quartos of Dekker's *The entertainment through London*, 1604, which were apparently divided between five and four printers respectively; and approximately one third of all the books printed by Snowdon and Okes in London in 1606-9 were shared with other printers.[15] Individual volumes of four collections of plays by Calderón were set at two or three separate printing-houses in Madrid in the 1670s.[16] The individual sheets of the 2- or 3-sheet octavo almanacs printed in very large impressions for the Stationers' Company in the seventeenth and eighteenth centuries were regularly put out to different printers.[17] Again, Charles Ackers printed 74 of the 120 quarto sheets of the 10th edition of Bailey's *Universal etymological dictionary* in 1742; 16 sheets of the 11th edition, 1745; and 25 sheets of the 13th edition, 1747; the remaining sheets in each case being printed elsewhere.[18] Printing may occasionally have been split up in this way for the sake of speed, but it is more likely to have been done as a rule in order to suit the productive capacity of the printers concerned, or in order to share out work equitably between the members of a partnership or the various owners of a copyright.

The other special form of concurrent production was when a journeyman, unable to get a full week's piecework from a single master, took a second job at another printing house, working (say) 3$\frac{1}{2}$ days for one printer and 2$\frac{1}{2}$ days for the other.[19]

STANDARDS

Influenced by the idealism of the nineteenth-century arts and crafts movement and by modern attitudes to workmanship, we are apt to think that the men who made the venerable and often beautiful books of the hand-press

[14] Bennet, T., *An answer to the dissenters pleas*, 2nd ed., Cambridge 1700 (McKenzie, D. F., op. cit. (1966), i, pp. 192-3); the strokes indicate payment periods which in some but not in all cases define the order within the periods.

[15] Greg, W. W., *A bibliography of the English printed drama to the Restoration*, i, London 1939, pp. 320-2, and see pp. 368-70 below; work in progress by P. W. M. Blayney.

[16] Cruickshank, D. W., 'Calderón's *Primera* and *Tercera partes*: the reprints of "1640" and "1664"', *The Library*, xxv, 1970, pp. 105-19.   [17] *Studies in bibliography*, xi, 1958, p. 112, n. 14.

[18] McKenzie, D. F., and Ross, J. C., op. cit., pp. 234-5.

[19] Moxon, J., op. cit., pp. 351-2; Savage, W., *A dictionary of the art of printing*, London 1841, p. 776.

period must have loved their work and have done it well for its own sake. But this is to misunderstand labour conditions in the craft industries. Printers have always liked working on special jobs, putting their best into them and taking their time; but such jobs were few and far between, and there is little evidence that, under the ordinary conditions of the trade, printers' journeymen (who were nearly all piece-workers in one way or another)[20] worked any harder than was necessary to meet their immediate needs, or any more conscientiously than the master-printer made them.

Incentives to earn more than a living were few, and if a man could get his bread by less than a whole week's work, he might well take the rest of the time off. Sometimes this was done simply by staying away (Saint Monday was always a popular feast in the trade), but perhaps more often by contracting with the master to work less. For his part the master could exercise some control over the men's hours by dismissing unsatisfactory hands, and by offering more or less work to those who remained, the degree of his control varying with the relative demand for work and workmen.

Standards of workmanship reflected the journeymen's attitude. Full-time work involved very long hours—a six-day, 72-hour week was common throughout the hand-press period, and even longer working weeks were known[21]—while the labour was repetitive and boring. If a man could increase his output and thus his earnings per hour by working less carefully, he would do so just so far as the master or overseer would let him; a critical and unsentimental examination of the detailed finish—and especially of the ink and the register—of a representative sample of books from any part of the hand-press period will quickly demonstrate that this was so. If some printers regularly produced work that was of a high technical standard, it was because the masters—Schoeffer, Estienne, Plantin, Baskerville, Bodoni—insisted on it, not because their men chose to do it.

Few masters cared, however, and there was in fact a steady and general decline in printing standards throughout Europe during the sixteenth and seventeenth centuries. The rate of decline was not the same everywhere, being least in the type-producing countries. French and Dutch printing was notably better than most in the seventeenth century, though even so it was plainly worse in 1700 than it had been 150 years before. Seventeenth-century English printing was mostly very poor, and there are few books

---

[20] The system whereby the journeyman contracted to produce so much in a day was also a form of piece work. Time hands were very rare in English printing before the nineteenth century.

[21] James Watson (*The history of the art of printing*, Edinburgh 1713, p. 21) suggested that English and Scottish pressmen might work a 17- or 18-hour day in the early eighteenth century. Not that piece-work journeymen normally complained about long hours—they characteristically asked for more hours, not fewer—but the effect of long hours on their standards was bad whether they wanted the work or not.

listed in Wing that were not set in ill-cast, battered type, clumsily arranged and carelessly printed in brown ink on shabby paper. This is sometimes said to have been the result of the exclusive protection afforded the English printers by the Stationers' Company, but it does not seem that they really lacked competition—as often as not they were short of work—while it may be observed that (for instance) the Spanish printers, whose standards were if anything even lower, had no protective gild. The true cause of the decline is likely to have been too much competition, not too little, with a superfluity of printers everywhere competing by offering ever cheaper products. It may be added that the period of decline in printing standards coincided with the great price revolution of the sixteenth and seventeenth centuries, when real wages and the standard of living also declined throughout Europe.

Only fine bespoke bindings, which were of course produced separately from the books they covered, continued to develop during the seventeenth century in the quality of their design and execution. The contrast between the fine feathers of these superb bindings and their jackdaw contents is often quaint.

A move towards a return to higher printing standards came at first from outside the ordinary trade, from the Imprimerie Royale du Louvre from 1640 onwards, and later in the century from the Oxford and Cambridge University presses and the French Royal Academy. The directors of these institutions sought and encouraged better-designed and better-made type, clearer typographical layout, and (with less success) improved presswork. By the early years of the eighteenth century the standards of trade printing itself at last began to rise, encouraging (and being in turn further encouraged by) the production of a variety of new types in all the major type-producing countries and, for the first time on anything but a very minor scale, in England and Scotland as well. The design of ordinary books was simplified and much improved thereby, but the quality of presswork generally left a good deal to be desired; presswork rates in Britain were low compared with rates for composition, and it may be that British pressmen in particular lacked pride in their work and took little trouble with it. The art of making good printing ink, moreover, was not recovered until after the end of the hand-press period, and it was not easy to print a good-looking sheet with the messy brown ink of the seventeenth and eighteenth centuries.

The English Book Trade to 1800

EUROPE AND ENGLAND[1]

It is not possible, unfortunately, to find room here for even a summary history of the European book trade in the hand-press period. Although printing technology remained fairly stable everywhere, the organization of publishing and bookselling was related to the various political, social, and economic situations of half a dozen different countries. What follow, therefore, are notes on particular aspects of the book trade as they affected book production, with special reference to the situation in England.

It must be said at once, however, that the English book trade in the sixteenth and seventeenth centuries was in important ways unlike that of the great book-producing countries of continental Europe. At the beginning of the sixteenth century England was a small, backward, and unimportant appendage of Christendom, where printing had arrived late and where it was deficient in technique and provincial in content. The increasing importance of England in Europe during the next two hundred years was not accompanied by a corresponding advance in its book trade, which remained small and backward, confined by tight political control and by the restrictions of a monopolistic trade gild. During the same two centuries the book trades of France, the Low Countries, Germany, and Italy, while differing in many respects from each other, were all organized on a much larger scale than the English trade, were relatively free of gild (if not of political) control, and operated a sizeable international market in which England took little part except as an importer of foreign books.

All this changed in the eighteenth century. The combination of an expanding home market, the relaxation of political and gild control of printing, and the development of native type-founding and paper-making enabled the English book trade to equal its European neighbours in both scale and quality during the first half of the century, and to surpass them during the second.

PRINTING PERSONNEL

Printing businesses of the hand-press period included up to five main grades of personnel.

(1) The master-printer owned the business, possibly in partnership with others; in a few cases the master was himself an employee of an institution such as a university, a superior overseer. Masters were usually trained

[1] See the bibliography, pp. 399–400.

printers, but some had been bred to another (usually related) trade, or occasionally to no trade at all, having been perhaps academics or merchants; and it was common for printers' widows to take over their husbands' businesses, at least until they remarried. The master would normally direct the whole business personally, taking its profit as his emolument, but if he or she were incompetent to do so a trained manager would be employed at a fixed wage. In a small shop the master would lend a hand with the work, certainly as a corrector and often as a compositor as well.

(2) Next came any senior employee who acted as the master's deputy, such as the overseer of a large shop who parcelled out the work amongst the journeymen and saw that it was properly done, and who might also work as a corrector. Overseers are scarcely heard of in English printing before the later eighteenth century, shops being generally too small to warrant their employment. Such a man was normally an ex-journeyman, but he was paid a regular wage and was responsible directly to the master. The warehouse keeper might also have some managerial responsibility, and he too was paid a fixed wage.

(3) The correctors were not as a rule trained printers, but were men of education specially employed, sometimes on a part-time basis; they too were rarely employed by English printers before the eighteenth century. Time wages were probably normal in the sixteenth century, piecework rates thereafter.

(4) The journeymen and apprentices were the most numerous class of printing workers, the labour force on which book production was based. Most journeymen served an apprenticeship to the trade, of at least seven years in England (but not so long elsewhere), after which they might take up employment with any master. Not all apprentices formally took up their freedom, but all who did so could themselves become masters and could bind apprentices. Journeyman printers generally specialized as compositors or pressmen and, although a compositor might on occasion take a turn at the press (especially in a small shop), few pressmen could set type efficiently.[2] Journeymen in employment were entitled (provided they had taken up their freedom) to bind apprentices of their own, but they seldom did so; on the other hand they did sometimes contract work out to other journeymen, as for instance when Plantin employed only one journeyman per press, paying him double wages and making him responsible for employing a second hand.[3] Pressmen would employ lads in the seventeenth and eigh-

---

[2] Seven of Bowyer's compositors in 1730–9 also worked at press, but only one of his pressmen also worked as a compositor; see p. 174.

[3] De Roover, R., 'The business organisation of the Plantin Press', *Gedenkboek der Plantin-dagen, 1555–1955*, Antwerp 1956, pp. 243–4.

teenth centuries (and perhaps before) to speed their work by taking the printed sheets off the tympan.[4]

Most journeymen were paid for piecework during the hand-press period. In France and the Low Countries (but not, apparently, in England) one or two senior compositors in a shop might be employed 'en conscience' to deal with imposition and odd jobs at time rates, while most of the men were paid 'à la tâche'; eighteenth-century French time hands, indeed, sometimes led small 'companionships' of piecework compositors (see p. 192). Until the later seventeenth century a special form of piecework payment was common in French and English houses, whereby journeymen contracted with the master to set so many pages or pull so many sheets in a day, if required to, for a fixed wage, being entitled to extra pay if they were asked to do more;[5] a similar system was used by Plantin, along with ordinary time and ordinary piece-rates.[6] From the later seventeenth until the mid eighteenth century (until the early nineteenth century in continental houses) compositors' piece-rates were calculated by the page, the sheet, or even the book, but then payment per 1,000 ens superseded the older system; and pressmen were paid for the number of sheets or tokens that they actually pulled.[7]

Journeymen traditionally had the perquisite of a free copy of each book that they had helped to print. In the sixteenth and seventeenth centuries these 'copy books' were claimed and promptly sold at bargain prices by the London workmen, who also on occasion used up defective sheets or even pulled a few sheets above the proper number in order to have extra copies to sell; but in 1635 the Stationers' Company substituted a payment of 3*d.* a week (later raised to 4*d.*) in lieu of copies.[8] Elsewhere the old custom persisted; Parisian journeymen were still selling their copy books in the 1820s.[9] Other perquisites might include payments for remaking the paper windows of the printing house at the time of the annual 'waygoose' celebration, and for cleaning the presses, besides occasional gratuities from authors.[10]

---

[4] Moxon, J., op. cit., p. 338.

[5] See McKenzie, D. F., 'Notes on printing at Cambridge *c.* 1590', *Transactions of the Cambridge Bibliographical Society*, iii, 1959–63, p. 101 and n.   [6] Voet, L., *The golden compasses*, ii.

[7] For a full discussion of these developments, with references, see McKenzie, D. F., *The Cambridge University Press 1696–1712*, Cambridge 1966, i, pp. 76–80, 84–90. C. M. Smith recorded the remarkable case of an untrained hand who in the 1820s bought galleys of set type from the compositors in a Parisian printing-office (Galignani's), corrected and imposed it, and passed the completed formes on to the employer at a small profit (*The working man's way in the world*, London 1853 (repr. London 1967), pp. 71–2).

[8] Johnson, F. R., 'Printer's "copy books" ', *The Library*, i, 1946–7, pp. 97–105. Copy books were not given to eighteenth-century journeymen in Scotland, although master printers there kept file copies of what they printed (printed papers in the case of Alexander Donaldson v. John Reid, Edinburgh 1769).

[9] Smith, C. M., op. cit., p. 94.   [10] McKenzie, D. F., op. cit. (1966), i, pp. 73–6.

Journeymen from foreign countries (known technically as aliens to distinguish them from foreigners, who were shop-keepers or craftsmen of English origin who were not free of the City of London) were quite often employed in English printing houses, at least until the early eighteenth century. Most of our earliest printers, indeed, were aliens, welcomed for their skills; and even after 1534, when aliens were denied full membership of the Stationers' Company, alien printers continued to reside as gild brothers.[11] Sixteenth-century Parisian printers employed many Flemish and German journeymen.[12] The Cambridge University Press at the end of the seventeenth century (which had special need for compositors in the learned languages) employed a Dutch manager and a majority of alien compositors;[13] while James Watson of Edinburgh brought over Dutch pressmen in the early eighteenth century in order to raise standards of workmanship.[14]

There was in any case considerable mobility of journeymen within the trade; men often changed masters, and even, in times of work shortage, took employment with more than one master at a time. The movement of employees at Bowyer's printing house during the 1730s is revealing. This shop normally employed from 16 to 25 journeymen at a time, but from March 1730 until August 1739, 92 different pressmen and 90 different compositors were taken on, more than half of the pressmen and about a third of the compositors staying for three months or less, and a few coming and going as part-time hands; seven of the compositors, moreover, did short stints at press, and one of the pressmen had a turn at composition.[15]

(5) Finally, a boy or two might be employed, in addition to any journeymen's devils, as messengers or cleaners. Unskilled employees were not supposed to do any printing, although it would be surprising if this rule was not occasionally broken.

GILD AND CHAPEL[16]

All printers—apprentices, journeymen, and masters alike—were in theory members of the printer-booksellers' craft gilds, such as those that were incorporated at Venice in 1548, at London in 1557, and at Paris in about 1570. In practice, however, the gilds were federations of master tradesmen who, in return for monopolistic privileges, co-operated with the govern-

[11] Blagden, C., *The Stationers' Company*, London 1960, chs. 1, 2.
[12] Febvre, L., and Martin, H. J., *L'apparition du livre*, Paris 1958, p. 196.
[13] McKenzie, D. F., op. cit. (1966), i, pp. 61–2.
[14] Watson, J., *The history of the art of printing*, Edinburgh 1713, p. 21.
[15] Information from Mr. K. I. D. Maslen.
[16] See the bibliography, pp. 400–1.

ment in its censorship of the press. The Stationers' Company of London, the most powerful and restrictive of all the European gilds from the later sixteenth until the end of the seventeenth century, controlled entry to the trade; regulated wages and conditions of employment; protected its members' copyrights; operated copyright monopolies for the benefit of its senior members; and limited the number of presses that might be used, and defined their location.

The journeymen, having no say in the affairs of the gild, organized their own associations within individual shops, which were known as chapels. The origins of this institution—part trade union, part friendly society, and part social club—are obscure, but chapels were well established by the mid sixteenth century in the larger continental shops. Their purposes were to ensure acceptable behaviour between the men and settle their disputes; to negotiate with the master; to accumulate and disburse a benevolent fund; and to exact contributions for drinks and parties. Chapels were 'closed shops', and all the journeymen in a business were obliged (by sanctions if necessary) to obey its rules and contribute to its funds.

The degree to which the chapel organization was used for combinations of journeymen against their masters varied a good deal; in France a series of journeymen's strikes resulted in official attacks on their chapels in the sixteenth and seventeenth centuries, whereas in England at the same period the printers' chapels seem to have operated chiefly as friendly and social societies. As a rule the masters encouraged the chapels—or at least tolerated them—not because they approved of trade unions but because the chapel, in regulating the behaviour of the interdependent journeymen, not only prevented quarrelsome men from causing their fellows to lose earnings, but also prevented them from upsetting the complex course of concurrent production; discipline in the workshop was essential to efficient working, and the masters preferred the men to apply it themselves.

SCALE AND FINANCE; BOOK PRICES

As we have seen, the economics of hand printing both kept edition quantities down and discouraged the hand printer from enlarging his plant to an extent that made him dependent upon a steady flow of large orders (pp. 106–2); and in fact most printing houses of the hand-press period were small ones. There were 20 printing businesses in Geneva in 1563, of which 85 per cent had 1 or 2 presses, and the rest 4 presses each; similarly in London in 1583, 87 per cent of 23 businesses had 1, 2, or 3 presses, the largest 5 presses; in Paris in 1644, 81 per cent of 75 businesses had 1, 2, or 3 presses, the largest 7 presses; and in London in 1668, 85 per cent of 26 businesses had 1, 2, or 3 presses, the largest 6 presses.[17] A few printers did build up larger businesses, but they were exceptional. Koberger of Nuremberg, whose great firm encompassed all departments of the book trade, owned 24 presses around 1500, and Plantin actually operated 16 presses in 1574;[18] there is no certain evidence, however, that any printer operated more presses than Plantin for at least another 200 years. Comprehensive figures for most of the eighteenth century are lacking, but the indications are that there were fewer small printing houses with 1 or 2 presses, but that businesses with 8 or more presses were still very rare. In Paris in 1701 there were 51 printing businesses, of which the smallest had 2 presses (one-press shops were officially discouraged); 45 per cent had 2 or 3 presses, 31 per cent had 4 presses, and the remaining 24 per cent had more than 4 presses, the largest having 9.[19]

The number of printing employees in a shop varied with the number of presses at work but, as we have seen (pp. 163–4), the number of presses owned by a printer was often—perhaps usually—greater than the number that he normally had working. The total number of printers per working press (master, compositors, pressmen, and apprentices together) was probably in the region of 4; Plantin's average was 3·7.[20] In Paris in 1644 there were only 2·3 printers per press, and in London in 1668 there were 3·0;[21] but in both cases it is known that a number of the presses were not in use.

There were only 198 printers altogether in London in 1668, of whom 75 per cent were journeymen, 13 per cent masters, and 12 per cent apprentices.[22] The total number of printers in London around 1600, when there may have been about 40 presses at work, was probably under 175; no doubt they all knew each other.

A printing business requires a large capital investment, chiefly because a lot of money has to be spent on wages and paper before the sale of books brings in a return. It was generally necessary to reinvest the profits from one job in the expenses of another, and printers of the hand-press period —especially the larger ones—regularly had difficulty in obtaining and paying for the amount of loan capital they required for expansion or to cover temporary shortages of money. Gutenberg himself appears to have been checked on this account and even Plantin, who was a shrewd man, was constantly plagued with problems resulting from excessive borrowing (the

[17] Geneva 1563: Chaix, Paul, *Recherches sur l'imprimerie à Genève de 1550 à 1564*, Genève (Thèse de la Faculté de lettres) 1954, p. 32. London 1583: Arber, E., [*Stationers' registers*], i, London 1875, p. 248. Paris 1644: Martin, H. J., *Livre, pouvoirs et société*, Genève 1969, i, p. 372. London 1668: P.R.O. SP 29/243.

[18] Hase, O. von, *Die Koberger*, Leipzig 1885, p. 54; and see p. 165.

[19] Martin, H. J., op. cit., ii, p. 699.   [20] See p. 165.

[21] Martin, H. J., op. cit., i, pp. 372–3; P.R.O. SP 29/243.   [22] P.R.O. SP 29/243.

investment in his business in 1565 being about 20,000 florins, then worth about £2,750 sterling, a considerable sum in the sixteenth century).[23] Consequently many books were financed in partnership (see the next section).

The cost of equipping a small printing house was not in itself enormous. A shop with 2 presses and 1,500 kg. of type with its related equipment could be set up for about £350 (mid-eighteenth-century prices),[24] but more than half as much again was needed to cover wages and overheads before any return could be expected. The cost of the paper (if the printer provided it himself) could be even more than the cost of printing on it, and unlike the labour, moreover, it had to be bought in advance of rather than during production. The distribution of the Plantinian investment in 1565 is instructive: 28 per cent of the total represented books in stock; 26 per cent unprinted paper; 24 per cent books in production; and only 19 per cent plant (the remaining 3 per cent being miscellaneous assets).[25] It was such considerations that encouraged the Elzeviers in the seventeenth century to exploit a vogue for miniature editions, whereby they found they could reduce their total costs of paper and production by about 75 per cent.[26]

The direct costs of book production, then, were printing paper (often about 75 per cent of the total in the sixteenth century, dropping to about 50 per cent by the eighteenth), wages (nearly all the rest), and supplies such as ink and candles. Rent, interest on capital, and replacement and maintenance of plant also added to the costs of production, but printers of the hand-press period were rarely skilled in cost accounting and did not include any accurate assessment of overheads in their financial calculations. Even Plantin, whose early partners kept elaborate books in double entry, did not calculate his actual overheads in fixing the prices of his products, while most other printers of the hand-press period, whose account books were generally simple journals of payments and receipts, were obliged to guess.

Printers' selling prices were therefore arrived at by rules of thumb that had proved themselves in practice. When the printer of a book was also its publisher (to use the modern term) he would fix a retail price that would cover production costs, overheads and profit, the discounts he would have to allow the trade, and risks such as slow turnover, loss in transit, and bad debts. This meant a retail price that was at least double the unit production cost, but there were also market factors to be taken into account—especially

[23] De Roover, F. E., 'Cost accounting in the sixteenth century', *Studies in costing*, ed. Solomons, D., London 1952, p. 64.
[24] Gaskell, P., *The decline of the common press*, Cambridge University Ph.D. thesis 2902, 1956, pp. 40-4 and app. C.
[25] De Roover, F. E., loc. cit.   [26] Martin, H. J., op. cit., i, p. 315.

the anticipated demand—and printer-publishers more often found it expedient to fix a retail price that was three or four times the cost of production (as Plantin sometimes did in the sixteenth century and as the Oxford University Press did in the seventeenth).[27]

When on the other hand a printer was employed by a publisher or publishers, which became increasingly common in the seventeenth century and was the normal practice in the eighteenth, he neither supplied the paper nor undertook any serious publishing risks. This meant that he had only to cover his own costs, overheads, and profit, and it was customary from the later seventeenth century (and perhaps earlier) for English printers to charge their customers labour costs plus 50 per cent;[28] French printers in the eighteenth century charged labour plus 75 per cent.[29] It was then up to the publisher to meet the costs of paper and of such things as editorial fees, and to settle the retail margin; and the printer became the publisher's dependant.

In England in the earlier sixteenth century books retailed at around $0.5d.$ a sheet;[30] and in 1598, when English production costs were characteristically in the range $0.15d.–0.25d.$ per sheet including paper, the Stationers' Company laid down maximum retail prices for ordinary books of $0.5d.$ a sheet for books set in pica and english type, and $0.67d.$ for those set in brevier and long primer.[31] The evidence is not very full, but sixteenth-century English retail prices may have been something like three times the cost of production. Books printed on the continent, where type and paper were cheaper than they were in England, cost rather less. Plantin, whose production costs in the 1560s were only about $0.125d.$ per sheet at the current rate of exchange, retailed some of his books (even those in small type) at no more than $0.25d.$ a sheet;[32] while a French edict of 1571 set the maximum price of Latin textbooks in large type at 3 deniers a sheet, then worth about $0.33d.$ sterling.[33]

Production costs of English books in the early and middle eighteenth century (when English printers, using native type and paper, became fully competitive with the continental trade) were usually around $0.5d.$ a sheet including paper, varying in the range $0.35d.–0.65d.$ according to the size

[27] Voet, L., 'The making of books in the Renaissance', *Printing and graphic arts*, x, 1966, p. 60; Johnson, J., and Gibson, S., *Print and privilege at Oxford to the year 1700*, Oxford 1946, pp. 147–8.

[28] Philip, I. G., *William Blackstone and the reform of the Oxford University Press*, Oxford 1957, p. 30.

[29] Mellottée, P., *Histoire économique de l'imprimerie*, i, Paris 1905, pp. 451–2.

[30] Bennett, H. S., *English books & readers 1475 to 1557*, Cambridge 1952, pp. 224–34.

[31] Plant, M., *The English book trade*, 2nd ed., London 1965, p. 221; Greg, W. W., and Boswell, E., *Records of the court of the Stationers' Company 1576–1602*, London 1930, pp. 58–9.

[32] Voet, L., op. cit., pp. 60–1.

[33] Pottinger, D. T., *The French book trade in the ancien régime 1500–1791*, Cambridge Mass. 1958, p. 205.

of the type, the quality of the paper, and the length of the run.[34] At the same time the retail price was normally about 2·5*d.* a sheet; it could be as little as 0·67*d.* per sheet of a cheaply-produced, popular book, and as much as 4*d.* a sheet (or even more) of a small luxury edition.[35] Thus the eighteenth-century retail price in England was about five times the cost of production, which is much the same margin as modern publishers allow.

Although retail prices could never be fixed in the hand-press period— it was always open to individual retailers to alter them—it is clear that there was considerable uniformity in pricing practice, even in the sixteenth century. There could of course be no one price for a book outside its place of origin, because the retail price had to include the cost of transport; but in general, retailers, who calculated their prices by the sheet, were sufficiently competitive to charge comparable prices all over Europe. To help with the calculations, French, Spanish, and Italian printers of the sixteenth and early seventeenth centuries often printed a note of the total number of sheets in a book on its title-page (a practice which was rare in England and Germany).[36]

By the early eighteenth century, the English book trade was sufficiently well organized to enable publishers and booksellers to advertise the prices of their wares, sometimes on the title-pages; though even then retailers would occasionally offer a discount, or lower the price if sales were going badly. Prices were still calculated by the sheet. Analysis of the advertised retail prices of 127 books printed by Ackers for various London publishers in the 1730s and 1740s shows a median price of 2·4*d.* per sheet with relatively little variation. The shorter books (under 10 sheets) were less uniformly priced than the longer ones, partly because of a greater tendency to price them in whole pence per sheet. Yet the standard deviation was only 0·63*d.* per sheet for the shorter books, and 0·50*d.* for those of 10 sheets and over; and it will be remembered that these prices were set by the various publishers, not by the one printer.[37]

PUBLISHING AND BOOKSELLING[38]

The traders involved in the production and distribution of a book have always been (1) a publisher (by which is meant one who owns or controls a text and who finances its production as a printed book); (2) a printer;

---

[34] There is copious evidence in the surviving ledgers of Bowyer, Ackers, and Strahan.

[35] The range for Foulis Press books in the mid eighteenth century was 0·67*d.*–3·5*d.* a sheet; by the end of the century a Foulis luxury edition was offered for 2*s.* 3*d.* a sheet; Gaskell, P., *A bibliography of the Foulis Press*, London 1964, pp. 53–4.

[36] W. A. Jackson in *The Harvard Library bulletin*, 1954, pp. 96–102, 363–4, and in *The Library*, xvi, 1961, pp. 197–201.

[37] Analysed from McKenzie, D. F., and Ross, J. C., *A ledger of Charles Ackers*, Oxford 1968, app. I.

[38] See the bibliography, pp. 401–2.

(3) a wholesale distributor; and (4) a number of retail booksellers. Now-adays there is a clear three-part division of the book trade into publisher-wholesalers, printers, and retailers, but in the hand-press period the functions of book traders overlapped to a much greater extent.

In the sixteenth century the English book trade was centred in London, and consisted chiefly of publishers (usually operating in small syndicates) who wholesaled their own books, but who were also retail booksellers handling a general stock, not all of their own publishing; printers, who were frequently members of publishing syndicates, and who generally had a retail shop as well; and retail stationers who would be likely to purvey both new and second-hand books and a variety of other goods. There were also binders, with or without a retail shop; wholesale stationers specializing in paper; and publisher-retailers specializing in the foreign trade. Apart from the university presses, there were no printers and scarcely any publishers in the provinces after the 1550s, only retailers (again trading in other goods as well as books and stationery) and retailer-binders.[38a] (It is confusing that both publishers and retailers were known indifferently as booksellers, and that any book trader might be referred to as a stationer.)

These arrangements did not alter fundamentally during the remainder of the hand-press period. From the later seventeenth century some printing and publishing moved into the provinces; the large London firms (especially the printer-publishers) got bigger, and there was tendency towards specialization in publishing; publishing syndicates became larger and better organized; and a larger proportion of retailers were able to concentrate on selling books and stationery. Publishers in the modern sense, however, did not emerge until the nineteenth century.

Partnership in publication is as old as printing. Book production makes great demands on capital resources before any return can be had, while distribution involves the publisher in the probability that turnover will be slow and the possibility that he may be able to sell no more than a fraction of an edition; it was obviously sensible to share both the outlay and the risk. Early partnerships appear to have been *ad hoc* arrangements between brother tradesmen, involving constantly changing combinations of partners. From the 1680s, however, initially as a result of the ending of protected copyright (see pp. 183–4), several large publishers formed a more perma-nent association which came to be known as the 'conger' (the name being variously derived from *congerere*, 'to bring together', and from the big eel which gobbles up the small fry). The first known conger, which survived until the early eighteenth century, was established to protect the copyrights of its individual members, which it did by controlling the greater part of the

---

[38a] For a list of English provincial presses up to the 1550s, see *Bibliographica*, ii, 1896, pp. 23–46.

wholesale trade in books. The conger system was found to be a profitable one to its members, and congers dominated the London book trade for the first half of the eighteenth century; in these later congers copyrights were usually jointly owned, and books were simultaneously published and distributed by the association.[39]

The early eighteenth century also saw the development of trade subscription sales, whereby publishers sold copyrights and blocks of copies of their books to wholesalers or large retailers, the price varying with the size of the block. By the 1750s the conger system was superseded by sales of this sort, dominated by the largest publishers; shared publication continued to be the resort of the smaller publisher-retailers for the rest of the eighteenth century, but separation between publishing and retailing was already beginning to take place.[40]

Publication by private subscription (which was quite different from distribution by trade subscription) was essentially a method of persuading customers to help with the cost of producing a book by offering them a substantial discount if they would agree to pay all or (more usually) part of the price in advance. Authors who could not find publishers to take their work by way of trade collected private subscriptions to finance their books in the mid sixteenth century, but it was not until the second half of the seventeenth century that the trade began to use private subscription as a means of finding capital for particularly costly works. Unable to find a bookseller who would publish his own costly *Guide into tongues*, John Minsheu was granted a Royal Patent in 1611 to collect contributions from private persons, and when the book was published in 1617 it included a list of over 360 subscribers.[41] An early example of commercial publication by subscription was Tonson's folio *Paradise lost* of 1688, and it too included a list of subscribers.[42] Printing for the author, which reached a peak in the 1730s, was not always as successful as the long subscription lists implied, since some subscribers might not complete their payments.[42a]

Serial (or part) publication was introduced in England in the later seventeenth century, appropriately enough by Joseph Moxon for the first appearance of his classic trade manual *Mechanick exercises*, which came out in 38 monthly parts at 6*d.* in the period 1678–83.[43] Serial publication was doubly attractive to the publisher of works which might be expected to appeal to

[39] Hodgson, N., and Blagden, C., *The notebook of Thomas Bennet and Henry Clements (1686–1719)*, Oxford 1956, ch. 3. Very important unpublished sources are Graham Pollard's Sandars Lectures for 1959, 'The English market for printed books' (typescript in Cambridge University Library); and Terry Belanger's Columbia University thesis 'Booksellers' sales of copyright', 1970.

[40] Hodgson, N., and Blagden, C., op. cit., p. 100.

[41] S.T.C. 17944.   [42] Wing M2146-7.

[42a] Maslen, K., 'Printing for the author', *The Library*, xxvii, 1972, pp. 302-9.

[43] Wing M3013-4; Moxon, J., op. cit., pp. xlv-xlix.

a wide audience, but which cost more than ordinary people were accustomed to spend on books. In the first place, production costs were met while they were being incurred; and in the second, it encouraged the poorer purchaser to buy by instalments a book which he could not (or would not) afford all at once. The second point is well made by Moxon's book, the total price of which was 19*s.*, about a week's wages for the artisans to whom it was chiefly addressed. The printer might also take the opportunity to adjust the edition size to the demand as the work progressed.

After a rather slow start, serially-published 'number books' became widely popular in the eighteenth century, reaching a peak in the 1730s with the general adoption of weekly rather than monthly publication of parts. They have generally survived as bound volumes, not obviously different from books published in the ordinary way; each number was normally made up of one or more whole sheets, sometimes with a reference figure printed in the direction line of the first page.[44]

It is not usually possible to sell more than a few copies of any one book at a single bookshop, and it has always been necessary to split editions up so that they can be retailed by as many booksellers as possible. Throughout the hand-press period publisher-wholesalers sold, bought, and exchanged blocks of copies of books for distribution both through their own retail shops and to other retailers or travelling salesmen. Unless the distance was short, the books travelled in sheets, unbound, packed up in chests or barrels.[45]

The flourishing international trade in books, which had its roots in the manuscript period, was largely between wholesalers, who dealt with each other either by post or by meeting at the great European book fairs, such as those of Frankfurt and Leipzig.[46] So far as possible the international traders exchanged books, but sometimes the balance was unequal and accounts were settled in money; the uncompetitive English book trade at the end of the seventeenth century imported twice as many books as it was able to sell abroad. Some of the early printer-publishers sent out salesmen to retail their wares in other countries.[47]

Books were advertised in the fifteenth and sixteenth centuries by means of printed publishers' lists, which were carried about by salesmen and were probably put up in retail shops; such lists were usually unpriced, since the retail price of a book partly depended on how far it had been

[44] Wiles, R. M., *Serial publication in England before 1750*, Cambridge 1957.

[45] Taubert, S., *Bibliopola*, Hamburg and London 1966, ii, p. 21 gives an illustration of a sixteenth-century German book-trader unpacking a barrel of books.

[46] Communications were poor; consignments between Antwerp and Rome could take nine months on the journey, and between Antwerp and Madrid a year or more—on one occasion more than *five* years (1625–30); Voet, L., *The golden compasses*, ii.

[47] See the bibliography, pp. 401–2; and especially Pollard, H. G., and Ehrman, A., *The distribution of books by catalogue*, privately printed, Cambridge 1965.

brought. They were followed by book-fair catalogues (from the later sixteenth century), retailers' catalogues, and collections of trade announcements, of which the most important English example was the series of 'Term catalogues' issued from 1668 to 1711. The title-pages of sixteenth- and seventeenth-century books were sometimes posted up in the street as advertisements; booksellers' lists were printed in books from about 1650, and were inserted at the ends of books from about 1685; and books were advertised in periodicals from the 1690s if not before, some retailers also using trade cards, handbills, book-labels, etc. A special form of advertisement was the printed Proposal, which developed in England in the mid seventeenth century from earlier notices of forthcoming publications, and which invited subscriptions for expensive books.[48]

AUTHORSHIP, COPYRIGHT, AND CENSORSHIP

Authors of the sixteenth century got little return for their work from the book trade. Agreements which ensured that the author got a return for his work proportional to its sales were virtually unknown, and substantial payments of any sort—enough, say, to support an author for a year—were most uncommon. Authorship did become a profession in the later sixteenth century, but with its income derived from patrons, not from the trade. There was nevertheless a symbiotic relationship between authors and publishers; they needed each other, and on the whole they worked together in amity.[49]

The root of the matter was that authors' copyright did not exist in practice before 1710.[50] Previously the only rights in copy were those granted as monopolies by royal patent, and those of a stationer to the exclusive and perpetual enjoyment of a copy which he had been the first to publish or had lawfully acquired. True, an author could sell an unpublished book to a publisher, or could be employed to write one for him, but he normally had to sell it outright for whatever the publisher chose to pay in cash or in printed copies. Once a book was out its copyright belonged to its trade publisher, so that if a pirate got hold of a text and published it before its legitimate 'owner' did, the pirate secured the copyright. No wonder that publishers would not pay much for a copy; under the circumstances Milton, who got £5 down for *Paradise lost* in 1667, with the promise of £5 more if the first edition sold 1,300 copies and of £5 each for a second and third edition (really a sort of royalty agreement) was well treated.[51]

---

[48] Pollard, H. G., and Ehrman, A., op. cit., *passim*.
[49] See the three volumes of H. S. Bennett's *English books and readers*, Cambridge 1952, 1965, 1970.
[50] See the bibliography, pp. 401–2; and especially Greg, W. W., *Some aspects and problems of London publishing between 1550 and 1650*, Oxford 1956, and Collins, A. S., *Authorship in the days of Johnson*, London 1927. [51] Parker, W. R., *Milton, a biography*, Oxford 1968, i, p. 601.

Publishers were supposed to enter their copies before publication in the register of the Stationers' Company, in order both to ease official control and to secure their own rights. For most of the sixteenth and seventeenth centuries, however, only two copies out of three were in fact entered, copyright being effectively secured by the fact of publication.[52]

All this was changed in the eighteenth century.[52a] The Licensing Act of 1662, in attempting to subject the press to censorship, had in effect protected its privileges, including publishers' copyrights. The Act was finally allowed to lapse in 1695 and, deprived of statutory support, the Stationers' Company was unable to protect its members' rights against those who chose to infringe them; it was indeed in anticipation of this development that the first wholesaling conger had been formed in the 1680s. The stationers petitioned for a copyright act, and in 1709 they got one. The new Act, which received the royal assent in 1710, was not entirely to their taste, however, for it ruled that copyright in a new book belonged not to its publisher but to its author.[53]

This immediately enabled a popular author to obtain, in one way or another, substantial payment for his work—Pope for instance got more than £5,000 for the first edition of his translation of the *Iliad* (1715–20),[54] quite a different matter from Milton's remuneration of half a century earlier— and the eighteenth century saw the development of various forms of agreement between author and publisher. Outright sale of copyright continued to be very common, but the prices given to popular authors rose steadily as the century progressed: Swift got £200 for *Gulliver's travels* in 1726, Fielding £1,000 for *Amelia* in 1752, and William Robertson the huge sum of £4,500 for *The history of Charles V* in 1769.[55] Alternatively copyright might be leased for a limited period of time—Pope was paid £200 for a year's lease of the *Essay on man*, 1733[56]—or for a particular edition; or the author and publisher might agree to share the profits, with or without a reversion of the copyright to the author. Thus Johnson, writing to the printer-publisher Strahan in 1759, suggested various agreements for the two volumes of *Rasselas*: 'The bargain which I made with Mr Johnson [W. Johnston, bookseller] was seventy-five pounds (or guineas) a volume, and twenty-five pounds for the second edition. I will sell this either at that price [i.e. outright] or for sixty, the first edition of which he shall himself fix the number, and the property then to revert to me, or for forty pounds,

---

[52] Greg, W. W., op. cit., ch. 4.

[52a] See the note at the foot of p. 185, opposite.

[53] Hanson, L., *Government and the press 1695–1763*, Oxford 1936 (repr. 1967), ch. 2; Plant, M., *The English book trade*, 2nd ed., London 1965, ch. 5.

[54] Nichols, J., *Literary anecdotes*, i, London 1812, p. 77 (quoting Johnson's *Life* of Pope).

[55] Collins, A. S., op. cit., pp. 33–4.   [56] Ibid., p. 133.

and I share the profit, that is retain half the copy.'[57] In the event Johnson got £100 for the copyright of both volumes, plus £25 for the second edition, which was £50 less than he had hoped to get for an outright sale.

Finally, a book might be published for the author on commission, the use of trade facilities being paid for as a percentage on each copy handled; this was said to be unpopular with the booksellers, but it was common ᵓough, generally financed by subscription. Failing to sell the first two volumes of *Tristram Shandy* to Dodsley for £50 in 1759, Sterne printed them at his own expense in York, and Dodsley sold them in London for the usual discount; they were so successful that Sterne was then able to sell the copyright of the same volumes to Dodsley for £250.[58]

A further result of the copyright Act of 1709 was that local piracy was virtually eliminated, although there was still damaging competition from piratical publishers overseas (especially in Ireland and Holland). Publishers still hoped to establish monopolies in individual books that were out of copyright, but this was eventually disallowed by a legal ruling of 1774. Thereafter only the Bible and the Prayer Book survived as privileged texts, as indeed they do still.

In meeting the stationers' demands for incorporation in 1557, the government provided itself with machinery for regulating the press, with the aim of preventing the publication of seditious books. To this end printing presses were limited in number and, with the exception of the university presses, were concentrated in the hands of the gild in London. The Company was given, and exercised in the later sixteenth and earlier seventeenth centuries, a right of search in order to seek out and destroy illegal presses and their products. Seditious books continued to appear, nevertheless, both from secret presses in England moving furtively from hideout to hideout, and from presses overseas which worked for the English catholics.[59]

A final attempt to control the output of the English press was embodied in the Licensing Act of 1662, whereby every publication was to be censored and awarded an official imprimatur. But the new regulations were both unpopular and ineffective, and were not renewed after 1695. From then on there was no organized general censorship of books in England.[60]

NOTE. The author's position was not so completely changed by the Copyright Act of 1709-10 as this section suggests. Publishers retained *de facto* copyright of most books until the 1760s, the big publishers being very much in control of the trade.

[57] Johnson, S., *Letters*, ed. Chapman, R. W., Oxford 1952, i, p. 124.

[58] Monkman, K., 'The bibliography of the early editions of *Tristram Shandy*', *The Library*, xxv, 1970, p. 18.

[59] Bennett, H. S., *English books and readers 1558 to 1603*, Cambridge 1965, ch. 3.

[60] Hanson, L., op. cit., *passim*.

BOOK PRODUCTION

THE MACHINE-PRESS PERIOD
1800–1950

Introduction

THE end of the eighteenth century saw a sharply rising demand for cheap print, associated with increases in population and in literacy which occurred all over Europe. Variations in demand became ever more extreme, and printers increased the scale of their operations, expanding their plant, taking on a larger proportion of cheap apprentice labour, and freely adjusting the number of journeymen in employment.

Next came the machines.[1] Hand printing was already an efficient means of mass-producing books, and its fundamental processes were not altered in any important way until the electronic revolution of the mid twentieth century; nevertheless it proved possible in the nineteenth century to speed the various processes by applying steam power to presswork, to binding, and to composition, in that order. The resulting vast increases in productivity led to further organizational changes. Printing houses became larger and more heavily capitalized, although security of employment was not achieved until late in the century; while publishers, now specialists linking the various elements of the book trade, grew in financial strength.

Although a nineteenth-century printing factory, with its hundreds of hands and its dozens of clattering machines, looked very different from a two-press shop of craft days, the technology of book production had really changed very little. It was usual until the introduction of composing machines in the last quarter of the century for individual metal types, just like Gutenberg's, to be set by hand and imposed in the traditional patterns; and it was not until the mid twentieth century that any appreciable number of books were printed otherwise than by inking the face of the metal, pressing sheets of paper on to it, and then folding and sewing them to make the sections of books. Not surprisingly books continued to look much the same as before. Paper was machine-made and smoother-surfaced; there was a wide range of new type-faces; presswork was cleaner; and an increasing number of books were cased in cloth. But these were minor alterations to what was basically the same thing, and it would be unwise to undertake the bibliographical investigation even of nineteenth- and twentieth-century books without a thorough understanding· of the book production of the hand-press period.

---

[1] In nineteenth-century Britain 'machines' were powered printing-presses of any sort, while 'presses' were hand-presses of wood or metal; in America, however, they were called 'power-presses' and 'hand-presses' respectively.

Nevertheless some of the printer's methods were changed to accommodate the new machinery, and several new processes were developed, which will be considered in the following sections. Lack of materials limits what can be said about printing practices, especially those of continental Europe, during the nineteenth century. What follows refers chiefly to the situation in Britain and the United States, which were in any case the originators of most of the technological advances of the machine-press period. During the earlier part of the nineteenth century, American printers largely followed English precedents, as they had done throughout the eighteenth. By 1850, however, the Americans were developing a new and advanced printing technology of their own, which in turn was imitated in England.

Survival and Change

THE EARLY-NINETEENTH-CENTURY BOOK HOUSE

Very few machine presses were used for book printing during the first quarter of the nineteenth century, and most book-printing businesses were really enlargements of their eighteenth-century predecessors. In 1826 the Glasgow University Printing Office had 35 compositors' frames, 17 iron hand-presses, and 8,800 kg. of type (there was also a stereotype foundry to supplement the modest allowance of 520 kg. of type per press). This office, which produced about 170 printed reams per week, was thus similar in size to Plantin's establishment in 1574, which employed 20 compositors, 16 presses, and 1,300 kg. of type per press. But whereas Plantin directed the foremost printing house in Europe, the Glasgow University office was no more than one amongst many shops of like size.[1]

COMPOSITION

The hand compositor's equipment and method of picking up type remained essentially unchanged in the machine-press period. Text type continued to be laid in pairs of cases in Britain and America, but a special individual case was developed in the mid nineteenth century in both countries to hold small founts of italic and decorated types.[2] This was the double or job case. It was of approximately the same dimensions over-all as each of the twin cases of the divided lay, but the whole of the lower-case pattern of boxes was squeezed into two-thirds of its width on the left-hand side, and half the upper-case pattern went into the remaining third. With the general adoption of composing machinery after 1900 many printers gave up the divided lay altogether, and kept all their founders' type, and small Monotype founts for correction, in double cases.

During the hand-press period, as we have seen, compositors seem normally to have worked on their own account, each man setting, imposing, and correcting by the sheet, the half-sheet, or the forme, and each writing his own bill for his work. Several compositors would work on a book, but only rarely would a man set less than a half-sheet or a forme at a time.

Individual working continued in the nineteenth century, though more commonly in the small houses than in the large. There was a tendency to

[1] *Specimens of types, and inventory of printing materials, belonging to the Glasgow University Printing Office*, [Glasgow 1826].

[2] Communicated from work in progress by Mr. L. A. Pryor. An American double-case lay is illustrated in *Studies in bibliography*, xxii, 1969, p. [134].

divide the work into smaller units, influenced perhaps by the companion-ship system and the use of long galleys (see pp. 194–5). The following routine for individual composition was usual in small English offices in the later nineteenth century.[3] The overseer handed out a taking of several leaves of manuscript to each compositor, and gave instructions as to type for distribution, margins, and length of page. When the compositor who had the taking from the beginning of the book had set all his copy he divided it into pages, and handed any extra lines beyond the last full page to the man who was setting the next taking; and then himself went on with setting a taking from later in the book. The second man used these extra lines at the beginning of his first page, and he too handed on any extra lines beyond his last full page to the compositor who had the third taking of manuscript; and so on. Each such transfer of lines was recorded in a line book as a credit and a debit to the compositors concerned, and the balance was added to or subtracted from each man's bill. Imposition was the responsibility of the man who had set most pages in a sheet.

In the larger British printing houses, however, individual piecework composition was superseded during the first half of the century by the companionship system, whereby a team of piecework compositors, led by one of their number, co-operated in the setting of a book and submitted a single bill for the work, the proceeds of which they then divided amongst themselves. A somewhat similar system had already been described in the *Encyclopédie* (s.v. *paquet*) in 1765 and was used at the Société Typographique de Neuchâtel in the 1770s.[4] Here from three to five piecework compositors (*paquetiers*) set up the text of a book that was wanted in a hurry, probably simultaneously, and delivered it to a time hand (*ouvrier en conscience*) who made up the pages and imposed the formes; payment for the whole job was made to the time hand, who paid the *paquetiers* according to the number of *paquets* equalling an octavo page that each one had set.

English companionships (or ships as they were usually called) were first described in Stower's manual of 1808,[5] but had probably been developed in late-eighteenth-century London for dealing with rush jobs in the larger printing offices. In the early days they differed from the French system in that the team leader, or clicker[6] was normally a piece-worker elected by his fellows, although later in the nineteenth century he was often appointed by the management.

<hr>

[3] Described in a number of late-nineteenth-century manuals, e.g. Gould, J., *The letter-press printer*, 6th ed., London [1892], pp. 35–8.

[4] *Encyclopédie*, xi, 'Neufchastel' 1765, p. 882; account books of the S.T.N. for the period 1779–82.

[5] Stower, C., *The printer's grammar*, London 1808, pp. 465–8.

[6] The term was originally late-seventeenth-century slang for a tout, and then for a foreman, in the shoe trade; it referred to the clicking of leather-cutting shears, not to a compositor's activities (*O.E.D.*).

There were two ways of organizing the ship.[7] In one, called working on time or in pocket, the clicker received copy and instructions from the overseer and divided the work among his companions. Each man then did whatever was most useful at each stage of the job, under the clicker's direction. A single bill was made out, and each man took an equal share of the payment, regardless of how many pages he had set; deductions were made only for failings such as unpunctuality.

The other method of organizing the ship, known as working upon lines, was more like the eighteenth-century French system, and appears to have been the one that was devised for use in cases of urgency; by the later nineteenth century, however, it was the normal arrangement in English houses for all classes of work. Again, the clicker received the copy, passed on the overseer's instructions about letter for distribution and typographical style, and handed out takings of manuscript. This time, however, he took care to see that copy was distributed fairly, and he kept an account of the number of lines that each man set, both in a line-book and by marking the copy. He himself set the headlines, etc., and made up pages as matter was delivered to him in galleys by the compositors. Imposition was then carried out either by the clicker, or by the men in turn. Formes were laid up after printing by the men who had imposed them, and matter for distribution was returned as far as possible to the compositors who had set it. Again one bill was made out for the whole job (or for the whole week's work by the companionship), but the clicker paid each man according to what he had set, keeping for himself a share equal to that of the most productive hand (a system that was often abused, for a grasping clicker would see to it that the fastest compositor got the easiest work). A single companionship of this sort would often have three or four works in production at the same time in a busy house, so that its members rarely stood idle for want of copy.[8]

Nineteenth-century American compositors organized themselves in very similar companionships, complete with clickers. The ship working in pocket was known but, according to Thomas MacKellar's *American printer* of 1866,[9] the more usual form was a variety of the ship working upon lines, in which the clicker set the headlines, etc., but the men made up the pages as they went along, and took it in turns to impose the formes. MacKellar mentions the companionship system in connection with hurried work, but

[7] Their development may be followed in Hansard, T. C., *Typographia*, London 1825, pp. 540-7; Savage, W., *A dictionary of the art of printing*, London 1841, pp. 175-7; and Southward, J., *A dictionary of typography*, 2nd ed., London 1875, pp. 16-18.

[8] But when work was short the members of a ship would 'throw for it' (Hansard, T. C., op. cit., p. 543) or 'figure for it' (Clarendon Press, late nineteenth century); both being ways of drawing lots, using pieces of type.

[9] McKellar, T., *The American printer*, Philadelphia 1873, pp. 204-8; first ed. 1866.

there is evidence that it was also used for ordinary work by the middle of the century. For instance, bibliographical investigation of two novels by Hawthorne has indicated that companionship systems were operated in the Boston printing house of Hobart and Robins in the early 1850s. In one case (*The house of the seven gables*, set in 1851) the marking of the manuscript copy suggests that each compositor, on reaching the end of the last type-page of his take, would continue setting up to the end of the current paragraph and would hand over the extra lines of type to the man who was setting the next take (who would have begun at the beginning of the first new paragraph in his copy). The other novel (*The Blithesdale romance*, set in 1852) was divided into rather longer takes, and in this case it appears that each member of the companionship, which included some of the same men as before, on reaching the end of the last type-page of a take, would stop setting and would hand over the marked final leaf of the copy to the next man; and that the next man, who had begun setting at the head of the next leaf of copy, would himself set the intervening lines.[10]

Printers of the hand-press period, as we saw, composed books by pages and took the first proof after the pages had been made up and imposed, not before. A different practice was developed in the newspaper offices of the later eighteenth century. There work was set and charged for by galleys-full of 5,000 long primer ens, and probably (though not certainly) slip proofs were taken from the type while it was still in galley, a practice that was normal in news work by the 1820s.[11] But, although proofing in galley offered the advantage that substantial corrections could be made to the type without the running-over that was necessary once the matter was made up into pages, the practice does not appear to have been common in book printing until the later nineteenth century.

Savage, who was careful to describe the latest developments in his *Dictionary* of 1841, made it clear that, although compositors working in companionships would often set more than a page before the type was made up and would use special large galleys for the purpose, slip proofs were not taken except in printing 'encyclopaedias, dictionaries of arts or sciences, and similar work, which frequently undergo great alterations in the proofs'.[12] Again, at the Harper establishment in New York, which was perhaps technologically the most advanced printing house in the world in the 1850s, books were first proofed after imposition, not in galley.[13]

There were early instances of galley-proofing, but they appear to have

[10] Bowers, F. T., 'Old wine in new bottles', *Editing nineteenth century texts*, ed. Robson, J. M., Toronto 1967, pp. 15-16.

[11] Howe, E., *The London compositor*, London 1947, pp. 57, 61, 177, ch. 15.

[12] Savage, W., op. cit., p. 774; see also pp. 249, 754.

[13] Abbott, J., *The Harper establishment*, New York 1855 (repr. Hamden 1956), p. 67.

been exceptional. A book printer in York seems to have been making slip proofs as early as 1773;[14] and Dickens, who corrected his part-issues heavily in proof, occasionally worked on slips: the first number of *David Copperfield* was sent to him in 1849 as slip proofs, although the remaining numbers were sent as page proofs.[15] In London a general change seems to have taken place in the 1870s and 1880s. In his *Dictionary* of 1870-1, Southward illustrated a galley press, saying that such presses were to be found 'in all newspaper offices, and in most bookwork houses',[16] but in the first edition of his manual, 1882, he makes it clear that it remained more usual in book-work to take first proofs after imposition, not before.[17] By 1892, however, the situation was reversed, Powell's revision of Southward making it equally clear that by then first proofs of books were made in slip or page before, not after, imposition.[18]

Piecework payment for composition continued throughout the nineteenth century, the rates per 1,000 ens set and corrected (or per 1,000 ems in America) varying with the difficulty of different sorts of work. The basic rate in London was $4\frac{1}{2}d.$ a thousand ens in 1785, and rose to $7\frac{1}{2}d.$ by 1891; apprentices would earn up to about half the journeyman's rate.[19] Fluctuations in the flow of work appear to have made it difficult for English compositors to average more than 1,000 ens per hour even when they were in regular employment, though some weeks were better than others; higher rates were possible, skilled American compositors being able to keep up 3,000 ens per hour in favourable circumstances.[20] 'Stab' (establishment) hands on weekly wages were also employed in the composing room, but more frequently in the late than in the early nineteenth century, and always in relatively small numbers; they worked the full week (which in English printing houses was about 72 hours in 1800 and about 55 hours in 1900). Time hands were employed on such jobs as authors' corrections, and were paid about as much as the average piecework hand actually earned.[21]

[14] Gaskell, P., *The first editions of William Mason*, Cambridge 1951, p. 18.

[15] Butt, J., and Tillotson, K., *Dickens at work*, London 1963, p. 21. (Confusingly for us, Dickens referred to his sheets of manuscript as 'slips'.)

[16] Southward, J., *A dictionary of typography*, London 1871, s.v. 'galley press'; the entry was repeated in the second edition of 1875.

[17] Southward, J., *Practical printing*, London 1882, pp. 154, 426-7. Southward also showed a slip-galley 'used principally in book work' which was two-sided and, as he said, could not be locked up for proofing, unlike his three-sided newspaper slip-galley (pp. 51-2).

[18] Southward, J., and Powell, A., *Practical printing*, London [1892], pp. 323-5 (a detailed schedule of the stages of proofing). See also Hargreaves, G. D., ' "Correcting in the slip": the development of galley proofs', *The Library*, xxvi, 1971, pp. 295-311 (which appeared while the present work was in proof and comes to the same general conclusions).

[19] Howe, E., op. cit., pp. 73, 328.

[20] Abbott, J., op. cit., p. 60.

[21] Scurfield, G., *A stickful of nonpareil*, privately printed, Cambridge 1956, pp. 21, 25.

IMPOSITION

The schemes of imposition that were used with the iron hand-presses of the nineteenth century were generally the same as those of the hand-press period. Most books were still folios, quartos, octavos, and duodecimos, the predominance of octavo becoming steadily more marked. Apart from the machine-press schemes described below (pp. 258–60), the only new imposition for ordinary bookwork was duodecimo without cutting, whereby a duodecimo sheet could be folded and sewn without the need to remove and quire-in an offcut. Duodecimo without cutting was known in the hand-press period—it was shown in an English manual of 1770[22]—but there appear to be no early records of its use; the trouble was that the top edges of four of the leaves were formed by the edge of the sheet, and the deckle edges of hand-made paper were frequently uneven. The appearance of machine-made paper in the early nineteenth century, with its clean-cut edges, made duodecimo without cutting more attractive, and the imposition is mentioned in all the nineteenth-century manuals. Fig. 70 shows a sheet printed in this way as it would appear on the open tympan of an iron hand-press; the position of the watermark on the border of the sheet was common at this period, but almost any position was possible.

The traditional 23-letter Latin alphabet remained the usual form for signing the gatherings in the majority of nineteenth-century books in English (and for a good number of those printed since 1900); small capitals were more commonly employed than large, and there was a tendency to drop all signatures after the first of each gathering. At the same time the practice of signing the gatherings with series of arabic figures rather than letters, which had scarcely been seen since the 1480s, was revived. A few forward-looking eighteenth-century typographers—Fournier, Bodoni—had occasionally used numerals as signatures, but numerals were unlikely to appeal to the trade so long as press-figures were used. Figures for signatures became gradually more common from the 1820s, but they did not become the normal form until the present century, when they were frequently associated with codes which identified the particular book to which each gathering belonged. The American stereotypers who signed sets of plates for more than one format (see p. 206) might use, say, letter signatures for the octavo series and figure signatures for the duodecimo.[23] Chittenden's edition of Newton's *Principia* (New York, *c*. 1846), which is in 8s, is signed numerically on the *last* recto of each gathering.

[22] Luckombe, P., *A concise history of . . . printing*, London 1770, pp. 413–14.
[23] *The Library*, iii, 1948–9, pp. 58–62, 224–9; vii, 1952, p. 134.

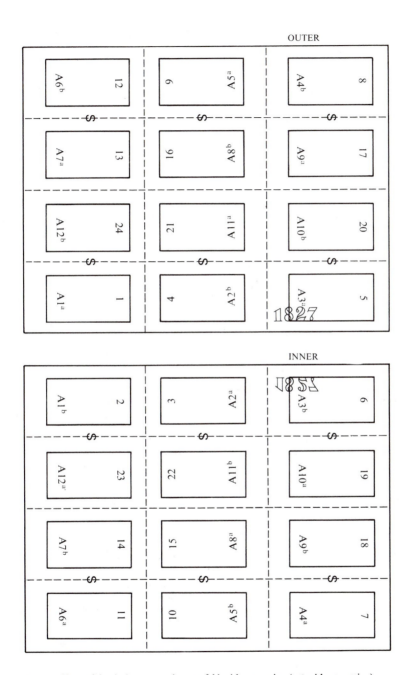

FIG. 70. Sheet of duodecimo, or twelves, to fold without cutting (12° without cutting).

IRON HAND-PRESSES

The old common press was a brilliant and deservedly successful invention, but by the end of the eighteenth century its limitations were beginning to seem irksome. There was need for a press that would give an impression sharp enough to do justice to the delicate neo-classic romans, and also one that could meet the rising demand for print by producing considerably more than 250 impressions per hour. Baskerville had achieved a sharp impression in the 1750s with well-built common presses, carefully operated with hard packing in the tympans, but such work could not be produced at speed by ordinary pressmen. Forward-looking printers realized that a machine of great precision was required, accurately made and sufficiently durable to behave predictably at every impression; and they also wanted it to print a whole forme at one pull, for they believed (wrongly, as it turned out) that a single-pull hand-press must work faster than one that had to be pulled twice at each impression.

Several attempts were made towards the end of the eighteenth century to build improved presses of this sort in wooden frames, but none were suitable for every-day use; they were difficult to operate, and the wooden frames were not strong enough to accommodate any large increase in power.[24] In 1800–3, however, Earl Stanhope built a hand press with a full-sized platen in a cast-iron frame, and the problem was solved.[25] The Stanhope, with its iron bed and platen, was rigid and accurate, and its iron frame was strong enough to contain the power of a screw augmented with compound levers. Used with a hard-packed tympan it could produce delicate impressions every time over the whole area of the forme. The only disappointment was the discovery that the extra effort required to work the full-sized platen and raise its counterweight (for there was no elasticity in the frame to return the bar at the end of the pull) tended to cancel out the advantage of only pulling once for each impression, so that its output was not much greater than that of the common press.[26]

The Stanhope and its lever-powered successors (the Columbian, the Albion, the Washington, etc.) were adaptations of the common press and incorporated no radically new principles. The iron press was worked by a

[24] See Chambers, D., 'An improved printing press by Philippe-Denis Pierres', *Journal of the Printing Historical Society*, iii, 1967, pp. 82–92, for an account of one of them; others are described in Gaskell, P., *The decline of the common press*, Cambridge University Ph.D. thesis 2902, 1956, ch. 3.

[25] Hart, H., *Charles Earl Stanhope and the Oxford University Press*, ed. Mosley, J., London 1966, pp. 398–404.

[26] The iron presses were originally praised for their power and precision, not for their productivity. Southward (*Progress in printing*, London 1897, p. 31), thought that iron presses were faster than wooden ones, but gave the top speed of a Columbian or Albion as only 200 impressions per hour. Experiment suggests that there is little to choose between one- and two-pull presses for speed.

FIG. 71. The impression assembly of a royal Stanhope press supplied to the Cambridge University Press in 1813. The power of the bar is augmented by the toggle action of the horizontal connecting rod which runs above the cast-iron staple (or frame) from the axle of the bar to the main screw. The small screw with eye and lock-nut at the end of the connecting rod is used for adjusting the depth of the impression.

team of two pressmen as before, one inking the type by hand for each impression, and the other pulling the usual sort of bar and working a carriage-assembly that had been taken over from the common press with scarcely any alteration. What was new about the iron-presses was their capacity for printing large formes with great delicacy.

The maximum type-area that was normally worked on a common press of the usual size measured about 49 × 39 cm., but early Stanhopes (of royal size) could manage a type-area of 58 × 45 cm.; and by the 1820s a graded series of iron hand-presses was available, in sizes up to double royal which allowed a type-area of 98 × 58 cm.[27]

The delicate 'kiss' impression of the iron presses, made through a hard, dry tympan, required a new sort of make-ready. The soggy tympan of the

[27] *Journal of the Printing Historical Society*, v, 1969, p. 12.

common press had ensured that all the type in the forme made a mark of some sort without special preparation, but now any type that was fractionally lower than the rest would print grey or not at all. The pressmen therefore patched the tympan with overlays of tissue paper wherever the type was low, a process that could take hours for a really uneven forme.[28] Another consequence of using a dry tympan was that ink from the side of the sheet that had been printed first would offset on to the tympan sheet during the printing of the other side, and then back again on to subsequent sheets of the reiteration; this was prevented by the use of set-off sheets, sheets of waste paper that were placed on the tympan behind the sheet being printed and changed as often as necessary, sometimes at each impression.[29] The earliest iron hand-presses were inked with balls in the traditional way, but balls were replaced by hand-rollers from 1813 (see p. 252).

The common press did not vanish overnight on the appearance of the Stanhope, but many—perhaps the majority—of the old machines had been replaced by iron hand-presses in the larger centres of printing by the mid 1820s. Stanhopes, closely followed by Columbians,[30] dominated the market at first, and both designs were manufactured in several European countries; during the later part of the century there was a preference for Albions.[31] Few iron hand-presses were used in America during the first quarter of the nineteenth century—printers there could buy an excellent new version of the common press by Ramage of Philadelphia—but from the 1830s the Washington press enjoyed great success.[32]

Iron hand-presses cost at least three times as much as common presses,[33] but they were extraordinarily durable. Until the middle of the nineteenth century even the larger machine printers kept numbers of iron hand-presses for working short runs, and many of these presses have survived in trade and private use up to the present day, a century or more after they were built.[34]

[28] Make-ready with overlays was also used at this time for fine printing on common presses with hard-packed tympans; Savage, W., *Practical hints on decorative printing*, London 1822, pp. 37–8.

[29] Savage, op. cit., p. 45.

[30] Moran, J., 'The Columbian press', *Journal of the Printing Historical Society*, v, 1969, pp. 1–23.

[31] Stone, R., 'The Albion press', *Journal of the Printing Historical Society*, ii, 1966, pp. 58–73; iii, 1967, pp. 97–9.

[32] Green, R., *The iron hand press in America*, privately printed, Rowayton, Conn. 1948.

[33] *Journal of the Printing Historical Society*, v, 1969, p. 12.

[34] Each make has its devotees. I have worked most types, but have found none to excel a royal Stanhope that was originally supplied to the Cambridge University Press in 1813 (fig. 71).

Plates

STEREOTYPE

It was realized in the hand-press period that, if casts of typeset matter could be made in the form of metal plates and put to press instead of the type itself, it might be possible both to store the setting of a book accurately and economically and to reduce type wear. This was an attractive prospect, since type was the costliest part of a hand-printer's equipment; its replacement was expensive, and few printers could afford to keep any but small books set up in type.

The origins of the process are obscure, but plate-making experiments were certainly carried out at the beginning of the eighteenth century by Johann Müller, a German pastor living in Holland.[1] Plates were made for several substantial books in the period 1701-18, which were probably true stereotypes and which undoubtedly worked; a massive Dutch folio Bible, for instance, was printed from a single set of Müller plates in 1718, in 1728, in 1757, and in 1791. A few years later William Ged of Edinburgh was casting stereotype plates in a plaster mould but, although his process was a practical one—he published a stereotype duodecimo Sallust in 1739 and in 1744—he was unable to overcome the very natural prejudices against it of the compositors and the typefounders.[2] No more was done until the 1780s, when the same process was re-invented in Scotland (by Alexander Tilloch) and in France (by F. I. J. Hoffmann and others); but again few books were printed from plates.[3]

Early stereotyping by the plaster-mould process suffered from two main disadvantages. One was that the moulds, each of which produced only a single plate, had to be made with skill and patience if they were not to damage the type; the other, which was crucial, was that stereotyping was rarely economic for the editions of a few thousand copies to which eighteenth-century printers were normally limited by the costs of hand presswork. It was simply not worth a printer's while to invest in the skill and plant necessary for stereotyping, and to overcome trade resistance, for the sake of increasing his profit on the small proportion of his output that could be in really large editions. Therefore stereotyping never got beyond the experimental stage in the eighteenth century.

[1] Westreenen van Tiellandt, W. H. J. van, *Verslag der naspooringen omtrent . . . der stereotypische drukwijze* (with parallel text in French), 's Gravenhage 1833.

[2] Carter, J. W., 'William Ged and the invention of stereotype', *The Library*, xv, 1960, pp. 161-92; xvi, 1961, pp. 143-5; xviii, 1963, pp. 308-9.

[3] Hart, H., op. cit., pp. 369-95.

Plaster-mould stereotyping was the only method of plate-making that was known up to the 1830s.[4] The pages that were to be stereotyped were set with spaces and quads that were rather taller than usual, so that there should not be hollows in the type-page from which it would be difficult to remove the mould. They were then framed with type-high bearers, and the face of the type was brushed over with a light oil. Plaster was mixed with water and poured over the type, and allowed to set; when it had hardened it was lifted off the page (the oil preventing it from sticking to the type), and baked hard in an oven. Next the plaster was placed face down on an iron plate, from which the face of the mould was separated by its raised edges. The iron plate was laid in a casting box, a covered iron

FIG. 72. Casting box for plaster-mould stereotyping. The box, with its lid locked on, is fixed in lifting tackle ready for immersion in the metal pit. The floating iron plate, on which the mould was placed face-down in the box, is shown separately on the left. (Hansard, T. C., *Typographia*, London 1825, p. 862.)

container with holes at the four corners of the lid. The whole box was then immersed for about ten minutes in a pit of molten metal, which flowed in at the corners, floated the iron plate and mould up against the lid, and filled the space between them with the metal that was to form the stereotype plate. After cooling, the plate and mould were removed from the box and the plaster was broken off and discarded. Next a 'picker' cleaned any re-

[4] Hansard, T. C., *Typographia*, London 1825, ch. 16. See also Dickens's excellent description of the plaster-mould process in *Household words* for 16 Apr. 1853 (*Uncollected writings*, London 1969, ii, pp. 471-5).

maining crumbs of plaster or metal from the face of the plate, and its back was turned to a smooth, even finish giving a thickness from face to back of about 4 mm. The plate was mounted for printing on a block of wood, metal, or composition which raised its face to type-height. Early nineteenth-century casting boxes could take only one large or two small pages at a time. The rate of casting depended of course on the amount of labour and plant available, but it is unlikely that casting could take place more than six times an hour at one metal-pit.

The introduction of the flexible paper mould and the pivoted casting-box made stereotyping much easier and cheaper. Flexible moulds made of

FIG. 73. Pivoted casting box for flexible-mould stereotyping. (*a*) The box open with a flong mould, pasted to a sheet of paper, on the horizontal bed; pica gauges are placed round the mould and another sheet of paper will be laid on top of them. (*b*) The box closed and pivoted upright for casting, the metal being poured between the two projecting sheets of paper. The gas burner heating the bed of the box ensures even setting. (Southward, J., *Practical printing*, 4th ed., London [1892], pp. 690-1.)

laminated paper called 'flong' were first used in Lyons in 1829, and were patented in England ten years later.[5] Flong was made of alternate layers of blotting and tissue paper pasted together, and the mould was formed by beating damp flong on to the face of the type. It was dried and hardened by heating while it was still in position, after which it could be lifted from the type without risk of damage. The overwhelming advantages of flong

[5] Patent no. 8159, 20 July 1839. Flong moulds were not generally used in England until the mid 1850s.

moulds were that they were both quicker to make and quicker to cast from than plaster moulds; that they could be up to four times the size of plaster moulds; that they were re-usable; and that they could be fitted into curved casting-boxes to make plates for rotary presses. It is true that they were not capable of reproducing such fine detail as were plaster moulds, which therefore continued to be used for making plates of wood engravings until the early twentieth century;[6] and that flong moulds were liable to shrink as they dried, often differentially according to the grain of the paper of which they were made. There had always been some shrinkage in stereotyping because the metal of the plate shrank as it cooled,[7] and printers could make use of it for the deliberate reduction of type areas; but the additional shrinkage of the wet-flong mould was merely a nuisance, which was eventually overcome by the general use of dry-flong moulds from about 1910.[8]

The casting-box for flong moulds was a flat iron case like a portfolio with one hinged lid, pivoted so that it could be turned from a horizontal to a vertical position; patented in 1844,[9] it was large enough to take the mould of a whole forme of duodecimo or small octavo. The metal was poured in when the mould and box were in the vertical position; it set almost immediately and the plate could be lifted out as soon as the box was turned flat and reopened.

Stereotype plates, normally mounted and imposed as separate pages, were printed exactly like ordinary typeset pages, and it is usually difficult to tell whether a particular book has been printed from type or plates. Plates could be corrected: faulty letters were cut or punched out, and pieces of type—or, later, Linotype slugs—cut off below the face were soldered in their place.[10] When impressions from a typeset page and from a stereotype plate made from it can be compared, shrinkage will usually indicate which is which, but it must be remembered that plates could be made from plates as well as from type, as was done for instance when a second set of plates was required after the original settings of type had been distributed, or when the first set of plates but not the type had been corrected. Another procedure (normal at the Cambridge University Press since the late nineteenth century and probably before)[11] was to make two sets of plates straight away of books that were likely to remain in demand; one set was put to press, but the other set was used only as a 'mother' from which further sets of plates could be made when the earlier ones wore out.

[6] Legros, L. A., and Grant, J. C., *Typographical printing surfaces*, London 1916, pp. 474–6.

[7] Hansard, T. C., op. cit., pp. 834–5.

[8] Information from Mr. Len Gray, C.U.P. Dry flong is a non-laminated material manufactured like paper.   [9] Patent no. 10,275, 29 July 1844.

[10] Hansard, T. C., op. cit., pp. 834–5. Later on stereo corrections were usually plated and soldered in ('mends'); soldering in pieces of type ('botching') was disapproved of in good houses because the metal was of a different quality and wore unevenly.   [11] Information from the University Printer.

Plaster-mould stereotyping made steady progress in Europe and America during the first quarter of the nineteenth century. Edition sizes were increasing, and many standard works were being stereotyped by the 1820s. Sale catalogues of printers' equipment increasingly listed sets of plates as part of the stock-in-trade;[12] the Glasgow University Printing Office, which had one metal-pit and fifteen casting-boxes in its stereotype foundry, was making 300 plates a week in 1826;[13] and by the mid 1820s there were specialist stereotyping firms in America which set and plated books for sale to printers in other towns, so that several shops might simultaneously print impressions of a book which none of them had set.[14]

Stereotype continued to be used for keeping standard works in print during the rest of the machine-press period, sometimes for many years. It is not uncommon even today to come across a new impression of a plated book that was set fifty years ago, while the privileged presses are in some cases using bible plates that derive from settings which are the best part of a century old. Plates were also made as a matter of course—sometimes in duplicate for printing two-up—for any book that was expected to sell more than a few thousand copies, although they were not necessarily kept for long if the expectation was disappointed. Some printers kept moulds in store rather than plates.

The process also came to be of fundamental importance in the printing of periodicals. By the mid 1830s *The penny magazine* reached the unprecedented sale of 200,000 copies in weekly and monthly parts, which could scarcely have been produced from type alone.[15] Stereo rotaries printed the major newspapers from the mid 1860s, when it also became common for flat column-stereos to be sent from London to the offices of provincial journals, so that local papers would include both typeset news of local origin and syndicated matter in plates from the capital.[16] Plates for magazines in book formats were larger than before, being made from formes of four or eight pages already imposed in the proper order and register, and sometimes (especially for rotary printing) they were fixed in the press in gangs of several pages rather than being cut up into individual pages as was normal for bookwork (see p. 260).

[12] e.g. the run of Hodgson's catalogues at the British Museum; the sale of 20 Jan. 1825 was devoted to sets of plates.

[13] *Specimens of types, and inventory of printing materials, belonging to the Glasgow University Printing Office*, [Glasgow 1826].

[14] Silver, R. G., *The American printer 1787–1825*, Charlottesville 1967, pp. 59–61.

[15] Altick, R. D., *The English common reader*, Chicago 1957, p. 393.

[16] The column plates were cast with longitudinal flanges, and were mounted at the provincial office on slotted softwood blocks.

ELECTROTYPE

Experiments in galvanism for printing, the electro-deposition of metal on to a mould in order to make a printing surface, were made in England and in Russia in 1839[17] and by the mid 1840s the process was in widespread use for the reproduction of engravings and for the piracy of type designs (see pp. 267 and 207).

The electrotyping of typeset pages was soon found to be practicable.[18] The type was set and prepared in much the same way as for stereotyping, either in single pages or in small formes, with the use of tall spaces and frames of type-high bearers. The mould was made of wax which was warmed and pressed firmly on to the face of the type; then it was brushed over with graphite to make it electrically conducting and immersed for several hours as an electrode in a bath of electrolyte. There it 'grew' a coating of copper which, peeled off, formed the face of the plate. The copper skin was strengthened by having a leaden backing cast into it to a thickness of about 4 mm. The completed plates were finally mounted and used in the same way as stereos. The process was slower and more expensive than stereotyping—the deposition of the copper took a long time, although a large bath could take many moulds at once—and plates were limited in size to about four pages of octavo, half the size of a large stereo plate; but the copper surface of an electro was harder than stereo metal, and the plates were much more durable.

In England electros were used chiefly for illustrations, but in America, where the practice of trading in sets of plates continued throughout the century, the new process largely supplanted stereotyping for bookwork. It is the remarkable fact that by the early 1850s the Harper establishment in New York was making electrotype plates for almost the whole of its great output of books and periodicals, and printing practically nothing from type.[19]

American printers who specialized in plate making sometimes signed sets for more than one imposition. Thus a set of plates might be signed both as an octavo with a signature series on leaves 1, 9, 17, 25 (etc.), and as a duodecimo in sixes with a different signature series on leaves 1, 7, 13, 19 (etc.). A printer who bought the set could then choose to print it either as an octavo or as a duodecimo, or could even print two impressions, one in each format.[20]

---

[17] Savage, W., *A dictionary of the art of printing*, London 1841, pp. 249–61.
[18] Southward, J., *Practical printing*, London 1882, pp. 569–77.
[19] Abbott, J., *The Harper establishment*, New York 1855 (repr. Hamden 1956), pp. 67–8, 96–102.
[20] *The Library*, iii, 1948–9, pp. 58–62, 224–9; vii, 1952, p. 134.

Type, 1800-1875

Text types continued to be made in the old way until well into the second quarter of the nineteenth century.[1] Punches were still cut by hand, for the most part by independent craftsmen working at home and producing two or three punches a day. The mechanical skill of the handful of men who supplied the trade—there were fewer than a dozen punch-cutters in Britain in the mid nineteenth century—was greater than ever, and indeed their work was so regular and precise as to appear machine-made. The punches were then struck at the foundry into copper matrices, which were justified at the rate of about four per workman per day; and finally letters were cast in hand-moulds at the old rate of around 4,000 letters a day. Type remained expensive, and there was a plain incentive to mechanize its production.

With one exception the methods of making punches and matrices were not much changed until after 1875, although the rate of production of ordinary matrices was slightly increased by the use of a screw press instead of a hammer for striking the punches, and of simple jigs for justification. The exception was the use of the electrotype process, from the mid 1840s, for making matrices from cast type. Electrotype matrices were neither so sharp nor so durable as ordinary ones, but they could be produced at less than a tenth of the cost of cutting and striking punches; and the method was widely employed in Europe and America for copying other people's type by founders who could not afford, or did not choose, to buy matrices or commission sets of punches for themselves.[2]

Hand casting was accelerated in England during the 1830s by the introduction of the lever mould, with which new-cast letters could be ejected without shifting the matrix by hand, and of the hand-pump (first used about twenty-five years earlier for casting elaborate display type) for forcing rather than pouring the metal into the mould.[3] The resulting increase in the hand casters' rate from about 4,000 to about 8,000 letters per day had little effect on the price of type, and it was not until an efficient mechanical caster was generally adopted that great reductions were made. A typecasting machine was developed in America by David Bruce in 1838 which was simple and effective.[4] Matrix and mould were pivoted and were brought

---

[1] Mayhew, H., *The shops and companies of London*, i, 1865, pp. 241-71.
[2] Johnson, J. R., 'On certain improvements in the manufacture of printing types', *Journal of the Society of Arts*, xxi, 1873, pp. 330-8.
[3] Mayhew, H., op. cit., pp. 264-6.
[4] Legros, L. A., and Grant, J. C., *Typographical printing surfaces*, London 1916, ch. 18.

up to the nozzle of a metal-pump for the moment of casting, and then swung back to eject the new-made letter. With a speed in normal conditions of around 20,000 letters a day, the Bruce pivotal caster was the model for most of its successors, including (by 1860) improved versions which dressed and finished the type after casting. The majority of British founders were slower than those of America and continental Europe to introduce mechanical casters, but by the early 1860s the new machines were in very general use.[5] In 1838 pica text types were selling in London at about 1*s*. 11*d*. per pound and long primer at about 2*s*. 4*d*. (the precise cost varying with the size of the fount and with discounts allowed for prompt payment, etc.); by 1868 these prices had come down to 1*s*. 0*d*. and 1*s*. 3*d*. respectively.[6]

Little progress towards the standardization of type sizes and of height-to-paper was made until after 1875, and printers everywhere continued to suffer the inconvenience of being unable on occasion to mix the types of different foundries (although, when ordering type, they could usually specify particular bodies and heights-to-paper). On the continent of Europe the Fournier and Didot point systems, with units of 0·349 and 0·376 mm. respectively, were quite widely used, but English and American standards continued to differ from founder to founder.[7]

International trade in cast type and in typefounding materials continued during this period, the chief exporters now being England and France. Much type was also produced in Germany and (from the 1820s) the United States, and in a smaller way in the Netherlands and Scandinavia, but here it was chiefly for use at home and for a few particular markets abroad. Other countries were mainly importers of cast type, or of matrices for use by small local founders.

Large types, especially the elaborate display letters which came into fashion soon after 1800, were difficult to make. Plantin had cast a 12-line (5 cm.) gothic type in sand for printing advertisements in the 1580s,[8] and two hundred years later the Caslon foundry was offering a sand-cast fount of 19-line (8 cm.) roman capitals for the same purpose;[9] but sand casting was slow and not easily adapted to the production of delicate designs.

Sometime in the later eighteenth century an ingenious version of stereotyping called dabbing was developed, whereby a pattern of wood or metal was dabbed into the surface of a quantity of type-metal that was half way between its solid and its molten state; the dabbed metal was then used as

[5] Mayhew, H., op. cit., pp. 268–71.

[6] Price-lists in Caslon specimens (St. Bride Library).

[7] Legros, L. A., and Grant, J. C., op. cit., ch. 7.

[8] Vervliet, H. D. L., *Sixteenth-century printing types of the Low Countries*, Amsterdam 1968, pp. 81–5. The normal measure for display bodies was the pica line of just over 4 mm.

[9] Wolpe, B., 'Caslon architectural', *Alphabet*, i, 1964, pp. 57–72.

a matrix for striking a copy of the original in similarly half-molten metal.[10] Dabbing continued to be practised, especially for the reproduction of small woodcuts, until the introduction of electrotyping in the 1840s. Also at the beginning of the nineteenth century, display letters were reproduced from wooden patterns by the polytype process, which like dabbing employed a matrix made from heat-softened metal.[11]

The problem of casting large metal type quickly and easily was solved in 1810 with the invention of the sanspareil matrix by William Caslon IV; each letter was cut out as a stencil in brass and mounted on a brass base.[12] Used with a large version of the hand mould fixed to a bench, with or without the addition of a hand pump for forcing in the metal, sanspareil matrices were soon in use for casting 16-line (6·7 cm.) display types, and by the 1820s for bodies as large as 20-line (8·4 cm.).

The largest types for placards had to be cut in wood.[13] Wooden letters had of course been used since the earliest days of printing, but being individually cut they were expensive and, compared with cast type, irregular. An American jobbing printer, Darius Wells, used a routing machine around 1828 to speed the cutting of wooden type, and then in 1834 William Leavenworth of New York attached the routing machine to a pantograph and so was able to cut wood types from three-dimensional patterns with speed and precision. The Leavenworth machine was widely imitated, and a wealth of wooden display letter was soon being cut in bodies ranging from 4-line (1·7 cm.) to 120-line (50·5 cm.). Fine-grained hardwoods were preferred, nearly always cut across the grain, although the largest sizes were sometimes cut on the plank. Wood letter was also produced in Europe from the middle of the century, but less copiously than in the United States, where later technical advances included die-stamping in place of pantographic copying, and wood letter with veneered and enamelled faces (all in trade use from the 1880s).

DESIGN[14]

Several neo-classic roman types, cut with considerable contrast, vertical stress, and unbracketed serifs, appeared in France, Italy, and England during the last years of the eighteenth century (see pp. 29–30); and during the early 1800s the new style rapidly became so fashionable as to supplant the

[10] The only account seems to be in *O.E.D.*, s.v. 'dab', sb[1], 9, which quotes a communication from T. B. Reed.

[11] Camus, A. G., 'Mémoire sur l'histoire et les procédés du polytypage et de la stéréotypie', *Mém. de l'Inst. Nat. des Sciences et Arts*, Littérature et beaux arts iii, Paris An IX (1801), pp. 433–527.

[12] Reed, T. B., *A history of the old English letter foundries*, rev. Johnson, A. F., London 1952, p. 321.

[13] See Kelly, R. R., *American wood type 1828–1900*, New York 1969, on the manufacture as well as the design of wood letter.

[14] See the bibliography, pp. 404–5.

earlier traditional forms almost completely. Bodoni himself, not the inventor but the definitive interpreter of the early neo-classic style, was immensely influential during the first quarter of the century, but he neither exported his type nor inspired imitators in Italy, and it was the punch-cutters of England and France who developed and popularized the modern face.

In England a number of uncompromisingly modern founts were cut very soon after the turn of the century.[15] These new designs were so different from the old that they could not well be used with them, so that from this time on it became usual to cut new faces as whole series of matching founts of different sizes, a procedure that had hitherto been exceptional. The demand for the old faces came to an abrupt end and the founders withdrew them from sale, some even destroying the old punches and matrices as so much scrap. Late-eighteenth-century transitional faces lingered for some years longer, but by the second decade of the nineteenth century English printers were using a preponderance of modern face. Printers in France were much influenced by English fashions in type, and a few of them may have imported founts from England, but in 1812 Firmin Didot cut a superb, restrained modern which set the French style in type design for the next half century.

The flamboyance of the earliest modern face proved evanescent, and it was a restrained interpretation of the design, combining elements of both the English and the French modern faces, that prevailed. During the 1820s and 1830s a machine-age vernacular of modern-face roman emerged and was generally adopted in Europe and America. It was unequivocally modern, with vertical stress and unbracketed serifs, but it was leaner and narrower than the early-nineteenth-century romans; contrast was reduced, and there was a hard brilliance in its mechanical regularity of cut.

Identification of particular mid-nineteenth-century founts is extremely difficult. The punch-cutters copied each other expertly, and literally hundreds of closely-similar series were produced, individual founders offering five or six at a time. Worse still, founts of cast type could be copied in facsimile (sometimes after emendation with a graver) by making electrotype matrices from individual types of each sort (see p. 207), a practice that was very common from the 1840s until late in the century; in 1851 the Imperial and Government printing establishment in Vienna possessed 36,500 matrices, of which no fewer than 11,000 were electrotyped, not struck from punches.[16]

---

[15] Notably by Thorne, 1800–3; Caslon and Catherwood, 1802–5; Fry and Steele, 1803–8; and Figgins, 1808–15. The 1808 specimens of Fry and Steele and of Caslon and Catherwood are included in Stower, C., *The printer's grammar*, London 1808 (repr. London 1965); and Figgins's 1815 specimen was reprinted in *Vincent Figgins type specimens 1801 and 1815*, ed. Wolpe, B., London 1967.

[16] *Geschichte der K. K. Hof- und Staatsdruckerei in Wien*, Wien 1851, p. 250.

a abcdefghijklmnopqrſstuvwxyz &

abcdefghijklmnopqrſstuvwxyz &

abcdefghijklmnopqrstuvwxyz &

b fait le grand honneur de dénommer *gothique Christian*. Il réalise, je crois, une harmonieuse combinaison des caractères gothiques au moyen desquels ont été imprimés en France, au XVᵉ siècle, un grand nombre d'ouvrages, et du

FIG. 74 (*a*). Three double pica alphabets from the Caslon foundry: the first by William Caslon I, *c.* 1732 (and later known as 'Double Pica No. 2'); the second by J. I. Drury for Mrs. Henry Caslon, 1796; the third is the 'Double Pica No. 3' of Caslon and Catherwood's 1821 specimen, probably cut *c.* 1810–15. (Savage, W., *Practical hints on decorative printing*, London 1822, pl. 21.)

74 (*b*). Firmin Didot's *caractères millimétriques* cut for the Imprimerie Impériale in 1812; Didot's commercial founts had conventional serifs, etc., but were otherwise similar in style. (Christian, A., *Débuts de l'imprimerie en France [etc.]*, Paris 1905, p. 139.)

a reign, first gave by charter to the city of London, the right of electing annually a mayor out of its own body, an office which was till now held for life. He gave the city also power to elect and

b screams of the young females who fled for protection to their weeping mothers, and whose ineffectual struggles tended only to inflame the passions of their violators. To these dreadful groans and

c THE Assyrian came down like the wolf on the fold,
And his cohorts were gleaming in purple and gold;
And the sheen of their spears was like stars on the sea,
When the blue wave rolls nightly on deep Galilee.

FIG. 75 (*a, b, c*). The development of modern face in England, 1820s and 1830s. (*a*) Caslon's pica no. 6 leaded (Henry Caslon, 1841 specimen). (*b*) Blake and Stephenson's pica no. 7 leaded (Stephenson, Blake, [1838–41] specimen). (*c*) Stephenson Blake's small pica no. 9 leaded (Stephenson, Blake, [1838–41] specimen).

From the 1840s there was a gradually quickening revival of interest in old-face romans. The first sign of the reaction against modern face was the use of original Caslon founts by the London printer Charles Whittingham (from 1840) for reprinting texts of the sixteenth and seventeenth centuries. At first few books were affected, but from the mid 1850s new founts were cut both in England and in France in adaptations of renaissance forms. The most influential of them, Miller and Richard's Old Style of 1860, was not a close copy of renaissance roman but was a modernized version of it; it was a hybrid letter, with the bracketed, inclined serifs of the old face combined with the vertical stress and sharp regularity of modern. It was a clever and successful compromise, and it found numerous imitators not only in Britain but also in France, Germany, and America.

guardians they had lost.   Agitated by these thoughts, he
cipitated his journey.   When he arrived in Edinburgh, wher
inquiries must necessarily commence, he felt the full difficul
his situation.   Many inhabitants of that city had seen and ki

Fig. 76. Miller and Richard's old style roman, 12-pt leaded (Miller & Richard, [1925] specimen).

The nineteenth century also saw an explosion of exaggerated and decorated letter forms intended for display. With few exceptions the new display types, which proliferated exuberantly during the first quarter of the century, were of three basic varieties. There were, first, the traditional serifed roman exaggerated by about 1806 into fat face by a great increase in contrast between thick and thin strokes. The second variety was a letter with slab serifs and little contrast, known as Egyptian, which first appeared in about 1817; it was the forerunner of the Ionics of the 1840s, and more importantly of Clarendon, a bold-face series designed in 1845 explicitly for use as an ancillary to the standard modern-face romans in such things as dictionaries and time-tables (the first new method of articulating a text since the subordination of italic to the position of a secondary face). The third main variety of display letter had little contrast and no serifs at all; known as grotesque or sans-serif (and confusingly in America as gothic), it first appeared in a type specimen in 1816, but was scarcely used until the 1830s, when it became immensely popular. There were also various mid-century decorated letters with forked or clubbed serifs which generally tended towards fat-face, but which might be intermediate in form.

Any of these three letter forms could be used without further alteration, but equally each could be varied endlessly by changes of weight and of proportion; by sculptural effects such as the engraving of lines within the strokes of the letters, or the addition of perspective shadows; and by the application of any amount of extraneous decoration. From the 1840s novelty in display types was increasingly achieved by adapting some exotic or more or less explicitly historical motif within this framework.

a **ad finem sese effrenata j**
ABCDEFGHIJKLMN

b **cite emulation in the !**
ABCDEFGHIJKLM

c **FLOWERS DRAWN FRO**

d **BIBLIOGRAPHICA**

NOVEMBER 1840.

NEW BRUNSWICK, NEWFOUNDLAND,

Fɪɢ. 77 (*a, b, c, d*). Nineteenth-century display faces: the three basic forms, and some decorated variants. (*a*) Fat face (Caslon and Livermore's double pica no. 5; Henry Caslon, 1841 specimen). (*b*) Slab serif (Caslon and Livermore's two-line english antique; Henry Caslon, 1841 specimen). (*c*) Sans serif (Stephenson, Blake's english two-line sans surryphs; Stephenson, Blake, [1838–41] specimen. (*d*) Decorated types from Stephenson, Blake's [1838–41] specimen: pica two-line shaded ornamented, which is a fat face; english two-line in ornament, a slab serif; and english sans-surryphs shaded, a sans.

Paper in the Machine-press Period

HAND-MADE PAPER AFTER 1800

In 1800 all paper was still made by hand from rags, and it was not until the 1820s that the production of machine-made paper exceeded that of hand-made, even in Britain. Early-nineteenth-century hand-made paper, however, differed from that of the hand-press period on account both of new methods of bleaching, and of changes in the form of the hand mould.

Chlorine, discovered in 1774, was first added experimentally to the pulp in the vat at British mills in the 1790s.[1] The new chemical was expensive, and in the early days it was often mishandled; much of the foxing of early-nineteenth-century paper was due to inefficient bleaching. Nevertheless the process had great economic potential. The supply of best-quality white rags for paper-making had always been precarious, and bleaching enabled the more abundant coloured and second-quality rags to be made into acceptable writing and printing papers. At first, paper made from bleached stock was not so handsome as the unbleached papers of the hand-press period had been—apart from any foxing, it tended to be greyish in tone—but the paper-makers, spurred on by the urgent need to increase their supply of raw material, eventually mastered the new technique. By the 1820s good white paper was regularly produced with the aid of chlorine bleaches, and the process has been used in the manufacture of virtually all white paper ever since.

The 1790s also saw a general change from laid to wove paper (see pp. 65-6), and by about 1805 nearly all British printing paper was made in wove moulds. Paper-makers elsewhere followed suit; hand moulds had a short life, and it cost relatively little extra to change from a laid to a wove mesh when a mould was replaced. Unfortunately the hand-made wove papers of the early nineteenth century offer few clues to the bibliographer. There are no chain-lines, although it is sometimes possible to detect very faint bar shadows, even in paper made in double-faced moulds; while the use of powerful hydraulic presses from the mid 1800s[2] could make the mould side of the sheet almost indistinguishable from the felt side. The watermark, moreover, was generally omitted from printing papers, which were now either unwatermarked or marked with a countermark alone. The countermark, which was commonly placed near one of the corners of the mould, usually took the form of the maker's name or initials, the date (of the mould,

---

[1] Coleman, D. C., *The British paper industry 1495-1860*, Oxford 1958, pp. 113-17.

[2] Hunter, D., *Papermaking*, 2nd ed., New York 1947, p. 201 n.

of course, not necessarily of the paper made in it), and occasionally the vat number.[3] Although paper was still made in the traditional sizes, the water-marks that indicated size were seldom used except for such writing papers as continued to be made in laid moulds.

As paper-making machinery was introduced during the first quarter of the nineteenth century the output of hand-made paper declined, not very quickly at first, for there was a continuing demand for the finest hand-made rag papers, which were not closely imitated by machines until the present century. Nevertheless, the total number of hand vats in Britain, which was about 750 at the beginning of the nineteenth century, was down to 100 at its end, and by that time they were producing less than one per cent of all British paper.[4] The use of hand-made paper for commercial book- and news-printing dropped away sharply during the 1820s, and it was scarcely seen after 1830 except in de luxe editions. The introduction of mould-made paper (which is a fine machine-made rag paper which looks like hand-made) in about 1910 reduced the production of real hand-made yet further, until by the 1950s there were no more than about a dozen hand vats at work in the whole of Europe.

A certain amount of writing paper continued to be made in laid moulds even in the early nineteenth century (some people would not believe that the new-fangled wove paper could be as good), though all moulds were double-faced by about 1810. Towards the end of the century a few makers exploited the antiquarian appeal of laid hand-made paper by reviving the single-faced laid mould.[5] Otherwise nineteenth- and twentieth-century hand moulds were made in the traditional way; the technique of attaching the watermark to the cover of the mould with solder rather than with wire, used in paper-making machines from about 1870, does not appear to have been much copied. Watermarks for special papers used for such things as bank-notes and bonds became increasingly elaborate, and in about 1848 the Englishman W. H. Smith devised a moulded, three-dimensional watermark which gave a light-and-shade effect in the paper;[6] but, although light-and-shade marks were later successfully adapted for machine-made paper, they were too expensive for normal use in hand moulds. Elaborate watermarks, moreover, did not show up well unless the fibres in the stuff were beaten very short, and short fibres made weaker paper than long ones.

[3] Balston, T., *William Balston*, London 1954, app. 4.

[4] Spicer, A. D., *The paper trade*, London 1907, apps. 6, 9.

[5] This was a speciality of Messrs. Barcham Green of Maidstone, who were apparently using a few single-faced moulds by the 1880s.

[6] Hunter, D., op. cit., pp. 297–308, 552–3.

PAPER-MAKING MACHINERY[7]

The urge to mechanize paper-making came at first as much from the paper-makers' desire to free themselves from dependence upon their skilled but rebellious workmen as from the pursuit of production economies. The French paper-makers had suffered more than most from journeymen's strikes during the later eighteenth century, and it was in France that the idea for what was to become the standard paper-making machine originated. The inventor was a Parisian, Nicholas-Louis Robert who, with the encouragement and financial backing of Leger Didot, constructed in 1796–9 a successful working model of a machine that made paper in an endless strip, or web. French technology was inadequate for the further development of Robert's machine, however, and Didot, who had an English brother-in-law, brought the model to London in 1801, where he secured the backing of the brothers Henry and Sealy Fourdrinier, wholesale stationers. Not being technicians themselves, the Fourdriniers were obliged to employ professional engineers, and soon engaged the young and extremely able Bryan Donkin to carry out the actual development work. Donkin had a prototype 'Fourdrinier' machine in operation in 1803, and by 1807 he was manufacturing an improved version of the machine that was in essentials the same as the paper-making machine that is still in general use today, and with which almost all modern printing paper is made. Bryan Donkin did so well that he was shortly able to set up his own engineering business, and to dominate the manufacture of paper-making machinery in Europe until the middle of the century. The Fourdriniers themselves had plunged too deeply in the venture and by 1810 they were bankrupt; and both N.-L. Robert and Leger Didot died poor.

The basic Fourdrinier machine worked in this way. Beaten stuff was dribbled steadily across the width of an endless belt of woven wire which carried it away from the vat in an even film. While the layer of pulp was on this wire, which corresponded to the vatman's mould, the water drained away and the wire was given a sideways shake as it moved along in order to lock the fibres of the stuff together. The web next passed under a light-weight belt or roller, which helped to consolidate it into paper, and was then transferred with the aid of a harder-bearing pair of couch rolls[8] on to another endless belt, this time made of felt, which corresponded to the coucher's post. Web and felt ran together between pressing rollers which, like the standing press, gave the paper its full strength, and the web alone

---

[7] Coleman, D. C., op. cit., ch. 7; Clapperton, R. H., *The paper-making machine*, Oxford 1967. Clapperton's book fully describes and illustrates all the early machinery mentioned here.

[8] In recent years the web has been couched by suction through the surface of the lower couch roll, and the upper couch roll is now usually dispensed with.

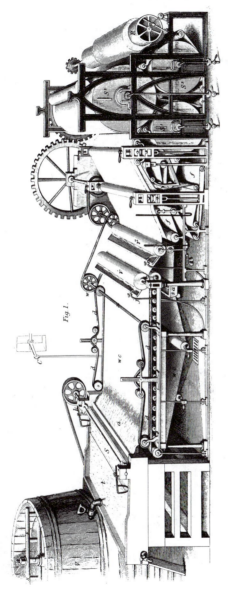

Fig. 1.

Fig. 78. A Fourdrinier machine, c. 1830, with primitive dry end. Stuff flows from the vat on to the machine wire (wc) at a, and is carried between the deckle straps, d, to two pairs of wet press rolls, r' and r"; the second pair of rolls couches it, now a coherent web of paper, on to the felt of the dry end of the machine, f. The web and felt then pass between two pairs of dry press rolls (not lettered) and round three steam-heated drying cylinders, and is finally reeled up at R. Later versions of the machine had a dandy roll in place of the first wet-press roll, more drying cylinders, and calender stacks adjacent to the reel-up. (Tomlinson, C., *Cyclopaedia of useful arts*, ii, London 1854, f. p. 365.)

was finally reeled up as it emerged from the machine, still wet, to be cut up later into sheets. The life of a machine wire depended on how it was used, but was characteristically 3–6 weeks.

Only one important modification was made to this wet end of the Four-drinier machine, which was the replacement of the light-weight belt or roller on the machine wire with the dandy roll, first used in 1825. The dandy was also a light-weight roller riding on the wire, but it was surfaced with wire mesh and it imposed its own watermark on the even wove texture that was made by the wove machine wire. The first dandy rolls were made in the laid pattern, and thus produced a machine-made laid paper, but wove dandies were also in use from 1828. Surprisingly the dandy roll was not used for watermarking designs in machine-made paper until 1839; from then on writing papers were commonly watermarked, from 1870 with marks that were soldered rather than wired on to the mesh of the dandy roll. Machine-made printing papers have seldom been watermarked, and until the mid nineteenth century were often made without a dandy roll; since then the use of a plain wove dandy roll has been normal. The right

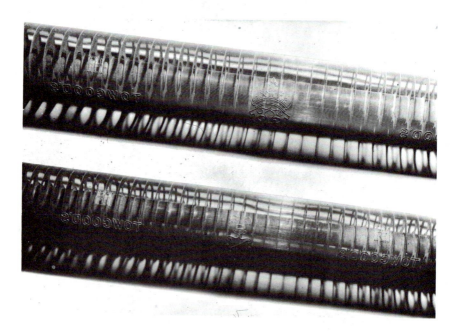

FIG. 79. Two laid dandy rolls from Towgood's mill, Sawston. The Strasbourg lily on the upper roll and the Strasbourg bend on the lower one are flanked by mill marks. The diameter of the roll varies with the size of the sheet it is to make (14·5 cm. for medium, 9·5 cm. for A4, etc.), but its length is governed by the width of the machine wire, in this case about 137 cm.

side of the machine-made sheet (the one from which the watermark is supposed to be viewed) was not the wire side but the upper-couch-roll side. Since the dandy roll worked on the right side, its watermark pattern was fashioned as a mirror image of what was to be seen in the finished paper. (In hand-made paper, the right side was the mould side, and again the watermark, being attached to the mould wires, was a mirror image of the finished result.)

From the 1820s a dry end was added to the Fourdrinier machine which dried and smoothed the web of paper as it emerged from the wet end. As the paper came out of the last set of wet-press rollers, it was led on felts round a number of steam-heated cylinders, and then through a stack of metal nipping-rollers (calenders), which successively dried the paper and gave it a smooth surface before it was reeled up. The dry end might also include devices for sizing or colouring the web, or (instead of a reel-up) a machine for cutting it up into sheets; they will be considered in the next section.

While Donkin was developing the Fourdrinier machine, John Dickinson (like the Fourdriniers, a wholesale stationer of London) was at work on the construction of a paper-making machine that operated on a different principle. This was the cylinder machine, which formed a web of paper not on an endless belt of woven wire but on a cylinder covered with wire mesh (looking like a large dandy roll) which revolved half-submerged in a vat of stuff. The water of the stuff poured into the middle of the cylinder through its wire-mesh cover, and was immediately pumped out from one end, leaving a film of fibres on the surface. This film was transferred as a

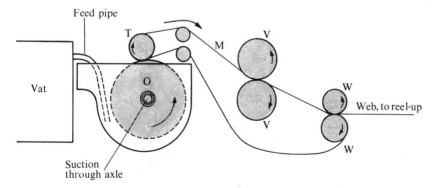

FIG. 80. Diagram of Dickinson's cylinder-mould machine, based on the early patent drawings of 1809-17. Water from the stuff was sucked into the mould cylinder, O, leaving the fibres on its surface. The web so formed was then 'licked' off the cylinder by the couch roll, T, and was carried by the felt, M, through two pairs of press rolls, V, W, to a reel-up (not shown).

web on to an endless felt which moved in contact with the top of the making cylinder, and then passed through the usual press rolls, etc., as on a Fourdrinier machine.

The cylinder machine had no shake mechanism (the device which locked the fibres together on the wire of the Fourdrinier machine) and, although it worked, its paper was neither so strong nor so thick as Fourdrinier paper if it was run at any speed. The earliest paper-making machines to be built in the United States (1817) were imitations of Dickinson's cylinder machine,[9] but they were superseded within ten years for making better-quality paper by faster Fourdrinier machines, and the cylinder machine was not at first a commercial success in Europe. Cylinder machines continued to be used for making coarse paper in America, and during the third quarter of the century multi-cylinder machines were developed there for making boards by building up several webs into one thick web. Another variant of the cylinder machine which had some success was the mould machine, introduced in England in about 1910 for making imitation hand-made (mould-made) paper from rag stock. It was similar to Dickinson's machine, but it had an agitator in the vat to prevent the fibres from being lined up parallel to each other by the action of the cylinder, and it was run very slowly, both to give the fibres a chance to lock together and to enable the machine to make an adequately thick sheet. The so-called moulds were ribs on the couching felt which divided the web into sheets and provided them with imitation deckle edges.[10]

The introduction of paper-making machinery certainly helped the masters to overcome the combinations of the skilled hand-vatmen, but its chief economic importance lay in its huge productivity. Even the earliest machine introduced an entirely new dimension into the industry. Donkin's second Fourdrinier machine of 1804 made a web 152 cm. wide, which was half as much again as the longer side of the largest sheet of printing paper that was normally made by hand. By about 1813 a typical machine would turn out as much paper as eight hand vats, and productivity per employee in a machine mill was already about two-and-a-half times that in a hand mill. An early development (at Aberdeen in 1811, for instance) was to organize shift working and run the machine night and day, for a good machine could average 23 hours' production in the 24 for weeks on end.[11] Machines

---

[9] The earliest American cylinder-machine book paper, made in Delaware by Thomas Gilpin and used for instance in C. V. Lavoisne's *A complete genealogical . . . atlas* (Philadelphia 1820, B.M. 1852. s. 10) was of excellent quality, comparable with the best printing paper then being made on Fourdrinier machines in Europe.

[10] Hunter, D., op. cit., pp. 368–73 (with illustrations).

[11] Clapperton, R. H., op. cit., p. 63. A common practice nowadays is to run the machine non-stop for six days, changing batches gradually by changing the stuff, and to stop it on the seventh day for maintenance.

for making book-printing and writing papers have not got much larger since the early days. Web widths of about 150-180 cm. (which enable the machine operator to reach in to the middle of the web from either side of the machine) are still normal. Machine speeds vary with the quality of the paper being made, the better the quality the slower the machine is run. During the middle and later nineteenth century such papers were made at speeds in the range 10-50 metres per minute; since then speeds have increased, but even today seldom exceed the range 40-90 metres per minute. Newsprint machines, on the other hand, have grown ever larger and faster, and there are newsprint Fourdriniers working today which can eject a web 1,000 cm. wide at speeds of up to 1,000 metres per minute (which is 60 k.p.h.).

MACHINE-MADE PAPERS

The early paper-making machines were dependent, as the hand vats had been, upon linen and (when they became available) cotton rags as their chief source of raw material; but the increasing demand for paper of all sorts, which the giant productivity of the Fourdrinier machine could easily meet, resulted in a parallel demand for rags which was soon outstripping the supply. During the first half of the nineteenth century rag prices rose sharply and rag imports increased, but by the 1850s there were fears of a serious shortage. The search for a substitute raw material, which had been pursued since the middle of the eighteenth century, was now intensified.[12]

Practically every known fibrous material had been tried at one time or another, and many new sorts of paper had been made experimentally, but none promised commercial success. The trouble was that vegetable fibres in their raw state contain not only the necessary strands of cellulose which can be converted into paper, but also other substances such as lignin which cause paper containing them to discolour and decompose after it is made. The conversion of flax and cotton fibres into thread and cloth has the convenient side-effect of eliminating these undesirable substances, and the problem therefore was to find a means of deliberately eliminating the lignin, etc., from some abundant natural fibre.

Some success was achieved in 1851 by boiling straw in caustic soda and mixing it with rag stock, but the resulting paper was still of poor quality and was little used by printers. Much more important was the development in 1860-1 of a similar chemical means of digesting esparto (a dune grass of the western Mediterranean); esparto paper, which is bulky and easy to print on, was made in commercial quantities in Britain from 1863, and quickly became popular with British printers who used it increasingly for

---

[12] On raw materials, see Spicer, A. D., op. cit., chs. 2, 3, and appendixes; Coleman, D. C., op. cit., chs. 8, 13.

bulking out thin books. The supply of esparto grass, however, even though it was little used outside Britain, was insufficient to meet the nineteenth-century demand for paper fibre, and it was the discovery in the middle years of the century of means of converting wood into paper that eventually solved the problem, for wood is not only a supremely abundant raw material, but it can also be made into a product which is second only to pure-rag paper for appearance, strength, and durability.

Woodpulp can be made either by grinding up untreated logs (when it is called mechanical wood, or groundwood), or by digesting wood chips chemically (chemical wood). Mechanical wood, used experimentally in America from about 1850, and commonly from 1867 (America) and 1871 (Europe), is the cheapest of all paper pulps, but none of the lignin is eliminated and paper made from it can be very unstable. With the addition of about 20 per cent of a purer fibre it makes acceptable newsprint, and with more additive a low-grade book paper, but light and heat soon cause it to discolour and even, in extreme cases, to break up. (The brown edges and characteristic smell of cheap paperbacks is familiar evidence of the use of mechanical wood.)

The early chemical woods, made by the soda process from the 1850s, were relatively stable, but paper made from them was poor in appearance and they were normally mixed with rag stock. It was chemical wood made by the later sulphite process that resulted in really fine, strong book papers of good stability. Sulphite chemical wood was made experimentally in the United States in 1866, and then on a commercial scale in Sweden (1874), England (1883), and the United States (1884), when it rapidly became the commonest of all the fibres used for making book-printing papers, either by itself or mixed with other materials.

Analysis of a considerable sample of nineteenth-century American books showed that up to 1849 all were printed on pure rag papers; that the period 1850-69 was transitional, with rag slowly giving way to wood; and that by the last thirty years of the century the transition was completed, nearly all book papers being made of mixtures of rag, straw, mechanical wood, and chemical wood in varying proportions.[13] The situation was probably similar in Britain, except that very little straw pulp was used, and a considerable amount of esparto. The papers chiefly used by English printers in about 1900 were (1) newsprint, largely made of mechanical wood; (2) cheap magazine and book papers, largely chemical wood with a small amount of mechanical wood; (3) medium book papers made of a mixture of chemical wood and esparto; (4) good-quality book papers mainly of esparto; and (5)

[13] Barrow, W. J., Research Laboratory, 'Strength and other characteristics of book paper 1800-1899', *Permanence/Durability of the book*, Richmond, Va. 1967.

a small quantity of rag printings, actually made of a mixture of rag, chemical wood, and esparto.[14] There were also writings of even higher quality, made either of pure rag, or of rag and chemical wood. (A curious technical term, 'woodfree', should be mentioned here: it refers to paper that contains no *mechanical* wood, but is made entirely of *chemical* wood.)

The characteristics of machine-made papers were determined not only by their constituent fibres but also by the processes of loading, sizing, coating, and finishing.[15] From the early years of the nineteenth century the beaten fibres of the stock were loaded with finely-divided mineral substances, chiefly china clay, which gave the paper additional body, weight, and opacity. Rag papers required relatively little loading, the clay seldom exceeding 5 per cent of the solids in the stuff, but esparto and woodpulp papers needed a heavier loading, and by the end of the century book papers commonly contained 10–15 per cent china clay.

Machine-made paper, like hand-made, had to be sized if ink was to be prevented from spreading along its fibres. At the same time as the Fourdrinier machine was being developed by Donkin, it was discovered in Germany that alum and rosin added to the stuff in the vat resulted in a paper that had a built-in size which was strong enough to resist printing ink; later starch was added as well. This process, known as engine sizing, was slow to be accepted—scarcely any American paper was rosin-sized before 1850—and sizing with the traditional material, animal gelatine, remained common. At first this was done in the old way by dipping cut sheets into the size tub by hand, but from 1830 it became usual to run the web through a trough of size, either in the Fourdrinier machine or by means of a separate tub-sizing machine which incorporated a drier.

Certain special-purpose papers were coated in the web. The papers coloured on one side that were used so freely in cased bindings from the 1840s to the 1890s had the colour applied as a clay-loaded coat at the calender end of the Fourdrinier machine, while art paper (the shiny paper used for printing fine-screen half-tones from the 1880s) had a coating of china clay applied in a special machine to one or both sides of a web of body paper.

The finishing or final surfacing of ordinary printing papers took place in the calender stack of the paper-making machine, when they were said to be machine-finished. If extra glazing was called for the web was run through a super calender, several times if necessary, to give an s.c. rather than an m.f. paper.

Finally the web was cut up into sheets (unless it was to be used on a web

[14] Spicer, A. D., op. cit., p. 51.

[15] Ibid., pp. 73–85. These processes are still normal practice in the trade, and are fully described in modern manuals, such as the B.P.B.M.A.'s *Paper making*, London 1949 and later editions.

rotary—see pp. 262–4—in which case it was divided longitudinally into a number of narrow reels). At first this was crudely done by cutting across the web parallel to the axis of the final reel and then slicing up the resulting slab of paper more accurately on a table, but from the 1820s various adjustable cutting machines became available which divided the web into sheets of even size.[16] What their dimensions were depended on the requirements of individual printing machines; usually they were multiples of the traditional paper sizes. If, for instance, a press could take 32 octavo pages together in a forme, then an octavo book would be printed on quad sheets (of double the usual dimensions in both directions), each of which would be cut up after printing and folded into four 8-leaf sections; while a smaller press, accommodating formes of 16 octavo pages, would use double sheets (of double the usual dimensions in one direction), each of which would yield two 8-leaf sections (see pp. 258–60). Table 5 shows some frequently-used sizes of paper in nineteenth-century British printing.

TABLE 5. *Paper sizes commonly used in nineteenth-century British printing*

Name	Dimensions	
	in.	cm.
Foolscap	$17 \times 13\frac{1}{2}$	$43\cdot2 \times 34\cdot3$
Double foolscap	27×17	$68\cdot6 \times 43\cdot2$
Quad foolscap	34×27	$86\cdot4 \times 68\cdot6$
Post	$19\frac{1}{2} \times 15\frac{3}{4}$	$49\cdot5 \times 40\cdot0$
Double post	$31\frac{1}{2} \times 19\frac{1}{2}$	$80\cdot0 \times 49\cdot5$
Quad post	$39 \times 31\frac{1}{2}$	$99\cdot1 \times 80\cdot0$
Crown	20×15	$50\cdot8 \times 38\cdot1$
Double crown	30×20	$76\cdot2 \times 50\cdot8$
Quad crown	40×30	$101\cdot6 \times 76\cdot2$
Demy	$22\frac{1}{2} \times 17\frac{1}{2}$	$57\cdot2 \times 44\cdot4$
Double demy	$35 \times 22\frac{1}{2}$	$88\cdot9 \times 57\cdot2$
Quad demy	45×35	$114\cdot3 \times 88\cdot9$
Royal	25×20	$63\cdot5 \times 50\cdot8$
Double royal	40×25	$101\cdot6 \times 63\cdot5$
Quad royal	50×40	$127\cdot0 \times 101\cdot6$

SOURCE: Southward, J., *Practical printing*, 4th ed., London [1892], facing p. 148.

[16] Sometimes but not always attached to the dry end of the paper-making machine. Clapperton, R. H., op. cit., p. 183, illustrates a mid-nineteenth-century cutter of a type that was used until *c.* 1920.

The paper-maker could vary the width of the web made on the Fourdrinier machine within the maximum capacity of its wire by setting the deckle-straps closer together. In filling a printer's order he would aim both to make a web of a width that could be cut into sheets of the required size with the minimum of trouble and waste, and to use as much as possible of the width of the machine wire, for the maximum economy of the machine was achieved only when it was running at full capacity. Thus if he was to make a batch of quad crown paper in sheets measuring 40 in. × 30 in. on a machine with a 70-in. capacity, he would prefer—other things being equal—to make a 70-in. web which would be cut into two strips 40 in. and 30 in. wide respectively; each strip could then be divided into quad crown sheets, the sheets from the 40-in. strip having their shorter edges parallel to the machine-direction (the direction in which the web moved through the paper-making machine), and those from the 30-in. strip having their shorter edges across the machine-direction.

Other things were not always equal, however. Machine-made paper has grain; the longer fibres tend to be lined up parallel to the machine-direction,

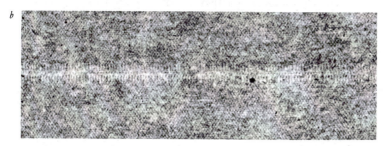

F_ɪɢ. 81 (*a*, *b*). A photograph (*a*) and a beta-radiograph (*b*), of a page in a nineteenth-century novel, showing the pattern of the machine wire and the seam where the ends of the wire were sewn together to make an endless belt. In this case the grain (or machine direction) of the paper runs up and down the page, parallel to the spine of the book, but elsewhere in the same copy it runs across the page. (Trollope, A., *Phineas Finn*, new ed., London 1871; author's copy, pp. 641, 481.)

with the result that the paper folds more easily along the machine-direction
—that is, parallel to these longer fibres—than across it. This characteristic
could interest the printer, who might specify in his order which way the
grain should run. For instance, he might want the machine-direction of
the paper to run parallel to the axis of the cylinder of his printing machine
so that the sheets would bend round it easily, or (more probably) he might
require the machine-direction of the paper to run up the spine of the
sections when the sheets were folded, so that they could be given a sharp
crease. Twentieth-century British book printers often specify the grain of the
paper they buy, generally in order that it may run up the spine of the book,
although occasionally a weak paper may be prevented from cracking at the
spine fold by running the grain of the paper across rather than along it.
Whatever the specification it could be a nuisance to the paper-maker as it
might require him to run his Fourdrinier machine at less than the full
capacity of the wire. In the nineteenth century, however, printers seem to
have cared little about the machine-direction of their paper. The paper
grain in English novels of the second half of the century seems to run
indifferently either down or across the page, often both ways in the same
book; and an unpublished survey (made by the W. J. Barrow Research
Laboratory in Richmond, Va.) of 50 books printed in America in the 1850s
showed that 16 of them were folded with the grain parallel to the spine and
34 with the grain running across the spine.[17]

Machine-made papers, then, can differ from each other in a variety of
ways: in their appearance by reflected and by transmitted light; in thickness
and in density; in the origin and final condition of the constituent fibres;
in sizing and in coating; and in grain. Bibliographers sometimes want to
investigate a particular paper in detail, or to compare one sample with
another in order to establish whether or not they are likely to derive from
the same making or batch. There are several more or less harmless diag-
nostic tests for paper which anyone can make and which will answer the
bibliographer's questions in many cases. (If there is still doubt a laboratory
analysis of the precise fibre content of a paper may be conclusive, but this
is expensive and it involves the destruction of a sample.)

The tests should be carried out in the following order. First come
five tests which can be made without doing any damage to the paper
that is being examined; then a further seven tests which do involve marking a small area of the paper, and which for this reason may have to be
omitted.

1. Consider the sample in a good light and assess its feel, surface texture,

---

[17] I have checked many English novels with inconclusive results. The W. J. Barrow survey was
kindly communicated to me by Mr. R. N. DuPuis.

and colour. If two papers are being compared, lay them side by side and look especially for differences of colour.

2. Use a raking light to find the wrong side of the paper and its wire mark, which should appear as a fine wove pattern in three dimensions. The wire mark may be almost obliterated in a well-calendered paper, but with practice it can usually be identified. Coated paper usually shows no superficial wire mark.

3. Hold the paper up against the light and measure the mesh of the wire pattern in wires per cm., and note its shape (square, oblong, or diamond). See which way an oblong or diamond wire-pattern is oriented; the longer dimension of the pattern is parallel to the machine direction, or grain, of the paper.[18] Assess the evenness of the substance of the paper, and the frequency of knots and impurities. Note any laid marks or watermarks.

4. Measure the thickness of about 20 leaves of the paper with a micrometer; a batch of machine-made paper, unlike one of hand-made, is generally of fairly even thickness.

5. If the papers of similar books in similar bindings are being compared, weigh the books to establish their relative densities, making allowance for any small differences in the number or dimensions of the leaves, and ensuring that the books are equally dry.

6. If the machine-direction has not been established by Test 3, make two folds in the sample at right angles to each other and parallel to the edges of the leaf. Examine the backs of the folds with a lens; the one that is sharper-edged than the other runs parallel to the machine-direction of the paper.

7. Test for the presence of mechanical wood (groundwood) fibre by applying a spot of phloroglucinol solution (1 gm. phloroglucinol in 50 cc. methyl alcohol and 50 cc. concentrated hydrochloric acid). It will immediately turn deep purplish red (Centroid 256) if the paper contains mechanical-wood fibres, the strength of the colour depending on the proportion of mechanical wood. (Note that no other chemical tests should be made within 2·5 cm. of the phloroglucinol test, as the chemical spreads invisibly in the paper and may invalidate their results; and that the solution should be tried out from time to time on newsprint, as it deteriorates with age.)

8. Test for acidity with a spot of chlorophenol solution (0·42 gm. chlorophenol red in 1,000 ml. distilled water). If the spot stays yellow the paper is decidedly acid (less than pH 6·0); an in-between colour (green, grey, grey-green, yellow-green) indicates mild acidity (pH 6·0–6·7); while if the

[18] Mid-twentieth-century machine wires usually have a square mesh, without a longer dimension of the pattern.

spot goes purple, the paper is near-neutral or alkaline (pH 6·7 or more). The precise shade of colour may distinguish between two samples.

9. Test for alum with a spot of aluminon solution (1 gm. aluminon in 1,000 ml. distilled water). When there is no alum present in the paper the spot will remain a very faint pink or will turn colourless; if alum is present it will turn a strong to deep pink (Centroid 2, 3).

10. Carry out the Raspail test for rosin. Place a drop of a saturated solution of sugar in water on the paper and dab up the excess liquid with cotton wool; then carefully apply a spot of concentrated sulphuric acid (96·6 per cent) on the same place. If a rosin size is present the spot will turn a dull purplish pink, but if there is no rosin the spot will remain colourless or turn brown. (Note that sulphuric acid is very dangerous and should be handled with great caution.)

11. Test for starch in the size with a spot of iodine solution (2·5 gm. potassium iodide, 0·5 gm. iodine, in 500 ml. distilled water). The presence of starch causes the spot to turn a dirty blue-grey, which in a few minutes becomes a muddy purple.

12. Finally, test the coating of a glossy paper by rubbing it with a piece of silver. If it is an art paper, coated with china clay, the silver will leave a grey mark on the surface; but it will leave no mark, or a very faint one, if the paper is an imitation art, loaded but not coated with clay.

These tests suggest various items for the bibliographical description of a machine-made book paper, which might include leaf size and thickness; machine direction; measurements of the wire mark and of any watermark; surface texture (rough, smooth, or glossy); colour; and the result of any chemical test that has been carried out. As with books of the hand-press period, measurements of the bulk or thickness of the whole book can be misleading since more or less pressure can alter the thickness by the sort of amount that might be caused by a change of paper.

THE NINETEENTH-CENTURY PAPER INDUSTRY

In 1800 all paper was made, rather expensively, by hand; in 1900 more than 99 per cent of it was machine-made; during the same period output increased about a hundred-fold, while prices went down by factors of about ten. It was of course paper-making machinery, and especially the Fourdrinier machine, which began this dramatic industrial revolution in the earlier part of the century, and the introduction of cheap raw materials, especially wood pulp, which supported the same high rate of expansion during its later part.

Paper-making machines were working commercially in England, as we have seen, by 1805, and it was English machinery that was first set up in most other countries: in France and Russia, 1814-15; Germany, 1818; Denmark, 1826; Sweden, 1831; Holland and Norway, 1838.[19] A locally-built cylinder machine was set up in the United States in 1817, but the first Fourdrinier in America (1827) was imported. Donkin's Fourdriniers continued to dominate the European market for paper-making machinery until about 1850; in America, however, a copy of an imported Donkin machine was built (with imported felts and wire) as early as 1830, and American machine-wires were available from 1847, and felts from 1864.[20]

Table 6 shows how paper output in nineteenth-century Britain was increased first by multiplying the number of paper-making machines at work, and later by increasing the speed of individual machines.

TABLE 6. *Nineteenth-century paper output in the U.K.*

Period	Average number of machines	Average total output (tons p.a.)	Average output per machine (tons p.a.)
1821-30	54	15,400	285
1851-60	305	77,890	255
1881-90	530	384,320	725
1901-3	536	735,800	1,375

SOURCE: Spicer, A. D., *The paper trade*, London 1907, apps. 6, 9.

At the same time the price of paper fell. At the beginning of the nineteenth century a fair book paper made (necessarily) of rags cost about 1s. 6d. a lb., whereas at its end an equivalent esparto paper cost only about 2d. a lb. The price in 1800 was made up of rags, 9d.; labour, capital charges, chemicals, etc., 4d.; and excise tax, 5d. Taxes on paper were successively reduced during the earlier nineteenth century, and were finally abolished in 1861; and the price in 1900 was made up of esparto grass, 1d.; and labour, capital charges, chemicals, etc., 1d.[21]

The chief paper distributor in the nineteenth century continued to be the wholesale stationer, although large printers would buy some of their paper direct from the maker (again a continuation of earlier practice). Small printers were discouraged from dealing direct with the mill because the paper-makers, who had to pay promptly for their raw materials, would not give the long credit that the wholesale stationer found it worth while to offer to his customers.[22]

[19] Clapperton, R. H., op. cit., *passim*.
[20] Weeks, L. H., *A history of paper-manufacturing in the United States, 1690-1916*, New York 1916.
[21] Spicer, A. D., op. cit., ch. 6.   [22] Ibid., pp. 125-32.

In the machine-press period, as in the hand-press period, economically advanced countries manufactured most of their own paper. There was some international trade in paper, but the major manufacturing countries rarely exported more than 20 per cent of their output of paper, or imported more than a similar proportion of their consumption; and imports and exports were usually at much lower levels than this. The article of international commerce was, not paper, but the raw materials from which paper was made: rags, esparto grass, and wood pulp.[23]

[23] Spicer, A. D., op. cit., pp. 133-43, apps. 1, 2, 4.

Edition Binding

INTRODUCTION

It will be remembered that throughout the hand-press period books were normally sent out to retail booksellers quired in sheets, or (if they were pamphlets) folded and sewn; and that, although trade binding by or on behalf of the retailer was common, edition binding by the printer or publisher was not (pp. 146–7). The reasons were economic—it actually cost more in the end, not less, to bind up a whole edition at once rather than by small batches—and economics prevailed, as always, despite the inconvenience to retailer and customer.

Edition binding was more attractive applied to books which could expect a large and rapid sale, and such things as school texts began to appear in modest edition bindings of paper boards by the mid eighteenth century. Paper boards, which attracted both retailers who could thus avoid the trouble of trade binding and customers who saved a few pence on the price of a book, spread to the generality of medium-priced editions in the period 1780–1820. But paper boards were neither very durable nor much cheaper than trade leather, and a considerable proportion of books (whether or not they had first been put into paper boards by the publisher) were trade-bound in leather by the retailer as before; often the leather cover was simply stuck on top of the paper boards.

The situation was entirely changed by various developments in binding technique which originated in the 1820s, developments which, although they were interdependent, may be considered under three headings. They were, first, the replacement of the traditional process of building up a binding for each book in turn by the speedier prefabrication in bulk of complete binding cases which were attached subsequently to the sewn and cut books. Secondly, the piecemeal mechanization of the binding processes which, while it was not completed until the twentieth century, immediately offered economies of scale, and combined with the technique of prefabricated casing to lower the unit price of binding, so that it became cheaper to bind a large than a small fraction of an edition at a time. Finally, the introduction of cloth as a covering material, which was stronger and more durable than paper, cheaper and more abundant than leather, and was regular and predictable in quality.

The binding trade altered its ways during the 1830s, and by 1840 the casing of large batches of an edition in cloth, generally for its publisher, had become the general rule in Britain and America. (Some classes of books, especially novels, were still 'subscribed' by wholesalers other than the publisher—see p. 181—but again the batches were generally large.) Cloth cases were never as popular in continental Europe as they quickly became in the English-speaking world, printed wrappers being preferred especially in France and Germany, but here too the binding of small batches by retailers gave way during the first half of the nineteenth century to large-scale sewing and wrappering by publishers or large wholesalers. Booksellers everywhere became simple retailers, purveying a finished product which would not be rebound except as a bespoke service to individual customers.

NEW PROCEDURES[1]

Most nineteenth-century books were gathered, folded, sewn, cut, rounded, backed, boarded, covered, and finished; for, with a few relatively unimportant exceptions (which are mentioned at the end of this section), the technological advances of the nineteenth century brought no fundamental change to the processes of binding. What did change was the order in which these processes were carried out, and their gradual mechanization.

Traditionally the case of a book had been built up during binding. The boards were first attached to the cords on which the sections were sewn, then a leather cover was stuck down over the boards and the spine, and finally the cover was finished with tooled lettering and decoration. With the introduction of cloth in the roll as a covering material, however, it was found that complete cases of cloth-covered boards could be cheaply mass-produced apart from the books they were to contain. The procedure, which was first carried out by hand and later mechanized, was to cut out boards, paper hollows for the spine, and cloth covers; to paste the boards and hollows into the covers; and to letter and decorate the outside of the cover. The books meanwhile had been sewn on to sawn-in cords, or on to tapes, and their spines had been lined with strips of muslin and paper. Cases and books were then brought together, and the muslin linings, together with the cords or tapes, were stuck down on to the boards under the paste-down endpaper. Even the earliest cloth-covered bindings of the 1820s appear to have been made with prefabricated cases, and there can be little doubt that this was the normal practice for cloth binding by the early 1830s.[2]

Another procedural change concerned the order of gathering and folding the printed sheets. In the early nineteenth century printers still normally delivered their work in the form of quires, with the individual books ready

---

[1] See the bibliography, pp. 406–7.

[2] The early accounts take the prefabrication of cloth cases for granted, e.g. Dodd, G., *Days at the factories, series 1*, London 1843, pp. 375–6.

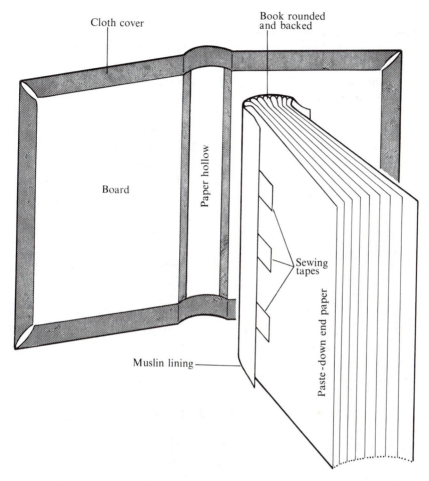

Cloth cover

Book rounded
and backed

Board

Paper hollow

Sewing
tapes

Paste-down end paper

Muslin lining

FIG. 82. A prefabricated cloth case and book ready for casing-in, which is accomplished by pasting the endpapers, with the tapes and lining beneath them, down on to the insides of the boards.

gathered, so that the binder did not have to gather but only to fold the sheets for each book. In London this remained the normal system until the early 1840s (as indeed was bound to happen so long as parts of editions were 'subscribed' to various wholesalers who had their batches bound up separately). Then books began to be delivered from the printers in ungathered heaps of separate signatures, just as they came from the printing machines, so that the binder gathered as well as folded the sheets;[3] this only happened, of course, when the publisher was going to be responsible for the binding

[3] Dodd, G., op. cit., pp. 367–8, says that both systems were used in 1843.

of all the batches of an edition. Because it is easier and quicker to pick up folded sections than unfolded sheets from the gathering table, books delivered to the binder in this way were normally gathered after folding, not before. The new practice quickly became established; at the Harper establishment in New York in 1855, which incorporated its own bindery, all books were gathered after folding, not before.[4]

'Stabbing', the stitching of small books from the outside through holes made alongside the spine fold (rather than in through the spine fold and back from the inside of the section) had been used for pamphlets since the sixteenth century, and the method became especially common during the earlier nineteenth century for the production of parts of novels, etc. Hand-operated stabbing machines, which forced three stabbing needles simultaneously through the side of a pamphlet, ready for subsequent sewing by hand, appeared early in the century; they were similar in principle to the desk punches used today for making eyelet holes in paper. By the middle of the nineteenth century stabbing machines were pedal-operated.[5]

The stabbing of pamphlets was superseded in the later nineteenth century by wire stapling. Wire staplers were first introduced in about 1875 in default of satisfactory book-sewing machines (which were not fully developed until 1882; see p. 237); the sections of a book were stapled to a coarse cloth backing, but unfortunately the staples soon rusted and became brittle. Consequently the book-stapling machines were generally replaced by sewing machines by the late 1880s; the stapling of pamphlets, however, had come to stay.[6]

An even more radical innovation was attempted in about 1840, when a method was devised for binding books without either sewing or stapling. The spine folds of the assembled sheets were simply cut off, separating all the leaves, which were then attached to each other and to a backing strip by a coating of flexible rubber solution, and cased in the ordinary way.[7] In time, however, the rubber on which these caoutchouc bindings depended perished, and the leaves fell out. The process was therefore abandoned from about 1870 until the middle of the twentieth century when it was revived, with a more durable plastic coating for the backs of the leaves, as the familiar (and to librarians deplorable) thermoplastic binding of modern paperbacks.

[4] Abbott, J., *The Harper establishment*, New York 1855 (repr. Hamden 1956), p. 130.

[5] There is an old hand-operated stabbing machine at the St. Bride Library; and Abbott, J., op. cit., p. 131, illustrates a pedal-operated machine.

[6] Leighton, D., *Modern bookbinding*, London 1935, pp. 33-4.

[7] Dodd, G., op. cit., p. 371.

BINDING MACHINERY[8]

At first all the processes of cloth casing were carried out by hand; then they were mechanized one by one until, by the early twentieth century, every one of them could be performed by machines. Mechanization came slowly to the binding industry, partly no doubt because of difficulties arising from the complexity of many of the processes, but perhaps also because the low wages paid to the women who performed all but the heaviest tasks in early-nineteenth-century binderies meant that there was little incentive to change. Similarly, scarcely any binderies were steam-powered before the 1850s, the earlier (and simpler) binding machines being hand-operated.

The earliest binding machine was not a new invention at all: it was the rolling press, familiar for more than two centuries as the copperplate printing press, which was adapted in 1823 with simple reduction gearing for pressing the sheets before folding, replacing the wearisome hand-beating of the folded sections. It immediately reduced the amount of labour required for pressing by a factor of six, and this was male labour, not female.

Next came machinery for preparing the covering cloth.[9] Plain calico makes a serviceable book cover but it looks better when it is coloured, and the earliest experimenters devised in about 1823 a method of calendering the cloth with dyed starch, which produced a covering material of fast, even colour, impervious to the adhesive with which it was stuck to the boards. (Cloth-makers' calenders are rolling presses.) Then, from about 1830, the covering material was further ornamented in an embossing machine. This was either a specialized calender of which the cylinders were engraved with a relief pattern (one positive and the other negative), or a press which nipped the cloth between a pair of flat engraved plates; heat was applied to one of the cylinders, or one of the plates, and the cloth took a permanent relief pattern from the engraved design (fig. 83).

Although binding cases could now be made with attractively coloured and textured material it still remained to find means of replacing the paper labels with which they were at first equipped by tooling in gold directly on to the cloth. The problem was solved in 1832[9a] with an improved size that was incorporated during the preparation of the cloth; and at the same time the arming (or embossing) press was developed, a machine similar to the iron hand-presses of the period with which a heated brass die could be

---

[8] On the progress of mechanization in the nineteenth-century binding industry see Leighton, D., op. cit., and Rogers, J. W., 'The rise of American edition binding', *Bookbinding in America*, ed. Lehmann-Haupt, H., New York 1967.

[9] See also Sadleir, M., *The evolution of publishers' binding styles 1770-1900*, London and New York 1930, and Carter, J. W., *Publishers' cloth 1820-1900*, New York and London 1938.

[9a] Pickering gold-blocked a cloth spine in 1830, but this was an experiment and was not repeated (McLean, R., *Victorian book design*, 2nd ed., London 1972, p. 6).

FIG. 83. Cloth-embossing machine in the 1840s. Lengths of book-cloth are passed between a pair of cylinders engraved (positive and negative) with one of the many conventional grains; the lower cylinder is heated by gas. (Dodd, G., *Days at the factories*, *series 1*, London 1843, p. 381.)

pressed into the cloth. Glair was applied to the pieces of cloth that were to be blocked, either before or after they were stuck to the boards, gold leaf was laid over them and they were run through the arming press one after another. Not only the spines but also the sides of the cases could be blocked, either gilt or in blind.

By 1832, then, trade binders in London had evolved a satisfactory but still largely manual technique for cloth casing, and they were quickly copied in America. No further developments in binding technology took place until the 1850s, whereafter most of the innovators were American, not English. In 1843 the great London bindery of Westley and Clark had a rolling press, two cloth-embossing machines, and three arming presses, but folding, gathering, sewing, rounding and backing, ploughing, case-making, and casing-in were all carried out by hand.[10] Even at the Harper establishment in New York, where all the latest machinery was installed after a fire in 1853, the mechanization of binding had not got much further: there were hydraulic instead of rolling presses, a simple machine for sawing

[10] Dodd, G., op. cit., pp. 364, 369.

slots for the sewing cords, and a powered guillotine in place of the hand plough, but still the greater part of the work—folding, gathering, sewing, rounding and backing, casemaking, and casing-in—was done by hand.[11]

Machines were developed for carrying out these remaining processes between 1856 and 1903, all of them American in origin: steam-powered folding machines (1856–80); sewing machines (1856–82); rounding and backing machines (1876–92); case-making machines (1891–5); gathering machines (1900–3); and, last of all, the casing-in machine (1903). In many commercial binderies the old methods tended to persist for some time after machinery became available, especially in England; not only were the new machines long in development, but even when fully developed they could not always justify their cost. The earliest sewing machines, for instance, were not entirely satisfactory and do not appear to have improved enormously on the work rate of an experienced hand-sewer (2,000–3,000 sheets a day); but the improved curved-needle machines developed in 1879–82 could do excellent work at the rate of 3,000–4,000 sheets per *hour* and they were soon widely adopted. On the other hand, although the gathering machinery of 1900–3 worked well enough, it was not worth using except for books of many sections, and even today commercial binders will gather short books by hand. Collating marks—usually black steps printed on the spine of each gathering —were commonly used from the 1890s.[11a]

In 1895, before the large-scale importation of the latest American machinery, a good London bindery would have the following machines: hand-fed folding machines, sewing machines, nipping machines (for pressing the sewn books before casing-in), cutting machines, rounding machines, backing machines, straight-knife trimming machines (guillotines), rotary board-cutting machines, power blocking presses, and hydraulic standing presses. The machinery would be belt-driven from shafting powered, probably, by a gas engine.[12]

From the printers' point of view the most important innovations in the binderies were guillotines which could cut right through the heap (introduced in the 1850s) and powered folding machinery (widely used by the 1880s). Together they could render the traditional imposition schemes obsolete; and, although the old work-and-turn impositions (mostly for octavo units) continued to be the commonest form, printers were increasingly obliged to follow the special imposition schemes required by particular folding machines.

[11] Abbott, J., op. cit., chs. 14, 16.

[11a] *American dictionary of printing and bookmaking*, New York 1894, p. 101; Southward, J., and Powell, A., *Practical printing*, 5th ed., London [1900], ii, pp. 222–3.

[12] Leighton, D., op. cit., p. 35.

PUBLISHERS' CLOTH IN BRITAIN AND AMERICA

Before considering the development of cloth binding styles, we may pause to establish methods of describing the colours and grains of binding cloths.

The system of colour nomenclature that is recommended for bibliographical use is the United States National Bureau of Standards' *ISCC–NBS method of designating colors* (NBS Circular 553) and its associated *Centroid color charts* (Standard sample no. 2106).[13] This system of nomenclature is based on ten names of hues and three names of neutral shades, with their adjectival forms; four adjectives indicating lightness; four adjectives indicating saturation; and three adjectives indicating combinations of lightness and saturation (see Table 7). The 267 colours named in this way are numbered and illustrated by colour 'chips' in the charts, in an arrangement of 29 main groups (see Table 8, p. 239).[14] There are of course more than 267 possible colours—there could be an infinite number of them— but this system does make it possible to assign any tint or shade to its place in what is known technically as the colour solid, and it will be found to be

TABLE 7. *Colour names and adjectives in the ISCC–NBS system*

Hues	*Lightness*
Blue; bluish	dark
Brown; brownish	light
Green; greenish	medium
Orange	very
Olive	
Purple; purplish	*Saturation*
Pink; pinkish	greyish
Red; reddish	moderate
Violet	strong
Yellow; yellowish	vivid

Neutral Shades	*Lightness and Saturation*
Black; blackish	brilliant (= light, strong)
Grey; greyish	deep (= dark, strong)
White	pale (= light, greyish)

NOTE: The *Centroid color charts* use abbreviations for colour names and adjectives, but some of them are ambiguous ('v.', for instance, stands for both 'very' and 'vivid'), and they are not recommended for use in bibliographical description.

[13] See Tanselle, G. T., 'A system of color identification for bibliographical description', *Studies in bibliography*, xx, 1967, pp. 203–34.

[14] It proved impossible to make chips for 16 of the 267 colours because of difficulties with dyes, but they are not likely to appear in book cloths.

TABLE 8. *The main colour groups and their Centroid numbers*

Pink	1–10	yellowish Green	129–38
Red	11–24	Green	139–57
yellowish Pink	25–33	bluish Green	158–66
reddish Orange	34–9	greenish Blue	167–75
reddish Brown	40–7	Blue	176–93
Orange	48–54	purplish Blue	194–204
Brown	55–65	Violet	205–15
orange Yellow	66–73	Purple	216–35
yellowish Brown	74–81	reddish Purple	236–45
Yellow	82–93	purplish Pink	246–53
olive Brown	94–6	purplish Red	254–62
greenish Yellow	97–105	White	263
Olive	106–14	Grey	264–6
yellow Green	115–22	Black	267
olive Green	123–8		

sufficiently precise in practice for the description of book-cloth colours. It avoids the ambiguity of such terms as 'beige'; and, although the form 'light greyish yellowish Brown (Centroid 79)' is rather lengthy (it is about the longest name in the system), it does define one of the several colours commonly called beige, both in words and by reference to a standard sample.

This system can of course be used for designating the colours of things other than book cloth: of paper, of ink, and of chemical stains, for example. In all cases colour matching should be carried out in daylight (but not in direct sunlight); and allowance should be made for differences of texture—the colour chips are glossy, most book-cloths are not—and for the possibility that the colour of a cloth or other substance has faded.

A great variety of book-cloths was manufactured and used from 1830 to 1850 (though no more than a few types of grain were really common), and the description of patterns is notoriously difficult. Bibliographers have generally used either descriptive names, or a letter code deriving ultimately from the specimen book of the Winterbottom Book Cloth Company of Manchester. Since the letter code is arbitrary and uninformative, verbal description is to be preferred, and it is suggested, following the work of G. T. Tanselle,[15] that the following scheme of classification should be used in conjunction with figs. 84–109 as a guide to description. In describing a grain the grain-type name will be referred to (or more than one name if it is of an intermediate type), with the addition of further verbal description if necessary. These names are used with modifying adjectives if the grain

[15] Tanselle, G. T., 'The bibliographical description of patterns', *Studies in bibliography*, xxiii, 1970, pp. 71–102. Some of Mr. Tanselle's illustrations (e.g. 124c, 204, 206) are printed upside down, with the light coming from the bottom of the picture rather than the top, which can be misleading.

is notably *fine* or *coarse*; if its pattern is *diagonal* to the edges of the binding case; or if it is *moiré* (i.e. like watered silk); the captions to the figures give examples. Frames and other patterns blocked in after the cloth was made up into a binding case are not included in the description of the cloth grain but are mentioned separately.

References are given in Table 9 to G. T. Tanselle's classification, who in turn gives tables of equivalences with earlier schemes. The classification given here does not include every known grain-type, some of which were

TABLE 9. *The Classification of Book-cloth Grains*

Classification	Fig.	Tanselle	Notes
REGULAR GRAINS, LINEAR PATTERNS			
lines and bands			
rib	84	102	Winterbottom T; diagonal fine rib and moiré fine rib were also common
ripple	85	104	Sadleir's 'fine ripple'[15a]
wave	86	106	Sadleir shows diagonal fine wave as 'ripple'
dotted-line	87	108	Winterbottom O
dot-and-line	88	110	
dot-and-ribbon	89	112	apparently always diagonal
checks			
net	90	118	also coarse
criss-cross	91	120	Sadleir's 'fine dotted diaper'
checkerboard	92	122	also fine
diaper	93	124	Winterbottom P; also fine and coarse
beads			
bead	94	202	Winterbottom D; also fine
beaded-line	95		Winterbottom BK; apparently always diagonal
REGULAR GRAINS, AREA PATTERNS			
hexagons			
hexagon	96	206	
honeycomb	97	208	
pansy	98	210	Sadleir's 'patterned pansy-face'
miscellaneous			
patterned-sand	99	410	the patterning may be unclear; cf. sand grain

[15a] Sadleir, M., *XIX century fiction*, London 1951.

TABLE 9 (*cont.*)

Classification	Fig.	Tanselle	Notes
IRREGULAR GRAINS			
cloth-texture			
calico	100(a)	302	Winterbottom R
linen	101(a)	304	Winterbottom AR
leather-texture			
morocco	102	402	Winterbottom DW; also fine and coarse
straight-grain-morocco	103(a)	404	Winterbottom G, N, AB, EE, TS; Tanselle's 'cord'; there is great variation in the linearity of the graining or ribbing
ribbed-morocco	103(b)	306	
crocodile	104		variant of Winterbottom LS
sand-texture			
sand	105	408	Winterbottom BW; merges with patterned-sand
pebble	106	406	Winterbottom E; also fine and coarse
bubble	107	204	Winterbottom W; Tanselle classifies as patterned
miscellaneous			
crackle	108		Winterbottom SW
frond	109		Winterbottom CW; one of several floriated grains

FIG. 84. Rib grain.

FIG. 85. Ripple grain.

FIG. 86. Wave grain.

FIG. 87. Dotted-line grain.

Fig. 88. Dot-and-line grain.

Fig. 89. Diagonal dot-and-ribbon grain.

Fig. 90. Fine net grain.

Fig. 91. Criss-cross grain.

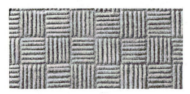

Fig. 92. Coarse checkerboard grain.

Fig. 93. Diaper grain.

Fig. 94. Bead grain.

Fig. 95. Diagonal beaded-line grain.

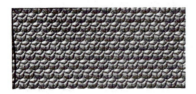

Fig. 96. Hexagon grain.

Fig. 97. Honeycomb grain.

FIG. 98. Pansy grain.

FIG. 99. Patterned-sand grain.

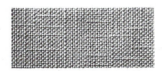

a

FIG. 100 (*a*). Embossed calico grain.

b

(*b*) Calico-texture cloth, not embossed.

a

FIG. 101 (*a*). Embossed linen grain.

b

(*b*) Linen-texture cloth, not embossed.

FIG. 102. Morocco grain.

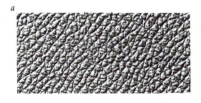

a

FIG. 103 (*a*). Straight-grain morocco grain.

b

(*b*) Ribbed-morocco grain.

Fɪɢ. 104. Crocodile grain.

Fɪɢ. 105. Sand grain.

Fɪɢ. 106. Pebble grain.

Fɪɢ. 107. Bubble grain.

Fɪɢ. 108. Crackle grain.

Fɪɢ. 109. Frond grain.

Fɪɢs. 84-109: *Sources: 84* ULC Rom. 66. 45 (1846); *85* ULC Nov. 133. 37 (1856); *86* ULC Nov. 6. 1ᵇ (1861); *87* ULC Nov. 46. 44 (1871); *88* ULC Nov. 20. 47 (1865); *89* ULC Nov. 20. 38 (1864); *90* ULC Rom. 74. 74 (1851); *91* ULC Nov. 28. 45 (1867); *92* ULC Nov. 86. 110 (1890); *93* ULC Nov. 70. 62 (1874); *94* ULC Nov. 3. 13ᵇ (1859); *95* ULC Nov. 23. 5 (1865); *96* ULC Nov. 22. 54 (1865); *97* ULC Nov. 7. 26ᵇ (1862); *98* ULC Nov. 29. 35 (1867); *99* ULC Nov. 65. 60 (1874); *100* (*a*) Winterbottom R; *100* (*b*) ULC Nov. 121. 59 (1906); *101* (*a*) Winterbottom AR; *101* (*b*) ULC Nov. 116. 96 (1898); *102* ULC Nov. 3. 43 (1861); *103* (*a*) ULC Nov. 6. 6ᵃ (1861); *103* (*b*) ULC Nov. 3. 14 (1859); *104* ULC Nov. 48. 103 (1885); *105* ULC Nov. 14. 66 (1868); *106* ULC Nov. 34. 79 (1883); *107* ULC Nov. 52. 2 (1872); *108* ULC Nov. 92. 115 (1892); *109* ULC Nov. 34. 105 (1883).

extremely rare, and only one form of each type is illustrated; most types are known in several variants. Much the commonest grains were rib, the various moroccos, sand, and pebble; while plain (ungrained) cloth was never rare. Next, of fairly frequent occurrence, came wave, dotted-line, diaper, bead, honeycomb, patterned-sand, and bubble. All the rest were relatively uncommon.

The development of publishers' cloth in England and America can be considered together owing to the very strong links between the binding trades of the two countries.[16] The experimental period, when the new materials and techniques were first developed, lasted from about 1823 to 1830. The earliest cloths in commercial use were coloured but, except for glazing, they were not artificially grained. Lettering was normally by means of paper labels pasted on to the spine.

The idea of using cotton cloth as a covering material for books probably originated with the London publisher William Pickering; and the earliest technical problems of colouring and dressing the cloth were solved by the binder Archibald Leighton. These were not quite the first trade bindings in cloth, for canvas had been used as a covering material for the trade binding of cheap school texts and chap-books since about 1770,[16a] but they were the first cloth bindings that were intended to compete with paper boards as seemly but inexpensive covers for ordinary books.

In 1830-2 the remaining technical problems—those of graining the cloth and of blocking its surface—were solved, Leighton again being primarily involved; and during the next ten years publishers' cloth spread rapidly to all classes of books. In considering particular developments, two points should be borne in mind. One, which is fundamental to any study of the chronology of cloth binding, is that editions were by this time bound up in batches over periods of months, years, and decades, so that the date on a volume's title-page is not always—or even usually—the precise date of its binding. The other is that for the greater part of the nineteenth century American binders bought virtually all their binding cloth, already coloured and grained, from British manufacturers; there was no effective competition from American binding-cloth manufacturers until 1883, and it was not until about 1900 that a majority of American books were cased in book-cloths of American manufacture; thus new cloth patterns appeared in England and America at approximately the same dates. It may be added here that at the end of the nineteenth century, when the manufacture of

---

[16] Carter, J. W., op. cit.; Rogers, J. W., op. cit.

[16a] D. Leighton's date. John R. Hetherington dates canvas a decade earlier; and also points out that calico back strips on boarded books were used as a trade style from *c.* 1800.

book-cloth was getting under way in America, the rest of the world was still supplied by a small handful of firms: one (Winterbottom's) in England, and two or three in Germany. English book-cloth was preferred in the British Empire, and in Austria-Hungary, the Netherlands and Japan; German book-cloth was preferred in Germany, France, and Greece; while both English and German cloths were used in Belgium, Denmark, Norway, Sweden, and Italy.[17]

The dates when some of the grains were probably introduced were as follows:[18]

morocco	1830
diaper	1833
fine rib	1836
coarse rib	1839
ripple	late 1830s
fine bead	1858
wave	1859
sand	early 1860s
dot-and-line	mid 1860s

Many of these grains remained in production for decades, and the ribbed cloths were still being used in the 1960s. Others, such as whorl grain (an irregular moiré pattern introduced in 1831) and the ribbon-embossed design (an irregular pattern on a sand-texture ground which flourished in the late 1830s) were soon discontinued.

The first attempt to letter cloth covers directly, without the use of labels, involved printing on them in ink (1829), a style which remained popular for reprint series until about 1840. But the advent of blocking in gold and blind with brass dies (1832) took cloth binding into a new dimension. At first the spines were simply lettered with pallets of binders' tools in the same way as trade leather, but some time in the mid 1830s (the precise date is uncertain owing to the difficulty of dating particular cases) dies began to be made for the decoration of individual books; and, spreading to the covers, dies became large, elaborate, and pictorial. Blind pictorial blocking was characteristic of the years around 1840, and was followed from 1842–4 by gilt pictorial blocking and combinations of gilt and blind.

Fashions in the decoration of book covers, like other fashions, changed from time to time during the remainder of the century; new themes, new elaborations, new restraints followed each other and were as characteristic of their periods as styles of dress. The most constant features up to the 1890s were cloths that were both coloured and grained; gold lettering on the spine; some form of decoration, usually in blind, on the covers; a reluc-

17 Rogers, J. W., op. cit., pp. 163–4.

tance to cut the edges of the book; the insertion, next to the last free end-paper, of a folded section of publishers' advertisements; and, from the 1840s to the 1890s, the use for endpapers of stock that was coated with colour on one side. (Towards the end of the century endpapers were occasionally printed with a pattern or with publishers' advertisements; and from about 1900 they might carry such things as maps related to the contents of the book.) The more fanciful styles of publishers' cloth included gilt blocking over the whole area of the covers; the use of several dies to block, not only in gilt and in blind, but in colour as well; and the incorporation in blocked cartouches of such things as photographs. These were superficial changes, however, and the basic techniques of cloth casing remained those of the 1830s.

It has been pointed out that editions were normally bound up in substantial batches as they were required for distribution. Separate batches might be bound up more or less simultaneously (perhaps by different binders), but more often they were bound seriatim, occasionally over long periods of time. When this happened the publisher did not as a rule require the binding of one batch to be repeated exactly in another; on the contrary, binding batches were frequently distinguished by binding cloths of different colours or grains, and by changes—usually simplifications—in the details of the lettering and blocking. There might also be changes in the inserted advertisements, which were generally dated (though this is evidence that should be approached with caution, as a sequence of dated advertisements could be used out of order).

OTHER STYLES OF PUBLISHERS' BINDING

Cloth rapidly became the commonest publishers' binding style of the nineteenth century, but it was not the only one. Leather, printed wrappers, printed paper boards, and exotic covering materials such as silk, which had all been used before cloth was introduced, all appeared as publishers' bindings during the cloth period, either in connection with particular classes of books, or as an alternative to cloth for a particular book.

It is hard to be sure when edition binding in leather began.[19] Many books had, of course, been offered in alternative bindings of trade leather or paper boards since the mid eighteenth century; the difficulty is to identify the transition from retailers' (or wholesalers') leather to publishers' leather. But edition binding in leather was at least as early as edition binding in cloth, and it continued to be offered as an alternative to cloth or printed paper boards for such things as poetical gift books, works of piety, and textbooks, commonly until the 1860s and sporadically thereafter; bibles, prayer books, and 'classics', may still be had in publishers' leather today.

[18] Rogers, J. W., op. cit., p. 160.   [19] Carter, J. W., op. cit., p. 41.

Leather bindings continued to be built up on the books, without the use of prefabricated cases, but binderies grew larger and there was much division of labour. It was found that it was quicker to cut large batches of the cheaper sort of book with a guillotine out-of-boards than to handle them individually in the traditional process of ploughing in-boards. Roan, a cheap sheepskin which supposedly resembled morocco, was the favourite covering for inexpensive edition bindings in the middle years of the century; Westley and Clark of London had a busy roan shop which mass-produced leather-bound school books.[20] At the same time a good deal of fine leather binding was carried on in the traditional way (though with an increasing use of hollow backs); and there was a steady output in the later nineteenth century of well-made prize bindings in gilt-tooled calf, which were slickly produced by specialist firms, again with much division of labour.

A few small books were put out in specially printed wrappers at Augsburg in the 1490s; it became common to equip pamphlets with wrappers (made by pasting a paper cover to the spine, and sometimes also to the endpapers, of the sewn booklet) from the mid seventeenth century; and from the mid eighteenth century pamphlet wrappers were often printed (pp. 151–2). The printed wrappers so characteristic of early- and mid-nineteenth-century pamphlets and part-issues were therefore no great innovation, but they carried their function of displaying and advertising the books they covered to greater lengths than before. Purely typographical wrappers remained common throughout the century, for instance on French books, which were very rarely cased, and on the Tauchnitz reprint series (the great German forerunner of the modern paperback); but a monthly part of a mid-nineteenth-century English novel had a wrapper of coloured paper, printed with a pictorial design in black and sometimes in another colour as well, and carrying advertising matter on the back cover for products unconnected with the book trade such as food or soap.

It was primarily for display, too, that printed paper boards were developed in the mid nineteenth century as an alternative to cloth, though they did offer the additional advantage of by-passing the 'cloth famine' caused in the 1860s by the American civil war. Like printed wrappers, printed paper boards had an early origin (there were Italian examples of the early sixteenth century), but the style remained relatively uncommon during the hand-press period. Paper boards with lettering and typographic decoration printed on the spine and covers began to appear at the end of the eighteenth century, and became increasingly common during the succeeding decades. It was not until the 1840s, however, that London publishers discovered that there was a large potential market for cheap reprints, and that the most effective way of selling them was to put them on railway bookstalls in pre-fabricated cases of paper boards printed with eye-catching coloured pictures. (The parallel with mid-twentieth-century pictorial dust-jackets and paper-back covers is obvious.) Books bound in this way came to be known as yellow-backs, after the ground colour of the paper most often used for covering them.[21]

The typical yellow-back of the mid nineteenth century was a cheap edition of fiction in small crown octavo, retailing at two shillings; its case was made of glazed coloured paper (usually yellow, but occasionally pink, green, blue, or grey) on strawboard, printed from two, three, or four colour blocks with a picture relevant to the contents of the book on the front cover, with decorative titling and perhaps another picture on the spine, and with advertisements on the back. Yellow-backs were thus startlingly different from the cloth-bound editions of the period, and at their best they were lively and attractive. Forerunners of the style appeared during the 1840s, but the main yellow-back period may be said to have lasted from 1855 to about 1870, during which time the production of colour blocks in London was dominated by the firm of Edward Evans. This was followed by a period of decline until the end of the century, when yellow-backs virtually disappeared, and when the quality of both cover designs and internal typography had become very poor.

Yellow-backs were a largely English phenomenon, but the fashion for annuals—generally anthologies, lavishly produced as gift-books—came to Britain from France and Germany around 1820, and was immediately imitated by British publishers. Produced until about 1840, the annuals were especially notable for their exotic bindings (also largely copied from abroad), which were covered with materials such as watered silk, velvet, deep-stamped leather, and papier mâché, sometimes enriched with chased metal, semi-precious stones, or pasted-on pictures.

THE TWENTIETH CENTURY

By 1900 nearly all the processes of casing could be mechanized, and little further progress in this direction was made before 1950. The largest mass-production units, nevertheless, were owned only by specialists in the binding of long runs, especially in America, and an English novel of the 1930s, bound in batches of 5,000 copies or less, was still gathered by hand and was otherwise bound with a series of small hand-fed machines which each performed a single process.[22]

[21] Sadleir, M., 'Yellow backs', *New paths in book collecting*, ed. Carter, J. W., London 1934, pp. 125–61.
[22] Leighton, D., op. cit., p. 50.

Cloth styles began to change in the 1920s with the introduction (originally in Germany) of plain uncalendered materials that made a virtue of showing the pattern of the weave. The old embossed cloths did not disappear overnight, but died out gradually during the 1930s, and with them went the blind blocking of the covers. At the same time spine lettering began to interest book designers, and it became both simpler and more closely allied to typography. Non-woven covering materials began to appear, one of the earliest being Linson, introduced in 1934.

But with the exception of the paperback revolution (which belongs rather to publishing than to binding history), the most striking innovation in the presentation of books in the first half of the twentieth century was the development of the dust-jacket as an advertising medium.[23] Printed dust-jackets began to appear sporadically during the nineteenth century; the earliest example was probably English (the printed paper jacket that protected Heath's *Keepsake* for 1833, an annual bound in watered silk and issued in the autumn of 1832), but they were also used occasionally in Germany from the 1860s.[24] However, the usual protection for a mid-nineteenth-century cloth-bound book—if it had any—was a plain paper jacket, sometimes cut with a window to show the lettering on the spine, and it was not until the 1880s that printed dust-jackets became common. The modern form of pictorial jacket, with printing on the flaps and blurbs to advertise the books they covered, and often other books as well, evolved between the late 1890s and *c.* 1907, simultaneously with the decline of pictorial casing. The early jacket illustrations usually repeated a picture from inside the book, but by the 1920s they were commonly new designs.

The bibliographical importance of twentieth-century dust-jackets is obvious enough, although librarians (and, more surprisingly, book collectors) often throw them away: it is that they may contain original material that is unavailable elsewhere. This is especially true of blurbs, frequently written by the author himself, and of original jacket illustrations, which might be prepared under his direction; but other features of modern jackets, such as biographical and bibliographical notes concerning the author, and his photograph, may also be of value.

[23] Tanselle, G. T., 'Book jackets, blurbs and bibliographers', *The Library*, xxvi, 1971, pp. 91-134.
[24] The early history of American printed jackets is obscure. The 'jacket' on W. E. Lord's *Poems* of 1845, is apparently a printed wrapper originally attached to the sheets.

Printing Machines

The early attempts to improve the common press of the hand-press period culminated as we have seen (p. 198) in Stanhope's iron press of 1800 and its essentially similar successors. The iron hand-presses, however, were not much more productive than the wooden presses which they replaced—their chief advantages lay in their greater precision and durability—and the output of early-nineteenth-century pressmen was much the same as had been that of their predecessors. If the productivity of the press was to be increased it had to be made larger, or faster, or both.

There were, it appeared, two ways in which this might be done. One was to employ steam power to work a flat platen of a larger size than was possible by hand. The other was to increase the effective size of the press by using a cylindrical platen, powered either by hand or by steam. In either case the speed of the press could be increased by the use of automatic inking apparatus and of semi-automatic feed and delivery mechanisms for handling the printing paper.

The first successful printing machines were based on the second, and perhaps less obvious, principle. An English inventor, William Nicholson, realized as early as 1790 that the effective size of a printing press could be increased by making the impression surface (or platen) cylindrical rather than flat. A flat platen must apply the effort of impression all at once to the whole type area immediately beneath it, which is thus limited in size by the amount of power available at a given moment. A cylindrical platen, on the other hand, applies the effort progressively as it rolls across the type area, needing only as much power at a given moment as is required to print the narrow strip of type beneath it; thus the type area can be as wide as the cylinder and of any length. The principle of the cylinder platen was hardly a new one even then—the rolling pin is an ancient device, and the copper-plate press used two cylinders working together—but no one before Nicholson had worked out its application to letterpress printing.

Nicholson's patent of 1790 specified the essential features of cylinder presses as they were later developed.[1] He described two flat-bed machines, a rotary, and the method of inking by batteries of rollers which became standard. He realized, however, that the engineering techniques available to him were inadequate, and the machines were never built.

[1] Patent no. 1748, 29 Apr. 1790; Savage, W., *A dictionary of the art of printing*, London 1841, pp. 449-55, reprints it with the drawings.

The first printing machines which actually worked were invented by a German, Friedrich Koenig.[2] Like Nicholas-Louis Robert (the inventor of the paper-making machine), Koenig was unable to obtain financial support for his development work at home, and in 1806 he migrated to London, where he was backed by the printers Thomas Bensley and Richard Taylor. Although he later denied it, Koenig was almost certainly influenced by Nicholson's ideas, and his successful presses were flat-bed cylinder machines with many Nicholson features. But he went further than Nicholson in designing machines for steam rather than hand power, machines which were in fact built while Nicholson's were not.

After an experimental period (he had a flat-platen machine working after a fashion in 1811, and a prototype cylinder machine in 1812), Koenig constructed two large cylinder machines for *The Times*, which started work in November 1814, and which marked the real beginning of machine printing. Then in 1816 he produced a perfector, with two impression cylinders which printed both sides of the sheet one after the other from two formes, capable in practice of turning out 900 perfected double-demy sheets per hour.[3] This may be compared with the maximum output of 150 such sheets per hour which might just be reached, with much effort, by a large iron hand-press. It was already plain that the future of printing lay with the machines.

Crucial to the success of printing machinery was the development of a satisfactory covering for the inking rollers. Attempts to use leather-covered rollers in place of ink-balls for hand-press work had been made soon after 1800, but they were frustrated by the unavoidable marks made by the seam with which the leather was sewn on; and Koenig had similar troubles with the leather-covered rollers of his first two machines. The solution (patented in 1813)[4] was found to be a composition of glue and treacle which could be cast, at first on to a cloth backing and later directly on to the roller stock, and which made a seamless, resilient surface that inked perfectly. A similar cloth-backed composition had been introduced a few years earlier for covering ink balls, and composition rollers were used in Koenig's *Times* machines of 1814.

The division of the printing trade into specialized book, news, and jobbing houses had already begun to take place by the beginning of the nineteenth century. If anything, the introduction of machinery accentuated the trend, for machine efficiency could be increased by specialization for particular sorts of work, while the high capital cost of machinery did not encourage diversity within individual businesses.

[2] The standard (but partial) biography is Goebel, T., *Friedrich Koenig*, Stuttgart 1883.
[3] Later developed by Applegarth and Cowper; see p. 262 and fig. 114.
[4] Patent no. 3757, 23 Nov. 1813.

Book printers wanted a machine that could achieve presswork of high quality over a sizeable type area, a press in other words of considerable power; speed of operation was a desirable but secondary consideration. At first there was a tendency, deriving perhaps partly from conservatism, to prefer flat-platen machines for high-quality bookwork, but flat-bed cylinder machines were also used, and by the 1860s were becoming the dominant form. The fact that the smaller cylinder machines were also suitable for turning out a country newspaper or a poster added to their popularity.

The newspaper printers of the metropolis, on the other hand, required presses that were above all productive. They wanted large, fast machines, and were prepared to accept a rather lower standard of presswork in order to get them. As we have seen, the earliest successful printing machines were specialized cylinder news presses of high capacity; and the rotary machine (pp. 262–4) was developed specifically for newspaper work.

The jobbing printer, finally, looked for different qualities again in his presses: ease of operation (especially in changing quickly from job to job) and speed, but not as a rule a large type area. It was to meet his needs that the 'platen jobber' was developed (pp. 263–5).

MACHINES FOR BOOK PRINTING[5]

The early history of book-printing machinery in England has not yet been investigated in detail, although research into nineteenth-century printers' records should eventually clear up some of the uncertainties. In outline, the course of events appears to have been that English book printers generally continued to do the bulk of their work on iron hand-presses until about 1830, although a few large firms also installed flat-bed cylinder machines during the late 1820s.[6] Then, from the late 1830s, the iron hand-presses were supplemented and eventually replaced by powered platen machines, which were thought to be capable of doing better work than the early cylinder machines. Finally, most of the platen machines were themselves replaced during the 1860s and 1870s by cylinder machines of improved design (known generically as Wharfedales) which continued to be used for most good-quality bookwork until the mid twentieth century.

The development of book-printing machinery in America followed similar lines.[7] No really effective machine was available, and even iron hand-presses were scarce, until the 1830s, when the Adams press was introduced. This was a powered platen machine, different mechanically from the English powered platens but like them a favourite for good-quality

---

[5] Wilson, F. J. F., and Grey, D., *A practical treatise upon modern printing machinery*, London 1888.

[6] But they did not necessarily use them for printing books, for book-printers large enough to buy machinery were likely to print periodicals as well.

[7] Green, R., 'Early American power printing presses', *Studies in bibliography*, iv, 1951–2, pp. 143–53.

bookwork in the middle years of the century. Then from the 1860s there was a further change, more gradual than in England, to cylinder machines, which were predominant everywhere by 1900.

Platen machines were essentially powered versions of the hand press. Type was imposed on a flat press bed, printing paper was positioned over the forme by a tympan-like frame, and impression was applied through a flat platen. Inking, however, and sometimes the delivery of the printed sheets, was automatic.

The mechanism could be arranged in various ways. In one simple version, known in England as the Scandinavian single platen machine (1841), the press bed and type were stationary throughout.[8] The inking rollers and tympan, which were arranged beside each other in one frame, were run automatically over the forme, and then when the rollers but not the tympan were clear of the type the platen was forced down to make the impression. A single operator fed and delivered the sheets by hand.

The single platen machine was small and not much used for book printing, but the English double platen machine, first manufactured by Hopkinson and Cope from about 1830 and then (probably from the 1840s) in an improved version by Napier, was widely employed for good-quality bookwork until the 1860s.[9] In this machine two formes were placed on the press bed, which moved in a carriage from end to end of the frame. There was an ink table at each end of the bed, and two sets of inking rollers were fixed in the frame at right angles to its movement, with the platen between them. As the bed moved back and forth, the platen was pulled down mechanically on to each forme in turn. Between each impression the tympan and frisket of the forme that was not being printed was thrown up automatically, the paper was changed by an operator and the inking rollers ran twice over the type; then the bed ran back to the other end, where the paper for the other forme was changed by a second operator. Thus the double platen was not a perfecting machine, but was in effect two single-sided machines sharing a platen; the two formes had no necessary connection with each other, and might belong to different books.

Another sort of platen machine was patented in America by Isaac Adams in 1830, and came to dominate American book printing during the middle years of the century.[10] Here it was the platen that was stationary, and the bed of the press (which did not move backwards and forwards) was pushed up to the platen to make the impression; the vertical travel of the bed was

---

[8] Southward, J., *Practical printing*, 4th ed., London [1892], pp. 348–50.

[9] Wilson, F. J. F., and Grey, D., op. cit., ch. 7.

[10] Abbott, J., op. cit., pp. 119–23; *The American dictionary of printing and book-making*, New York 1894, pp. 8–9; *Printing impressions*, xii, 1969, pp. 68–9.

FIG. 110. Napier double platen machine. The platen is the ribbed structure in the middle, which is pulled down on to each forme in turn. In this picture one forme is beyond the inking rollers on the left, and its tympan and frisket are lying on the guides leading up to the left-hand feed board; the other forme, with its tympan and frisket, is under the platen. (Wilson, F. J. F., and Grey D., *Modern printing machinery*, London 1888, p. 145.)

FIG. 111. Adams platen machine. Sheets of paper are transferred from the feed board, upper right, to the frisket on the apron in the middle of the machine, which draws them back under the platen beneath the feed board. The forme, which is under the platen, having been inked by the moving rollers on the right, is pushed up against the platen to make the impression; and the printed sheet is then carried on tapes under the apron to the fly of the automatic delivery on the left. (*The American dictionary of printing and bookmaking*, New York 1894, p. 9.)

considerable, since there had to be room between the face of the type and the platen for the passage of the inking rollers. The machine required only one operator, who fed the sheets via grippers to a frisket; delivery was completely automatic, the printed sheets being blown on to endless tapes for transfer to the heap.

Although these platen machines were both slower and smaller than the cylinder machines that were available during the second quarter of the nineteenth century, they were preferred for the quality of their work. The Adams press ran at about 500 impressions per hour with one operator, the Napier rather faster (up to about 800 per hour) with two operators, and both took sheet sizes up to double royal (about 102×64 cm.). The early single-sided cylinder machines could run at 1,000 impressions per hour (and the perfectors at 2,000), and could be made to take sheets in sizes up to quad demy (about 114×89 cm.), usually with two operators. But the early cylinder machines worked less accurately than the platens, tending to slur the impression and batter the type. Indeed, the Clarendon Press kept a Napier double platen machine at work until 1950 for the sake of its gentleness with the delicate kerns of Fell italic.

Meanwhile cylinder flat-bed machines suitable for book printing were being developed. Like their predecessors (which were mostly news presses) they had reciprocating carriages with ink tables at the end and inking rollers fixed at right angles across the frame, an arrangement analogous to that of the English double platen machine; the impression cylinder was in the middle, geared to turn as the carriage moved under it, pressing down on one traverse but clearing the type on the return; while feed and delivery of the paper were partly automatic.

Up to the 1830s the few book printers who used machines were chiefly equipped with Applegath and Cowper perfectors, advanced two-cylinder machines that had been introduced as news presses in *c.* 1820 (pp. 262-3); but the cylinder machines that replaced the platens for the better class of work during the third quarter of the century were single-sided, not perfectors. Their ascendancy may be traced through the Main or tumbler machine of *c.* 1840, Payne's Wharfedale stop-cylinder machine of 1858, and the improved Wharfedales produced by Payne and others in the mid 1860s. These machines did not incorporate radically new features but, by combining minor improvements with new standards of mechanical accuracy, they first challenged and then overcame the lead enjoyed in the mid nineteenth century by the platen machines.

The improved Wharfedale of *c.* 1865, which was built by a number of makers, will serve as an example.[11] There were the usual three parts, frame,

---

[11] Wilson, F. J. F., and Grey, D., op. cit., ch. 3.

carriage, and platen (cylindrical, of course, not flat). The carriage was moved mechanically to and fro in the frame, so that the forme on the bed was carried twice under the inking rollers and twice under the impression cylinder during each complete cycle of the machine. The inking rollers, which were fixed across the frame, took ink from a table at one end of the carriage and inked the type both during its movement towards the cylinder and during its return. The hollow impression cylinder had a segment parallel to its axis cut out, and was geared to roll over the forme as the carriage moved towards it from the inking rollers, and then to stop with the cut-out facing and clearing the type as the carriage returned. Thus the paper, which was fed sheet by sheet into grippers on the cylinder by an operator, was printed as the cylinder rolled over the forme, and was then discharged automatically while the carriage was returning to the roller end.

Fig. 112. A large stop-cylinder machine with double inking developed from the Wharfedale (the Franco-Bremner of *c.* 1870). The paper is taken round the cylinder and printed as the forme moves under it from left to right, and is delivered automatically to the heap under the feed board. The cylinder then stops with the cut-out downwards as the forme moves back from the supplementary ink table on the right to the main inking and distributing rollers on the left. (Wilson, F. J. F., and Grey, D., *Modern printing machinery*, London 1888, p. 107.)

Single-sided cylinder machines of this sort were made in sizes from foolscap folio (to take sheets of up to 33×25 cm.) to double quad crown (152×102 cm.), but a book printer would normally want machines of intermediate size. Typical was the double demy Wharfedale, which printed sheets of up to 91 × 61 cm., and could reach speeds in the range 800-1,200 impressions per hour, equivalent to 1,600-2,400 ordinary demy impressions per hour, eight times the speed of a hand press. But it should be added that these high speeds were not usually maintained: 'There are cylinder machines that have done, and can do, on long runs, 10,000 impressions in a day of ten hours, but we also know that the average performance of cylinder machines in jobbing offices, on long and short runs, rarely exceeds 3,500 impressions a day, and oftener falls below that number.'[12]

MACHINE OPERATION[13]

The workman who was in charge of a machine was known as the machine-minder, or machineman. In all but the smallest offices he would have several machines in his charge, which he made ready but which were operated during the run by boys (or often in America by girls) known as layers-on and takers-off. There was always a layer-on to feed in the paper, but machines with automatic delivery did not need a taker-off.

Although platen machines differed mechanically from single-sided cylinder machines, they were prepared and operated in similar ways. In both cases the machine-minder received a forme from the composing room (or plates from the foundry) and imposed it on the bed of the machine, made ready with overlays, set up the automatic inking apparatus and, having cleared a proof with the machine-room overseer, got the run under way. And in both cases the machine was then left in charge of the boys or girls who operated them during the run.[13a]

Virtually any of the familiar imposition schemes could be used on a machine, but much the commonest arrangements were octavo and duodecimo work-and-turn schemes, which were analogous to half-sheet imposition in hand-press work.[14] To take a typical example, all sixteen pages for a demy octavo sheet would be imposed together as a half-sheet of sixteens in a single forme; the same forme was then printed on both sides of double demy paper, the heap being turned from end to end as well as over for perfecting; and finally each double sheet was cut in half to give two demy octavo whole sheets. Similarly, the twenty-four pages for a sheet of duodecimo would be imposed as a half-sheet of twenty-fours and printed on double-sized sheets to give two duodecimo whole sheets each. The larger machines were used with multiple work-and-turn schemes whereby impositions for double sheets (such as those just described) were combined to make quad, octuple, etc. schemes (fig. 113). It should

---

[12] Southward, J., *Modern printing*, iv, London 1900, p. 87.   [13] See the bibliography, p. 407.

[13a] There might also be an adult labourer who turned the ink duct, and washed up after the run.

[14] Recent examples are worked out in Steele, O. L., 'Half-sheet imposition of eight-leaf quires in formes of thirty-two and sixty-four pages', *Studies in bibliography*, xv, 1962, pp. 274-8.

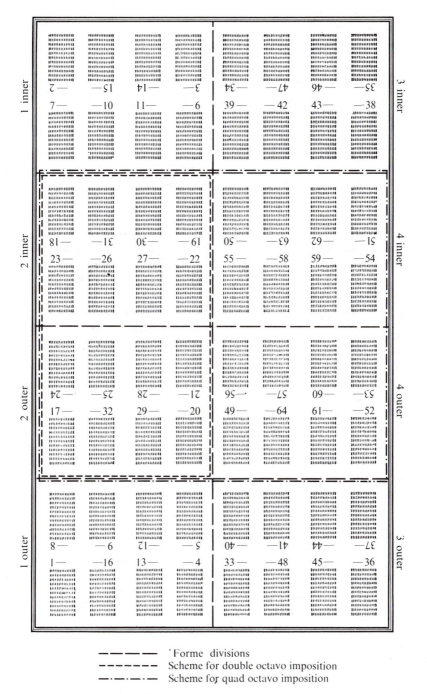

— — — — `Forme divisions
— — — — — Scheme for double octavo imposition
— · — · — · — Scheme for quad octavo imposition

FIG. 113. Octuple octavo imposition scheme for a small format on a large machine: the 64 type pages or plates for four whole sheets of octavo imposed together in one chase for work-and-turn. The perfected sheet will be cut into eight to give two copies each of signatures 1, 2, 3, and 4. For a larger format or a smaller machine a fraction of the scheme might be used, e.g. 2 outer + 2 inner for a double scheme, or 2 outer + 2 inner + 4 outer + 4 inner for a quad scheme. (Adapted from De Vinne, T. L., *Modern methods of book composition*, New York 1904, p. 341.)

be borne in mind, however, that some folding machines were made for sheet (not half-sheet) work, and that others required special impositions.

When a book was to be printed from type the pages were locked up in the composing room, usually with wooden furniture and quoins although metal furniture and mechanical quoins were used increasingly from the mid century. All the machine-minder had to do was to fix such formes against gauges on the bed of the press and plane them down in preparation for make-ready. On stop-cylinder machines the orientation of the chase was commonly with page 1 away from the cylinder and towards the primary ink-table.[15]

If plates were used instead of type they were usually delivered to the machine room unmounted, and it was the machine-minder's duty to mount them—usually by means of clips or catches on the mounts, occasionally with screws—and to impose the mounted plates as a forme. In printing houses where much work was printed from plates, formes of mounts were kept in the machine room ready locked up, so that the machine-minder had only to fix the plates on to the right mounts.[16] By the end of the nineteenth century plates were sometimes made and mounted in 'gangs', primarily for printing on rotary presses: these were groups of pages cast together as large single plates, sometimes signed with special numbers in addition to the ordinary signatures (numbers which were supposed to be deleted from the plate before printing).[17] Imposition, whether of type or plates, by the machine-minder rather than by the compositor was of course a departure from traditional practice.

The impression was made ready, as on the iron hand-press, by pasting overlays of paper on to a sheet inserted between the impression surface and the printing paper. On the platen machine, this overlay sheet was placed in the tympan (again as on the hand press), but on the cylinder machine it was stretched round the cylinder itself and was then covered with another sheet of paper or with a fine blanket.

Inks for machine printing differed little from those for the hand-press period.[18] Linseed oil reduced by boiling, with a proportion of resin, continued to be the main constituent of the varnish, and lampblack was still used for the colouring of black ink. The chief differences were the occasional use of thinners to weaken the ink, and of dryers to avoid problems of offset when machine speeds were high. Inking was of course entirely automatic. A duct at one end of the frame deposited a small, regular quantity of ink

[15] Southward, J., *Practical printing*, London 1882, p. 465.

[16] Ibid., p. 499.

[17] Bruccoli, M. J., and Rheault, C. A., 'Imposition figures and plate gangs in *The Rescue*', *Studies in bibliography*, xiv, 1961, pp. 258–62.

[18] Bloy, C. H., *A history of printing ink*, London 1967.

on to the ink-table after each impression, where it was spread by a set of distributing rollers before being picked up by the inking rollers and transferred to the type.

It will be remembered that the platen machine had not only a tympan but also a frisket, usually a frame with cross wires on which the printing paper was laid sheet by sheet; the cylinder machine had neither tympan nor frisket, the paper being held in place on the cylinder by the grippers. Machine-made paper, provided that it was dry, could be laid on with sufficient accuracy for register to be made with no more ado than adjustment of the forme for the second run. But damp paper was still preferred for much ordinary printing until late in the nineteenth century, partly because damp paper was easier than dry to ink, and partly because it evened out the minor inequalities of used type (and of plates made from used type) in the days before the introduction of hot-metal composing machines which cast type afresh for each job.[19]

Damp paper is difficult to lay accurately as its dimensions are changed by wetting, and points continued to be used for some machine work, as for hand-press work, at least until the 1880s.[20] In platen machines the points were incorporated in the frisket frames, in cylinder machines they projected through the feed board. They were forced through the printing paper by the operation of the machine on the first run, and the layer-on located the sheet on the points for the second.

COLOUR PRINTING[21]

Nineteenth-century colour printing was both more complex and more precise than the two-colour work of the hand-press period, frequently involving elaborate ornamentation in three or more colours. Specialist colour printers used special multi-colour cylinder machines; while new techniques for letterpress printing in colours with ordinary equipment were developed during the second quarter of the century. There were two main departures from the earlier method of working two colours from a single forme (pp. 137-8). Machines could not accommodate the overlays (or underlays) of traditional two-colour work, and cylinder machines were not equipped with frisket masks. It was therefore necessary to make up separate formes for each colour, and then to work them off one after another. Secondly, special points were used to ensure accurate register. If, for instance, there

[19] High-class magazine work was printed dry in America from *c.* 1870, but ordinary printing paper was still damped in England in 1888; English books were printed dry from the early 1890s, newspapers rather later (Wilson, F. J. F., and Grey, D., op. cit., p. 365; Southward, J., *Progress in printing*, London 1897, pp. 20-1, 39-40).

[20] Southward, J., *Practical printing*, London 1882, p. 500.

[21] Wilson, F. J. F., and Grey, D., op. cit., ch. 24.

were to be three formes for printing a job in three colours, two clusters of two points each were tacked to the furniture of the first forme, positioned so that they were pressed through the paper by the operation of the machine at two opposite edges of the sheet, each cluster making two holes. No points were attached to the other two formes, but for the second run the two ordinary points of the machine were placed so that they made register when they were used with one of the two holes made at each end of the sheet during the first run; and for the third run the points of the machine were adjusted to make register with the other two holes made during the first run. Thus a new pair of holes was used for each forme, and the register was not spoiled as it might otherwise have been by damage to the point holes. Neither was the paper disfigured, for all the holes were placed at the very edge of the sheet and were subsequently trimmed off. (The clusters of points that were attached to the first forme did not always contain two points each, of course, but as many points as there were formes after the first.)

OTHER PRINTING MACHINES

As well as the platen machines and the single-sided cylinder machines that have already been described, the nineteenth century saw the development of three other main classes of printing machines. These were the flat-bed perfectors; the rotaries; and the platen jobbers. They were not primarily book-printing machines, but examples of each sort were used for printing books.

The best of the early perfectors was the Applegath and Cowper two-cylinder machine of *c.* 1820, developed from Koenig's second *Times* machine.[22] The two formes of the sheet were imposed on the bed of the reciprocating carriage where they were inked by two sets of rollers, one at each end of the frame. The printing paper was fed on to endless tapes which carried it first round one impression cylinder and then, via a pair of reversing cylinders, round a second impression cylinder; thus the sheets were printed successively on each side during one complete cycle of the machine, and perfected sheets were delivered to a taker-off. This was a fast machine for its period—700–1,000 perfected sheets per hour were typical rates in book houses of the 1830s—and for a while it was used in many of the largest printing shops, not only in Britain but also in America and in continental Europe. Later there were improved flat-bed perfectors (such as the 'Anglo-French' machine of 1865, which dispensed with the reversing cylinders),[23] but by that time book printers were using other machines.

Rotary presses are like wringers, the printing paper being nipped between

---

[22] Frequently described, e.g. [Knight, C.], *Guide to trade, the printer*, London 1839, pp. 48–53 and plate.   [23] Wilson, F. J. F., and Grey, D., op. cit., ch. 7.

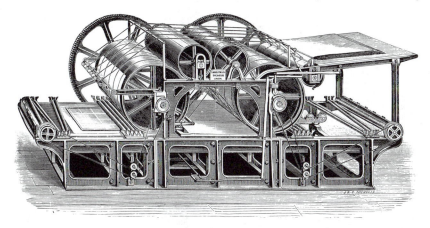

FIG. 114. Middleton's fast perfecting machine, a copy of the Applegath and Cowper machine of *c.* 1820, which was itself based on Koenig's perfector of 1816. The machine-bed carries two formes backwards and forwards between ink tables at either end of the frame. Paper from the feed board, upper right, is carried between two sets of tapes round the right-hand cylinder and is printed on one side from the inner forme (not visible here); it is turned at the two reversing drums at the top, then passes round the left-hand cylinder and is printed from the outer forme, shown emerging at the left. The completed sheets are delivered to the board lying across the frame between the cylinders. (Wilson, F. J. F., and Grey, D., *Modern printing machinery*, London 1888, p. 151; see ibid., p. 315 for a diagram of the tape travel.)

two cylinders, one of which has the inked type imposed round its curved surface while the other supplies the impression; paper from a web (or roll) is fed between the cylinders, giving them very high speeds. Nicholson patented a rotary press in 1790, and various primitive rotaries were built from 1813 onwards, but none of the earlier machines was entirely satisfactory. The trouble lay in the difficulty of imposing type on a curved surface. The solution to the problem proved to be a curved stereo plate, cast from a flong mould bent to the shape of a curved casting-box, and first patented in France in 1845. Technical difficulties persisted for a few years longer, and it was the web rotaries of the 1860s, which achieved outputs of the order of 10,000 complete eight-page newspapers per hour, that first realized the potential of the machine.[24] Even the fully-developed rotary, which soon included devices for cutting and folding the paper as well as for printing and perfecting it, remained fundamentally simple. The basic printing unit (which might be duplicated) consisted of a plate cylinder mounted adjacent to an impression cylinder, with a battery of inking rollers on the other side. There were no major reciprocating parts, and speed was limited in practice only by the fragility of the web of paper.

Finally there was the platen jobber, a brilliant answer to the widespread

[24] Wilson, F. J. F., and Grey, D., op. cit., Part 2.

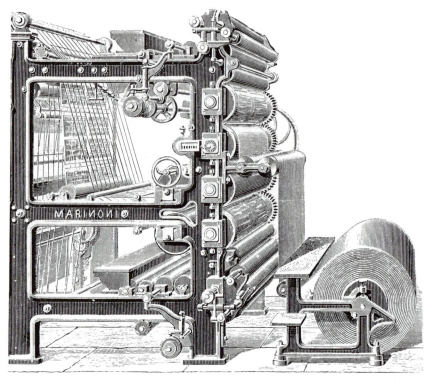

FIG. 115. Marinoni rotary perfecting machine, *c.* 1872. The web of paper is fed from the right to one of the two impression cylinders in the middle of the stack; on either side of them are the two plate cylinders, with sets of inking rollers top and bottom. Completed, cut sheets are delivered on the left. (Wilson, F. J. F., and Grey, D., *Modern printing machinery*, London 1888, p. 234.)

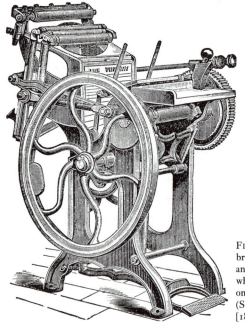

FIG. 116. 'Minerva' platen jobber. The treadle drive brings forme and platen together for the impression and operates the inking rollers between impressions, while the operator delivers the printed sheets with one hand and feeds fresh paper with the other. (Southward, J., *Practical printing*, 4th ed., London [1892], p. 352.)

need for a cheap, simple machine for dealing with the minor jobs such as billheads and cards for which the hand-press was too slow and the full-sized printing machine too large to be economic.[25] Invented around 1850 by the Americans Stephen Ruggles and George Gordon, the platen jobber worked after the fashion of a bivalve shell. A small forme was fixed in a vertical bed, where it was inked automatically between each impression by rollers which took ink from a revolving disc at the top of the machine. The platen faced the bed and was pressed against the type by toggle-action levers, which moved either the platen or the bed, or both. The operator worked the press by means of a handle or (more commonly) a treadle, and at the same time laid the paper on the platen by hand (and delivered it) between each impression. Platen jobbers were relatively small—the foolscap folio machine with a chase measuring only 33 × 23 cm. inside was the most convenient size, larger machines needing belt drive—but they were cheap, they required scarcely any make-ready, and they were fast. A boy could work a platen jobber at the speed of 1,000–1,200 impressions per hour, and output could easily be increased by making several stereo plates of the same job and working them together.[26] Platen jobbers poured on to the market in the 1880s, and they remained standard equipment in all small offices until the 1950s.

A word may be added here about standards of workmanship. Led by masters such as Bulmer, Bensley, and the Didots, the hand printers of the early nineteenth century did work with the new iron hand-presses that was a great improvement in clarity and precision over the presswork of the eighteenth-century common press; and the operators of cylinder and platen machines found that they could produce work of even higher quality. Mid-nineteenth-century printing was indeed marred on occasion by weak design, and by the use of worn plates and of poor-quality paper and ink, but by the 1850s the generality of printers were reaching a standard of presswork that had hitherto been achieved only exceptionally; a crisp, even impression became the norm, along with the use of respectable paper and ink, and of type that was not noticeably worn. This represented a real change in standards, for even the best of machines would not do good work if they were carelessly handled or fed with second-rate materials.

[25] Green, R., *The history of the platen jobber*, privately printed, Chicago 1953.
[26] Southward, J., *Practical printing*, 4th ed., London [1892], p. 352.

Processes of Reproduction[1]

DEVELOPMENTS in the processes of graphic reproduction were as remarkable as any of the technological advances that affected printing during the nineteenth century. The traditional relief and intaglio processes were continued without fundamental change; but lithography involved an entirely new method of transferring an image from printing surface to paper; while the application of photography to printing introduced a method of reproduction that was potentially as important as printing itself, and which was eventually to penetrate if not to control every department of book production.

ENGRAVINGS

Blocks and plates continued to be cut in the nineteenth century in the same ways as before (see pp. 154-8), although the influence of Bewick led to a general improvement in the techniques of engraving, and especially in the fineness of line mastered by ordinary engravers.

Wood engravings succeeded copper plates as the chief medium for good-quality book illustration during the first decade of the century and, despite competition from steel plates in the 1830s and 1840s, they retained their position until satisfactory photographic blocks became freely available around 1890. The normal procedure was for the artist to make a reversed drawing for an illustration directly on to the face of the block, and for the engraver to cut through the drawing, interpreting the shading, etc., in his own way. The work was laborious, a detailed illustration sometimes taking ten or twelve working days to cut, but the best engravers were more than mere copyists; some indeed made blocks that were works of art in themselves, as well as being miracles of skill. From 1866-7 it became usual to photograph the original drawing on to the face of the block (which was sensitized for the purpose) as a guide to the engraver, but blocks were cut by hand until well into the 1890s.[2]

The life of a block could be prolonged indefinitely by making an electrotype of it with the use of a wax mould, in the same way as making an electro of a page of type (p. 206). This practice does not appear to have been common in England until the later nineteenth century, but at the Harper Establishment in New York, all blocks were electrotyped by the mid 1850s,

---

[1] See the bibliography, p. 408 and, for a convenient illustrated summary, Twyman, M., *Printing 1770-1970*, London 1970, ch. 2.

[2] Southward, J., *Progress in printing*, London 1897, p. 21; Fildes, Sir P., 'Phototransfer of drawings in wood-block engraving', *Journal of the Printing Historical Society*, v, 1969, pp. 87-97.

in the forme along with the type.[3] Blocks could of course be duplicated in the same way, and by about 1850 type-founders were offering their standard cuts as electros.

Colour printing from suites of wood blocks, used hitherto chiefly for separate prints, became common for book illustration in the 1840s and soon afterwards for the printed covers of yellow-backs.[4] The technique was to cut the design in the ordinary way for printing in black, then to transfer it from this key block to the faces of the several colour blocks by setting-off wet pulls on to them. The colour blocks were next cut to give the necessary tints to various parts of the picture; and finally the suite was printed in the way outlined (pp. 261-2) above.

The chief technical problem in printing from copperplates was, as always, that of preventing noticeable wear, and steel plates were substituted for copper around 1820.[5] They could be softened for engraving and then retempered for printing; or they could be etched without softening. Sometimes the shaded portions of a picture were worked mechanically with a sort of 'rose engine'. Copperplates, both engraved and etched, were used again for book illustration from the mid century—in some of Dickens's novels for instance—especially after 1858 when it was found that a durable skin could be grown directly on to the surface of the plate by the electrotype process, which gave it a life comparable to that of a steel plate.[5a]

LITHOGRAPHY[6]

The principles of lithography were established in Germany by Alois Senefelder in 1798, and the methods he developed during the succeeding twenty years were those chiefly used by his successors. Water, he saw, will not lie on a greasy surface, but a greasy printing ink will. The lithographer therefore draws a design with a grease pencil or a greasy ink on a flat surface that is sufficiently porous to retain the marks; a fine-grained limestone is especially suitable, and it can be surfaced with different grades of abrasive to produce a more or less toned effect in the design. The drawing is next fixed with an acid solution, which also slightly etches the unmarked parts of the surface. Then the whole stone is washed over with water, with the result that a film of water lies on the unmarked parts of the stone, but not on the greasy marks of the design. Next the stone is rolled with a greasy printing ink, which is repelled by the water on the unmarked part of the surface but

---

[3] Abbott, J., op. cit., p. 96.

[4] Evans, E., *Reminiscences*, ed. McLean, R., Oxford 1967.

[5] The steel-plate process was patented in 1810 (no. 3385, 1 Oct. 1810) but was not used commercially for ten years.

[5a] The process of steeling copperplates was patented on 29 March 1859 (no. 667), from a communication by H. Garnier.   [6] Twyman, M., *Lithography 1800-1850*, Oxford 1970.

is accepted by the greasy marks. Finally a sheet of printing paper is laid directly on to the surface of the stone and run through a suitable press, where it takes a reversed impression of the design.

Lithographic stones are easy to prepare, they can give a very large number of impressions, and they can be resurfaced by polishing with an abrasive. Senefelder also anticipated lithographic printing from grained zinc plates, which were cheaper though slightly coarser than the best lime-stone, and the use of transfer-papers on which unreversed designs could be drawn and then transferred to the stone or plate in a press. The zinc-plate and transfer methods proved to be especially valuable in photolithography, but plain lithography was generally preferred for art work.

Lithography was well established in Europe and America by 1820 for the reproduction of music, maps, and decorative prints. It was less well suited to book illustration, having to be printed separately from the letter-press, and it did not seriously challenge wood engraving except in the specialized fields of technical and scientific illustration where particularly fine detail was required.

Coloured lithographs were another matter, and they virtually created a market for high-quality colour-plate books in the 1840s, and were then widely used up to the 1890s for such things as the frontispieces to children's books and for works of popular information.[7] Some colour had been commonly added to decorative lithographic prints from about 1818 by means of a tint stone, with which a transparent colour—usually pale buff—was printed over the whole or part of the design. But in the late 1830s Engelmann in France and Hullmandel in England developed processes of 'chromolithography' whereby pictures in full colour were printed from suites of stones. Engelmann's technique was based on the analysis of the constituent primary colours of the picture to be reproduced, and used only three colour stones (red, yellow, and blue) to make a full-colour print, with perhaps a black stone added for depth. But for the most part chromo-lithographers combined the three-colour method with the superimposition of flat tones (as in colour printing from wood blocks) and used a larger number of colour stones than the basic three.

Nineteenth-century lithography was a separate trade, with its own draughtsmen and printers, analogous to the copperplate trade of the hand-press period; and by the early 1820s a lithographic hand-press was in general use that was similar to the copperplate press except that the printing surface was run under a scraper rather than a roller.[8] Towards

---

[7] McLean, R., *Victorian book design & colour printing*, 2nd ed., London 1972.

[8] Twyman, M., 'The lithographic hand press 1796-1850', *Journal of the Printing Historical Society*, iii, 1967, pp. 3-50.

the end of the century, however, powered lithographic cylinder machines were developed which had a productivity comparable with that of the letterpress machinery of the period, and they were followed around 1900 by lithographic rotaries which ran at yet higher speeds. These new machines, used in conjunction with photographic transfer methods of plate preparation, pointed the way to the integration of lithographic with general letterpress printing which took place during the first half of the twentieth century.

Anastatic printing was a form of transfer metal-plate lithography which, as well as being a cheap method of duplicating specially-written documents, offered the interesting possibility of making prints direct from letterpress originals.[9] A printed woodcut or page of type-printed matter could be soaked in nitric acid and then pressed on to the surface of a metal plate, which was attacked by the acid in the paper except where it was inhibited by the original printing ink. The plate, lightly etched in this way, could then be used to make lithographic prints which were direct mechanical copies of printed originals, not hand-drawn facsimiles; and the process was intended to be used for reproducing old printed documents as well as recent ones. (Anastatic prints have the characteristically flat appearance of lithography, and are unlikely to be confused with letterpress originals.) In fact it appears that few early originals were copied in this way; the process was used in England in a limited way for duplicating and for reproducing illustrations from about 1845 to about 1870, but then lost ground to photolithography and to cheaper methods of planographic duplication.

PHOTOGRAPHIC PROCESSES[10]

The early photographically-illustrated books (of which Fox Talbot's *The pencil of nature*, London 1844, was the first) contained actual photographs mounted on the pages, and the first ink-printed photographs were pictures of works of art reproduced by means of intaglio plates for sale as prints. Daguerrotypes had been etched to make plates from which a few prints could be taken as early as 1839, but it was not until the 1850s that Fox Talbot in England and Pretsch in Vienna developed methods of photoengraving intaglio plates that had commercial possibilities.

The appearance of Pretsch's *Photographic art treasures* (London 1856-7), which consisted of large prints made by 'photogalvanography', showed the potential of the new process. A photographic exposure was made on a surface of gelatine treated so that it reproduced the picture in negative relief,

[9] Wakeman, G., 'Anastatic printing for Sir Thomas Phillipps', *Journal of the Printing Historical Society*, v, 1969, pp. 24-40; idem., *Aspects of Victorian lithography*, Wymondham 1970.
[10] This section is based primarily on Eder, J. F., *History of photography*, trs. Epstean, E., New York 1945; and Gernsheim, H. and A., *The history of photography . . . up to 1914*, 2nd ed., London 1970. See also [Wood, H. T.], *Modern methods of illustrating books*, London 1887.

tone resulting from the reticulation of the drying gelatine; the surface was then moulded in rubber, the mould was electrotyped to make a copper matrix, and this matrix was itself electrotyped to make a positive intaglio plate for printing on a copperplate press. The process was very expensive —the preparation of a plate took about six weeks—and books continued to be illustrated with actual photographs, not mechanical prints.

Experiment continued vigorously until, in 1879, Karl Klič of Vienna perfected photogravure, an extremely faithful—though still expensive— method of etching the image of a photograph directly on to a copper plate which was grained with resin dust for the reproduction of tone. Of greater relevance to ordinary printing were two later developments in which Klič was again prominent: these were the toning of the plate by interposing a net of fine lines (the half-tone screen, pp. 271-2) between the projected image and the plate; and the development of a rotary press for gravure printing on which a scraper (the doctor) removed the excess ink from the surface of the intaglio plate. Rotogravure, as the fully developed process was called, was established in 1890-5, and was used for the reproduction of the highest class of book and magazine illustrations during the rest of the machine-press period.[11]

The 1850s also saw the appearance of photolithography, whereby a chemical film spread on the surface of a litho stone or plate was rendered insoluble and water-repellent by exposure to light; so that the image of a photograph projected on to it became the equivalent of a design in grease pencil, tone being supplied by the grain of the underlying surface. The bitumen (or asphalt) photolitho process of Lemercier and others (1852) gave only a handful of prints from each stone, but the bichromate process of Poitevin and Lemercier (1855) could give as many as 700 prints from a single stone, and could be used with photographic transfers. The early photolitho books of 1856-7 were again collections of reproductions of art photographs, but in 1858 there was an event of greater bibliographical significance: the production of a photolitho facsimile of a printed book. The subject was the Duke of Devonshire's copy of the first quarto of *Hamlet*, of which 40 facsimiles were photolithographed on behalf of the Duke by J. Netherclift, working under the direction of the Shakespeare scholar (and forger) J. Payne Collier. This facsimile and its twin (Q2 *Hamlet*, 1859) were remarkably well done—there was little retouching, and the results are closer to the originals than were the Griggs-Furnivall photolitho facsimiles of the 1880s—and they were moreover the forerunners of a method

---

[11] The essence of photogravure is the employment of intaglio plates, not relief blocks. There are various ways of introducing tone in photogravure, the half-tone screen now being the most usual; but the term 'half-tone' by itself means a toned relief block (pp. 271-2).

of book production that was to challenge letterpress printing itself a hundred years later. Meanwhile photolithography by the zinc-plate transfer process was firmly established in the early 1860s for the printing of maps and music.

Collotype, which was also originated by Poitevin in 1855 but not immediately developed, was a version of bichromate photolithography in which tone was given by reticulation of the gelatine in the chemical film rather than by graining the underlying surface. Collotype plates could thus be made of any smooth material to which the film would adhere (finely-ground glass was an obvious choice), and commercial versions of the process appeared in 1868-70 which offered extremely faithful reproductions of photographs but which were relatively cheap; professional photographers, indeed, who needed a hundred or more copies of a photograph in the mid 1870s found it cheaper to have them printed from a collotype plate than to print them photographically from a negative. By that time 1,500 impressions from a single plate could be printed on a hand press at the rate of 200-300 a day (finished book illustrations were available at no more than $1\frac{1}{2}d$. each), and higher speeds were to be available in the mid 1880s from powered lithographic machinery. Colour collotypes were also introduced in the 1870s; each colour plate was made from a separate colour-filtered negative, and the suite was then printed in the same way as a chromolithograph.

The last, but from the letterpress printer's point of view the most important, of the photographic processes to appear was the photo-etching of zinc blocks in relief. In fact the earliest 'zincographs', pioneered in Paris by Firmin Gillot in the early 1850s, were not made photographically but by transferring a line drawing in a greasy and acid-resistant ink on to a zinc plate and then etching it; the ink protected the lines of the design from the acid and left them standing in relief, while the whites were etched, and subsequently routed, away so that the plate could be mounted and printed like a wood-cut. The technique was similar to that of making zinc-plate lithographs by the transfer method, the difference being in the degree to which the plate was etched, and in Paris it largely replaced wood engraving for book and magazine illustration during the 1850s. Gillot continued to be prominent in the development of the process, making zincographs with photographic transfers in the mid 1860s, and proceeding in 1872 to make a line (or process) block as we know it today, by projecting a reversed photographic negative directly on to a sensitized zinc plate and then etching out the whites. Again the plate was routed mechanically and mounted for printing.

Photo-etched blocks with tone (half-tones) soon followed. Experiments with hatched screens to divide an image into small units to give tone had been made in the 1850s, and screens were now developed for use with photographic relief blocks by Jaffé in Vienna (1877), Horgan in New York (1880), and Meisenbach in Munich (1882). A piece of glass marked with fine crossed lines was interposed between the negative and the sensitized plate on to which it was projected. The light which penetrated the interstices of this screen made dots on the emulsion (and later on the etched plate) which varied in size according to its intensity, so that when the block was printed the dots merged in the eye of the beholder to give the effect of tone. The mesh of the screen was suited to the texture of the paper on which the block was to be printed, a screen of 30 lines per linear centimetre (about 75 lines per inch) being used for rough-surfaced newsprint, and screens of up to 70 lines per cm. (about 175 lines per inch) for coated papers.

The use of half-tone blocks in newspapers and magazines spread gradually during the period 1885-95, and by the early 1890s they were being used for book illustration as well, usually in the form of inserted plates on art paper; the same decade saw the demise of commercial wood engraving. There were also experiments in the 1890s with three-colour half-tones (three plates being made with red-, yellow-, and blue-filtered negatives, usually with the addition of a black plate for depth), and with multicolour photogravure.[12]

IDENTIFICATION

The identification of the various reproduction processes in books of the machine-press period can be difficult.[13] Letterpress blocks (wood engravings and photo-etched relief blocks) were printed in the forme along with the type and generally show some impression on the back of the leaf. Lithographs and intaglio plates, on the other hand, were printed separately from the type, often on a different paper from the ordinary sheets, and show little or no impression on the verso (although a well-etched lithographic tint stone may show a perceptible edge). Intaglio plate marks were seldom allowed to show, but there is often a slight roughness to be felt on the surface of a picture printed from copper or steel. It is not usually possible to tell a wood engraving from an electro of an engraving, or a stone lithograph from a zinc-plate lithograph.

The detail of all but the very best photographic line blocks tends to be slightly rougher at the edges than that of wood engravings or electros of engravings. The flatness of a lithograph is apparent under a magnifying glass, and there is often a slight greyness about lithographic ink when compared with letterpress ink. The texture of a half-tone block is easily

---

[12] See Southward, J., *Modern printing*, iii, London 1899, chs. 17-23.

[13] A good lens (at least × 10) is an essential tool. Better still is a compound magnifier such as the Seibert Emoskop which gives magnification in the range × 20- × 30.

resolved with a glass into its constituent dots, which are plainly round. Photogravure dots, on the other hand, tend to be rectangular and to string together in lines; and the photogravure screen appears under magnification as a white net. The magnified images of the dots of colour half-tone and colour gravure have similar characteristics.

The reader is warned, however, that there were various other processes of reproduction (seldom, in fact, used by book printers) which can be extremely difficult to distinguish from the major processes and from each other.[14]

---

[14] Harris, E. M., 'Experimental graphic processes in England 1800-1859', *Journal of the Printing Historical Society*, iv, 1968, pp. 33-86; v, 1969, pp. 41-80; vi, 1970, pp. 53-89.

Mechanical Composition,[1] and type 1875–1950

COLD-METAL MACHINES

By the early 1820s high-speed printing machines were a reality, but type was still set by hand and it was already plain that composing machinery, if it could be developed, would be a valuable complement to the new cylinder presses. The first composing machine to be patented (1822)[2] was the invention of an American resident in England, Dr. William Church; and it was followed later in the century by a number of similar machines which, while they differed from Church's original design in detail, all worked on the same basic principle. They were cold-metal machines, which set pre-cast type, as distinct from the later hot-metal machines which cast fresh type as they went along. Ordinary type was stored in magazines (one for each sort) at the top of the machine, and the operator used a keyboard to select and release the pieces of type one by one, which slid down a series of channels to a collecting tray, each line then being justified by hand. These machines worked—skilled operators of the 1850s could set type at speeds in the range 5,000–7,500 ens per hour[3]—but, since the matter still had to be justified and eventually distributed, the saving in wages was not great; and there was besides vehement opposition to the machines from the hand compositors. Most of the printers who used cold-metal machines, therefore, were those to whom an increase in the speed of composition was especially important, namely the printers of periodicals.

There appears to be no record of the use of Church's original machine, but a development by Young and Delcambre was used to set the *Family Herald* in 1842;[4] and Hattersley machines (patented in 1857)[5] were still in use for setting the *South Wales Daily News* in 1915.[6] Later versions (such as the Thorne of 1880) incorporated apparatus for distributing the type into the magazine and, less successfully, for justifying the lines; the *Manchester Guardian* was using eighteen Thorne machines around 1890, which reached speeds approaching 10,000 ens per hour.[7] Few nineteenth-century book printers used cold-metal machines, but one who did was Trow of New York, who installed Mitchell machines in 1855, the first appearance of mechanical composition in America.[8]

---

[1] See the bibliography, pp. 408–9.   [2] No. 4664, 24 Mar. 1822.
[3] Legros, L. A., and Grant, J. C., *Typographical printing surfaces*, London 1916, pp. 325, 327.
[4] The machine had already been used to set a book: Binns, E., *The anatomy of sleep*, London 1841.
[5] No. 1794, 26 June 1857.
[6] Legros, L. A., and Grant, J. C., op. cit., p. 327.   [7] Ibid., p. 370.
[8] Lehmann-Haupt, H., *The book in America*, 2nd ed., New York 1952, p. 85.

FIG. 117. Kastenbein cold-metal composing machine, *c*. 1870, used for setting the London *Times*. Operation of the keyboard releases pieces of pre-cast type from the magazine above it, which are delivered on a type-race to a second operator on the right who justifies them into lines. (Legros, L. A., and Grant, J. C., *Typographical printing-surfaces*, London 1916, pl. 27.)

HOT-METAL MACHINES

The weaknesses of the cold-metal machines were that they did not justify the lines automatically as part of the type-setting process, and that they used pre-cast type which had to be distributed for re-use (it was of course possible to recharge the machines with nothing but new type, but this could cost even more than distribution). The solution that was eventually discovered was to equip the machine with matrices, rather than pre-cast type, which could be assembled for the casting of a justified line—either as separate letters or as a single slug—in the machine itself, and to return the type after printing to the machine's metal pot for recasting. Thus separate justification and separate distribution, whether by hand or by machine, were eliminated, and printing always took place from fresh, undamaged type.

There was one difficulty however, which could have been crucial: the new machines, if they were to be produced in any quantity, would require huge numbers of matrices, which in turn needed large numbers of punches, far more indeed than could be produced by all the punch cutters then at work. At this point, however, a Milwaukee engineer named Benton needed a machine to cut master type on which electrotype matrices could be grown (he was concerned with the development of self-spacing type, and needed an exceptional number of matrices). For this purpose he refined Leavenworth's pantographic wood-letter cutter of 1834 (p. 209), and by 1884 had produced a machine which could cut not only master types from patterns, but also steel punches.[9] Benton's self-spacing type was no great success, but his punch-cutting machine was the essential prerequisite for the exploitation of hot-metal composing machinery, and primarily of the Linotype machine.

The slow, complex development of the Linotype occupied most of the 1880s, the engineer Ottmar Mergenthaler of Baltimore being its chief (though not its only) progenitor. Early versions were in commercial use by 1886, and design work on the final version of the machine was largely completed in 1888. It was not until Mergenthaler and his associates obtained Benton punch-cutters in 1889, however, that they were in a position to produce the Linotype in quantity, and large-scale series production eventually began in 1890.[10]

The Linotype was a self-contained hot-metal machine, with matrices stored in a magazine at the top. The matrices were selected by means of a keyboard and assembled, via slides and a conveyor belt, into lines, the

[9] Legros, L. A., and Grant, J. C., op. cit., ch. 12.

[10] Bullen, H. L., 'The origin and development of the Linotype machine', *The inland printer*, Feb.-Mar. 1942 (repr. in Howe, E., '*The trade*', London 1943, pp. 97-108); for technical development, see Legros, L. A., and Grant, J. C., op. cit., pp. 421-35; and for an early printer's assessment see Southward, J., *Modern printing*, ii, London 1899, ch. 16.

space key inserting a spacing wedge between each word. When the line was approaching the pre-set measure the operator ended (or if necessary broke) the word he was setting, and pressed a lever. This caused the spacing wedges to be pushed down between the words, giving equal spacing to the whole line, and the line was cast as a single type-high-slug. The slug was automatically trimmed and delivered to a galley, while at the same time the matrices were directed (by means of keyways cut in them) back into the boxes from which they had come, and the operator got on with setting the next line. (The Linotype could not of course cast the equivalent of kerned type, so that 'f' and 'j' had to be designed for it with abbreviated projections (f, j), a point which conveniently distinguishes the work of a slug-caster.[10a])

The Linotype keyboard grouped the characters according to frequency of use and ease of combination, but not in the familiar typewriter pattern. There were ninety keys arranged in fifteen near-vertical files of six; the

a

b

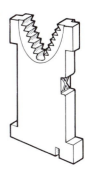

Fig. 118 (*a*). 'Square-base' Linotype machine of 1890, a design which has remained essentially unaltered. The matrix magazine is above the keyboard, and slugs are delivered to a sloping galley on the operator's left. (Legros, L. A., and Grant, J. C., *Typographical printing-surfaces*, London 1916, p. 424.)

118 (*b*). Single-letter Linotype matrix, made of brass and 32 mm. high. The teeth at the top are coded to guide the matrix back into the right part of the magazine after casting.

[10a] But see p. 279, note 12[a], below.

first five files on the left controlled the lower-case matrices, the five files in the middle the points, figures, and small capitals, and the five files on the right the capitals. The magazines contained either single matrices, in which case one key set one letter, or double matrices, when each key controlled two letters, usually the roman and italic of the same character. The arrangement shown here was the English-language pattern, used in Britain

FIG. 119. Linotype keyboard layout, English-language pattern; the hatched keys are coloured blue. (Legros, L. A., and Grant, J. C., *Typographical printing-surfaces*, London 1916, p. 294.)

and America; there were different patterns of Linotype keyboard for French, for German, and for other languages.

The introduction of the Linotype brought entirely new speeds of work into the composing room. The normal rate of an average operator was 6,000 ens per hour, and this was of course a net rate; there was no further time involved in justification or distribution, and even correction was not difficult: the operator simply keyed a new line to replace the slug containing an error. A skilled operator working under good conditions would average 8,000–10,000 ens per hour, and at typesetting competitions held in the United States in 1900 speeds in the range 12,000–17,200 ens per hour were achieved.[11]

The Linotype was quickly successful. When Mergenthaler died in 1899 more than 6,000 of his machines were in use, having faced and overcome the opposition of the hand compositors. A majority of them were in the larger American newspaper offices, but Linotypes were already being built under licence in England and Germany; and there were soon to be other slug-casters, such as the Intertype, which were variants of the basic Linotype. In America the Linotype was soon used for setting books as well as newspapers, and it has remained the principal composing machine there for all purposes. In Europe, however, printers did not manage to get such

[11] Legros, L. A., and Grant, J. C., op. cit., pp. 429–30.

good results from their Linotypes as did their American contemporaries, and Linotypes were not much used by the book houses.

The other important hot-metal machine, the Monotype, worked on different lines.[12] It was really two separate machines, the keyboard and the caster, which were worked apart from each other, usually in different rooms. Operation of the keyboard punched holes in a roll (or spool) of paper, the positions of the holes indicating the various characters; the spool was in fact a set of coded instructions like a pianola roll or a punched computer tape. When he came towards the end of a line, the operator finished or broke the last word according to its length, and calculated (with the aid of a device on the machine) the amount of space that would be required between each word to fill the line out to the measure; then a coding for the spaces was punched in, and he proceeded to key the next line. If he was conscious of having made a mistake, the operator could paste a patch over the wrongly punched holes, and punch them again.

The finished spool then went to the casting room. The heart of the caster was the matrix case, a metal plate which held a grid of 225 matrices, one for each key of the keyboard and for each character of a fount. Air blown through the holes in the paper of the punched spool caused the matrix case to be pushed back and forth and sideways, each coding of punched holes bringing the correct matrix into position over an adjustable mould. A separate type was then automatically cast in the mould, its width being determined by the position of the matrix in the grid. In order that each line should be properly spaced the spool was run through the caster backwards, the last character to be keyboarded being the first to be cast. In this way the machine came to the coding for the spacing of a line before setting it, and was enabled to cast a space of the proper width between each word.

The caster produced a galley of type which, although it came out of the machine last line first, was otherwise very like a galley of hand-set founders' type. Kerned type could be cast as freely by Monotype as in a hand mould;[12a] and correction of the set type by individual characters could be carried out in the ordinary way. There were the further advantages that a punched spool could be used with different grids of matrices (inexpensively hired from the manufacturers) to cast a text in different founts, and that it could be stored for recasting at a later date.

The Monotype was also an American invention (the work primarily of Tolbert Lanston and J. S. Bancroft),[13] but it found its greatest success in

---

[12] Ibid., pp. 393-404.

[12a] The earliest Monotype founts had kernless f and j, but kerning was introduced in 1905-8 (information from Nicolas Barker).

[13] 'The pioneer days of "Monotype" composing machines', *The Monotype recorder*, xxxix, 1950, no. 1.

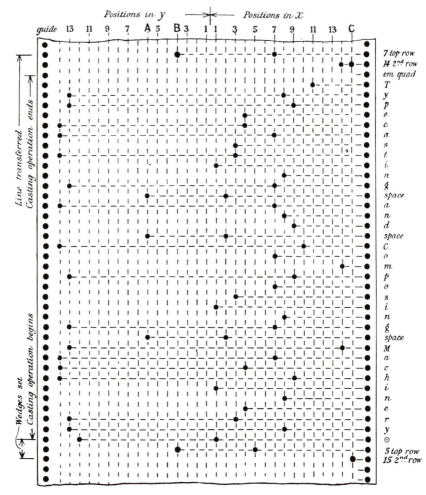

FIG. 120 (*a*). Perforated ribbon from a Monotype spool of 1901–7, with the 'C' code for the line 'Type-casting and Composing Machinery.'. The line is keyboarded from top to bottom, ending with spacing instructions; the caster begins at the bottom, taking the spacing instructions first and casting the letters in reverse order. The code can be deciphered by comparing the positions in *x* and *y* with the co-ordinates of the matrix grid shown in (*b*). (Legros, L. A., and Grant, J. C., *Typographical printing-surfaces*, London 1916, p. 399.)

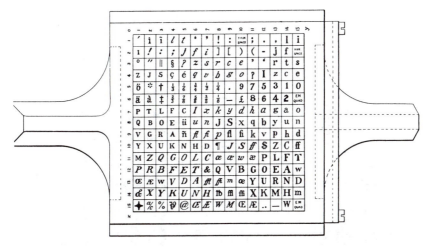

120 (*b*). Plan of a Monotype matrix case, pattern C. The matrices, which are blocks of bronze about 7 mm. square at the face, were re-arranged for the D keyboard, but the relationship between the keyboard code and the grid remained essentially the same. (Legros, L. A., and Grant, J. C., op. cit., p. 400.)

Europe, where book printers were attracted by the fact that its individual types could be handled and printed in the same way as hand-set type; with few exceptions they looked down on the Linotype as being incapable of the best work, ignoring American proofs to the contrary. Technical difficulties beset the development of the Monotype through the 1890s, and it was not until 1901 that the English Monotype Corporation could offer American-built machines in quantity. Even then they moved fairly slowly, partly because the Monotype was not so economical as the Linotype (the Monotype keyboard operator worked at much the same speed as the Linotype operator but did only half the work, since the spool then had to be cast at another machine), and partly because the layout of the keyboard was at first very awkward. Until 1907 the Monotype keyboard was arranged not according to the frequency of use of the keys, but to the thickness of the types they controlled; the file of keys (from top to bottom) on the left-hand side controlled the thinnest letters, the file on the right the thickest—and, worse still, a change of fount might mean a change of keyboard layout. In 1908, however, the 'D' keyboard was introduced, with a standard layout based on the typewriter pattern. The change from hand-setting to machine-composition accelerated and by the early 1920s, when a wholly English-built machine was marketed, most of the large book houses in Britain were using Monotype.

Small printers who could not afford composing machinery of their own could still take advantage of the economies it offered by sending copy to

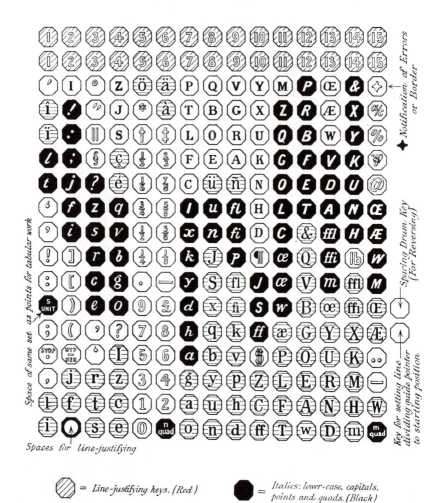

= Line-justifying keys. (Red)

= Italics: lower-case, capitals, points and quads. (Black)

= Small capitals, points, peculiars, figures & fractions. (Blue)

= Roman: lower-case, capitals and lower-case accents. (White)

Fig. 121 (*a*). Layout of the Monotype C keyboard. (Legros, L. A., and Grant, J. C., *Typographical printing-surfaces*, London 1916, p. 292.)

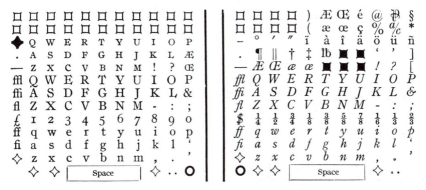

Fig. 121 (*b*). Layout of the Monotype D keyboard; the unlabelled keys at the top are for line-justifying. (Legros, L. A., and Grant, J. C., op. cit., p. 293.)

be set at the composing machines of larger firms; they would get back set type in galleys, which they would then make up and print themselves, thereby saving both compositors' wages and investment in founders' type. Some of the larger English newspaper offices, whose Linotypes otherwise stood idle for much of the day, were offering typesetting services of this sort by the mid 1890s; while Monotype services were even more attractive to small printers since it allowed them to correct the type themselves.

TYPE SINCE 1875[14]

The general use of casting machinery from around 1860 (pp. 207–8) lowered the price of type, but had little effect on its design. Even the appearance of the punch-cutting machine in 1884 did not immediately prompt the production of new founts of text type by artists who were not punch-cutters; the moderns and old-styles that had appeared by the 1860s continued to dominate commercial printing until the end of the century.

This period did, however, see the long-overdue standardization of type dimensions and units of measurement.[15] It has already been mentioned that the Fournier and Didot point systems were widely adopted in continental Europe during the mid nineteenth century, initially with Fournier's unit of 0·349 mm., and later with the Didot point of 0·376 mm.; and at the same time there was a gradual adoption in Europe of the French height-to-paper of 23·566 mm. Anarchy persisted for longer in the English-speaking world. In 1886 the leading type-founders of the United States agreed to use as a standard the pica of Mackellar, Smiths, and Jordan (the firm that was the descendant of the first important native founders in America,

14 See the bibliography, p. 405.

15 Legros, L. A., and Grant, J. C., op. cit., ch. 7; Figgins, J., *Type founding and printing during the nineteenth century*, London 1900, *passim*.

Binney and Ronaldson), dividing it into 12 points of 0·351 mm. each; this was significantly less than the European standard point of 0·376 mm. At the same time the Americans adopted a standard height-to-paper of 23·317 mm., again significantly different from the European standard. The amalgamation, under pressure from Linotype competition, of the major American type-foundries into the American Type Founders Company (A.T.F.) in 1892 gave added authority to the new units, and they were gradually adopted by the English trade in the period 1898–1905. Standardization never became quite complete, especially as regards height-to-paper; the Clarendon Press, which until the late nineteenth century used two different heights for different sorts of work, sturdily retains the so-called Dutch height of 23·851 mm. to this day, and various aberrant heights may still be found in Europe. There have been fewer differences in body units. Fournier points lingered in northern France and a few other places in continental Europe until the First World War, and the Monotype Corporation at first used a private point system, but there has been little variation from the two main standards since the 1920s.

A further refinement was the development around 1905 of standard line. The baseline of a fount (see fig. 1 (b), p. 9) had hitherto been placed in a haphazard position on the body, relative to the front and back of the type; consequently different founts of the same body seldom lined alike, and could not be set tidily together. Now a standard line was agreed, first in America and soon afterwards in Britain; and a similar but necessarily different standard was proposed in Europe for use with Didot bodies. There was a common line for ordinary founts, and a title line for titlings without descenders.

This standardization, together with the widespread use of electrotype matrices, meant that founts of type from different foundries could not be told apart, incredible as this may seem to students of the type of earlier periods. Legros and Grant devised a simple test to prove the point. They set four stanzas of doggerel 'in type from three different foundries using different matrices, different moulds, and different machines. In one verse the product is entirely that of foundry A; in another it is mixed with sorts from foundry B; in yet another it is mixed with sorts from foundry C; while in the remaining verse the products of the three foundries are mingled.' Legros and Grant successfully defied the experts to say which type was which—a task in which they themselves, and the compositor who had set the type up, also failed—and it is difficult to avoid their conclusion that 'to distinguish which individual type is the product of which individual type-foundry is probably beyond the limits of human achievement'.[16]

---

[16] Legros, L. A., and Grant, J. C., op. cit., pp. 117-18.

I.

The expert is a man of worth,
   Far above me and you;
For he knows everything on earth
   From China to Peru!

II.

Should you engage him on the spot
   To criticize you this,
You'll find his criticism not,
   The thing he thinks it is.

III.

Suppose he says, "It's clear as day,"
   The thing he's asked to do,
Well, it's been done the other way:
   We've different points of view.

IV.

Which type is which? "Aye, there's the rub!"
   Come Experts to the test;
From London even to the "Hub"
   And do your very best!

FIG. 122. Old-style roman from three different foundries: which is which? (Legros, L. A., and Grant, J. C., *Typographical printing-surfaces*, London 1916, p. 117.)

The influence of William Morris on the typography and presswork of the twentieth century was great, but it was influenced at second hand.[17] The private-press movement, of which Morris's Kelmscott Press (1884–96) was the chief (but not quite the only) begetter, showed how different and how magnificent a book could be when it was printed in type cut in a medieval or renaissance manner, with boundless care for layout, paper, ink, impression, and binding; but it did not offer a practical model to the trade. The private-press books were in general idiosyncratic, uneconomical, and unreadable, and the same may be said in particular of the private-press types. These extraordinary books, nevertheless, did profoundly impress the generation of designers and printers who were to be responsible for commercial book production after the First World War, and it was then, a quarter of a century after his death, that Morris's teaching and example had its greatest effect.

Meanwhile commercial book printers, with few exceptions, continued to favour the modern faces and old styles that they had inherited from the

[17] For an excellent short survey of twentieth-century typography, see McLean, R., *Modern book design, from William Morris to the present day*, [2nd ed.], London 1958.

nineteenth century. Punch-cutting machines were increasingly used from the late 1890s for the production of new founts, most of them intended for use in periodicals and display. There were already distinguished designers at work—F. W. Goudy in America, de Roos and van de Velde in Europe, all influenced by Morris; and Auriol and Grasset working for Peignot in France, their styles deriving from *art nouveau*—but the typical new type of the period was Cheltenham, an old-style magazine and display series designed by Bertram Goodhue of New York in 1896, a mechanical design that is given a spurious air of antiquity by its quaint g and r.

The expert observer, the man with the discerning eye, is the man who " picks up " what other men miss. The point at which real value is reached is that behind the obvious. And that is the point for young business men to aim at.

FIG. 123. Caslon's Cheltenham old style, 14-pt. solid. (H. Williams & Son, [1909] specimen.)

The makers of the hot-metal composing machines also began by giving the trade what it was used to: more copies of the nineteenth-century moderns and old styles. The type faces offered by Linotype remained undistinguished —and almost indistinguishable from their models—until the appointment of C. H. Griffith as typographic Director in New York in 1916.[18] During his long reign—he retired in 1949—Griffith oversaw the development of a satisfying range of new and revived faces for Linotype, but during the same period the English Monotype Corporation undertook an even more adventurous typographical programme, and it was Monotype that established itself as typographical leader of the English-speaking world in the second quarter of the twentieth century.[19]

Monotype's first two faces (Series 1, Modern No. 1, 1900, and Series 2, Old style, 1901) were as typical of the period as was Cheltenham and gave no hint of what was to come. The initiative in taking the opportunity offered by the commercial success of composing machinery to pursue the typographical ideals of the private-press movement came in the first place from two publishers, J. M. Dent who commissioned Series 59 Veronese (1911), a mannered Venetian deriving from Morris, and G. T. Meynell who specified the much more successful Series 101 Imprint (1912), an excellent variation of Caslon that was given a strength and regularity that suited it

[18] Information from Mr. Jackson Burke.
[19] 'Fifty years of type cutting', *The Monotype recorder*, xxxix, 1950, no. 2.

for machine printing. The Corporation's own first venture with a new face was the equally fine Series 110 Plantin (1913), a powerful version of the 'Garalde' roman, and the first commercial attempt to make a scholarly interpretation of an early design. But these efforts to reform typography had little general effect, and when the First World War slowed further development the work of trade printers everywhere was still based on nineteenth-century faces.

The art of book design lies mainly in relating size and x-height to the

FIG 124 (*a*). Monotype series 1, Modern No. 1 (1900), 11-pt.

The art of book design lies mainly in relating size and x-height to the

FIG. 124 (*b*). Monotype series 2, Old Style (1901), 11-pt.

The art of book design lies mainly in relating size and x-height to the

FIG. 124 (*c*). Monotype series 101, Imprint (1912), 11-pt.

The art of book design lies mainly in relating size and x-height to the

FIG. 124 (*d*). Monotype series 110, Plantin (1913), 11-pt.

Then in 1922 the English Monotype Corporation initiated a typographical programme of great originality—much to its credit, for there was little competition in the expensive business of raising typographical standards. Under the direction of H. M. Duncan and W. I. Burch, and with the all-important services of Stanley Morison as typographical adviser, the next seventeen years saw the creation of a wonderful collection of revived and original type faces. Their effect on traditional printing everywhere was profound; and, as far as the English-speaking world is concerned, their use is still so widespread that it is unnecessary to do more than name a few of them: first, six revivals from the hand-press period, Series 156 Garamond (1922); 169 Baskerville (1923); 185 Fournier (1925); 270 Bembo (1929); 341 Bell (1931); and 453 Ehrhardt (1938). Secondly, four new designs: Series 239 Perpetua (1929, Eric Gill); 327 Times (1931, Stanley Morison); 262 Gill Sans (1933, Eric Gill); and 481 Albertus (1937, Berthold Wolpe).

But originality in type- and book-design between the wars was not confined to England: there were notable typographers in France, Germany, Holland, Sweden, Switzerland, and the United States, whose work tended to accentuate the national style of book production in each country. The style of the German Bauhaus (Dessau, late 1920s) was to have a more than local influence, shifting the typographical emphasis from the design of the type-face to the placing of the printed images on the page, but it was slow to spread and had little general effect before 1950. Meanwhile the typographical revival deriving from Morris took hold at last in commercial book-production, under the direction of a new type of professional, the publisher's designer. Hot-metal composing machines were used everywhere, and the old type-foundries, no longer supplying large founts for setting books and periodicals, contracted and amalgamated into the few firms that survive today supplying display founts to jobbing printers.

Printing Practice in the Machine-press Period[1]

THE complex history of the development of the printing trade during the machine-press period from a medieval craft into a mechanized industry, with all the differences of scale and emphasis that occurred in various countries, cannot of course be followed in detail here. Two aspects of this history, however, are of particular concern to bibliographers: the characteristics and quality of the workforce employed by the book printers, and the production routines that they habitually followed.

PERSONNEL

By the mid nineteenth century printing offices varied widely in size. At one end of the scale were a large number of small shops that had scarcely changed since the eighteenth century but for the introduction of iron hand-presses and perhaps of a small cylinder machine or a platen jobber; at the other were a small number of large factories in the cities, with shifting workforces, hours often geared to the deadlines of periodicals, and the flow of production dependent upon rows of clattering machines tended by tired children.

The small shops were still worked by ten or a dozen men each, but the large numbered their workers by hundreds. In 1850 the Imperial and Government Printing Establishment in Vienna had 46 cylinder machines, 50 iron hand-presses, 150,000 kg. of type, and a workforce of 868; the weekly output approached 4,000 printed reams.[2] At that time there were no British or American printing factories that were quite so large, but in 1843 Clowes of London, a firm which combined book and magazine printing, used 24 Applegath and Cowper perfectors and 24 hand-presses to print 1,500 reams a week; the works included type and stereotype foundries, and kept in store 2,500 tonnes of stereo plates and 80,000 woodcuts; in 1864 the same firm had 27 machines and a workforce of 568.[3] The Harper Establishment of New York, another combined book and magazine house, was of comparable size in the mid 1850s: there were 28 Adams platen machines with a probable output of about 1,250 printed reams a week; all work was electrotyped, and the factory included both a type-foundry and a bindery.[4]

[1] See the bibliography, pp. 409–10.

[2] *Geschichte der K.K. Hof- und Staatsdruckerei in Wien*, Wien 1851, *passim*.

[3] Dodd, G., *Days at the factories, series 1*, London 1843, pp. 326–60; 'Children's employment Commission (1862), 5th report of the Commissioners', *Parliamentary papers 1866*, xxiv, Evidence, p. 14.

[4] Abbott, J., *The Harper establishment*, New York 1855, *passim*.

The broad division of printing personnel into managerial staff (owners and overseers), correctors, skilled journeymen (compositors and pressmen), and apprentices continued into the machine-press period, but the situation was complicated by an increase in the proportion of apprentices to journeymen, and by the introduction of printing machinery which required the services both of skilled machine minders and of unskilled machine boys. In the hand-press period the proportion of apprentices to journeymen had been limited by trade custom and gild rules but, with the demand for print increasing in the later eighteenth century, the old restraints were ignored and by the beginning of the nineteenth century many British printers had come to rely for most of their work on relays of apprentices, who were simply discharged at the end of their terms and replaced by new apprentices; the old-time indoor apprentices, who had boarded and lodged with the master and received only nominal wages, were mostly replaced by outdoor apprentices who found their own board and lodging and were paid wages according to their skill and experience (characteristically from a quarter to a half of the journeyman's time rate).[5] Since the outdoor apprentice became a competent compositor or pressman after no more than one or two years but was bound for seven, his labour was both convenient and cheap.

The journeymen suffered endemic unemployment. Charles Manby Smith, who completed his apprenticeship at Bristol in 1826, could find no work there and came to London with no better result. 'In vain I walked from one end of London to the other, and trod the "stony-hearted streets" from morning to night, day after day. . . . Sometimes of an evening, after my miserable journeyings through the day, I would stand for hours in the Strand, leaning against the shutters of a closed shop, and watching the compositors at work by gaslight on the opposite side of the way, upon a morning paper. How I envied them. . . .'[6] Smith eventually found employment in Paris.

Printing machines were operated by two new grades of worker, machine minders and machine boys. Machine minders were skilled but were not as a rule ex-pressmen, and not all of them served a regular apprenticeship, in spite of the protests of the journeymen; some of them had been machine boys. The boys themselves, who in mid-nineteenth-century London might begin work at the age of 11 (but more usually 12 or 13) were not apprenticed. They came from poor homes—many indeed were illiterate—and did no more than feed paper into the machines and take delivery after printing, tasks of appalling monotony. They were paid so little that it was cheaper

---

[5] Howe, E., *The London compositor*, London 1947, ch. 4.
[6] Smith, C. M., *The working man's way in the world*, London 1857 (repr. London 1967), p. 18.

to hire boys than to fit the automatic delivery mechanisms that were already available.[7]

Hours of work were anything but regular. In news and periodical offices night work was so usual as to be the rule, and even book houses which nominally worked set hours during the day rarely avoided night work entirely. From 1810 normal hours were down from the eighteenth-century 72 per week to about 60; a typical week would be 8 a.m. to 8 p.m. on Mondays to Fridays with 1½ hours off each day for meals, and 8 a.m. to 2 p.m. on Saturdays. But in practice compulsory overtime to 10 p.m. or midnight was a very common occurrence, with all-night working when there was a rush on. Overtime was supposedly voluntary, but in practice the men could not risk their employment by refusing it. In March 1864 Thomas Meek, a machine boy at the Clowes works in London, told a member of the Children's Employment Commission: 'Am 12 next week; have been eight months here; have worked five times all night; can't recollect how often until 12. p.m. . . . Last week I worked till 8 p.m. on Monday; till 10 p.m. on Tuesday and Wednesday; on Thursday the machine was stopped a good part of the day, and I left at 8 p.m.; on Friday I worked till 12 p.m., and on Saturday left at 3 p.m. Have never been to day school or a Sunday school; can't read. . . .' The Commission added: 'This boy [a printer's son] is said to be one of the best workers in the room.'[8] In 1872 the men secured a 9-hour day, 54-hour week, but overtime remained common.

The environment was often unpleasant.[9] Printing houses—apart from the few that had been built for the purpose rather than converted from something else—were generally filthy and badly ventilated. Even by day artificial light was usually needed and, since the men refused to open the windows, the heat and fumes from gaslights rendered the air scarcely breathable; mid-nineteenth-century printers died earlier than workers in other trades, and the death rate from consumption in particular was double the average. There is an astonishing account in Charles Manby Smith's autobiography of the rushed production of parliamentary blue books at Hansard's printing office in the late 1830s, when the compositors worked non-stop, breaking off only to eat, for the almost incredible period of fifty hours: two days and two nights without rest 'in an atmosphere that would poison a vulture'.[10]

But the men's unions, which had been relatively powerless in the early years of the nineteenth century when union activity was prosecuted as conspiracy, had been growing in strength from the 1820s to the 1860s, and

[7] The best accounts of the boys' conditions are in the reports of the parliamentary inquiries of 1843 and 1862; see the bibliography, p. 409

[8] 'Children's employment Commission (1862)', loc. cit., p. 15.

[9] 'Report by Dr. Edward Smith on the sanitary circumstances of the printers in London', *Parliamentary reports 1864*, xxviii, pp. 383-415.   [10] Smith, C. M., op. cit., pp. 241-4, 272-9.

were then able to add their weight to the authority of the parliamentary investigators in bringing the worst excesses of unregulated apprenticeship and of poor working conditions under control. Henceforth the emphasis of union activity shifted to the questions of better wages and shorter hours.

Piecework composition remained the normal practice of the trade in Britain and America throughout the nineteenth century, together with a few stab hands on time rates (p. 195).[11] In 1785 the London journeymen were able to establish a scale of piecework prices which was continued and improved on during the nineteenth century, but of course a scale did not guarantee the average earnings of a man in intermittent employment. Very wide fluctuations in earnings were still possible. In the early 1860s, when London stab hands were paid 33–38s. per week and piecework compositors were averaging 30–36s. per week, the compositors in one shop averaged £9 per man in one week—more than *five times* the average—'while composing some unusually remunerative parliamentary (not government) work, and working almost night and day'.[12] At the same period piecework pressmen were averaging 25–30s. per week, machine minders (who were time-hands with much overtime) 36–50s. per week, and machine boys 5–8s. per week (taken in most cases by their parents). The early years of the twentieth century saw a temporary move to time rates for all, but since the Second World War the introduction of bonus schemes has brought back the reality (if not the name) of piecework.

PRODUCTION ROUTINES

The complex patterns of concurrent production were continued from the hand-press into the machine-press period, and managements continued to adjust the labour force to demand by hiring and firing journeymen (especially compositors), making use of the permanent pool of unemployed printers.

No discussion of production routines can apply to every case, for the printing offices of the period differed from each other not only in the size of their output, but also in their premises, plant, and organization. We lack, moreover, detailed studies of the actual working arrangements of particular nineteenth-century firms. It may nevertheless be helpful to follow an imaginary book through the works of a large London printer of the 1870s, referring for much of the detail to John Southward's *Dictionary of typography* (London 1871), and the first edition of his *Practical printing* (London 1882).

We will assume that our book was to be a straightforward octavo, and

<hr/>

[11] For London, see Howe, E., op. cit., *passim*.
[12] 'Report by Dr. Edward Smith', loc. cit., p. 397.

that its manuscript was sent from the publishers' office with instructions as to format, paper quality, and edition quantity; indeed the publisher might have required the printer to set a specimen page in advance. The manuscript arrived, then, in the office (or counting house) of the printing works, and was forwarded via the manager's office (or closet) to the overseer of the composing department, together with instructions concerning type (say 'two-nicks long primer', type-faces not being specifically distinguished) and format (post octavo); it was of course hand-written.[13] Unless a specimen had been set and passed, the overseer would himself decide the measure and margin; the publisher had already calculated the length of the whole manuscript, and it was no longer customary to cast it off in the composing room. The overseer therefore called his clickers together and handed them batches of copy, explaining how it was to be set. The clickers in turn got their men together, and divided the batches of copy into individual takings for the members of the ship, the length of the taking varying but being typically from one to four leaves of a manuscript written on one side of 'quarto' paper; at the same time the men were given letter for distribution and told the measure. As they set to work (upon lines at this period, see p. 193), the clickers collected chases and furniture from the quoin-drawer man—a stab hand—and made the matter up into pages as it was delivered galley by galley, by the compositors, marking the copy appropriately as they did so. The pattern of composition of a companionship job, as revealed by surviving copy marked up both by the individual compositors and by the clickers, was complex, not surprisingly since the six or eight members of a ship worked simultaneously on takes of different length, and probably had three or four different books on hand at a time.

Although most London book houses owned galley presses for making slip proofs by the 1870s, it appears that companionship bookwork was generally made up into pages and imposed before proofing until the mid 1880s. This being the case, the clickers took the formes as they were finished to a hand press, which might be situated in the composing room itself, where proofs were pulled, folded, and given together with the relevant copy to the overseer for delivery to the reading department. (It should perhaps be emphasized that it was the universal practice to proof and correct the sheets in the printing house before sending out proofs to the publisher or author, who were not expected to have to correct the compositors' literals; and also that when the corrected proofs of the final sheets of a book were sent to the author it was not normally possible for him to make retrospective corrections to the earlier sheets of the same book because they would already have been printed off and the type distributed.)

[13] At any rate before 1874, when the first reliable typewriter was put on the market in America.

The head reader (who was normally responsible to the management, not to the overseer of the composing department) distributed proofs and copy to his staff, which until the early years of the present century continued to be organized in teams of readers and reading boys, who corrected the proofs by the method of reading the copy aloud (pp. 112-13). This meant, of course, that although substantive variations and literal errors were observed by the reader, compositorial normalization of spelling, etc., was not.

After correction the first proofs were returned to the clickers in the composing room, who called each man up in turn to correct the matter which he had set, the clicker himself being responsible for correcting the headlines, page numbers, and imposition. Revises were then pulled, and these having been passed by the composing department overseer—or in some houses by the reading department—clean proofs were dispatched to the publisher for forwarding to the author; surprisingly, they were not always accompanied by the copy. When these proofs were returned they were likely to be corrected by a stab hand, not by the piecework compositors. Eventually, perhaps after further proofing, the first formes of the book were ready to go to the machine room or the stereotype foundry.

Although a book might be printed from type alone, it was usual to make at least one set of plates if the edition quantity was to exceed a thousand or two. There were then various ways in which the machining might be organized. One method was to use the typeset formes for the first impression and then to distribute them, the plates being reserved for later impressions. Alternatively, two or more impressions might be printed simultaneously on different machines—or even at different printing houses—one from type, the others from plates. Then there was an economical method, often preferred when later impressions were not likely to need further correction, which was to return the typeset formes to the composing department immediately after plating, and to print from plates alone; this saved wear and tear on the type and recycled it without delay. The simultaneous use of duplicate sets of plates was common, especially for printing half-sheets in duplicate at a single machine.

Type or plates, then, for the early formes were delivered to the machine-room overseer, an important man who ran the hand-press department as well as the machine-room, and who fitted the jobs as they were delivered into the work-pattern of his shop. He allotted formes to individual machine-minders and ordered up the necessary paper—still damped at this period (see p. 261)—and the machine-minders proceeded with make-ready as machines became available. Make-ready was a lengthy process—it could occupy most of a working day—and, in the case of a plated book, it probably included the mounting and imposition of the plates (p. 260).

While this was going on a rough proof from the machine was scrutinized by the press reviser, whose task was to ensure, not so much textual purity, as the accuracy of headlines, page numbers, margins, and imposition. If he found a mistake, or if type or plates were subsequently damaged, it was normal to call a stab hand down from the composing room to make corrections; the machine-minder corrected the imposition, but not the type. Plates that needed correction were returned to the foundry for emendation or recasting. Finally, the machine-room overseer scrutinized a press proof after make-ready, and authorized the beginning of the run.

There was not much more for the machine-minder to do. He started the machine, checked inking and impression, and left it in charge of his machine boys; and the boys, regular apprentices by this period, could be trusted to call him if the quality of the work deteriorated or if a sheet went wrong and blocked the machine. For perfecting with one of the normal work-and-turn impositions the heap was simply turned over and end to end; there was no need to make ready again.

As each edition sheet was finished the heap was sent to the warehouse, just as it came from the machine, where it was dried if necessary and stored until all the sheets were done. It sometimes happened that further alterations were called for at this stage by the publisher or author, in which case cancels had to be made. Much the commonest method was to print a cancel sheet or half-sheet, substituting a new or corrected plate for the faulty one (although it should be remembered that a new or corrected plate might have been put into the forme during the original run, giving the appearance of cancellation). The other traditional methods of making cancels were also used occasionally: the cancellation of individual leaves and of conjugate pairs, the cancellantia being printed from sets of plates cast in duplicate or quadruplicate; the pasting-on of cancel slips; and overprinting. The formes, meanwhile, were returned to the composing department for storage or distribution, and the plates were sent to the plate store.

Finally, when all the sheets were printed, the heaps were sent to the bindery, or if—as was more likely—the book was to be bound up in batches, so many sheets were taken off the top of each heap and sent for binding. It might seem that the sheets at the tops of the heaps, which would go first into the binding machinery and thus make up the first bound copies of the edition, would show the type or plates in their final state, since they were the last to emerge from the machine, but in fact the situation was not so simple. The use of work-and-turn impositions, normal for all machine-printed bookwork, resulted in complex patterns of type state. To take the simplest case, all sixteen pages for an octavo gathering were printed on one side of the paper, and the heap was then turned over and round, and the same sixteen pages were printed on the other side (see fig. 113, p. 259). Thus the first sheet of paper to go through the machine, the one that would end up at the bottom of the heap, had the sixteen pages in their earliest state on one side; and the same sixteen pages in their half-way state (i.e. at the beginning of the perfecting run) on the other side. When this sheet was cut in half to yield two similar copies of the octavo gathering, one copy had page 1 (etc.) in the earliest state of the type and page 2 (etc.) in the half-way state; while the other copy of the gathering had page 1 in the half-way state and page 2 in the earliest state. Similarly, the last sheet to go through the machine, the one on the top of the heap, gave copies of the gathering showing the half-way and the latest states of the type in two combinations; and a sheet from the middle of the heap gave copies showing the quarter-way and three-quarter-way states, again in two combinations.

Consequently there could be no such thing as a copy of the book showing a consistently early or a consistently late state of the type; every gathering necessarily showed pages that were separated from each other in printing order by half the total run. Any residual regularity (such as all the gatherings in a copy being from top sheets and therefore showing half-way and latest states only) was likely to have been disturbed by the accidents of real printing, such as the sorting of subdivisions of the heaps during the drying process, or the mixing of batches of gatherings after the double sheets were cut in half. E. B. Browning's *A drama of exile*, New York 1845, shows that sheets were sometimes mixed in this way: every copy examined by Mrs. Browning's bibliographer was found to contain a different combination of variant states (see pp. 378–9).

Although machine speeds were high, the rate of book production was still limited by the speed of hand composition and of proofing. In cases of urgency a full-length book could be produced in no more than 2–3 days; this was done either by applying a large number of compositors to a single job—all of Hansard's ninety compositors, for example, would be put on to setting an individual parliamentary blue book in the 1830s, and would be kept at it until it was finished—or by dividing a work for simultaneous production by several printing houses, as when four printers shared the three volumes of Bulwer's *Rienzi* in 1835.[14] Once in 1837 Bentley got through all the stages of producing a novel, from reader's report to publication, in four days; but the usual rate of production was 3–4 sheets per week, which meant that a three-volume novel of the usual length in 50–60 sheets took about four months to print.[15]

[14] Smith, C. M., op. cit., pp. 241–4, 272–9; *The Library*, xviii, 1963, p. 117; [Saunders, F.], *The author's printing and publishing assistant*, 2nd ed., London 1839, p. 6 n.
[15] Gettmann, R. A., *A Victorian publisher*, Cambridge 1960, p. 198; [Saunders, F.], loc. cit.

The Book Trade in Britain and America since 1800[1]

THE STRUCTURE OF THE TRADE

The familiar three-part division of the modern book trade into publisher-wholesaler, printer, and retail bookseller was established in Britain during the early years of the nineteenth century. The old method of publication by syndicates of retail booksellers (who might also be wholesalers and/or printers) remained normal during the last quarter of the eighteenth century, but syndicates tended to become smaller as their members gained in financial strength and in the ability to bear greater proportions of the risk; and around 1800 a few of the larger men—Murray and Cadell & Davies in London, Blackwood and Constable in Edinburgh—began to publish on their own. The process is exemplified in the early editions of Burns: the first London edition of the *Poems*, the third edition of 1787, was published by Creech of Edinburgh, by Strahan of London, and by Cadell of London; the editions of 1793, 1794, 1797, 1798, and 1800 were published by Cadell (later Cadell & Davies) of London and Creech of Edinburgh; and the four-volume *Works* of 1800 was published by Cadell & Davies alone.[2]

Similar developments took place in America, but half a century later. There the small-town book trader of the eighteenth century, still dependent upon Europe for most books and combining in one firm the businesses of printer, binder, newspaper proprietor, wholesale stationer, and retail bookseller, grew larger along with his town but specialized only gradually. Books were indeed published by individual firms in the earlier nineteenth century, but the firms were not solely publishers. Even in the 1850s, when such firms as Ticknor & Fields of Boston were developing as specialist publishers, the Harper establishment of New York was still an omnibus firm which not only published large numbers of books and periodicals but also printed, bound, and wholesaled them as well.[3]

Henceforth the central figure in the trade was the specialist publisher, who wholesaled his own books but usually not those of other publishers; who was not a wholesale stationer and who might not even have a retail bookshop; and who (with few exceptions such as the University presses) was not a printer or a binder. The specialist publisher organized the production, advertising, and wholesaling of editions, usually at his own risk

---

[1] See the bibliography, pp. 410–11.

[2] Besterman, T., *The publishing firm of Cadell & Davies*, Oxford 1938, pp. xxi–xxii.

[3] Lehmann-Haupt, H., *The book in America*, 2nd ed., New York 1952; Tryon, W. S., and Charvat, W., *The cost books of Ticknor & Fields*, New York 1959; Abbott, J., op. cit.

but sometimes on commission for authors; and he financed the publication of editions of which he owned or leased the copyright. His position was pivotal because he was not only the organizer but also the financier and indeed the speculator of the book trade.

Backing his own judgement the publisher risked his capital in financing the publication of books which might or might not prove successful, and no publisher was immune from making mistakes. Those publishers who made least mistakes gained a fair living, while those who lacked judgement failed, as Constable did for the very large sum of £250,000 in 1825; hardly any made their fortunes.[4] As Ruari McLean put it, 'publishing had been considered, like the wine trade, an occupation permissible for gentlemen, perhaps from the fallacy that the most necessary qualification was an appreciation of literature. In fact, then as now, a publisher, to achieve success, needed charm, financial acumen, a knowledge of the future, a stony heart, and a very rich wife.'[5] Wise publishers, moreover, tried to put at least part of their capital into steady-selling educational and technical works, which were less glamorous but safer than poems and novels.

The degree of risk a publisher took was determined by the agreements he made with his authors. With the exception of percentage royalty contracts, all the main types of agreement that became characteristic of the machine-press period had been tried out in the eighteenth century, and even royalty agreements were known in a slightly different form (see pp. 183–5). They may be divided into five groups: outright sale of copyright; limited sale of copyright; profit sharing; royalty agreements; and commission publishing. In addition agreements were sometimes made which combined elements from different groups. Apart from commission publishing (which remained a small but regular proportion of the whole), outright sale of copyright was still the most usual form of agreement in the early part of the nineteenth century; to be succeeded in popularity during its middle years by limited sale of copyright and profit-sharing agreements; and later in the century by the royalty agreements which have remained the dominant form.

When an author sold his copyright to a publisher he had no further rights in or control over his work, although publishers sometimes paid a bonus if a book proved unexpectedly successful. In its simple form outright sale did not benefit the average author: it tempted him to sell at a low price for the sake of an immediate reward, it deprived him of a regular income, and it frequently gave the publisher a disproportionately large share of the profits. Of course the publisher did not always win; Melville, known in 1850 as the author of exotic romances, got £200 from Bentley

4 Gettmann, R. A., *A Victorian publisher*, Cambridge 1960, pp. 9–10.
5 McLean, R., *Victorian book design*, London 1963, p. 4.

for the copyright of *White jacket*, and Bentley lost £173 on the book.[6] But by then outright sale was becoming less common, although it was favoured by some mid-century authors—Fenimore Cooper, Mrs. Gaskell—for the sake of its simplicity.[7]

Sale of copyright for a limited period of time ensured that an author would profit by a work that achieved steady sales, although it could lead to difficulties. Charles Reade sold the copyright of his first major novel, *It's never too late to mend*, to Bentley for a period of two years from 1856, and the book was a success. Reade was annoyed, however, when Bentley followed the three-volume edition with reprints at 5s. and 2s., feeling that they cheapened his novel; while Bentley, who considered that he had made Reade's name with but little profit to himself, was hurt because Reade would not offer a good price for the unsold stock (which Bentley was no longer entitled to sell) at the end of the two years.[8]

When a profit-sharing (or joint-account) agreement was made, the publisher met the whole cost of publication and then, when costs were covered by sales, shared subsequent returns with the author. The shares were usually equal, although a successful author might get as much as three-quarters of the profit. The disadvantage from the author's point of view was that payment was necessarily much delayed; and there was besides an understandable (if often mistaken) tendency to distrust the publisher's accounts. Publishers tended to use this form of agreement for books in which they had only limited confidence, for it relieved them of the need to pay the author unless there was a certainty of profit.

The royalty agreement with which we are nowadays most familiar was a natural extension of profit sharing, and began to supersede it around the 1860s. A royalty—either a fixed sum or a percentage of the retail price—was paid to the author on each copy sold. Thus the author's rewards were at last proportional to his sales; while the publisher could decrease his commitment by withholding royalty payments until a certain number of sales had been achieved, or could increase it by paying the author an advance on future royalties (which was normally not repayable). For instance, a nineteenth-century author might get 2d. a copy on a 2s. reprint (offered by Bentley to Reade in 1857), or 10 per cent on each copy sold (paid by Cassell's for *Treasure island* in 1883).[9]

Publishing on commission, when the author paid all the costs of production and allowed the publisher a percentage of the gross receipts (typically 10–12½ per cent) as a payment for producing and handling the book, had been used since early times for specialist publications such as works

---

[6] Gettmann, R. A., op. cit., p. 83.   [7] Ibid., p. 79.
[8] Ibid., pp. 89–90.   [9] Ibid., pp. 116, 117.

of local history, and was relatively common in the eighteenth century when authors would finance publication by collecting subscriptions. Commission publishing continued in a relatively small way in the nineteenth century, being commonly the resort of authors who could not otherwise persuade a publisher to undertake their work, and of undercapitalized publishers. There were exceptions, as when an author who was sure of his sales (such as Bernard Shaw, who would of course have been the pride of any publisher's list) chose to publish on commission and take the publisher's profit for himself.

FORMS IN NINETEENTH-CENTURY PUBLISHING

There was a good deal of convention in the forms of various types of books in the nineteenth century: shapes, sizes, and binding styles that were characteristic of novels, of poems and of biography, of atlases, encyclopedias, and time-tables amongst many others. Literature, moreover, especially fiction, was published not only in book form but also in monthly parts and as serials in magazines. An understanding of these forms is valuable since they inevitably had some effect, if not always a strong one, on what authors wrote.

The influence of publishing forms was probably greatest upon fiction. There had been a marked tendency for eighteenth-century novels (some of which had been of considerable length) to appear in several small volumes, and this practice was carried over into the early nineteenth century, the number of volumes per novel being anything from one to six (though with an increasing preference for three). The physical dimensions of novels then tended to increase, and during the 1820s a standard form of three substantial volumes—the three-decker as it was later nicknamed—became established, and dominated the production of English fiction in book form from the 1830s to the 1880s.[10]

The standard retail price for a volume of fiction was half a guinea, so that a three-decker at £1. 11s. 6d. (the weekly wage of a skilled workman) was extremely expensive. Despite occasional attempts at price cutting, however, the trade maintained the price for commercial reasons. Then as now most people did not buy novels but borrowed them from lending libraries, the most important of which in the mid century were the subscription libraries led by Mudie's.[10a] The high price enabled the publisher to produce a lengthy book in a small edition—he could always put out a cheap single-volume reprint later if it was successful—while the multivolume form was attractive to the lending libraries, where subscriptions

[10] Lauterbach, C. E. and E. S., 'The nineteenth-century three-volume novel', *Papers of the Bibliographical Society of America*, li, 1957, pp. 263–302.
[10a] Griest, G. L., *Mudie's circulating library and the Victorian novel*, Bloomington 1970.

were proportional to the number of volumes that could be borrowed at a time.

The mid-nineteenth-century English three-decker was typically a cloth-cased post octavo with about 20 gatherings, 320 pages, per volume. The edges were often uncut, and the type was small pica, or less commonly pica, with up to a nonpareil of lead between the lines (i.e. 10 or 12pt., up to 6pt. leaded). There were 900–920 pages of text, containing 150,000–200,000 words, padded out with heavy leading, wide margins, and extravagant chapter divisions. The median length of a large sample of three-deckers was actually 168,000 words, divided into 45 chapters.

It would be wrong to overstress the influence of the three-decker upon literary composition—there is no reason to suppose that nineteenth-century authors would often have preferred to write shorter or longer novels than they generally did—but there certainly was some pressure upon novelists to conform. Contracts between authors and publishers often specified the number of pages to be filled; an authors' manual of 1839 remarked that the proper quantity of pages for a volume of a novel was 300, each containing 22 lines of 8 words (making a book of 148,400 words less chapter divisions); and in 1883 George Bentley told one of his authors that a novel consisted of 920 pages, averaging $21\frac{1}{2}$ lines of $8\frac{1}{2}$ words (or 187,810 words less chapter divisions).[11] There were also cases of authors being urged to add to a book in order to fill the last volume, or to increase the number of chapter divisions (each of which made an extra page).

Not all mid-nineteenth-century fiction was first published in three-decker form. About a third of the novels that were first published in book form came out in one or two (or very occasionally four) volumes, while the works of established authors were often brought out periodically, either as part-issues or as magazine serials. Part issue, which we met in the hand-press period as a method of spreading production costs and retail payments over a period of time (pp. 181–2), survived in the early nineteenth century chiefly as a device for selling illustrated books and sets of plates; but in 1836 the then obscure Charles Dickens was commissioned to write a text to go with plates by the better-known artist Robert Seymour for issue in parts. The resulting *Posthumous papers of the Pickwick Club* was so successful as to initiate a vogue for the part-issue of novels by best-selling authors which lasted from the late 1830s to the early 1870s. There were variations, but a typical part-issue novel consisted of 20–24 monthly parts of 2 octavo gatherings (32 pages), each illustrated with one or two plates by a popular artist, retailing at 1*s.* each in wrappers; a cased issue at 9*s.*–12*s.* per volume, printed from the same stereo plates and complete with illustrations, was

[11] Gettmann, R. A., op. cit., ch. 8; [Saunders, F.], op. cit., pp. 35–6.

then put out shortly before the appearance of the final (usually double) part.[12]

The serialization of fiction in magazines had also taken place in the hand-press period, but with few exceptions before the 1820s the novels published in this way were reprints, not new books; the reason being that before 1819 magazines containing previously unpublished material were counted as newspapers and were liable to stamp duty, but not if they contained only reprinted matter. The serialization of new fiction in half-crown monthly magazines such as *Blackwood's* started in a small way in the 1820s, and grew in importance during the following decade. The success of the shilling part-issues of the 1840s, however, which seemed better value than half-crown magazines or one-and-a-half-guinea three-deckers, prompted the appearance of shilling magazines carrying two or three serialized novels in each monthly number, and these in turn recaptured the bulk of the serial fiction market from the part-issues during the 1860s. The innovator was *Douglas Jerrold's shilling magazine* (1845–8), but the greatest success came with *Macmillan's magazine* (November 1859) and *The Cornhill magazine* (January 1860). Thackeray's *Cornhill*, which serialized both his own *Lovel the widower* and Trollope's *Framley parsonage* from the first number, sold 100,000 copies, more than double the number of the most popular of Dickens's novels in part-issue form.[13]

The effect of part-issue and magazine serialization upon what the novelist wrote was of course considerable, since the author had to keep not only the design of the whole work in mind, but also the identity of the individual numbers, each of which had to lead to a climax or at least to a point at which the reader could reasonably leave the story for a month. There could also be important interaction between text and illustrations, Dickens for instance specifying minutely what the artist should draw and deliberately using the plates as an adjunct to the story.

Some novelists—especially Dickens, again, who wrote each number as it became due for publication—thought that the difficulties of writing for serialization were worth overcoming, since part-issue encouraged a close relationship between author and reader as the story grew from month to month; but others—Trollope, for instance, who disapproved of starting publication of a serial until the whole book was written—disliked the form, and their work was probably the worse for it.[14]

The part-issue form faded out in the 1870s, but magazine (and later

[12] Dickson, S. A., *The Arents collection of books in parts*, New York 1957.

[13] Pollard, H. G., 'Serial fiction', *New paths in book collecting*, London 1934, pp. 245–77.

[14] Butt, J., and Tillotson, K., *Dickens at work*, London 1963; Trollope, A., *An autobiography*, ed. Sadleir, M., Oxford 1950.

newspaper) serialization of fiction continued into the present century, although used less commonly for the first publication of novels by major writers after 1890. The three-decker declined gradually during the 1880s and then, attacked simultaneously by authors, booksellers, and public librarians, expired in the mid 1890s and was succeeded for the first publication of novels by single volumes at 6s.

So far we have discussed only fiction, but there were also conventions for the forms of other sorts of books on the publishers' general lists. The authors' manual already referred to remarked that 'Pica is the Type usually employed in Printing works of History, Biography, Travels, &c., in the Demy octavo size; Small Pica, in Novels, Romances, &c., in the Post octavo size; and Long Primer, Poetry, in the Foolscap octavo size'.[15]

Besides the various forms in which new books were published, there were many series of cheap reprints. Again there had been eighteenth-century precedents—John Bell's *Poets of Great Britain*, 109 duodecimo volumes at 1s. 6d. each (1776-92) was the first great reprint series—but the nineteenth-century vogue for cheap series was due chiefly to the vision of Archibald Constable, as he described it to Scott in 1825: 'a three shilling or half-crown volume every month, which must and shall sell, not by thousands or tens of thousands, but by hundreds of thousands—ay, by millions! Twelve volumes in the year, a halfpenny of profit upon every copy of which will make me richer than the possession of all the copyrights of all the quartos that ever were, or will be, hot-pressed! Twelve volumes, so good that millions must wish to have them, and so cheap that every butcher's callant may have them, if he pleases to let me tax him sixpence a-week!'[16] The eighty volumes of Constable's Miscellany (as the series was called) ran from 1826 to 1835 at 3s. 6d. a volume, mostly reprints but including significantly several new books specially written for the series.

The Miscellany was soon imitated by other publishers, notably by John Murray, whose Family Library edited by Lockhart was launched in 1829. The market for non-fiction series, however, was soon saturated (the stock of the Family Library was remaindered in 1834), and it was the series of cheap reprints of recent fiction initiated by Colburn and Bentley with their Standard Novels that were to prove the most successful form of series publishing.[17] Physically the Standard Novels were based on Cadell's 'Author's edition' of Scott's Waverley Novels (begun in 1829 as a series of cloth-cased volumes in royal 18°, 17 × 10·5 cm., selling at 5s. each), and the

[15] [Saunders, F.], op. cit., p. 35.
[16] Lockhart, J. G., *Memoirs of the life of Sir Walter Scott, Bart.*, vi, Edinburgh 1837, p. 31.
[17] Sadleir, M., *XIX century fiction*, London 1951, vol. 2; Gettmann, R. A., op. cit., ch. 2.

main series comprised 126 volumes, published from 1831 to 1854, selling at 6s. per volume complete with frontispiece.

The reprint series got steadily cheaper as the market expanded, and of course they are still very much with us. Outstanding amongst those who specialized in series publication were Tauchnitz of Leipzig, who for a century from the early 1840s bought English (and later American) copyrights and by the later nineteenth century was putting out 100 paperbacks a year, reprinting English literature for sale on the continent at 1s. 6d. per volume;[18] Beadle and Adams of New York, who ran more than forty fiction series during the last quarter of the nineteenth century and whose 'dime and nickel novels' included both new books and pirated English novels retailing as paperbacks at 10 cents a volume;[19] Joseph Dent, who established the Everyman Library in 1905 with the intention that it should consist of all classes of literature for every class of reader, in well-printed bound volumes at 1s. each;[20] and Penguin Books, founded by Allen Lane in 1935, which began by reprinting good-quality fiction and marketing it in department stores as well as book shops at 6d. a paperback volume.[21]

EDITION QUANTITIES AND PRICES

In the hand-press period it had been uneconomic to print editions of ordinary books in quantities of more than about 2,000 copies, since unit costs then began to increase with quantity. With the introduction of powered printing machinery, however, the unit cost not only of composition but also of machining varied inversely with edition quantity up to about 10,000 copies—the more that were printed the lower the price of each—whereupon the curve flattened out, the unit cost for 100,000 copies being much the same as for 10,000.[22] Of course there was no point in printing 10,000 copies of a book cheaply if it could find no more than 1,000 purchasers at any price, but the capacity was available; there were positive savings to be made on editions of up to about 10,000 copies, and no harm in printing 100,000 copies if they could be sold.

The result was a parallel increase in the range of edition quantities of nineteenth-century books and periodicals. Most new books continued to be published in small editions, the first printing of works of fiction, history, biography, travel, etc. still being normally in the range 750–1,250 copies.[23]

[18] Nowell-Smith, S., *International copyright law and the publisher in the reign of Queen Victoria*, Oxford 1968, ch. 3.

[19] Johannsen, A., *The house of Beadle and Adams*, Norman, Okla. [1950].

[20] McLean, R., *Modern book design*, [2nd ed.], London 1958, pp. 36–7.

[21] Williams, W. E., *The Penguin story MCMXXXV–MCMLVI*, Harmondsworth 1956.

[22] This was true, at any rate, for book printers of the 1920s and 1930s, and there is no reason to suppose that it was not equally true for nineteenth-century book printers with their essentially similar machinery.   [23] Gettmann, R. A., op. cit., ch. 5.

A relatively small number of books by established authors were printed in much larger quantities: the sales of some of Dickens's part-issues reached 50,000 copies, and the first edition of Tennyson's *Enoch Arden* was of 60,000. Periodicals reached even larger quantities: the *Penny magazine* sold 200,000 copies a week at its peak in the mid 1830s, and the literary *Cornhill* averaged 84,000 a month during 1860–2.[24]

To take George Eliot as an example, her first work of fiction *Scenes of clerical life*, was serialized in *Blackwood's* and then put out in book form in an edition of 1,000 copies (2 volumes 1858); there was no immediate cheap reprint. In the following year *Adam Bede* appeared in three volumes in an edition of 2,100 copies, and was quickly followed by about 10,000 copies of a cheap one-volume reprint. At the height of her fame *Middlemarch* was published in the unusual form of eight half-volume parts in editions of about 5,000 copies each; then in four volumes and about 3,000 copies in 1873; and in one volume and about 13,000 copies in 1874.[25]

Books in cheap reprint series were not necessarily produced in very large numbers; the average edition quantity of the first nineteen titles (1831–2) in Bentley's Standard Novels was just under 4,000 copies each,[26] and the Tauchnitz reprints seem to have averaged no more than 2,000 copies for their first printings.[27] Later series, of course, were produced in huge quantities; 20,000 and 30,000 were not unusual printings for the early Everyman titles, while paperback editions following the Penguin revolution rapidly moved into six figures.

Gross differences in production costs have of course always been reflected in the prices of books, but at the same time there has been a tendency towards the systematization of book prices. In the hand-press period the price of a book was generally related to the number of gatherings it contained (see pp. 178–9), and there was also an inclination to standardize the prices of particular types of books, logically enough since editions of a particular type were likely to have comparable production costs. The next stage, which developed gradually in Britain during the eighteenth century, was for publishers and booksellers to agree to maintain prices, that is not to retail books at a discount on the listed or advertised price. List prices were not in practice always maintained, for many booksellers would surreptitiously give a discount rather than lose a sale, but the system was working well enough by the 1780s for the trade to be alarmed by the price-cutting of James Lackington, who established a large and successful retail

---

[24] Altick, R. D., *The English common reader*, Chicago 1957, app. B, collects the statistics of Victorian best-sellers.

[25] Haight, G. S., *George Eliot, a biography*, Oxford 1968, *passim*.

[26] Gettmann, R. A., op. cit., pp. 52–3

[27] Nowell-Smith, S., op. cit., p. 58.

book-warehouse in 1780–98 with the motto 'Small profits do great things'.[28] Trading for cash, not credit, Lackington cut his profit on new books to less than half of what booksellers normally took, and relied on the size of his turnover to make his fortune; he was not disappointed. Another of Lackington's innovations, which found several early-nineteenth-century imitators, was to buy up blocks of recent books at trade auctions and sell them as remainders at a fraction of the advertised price, and, although this infuriated the rest of the trade, there was not yet general agreement as to what was and what was not a remainder.

The next stage resulted from a combination of publishers and large booksellers in 1829, when it was agreed to withhold supplies from booksellers who offered new books at a discount greater than the 10 per cent usually allowed for cash, defining as new any book that had been published or reprinted within two years or which was protected by copyright; and, since by this time the majority of new books were retailed in Britain by specialist booksellers, the combination succeeded in controlling retail prices, generally at their existing high level.[29] The increasing efficiency of machine printing did reduce the average price of reprints and of popular works even so, but new literature remained disgracefully expensive; the standard price from the 1830s of 10s. 6d. for each volume of a novel, which was generally quite unrelated to production costs and may be thought of as more than £5 at today's prices, was plainly an abuse.

In 1852 free-trade agitation led to a judgement against the legality of price-fixing by publishers and booksellers, and the practice came to an abrupt end.[30] For the rest of the nineteenth century booksellers were at liberty to offer their customers whatever discounts they pleased and, although publishers' prices were still listed (for instance in the catalogues commonly tipped in when books were cased), it was the standard practice for British booksellers to allow discounts of from 5 to 20 per cent off the advertised figures.

Typical list prices for novels during the third quarter of the nineteenth century were, for a three-decker in post octavo, 31s. 6d.; for two volumes demy octavo, illustrated and printed from serial or part-issue plates, from 18s. to 24s. depending on length; for two volumes post octavo, from 12s. to 18s.; and for one volume, post octavo, from 8s. 6d. to 12s.

The old inflated prices finally collapsed in the 1890s. Three-deckers were replaced by single-volume novels at around 6s., and prices in general became more competitive. At the same time publishers and booksellers combined once more to fix retail prices, concluding in 1900 a 'net book

[28] Lackington, J., *Memoirs*, London [1791]-4.
[29] Barnes, J. J., *Free trade in books*, Oxford 1964, ch. 1.   [30] Ibid., chs. 2–4.

agreement' that was in essentials similar to the agreement of 1829: book-sellers were forbidden to retail new books, other than bona fide remainders, at less than list prices, under threat of being black-listed and refused further supplies.[31]

Despite what amounts to undercutting by direct-sale publishers calling themselves 'book clubs' the British net book agreement has remained in force until the present day. The argument for its retention (which was accepted by a court in a case brought under the Restrictive Trades Practices Act in 1962) has been that, without resale price maintenance, the trade could afford to purvey only best-sellers, in which case all other sorts of books would suffer.[32]

Things have developed differently in America, where the trade has always depended less on specialist booksellers than it has in Britain.[33] There were specialist American booksellers even in the mid nineteenth century, but the majority of books were retailed over the vast extent of the country through general stores which handled them as a side line, and there was also a strong tradition of direct sale from publisher to reader. There was an attempt by the specialist booksellers to organize resale price maintenance in the 1870s, but it failed; the major outlets were not interested, and there were the further complications of competition from paperbacks retailing at 5 to 10 cents, and of the practice (even then) of general stores using books as loss leaders.

A more determined attempt by both publishers and booksellers to intro-duce an American version of the net book agreement was undertaken in 1900, but it too failed when Macy's, the New York department store, brought an action against the publishers under the anti-trust laws, and won it in 1914. That ended price fixing in the American book trade, where the majority of books are still retailed through outlets other than specialist bookstores, where publishers still sell direct to the public, and where books are still used as loss leaders in department stores and supermarkets.

COPYRIGHT, NATIONAL AND INTERNATIONAL[34]

The complicated progress of nineteenth-century copyright legislation is not always easy to follow in detail, but from the point of view of the British or American author copyright in his own country it was simple enough. Subject to the completion of certain formalities (chiefly the deposit of printed copies) copyright in a publication was secured to its author for a

31 Kingsford, R. J. L., *The Publishers Association*, Cambridge 1970.
32 Barker, R. E., and Davies, G. R., *Books are different*, London 1966.
33 Lehmann-Haupt, H., *The book in America*, 2nd ed., New York 1952, *passim*.
34 Nowell-Smith, S., op. cit., summarizes nineteenth-century developments.

fixed period of time. Thus in Britain at the beginning of the century, copyright was still based on the Act of 1709-10, and lasted initially for 14 years, plus a further 14 years if the author was still alive; in 1814 the period of copyright was extended to 28 years or the life of the author, whichever was longer; in 1842 to 42 years, or the life of the author plus 7 years; and finally in 1911 to the life of the author plus 50 years, which remains the law today. Early American copyright law followed English precedent, the first Federal enactment specifying copyright lasting for two successive periods of 14 years; this was extended in 1831 to 28 years, plus a further 14 years if the author, his wife, or his children were still alive; and in 1870 to two successive periods of 28 years on the same conditions as the rule of 1831, and this is still the case in America now.

International copyright, however, was another matter. In Europe a long series of international agreements, beginning with a Prussian law of 1837 and culminating in the Berne Convention of 1887, secured reciprocal copyright privileges for the authors of the countries concerned (Britain included) which gave them much the same protection abroad as they had at home. America, however, joined in none of these agreements, naturally enough since the majority of the profitable nineteenth-century books in English were of British origin, not American, and the American book trade had nothing to gain and a good deal to lose by allowing copyright protection to the works of British authors.

Until 1891 copyright in a printed book could be acquired in the United States only by a citizen or a resident, which meant in practice that a book by a British author could not be protected there, and was free for anyone to print. The best that a British author or publisher could do was to authorize an American publisher to bring the book out in America for whatever fee could be obtained, giving him an advance copy of the text so that he could get in ahead of the field; even then there was nothing to stop another American publisher from reprinting the book if he thought it worth his while, a practice that was known as piracy although it was in fact legal. Similarly an American author could acquire British copyright only by residence and first publication of his work in British territory.

In 1862 Trollope agreed to send Lippincott of New York early proofs of the projected Chapman & Hall edition of his *North America*, Lippincott undertaking to publish an American edition and to pay Trollope a royalty after the sale of the first 2,000 copies; but in fact Harpers of New York managed somehow to get hold of a text of the book in time to rush out an edition for sale at 60 cents, so that Trollope never got a penny from the considerable American sales.[35] Hardy, on the other hand, sold the rights of

[35] Sadleir, M., 'Anthony Trollope and his publishers', *The Library*, v, 1924-5, pp. 229-30.

serialization and of domestic book production of *The Woodlanders* to Harpers in New York and to Macmillans in London. In order to forestall piracy, the two publishers brought out the magazine serials in parallel (May 1886 to April 1887), and the book issues within ten days of each other in March 1887 (i.e. before the appearance of the final serial number). Hardy's part was to send over advance proofs of the English setting for resetting in America; there was time to correct them only superficially, so that the English text, which he corrected more fully at leisure, was in a later state of revision than the American text.[36]

In the case of an author (such as Henry James) who was a citizen of one country and resident in the other, it was possible to secure copyright in both Britain and America, although the formalities presented their own difficulties: to obtain British copyright first publication had to take place in British territory and a copy had to be deposited in the British Museum within a month, while in America the title-page of the book had to be deposited in Washington before publication anywhere, and a copy had to be deposited within ten days of publication in America. Still, James was relatively lucky; there was justice in Dickens's complaint that his books would have made him many thousands of pounds in America if he had been able to copyright them there.

America has never signed a fully reciprocal copyright agreement with Britain, but the international copyright act passed by Congress in 1891 (the Chase Act) did at last afford protection in America to the works of British and other foreign authors, enabling them to obtain a fair return for their work. Even so the conditions were irksome: publication had to take place simultaneously in Britain and America, and the American edition had to be printed from type set in America or from plates made from such type; further legislation of 1909 relaxed the time limit for the publication of British books in America, but ruled that to secure copyright the American edition had to be not only set but also machined in the United States. From 1891, therefore, copyright American issues of British books could not be made from British plates or British sheets, as had sometimes happened before, but occasionally both British and American issues of a British book were printed from American plates.

The requirement for the complete manufacture of copyright books in the United States remained in force until 1957, when the Universal Copyright Convention was ratified, and British books that could expect a large American sale were so manufactured. A few specialist books, British as well as American, were reproduced photolithographically for transatlantic sale

[36] Kramer, D., 'Two "new" texts of Thomas Hardy's *The Woodlanders*', *Studies in bibliography*, xx, 1967, pp. 135-50.

by about 1930; these were chiefly technical and academic works which, because they would have been expensive to manufacture in relation to their expected sales, were unlikely to become the subjects of unauthorized reprinting even though they were technically out of copyright. Works of literature continued to be reset as a rule right up to the late 1950s, though latterly this was as much for editorial as for copyright reasons.

BIBLIOGRAPHICAL APPLICATIONS

THIS last section approaches the heart of the matter: textual bibliography, or the use of an understanding of books as material objects in the production and distribution of accurate texts. But two technical questions must be considered first: how to identify and to describe the material objects themselves.

Identification

EDITION, IMPRESSION, ISSUE, AND STATE

Before discussing the techniques of bibliographical identification we must deal with the technical terms which are used to define the relationship between different copies of the same work.[1] An *edition*, first of all, is all the copies of a book printed at any time (or times) from substantially the same setting of type, and includes all the various impressions, issues, and states which may have derived from that setting. As to the meaning of 'substantially the same setting of type', there are bound to be ambiguous cases, but we may take it as a simple rule of thumb that there is a new edition when more than half the type has been reset, but that if less than half the type has been reset we are probably dealing with another impression, issue, or state.

Editions of the hand-press period are usually easy to identify. Resetting by hand, even when the compositor follows the spellings and abbreviations of printed copy word for word and line for line, always results in identifiable differences of spacing between the words, and the random pattern of damaged types is likewise different. With practice, two very similar settings can be told apart at a glance when copies are laid side by side, something that is usually easy to arrange with the aid of photocopies. If it is not practicable to compare copies or photocopies directly, resetting will normally be revealed by comparing notes of the precise positions of signature letters relative to words in the lines immediately above them.

Editions of the machine-press period, however, are not so readily defined. Resetting by hand is still easily identified, although resetting of Linotype by Linotype, where the spacing is mechanical, may be very difficult to detect. But the problem of defining editions of the machine-press period is not so much that of identifying new settings of type as of classifying reprints made *indirectly* from one setting, one act of composition.

Let us start with plates. Stereos and electros are three-dimensional models of the original setting, which may not itself have been used for printing at all. Copies printed from plates must therefore be regarded as part of the original edition. This is true, moreover, even if there are long pauses in a book's printing history. If a book is reprinted from standing type, the reprint is part of the original edition, even if it is not part of the original series of publishing units; and if a book is reprinted from an old set of plates, the result is again part of the original edition.

Which leads us on to the much more difficult question of photographic reprinting. It is evident that the photolithographic version of a current

---

[1] See Bowers, F. T., *Principles of bibliographical description*, Princeton 1949 (and later impressions), chs. 2, 11.

book—made for the American issue, say, of a work printed from type or plates in England—has to be considered part of the original edition. But once this is granted, and bearing in mind that a long pause in a book's printing history does not in itself make a new edition, it is difficult to avoid the conclusion that *any* photographic reprint is part of the edition from which it derives, and that this includes modern photographic facsimiles of early books and even individual photocopies. While this conclusion makes for some absurdity (for one cannot seriously consider a xerox of Q1 *Hamlet* to be part of the first edition of *Hamlet*), it is necessary for dealing with commercial photolithographic reprints in multiple copies (which will normally bear an additional imprint, and where parts of the original may have been suppressed or added to), and with such modern possibilities as the transmission of settings by line for photolitho printing at a distance.

We see, in fact, that in the machine-press period the edition may be defined by the image of the setting as well as by the setting itself. Similarly with Monotype, the edition is defined not by any particular setting of type but by the programme for a setting punched on a paper spool. The Monotype spool can be run through the caster several times to produce several duplicate settings of type which, although not physically identical, are in practice indistinguishable from each other; and copies from any of these duplicate settings must be thought of as part of the one edition defined by the spool since they derive from a single act of composition. What is more, if the Monotype caster is fited with a different matrix case for one of these settings, so producing it in type of a different design from the rest, copies printed from this different type are still part of the same edition, deriving from one spool, one act of composition.[1a] Similar considerations will apply to programmes of composition recorded in other ways, for instance on magnetic tape.

For books of the machine-press period, therefore, an edition may include not only all the copies of a book printed at any time (or times) from substantially the same setting of type, but also copies printed from relief plates made from that setting; copies reproduced photographically; and all the copies deriving from a particular Monotype spool, computer tape, or other programme of composition, however reproduced.

Impression, which means all the copies of an edition printed at any one time, is as a concept less ambiguous than edition, but impressions can be very difficult to identify. In the hand-press period it was normal to distribute and re-use the type from each sheet as it was printed off, so that at that time the edition and the impression were generally the same thing; even then there were exceptions, as when the type for a small or successful book was kept standing for reprinting later. One of the chief advantages of stereo

[1a] For instance the same spool can be used for casting either series 101 Imprint or series 110 Plantin.

and electro plates, however, was that they could be kept and used to print further impressions after the first, and it was not unusual in the nineteenth century for stereos to be used for ten successive impressions, and for electros to be used for as many as thirty; while, if a set of plates was kept as a 'mother' from which further sets could be made, the number of successive impressions of an edition that could be printed from plates was virtually unlimited.

New impressions were sometimes marked by special symbols, if not by new signatures; and in the eighteenth century press figures were normally altered. Less obviously the relative position of the pages or plates in the forme may have been altered, or the lines of a typeset page may have shifted slightly if it was re-imposed with new furniture. In the absence of any typographical differentiation, the best clue is likely to be found in the paper used.

Before considering issue and state, the bibliographical concept of 'ideal copy' must be introduced. Since different copies of an edition may vary from each other in a number of ways, the bibliographer examines as many copies as possible in order to construct a notional ideal copy of the edition he is studying. A description of this ideal copy would note all the blank leaves intended to be part of its gatherings, and all excisions, insertions, and cancellantia which belonged to the most perfect copy of the work as originally completed by its printer and first put on sale by its publisher. This is the basic ideal form; and the description of ideal copy is completed by the addition of notes of any subsequent changes made by the printer or publisher to improve the book or to modify the conditions of its sale, and of any unintentional alterations to its form. Roughly speaking, different publishing units within the one edition are called issues, while parts of an edition embodying changes to the text, whether intentional or not, are known as variant states. Sometimes these differences were introduced during the course of a single printing, sometimes they were connected with the production of a new impression.

An *issue* is all the copies of that part of an edition which is identifiable as a consciously planned printed unit distinct from the basic form of the ideal copy. The criteria are that the book must differ in some typographical way from copies of the edition first put on the market, yet be composed largely of sheets deriving from the original setting; and that the copies forming another issue must be a purposeful publishing unit removed from the original issue either in form (separate issue) or in time (reissue).

Cases of *separate issue* would be: the alteration of title-pages to suit the issue of a book simultaneously in two or more different forms; the reimposition of the type pages to produce copies in different formats; impressions on special paper distinguished from ordinary copies by added, deleted, or substituted material. (Special-paper copies not distinguished typographically from those on ordinary paper—or distinguished only by altered margins—are said to be of a different state, not of a different issue, even though they represent a purposeful publishing unit.) *Reissue* normally involves a new or altered title-page, and includes cases such as: the cancellation of the title-page to bring old sheets up to date; a new impression with a new title-page; and collections of separate pieces with a new general title.

The term *state* is used to cover all other variants from the basic form of the ideal copy. There are five major classes of variant state. (1) Alterations not affecting the make-up of the pages, made intentionally or unintentionally during printing, such as: stop-press corrections; resetting as the result of accidental damage to the type; resetting of distributed matter following a decision during printing to enlarge the edition quantity. (2) The addition, deletion, or substitution of matter, affecting the make-up of the pages, but carried out during printing. (3) Alterations made after some copies have been sold (not involving a new title-page) such as the insertion or cancellation of preliminaries or text pages, or the addition of errata leaves, advertisements, etc. (4) Errors of imposition, or of machining (e.g. sheets perfected the wrong way round; but not errors of folding). (5) Special-paper copies not distinguished typographically from those on ordinary paper. Apart from class (5), differences of state are generally the attributes of individual formes, or sometimes of individual sheets.

These terms are used with reference only to the printed sheets of a book, and are not affected by binding variants. An exception might be made of printed wrappers which are peculiar to an edition, for they sometimes did duty as supplementary title-pages and were printed along with the sheets. Variant binding cases of the machine-press period may suggest re-issue, especially when they are related to particular inserted advertisements, but they cannot normally prove it.

ASSESSING THE EVIDENCE

Turning, then, to the techniques of bibliographical identification, when an editor or librarian is confronted with a more or less mysterious volume he will want to know the name of the author and of the work, the names of printer and publisher, the places and dates of printing and publication, and the place of the volume in the printing history both of the work as a whole and of the particular edition to which it belongs. Usually he will already know, or can easily look up, most of these facts, but occasionally one or more of them may prove difficult to establish, and the following notes suggest ways in which such questions may be answered.

Most books have title-pages, and sometimes imprints and colophons as well, which supply the author's name, the title of the book, the name of the printer or publisher, and the place and date of publication. Sometimes this information is partly or wholly lacking, however, and sometimes it is given wrongly, when it is the bibliographer's task to supply it as best he can. He does so by weighing the information that is given in the book against its physical make-up, referring at the same time to any external evidence that is available. As far as author and title are concerned the search must normally be made externally, both in contemporary sources such as the Stationers' Register, the Term Catalogues, and the trade-sale and publishers' catalogues of the eighteenth and nineteenth centuries, and in modern bibliographies and reference books.[2] It is also worth remembering that the author's name or initials may be found in the body of the book (commonly at the end of a fore-word or preface) and that the title may be used for running headlines.

Edition statements should be received with caution. The term 'edition' has always been used in the trade for 'impression' or 'issue' as well as for edi-tion in the bibliographical sense; a book that is advertised as a 'new edition' may indeed represent a new setting of type, but it may be a reimpression from standing type with or without correction, an impression from plates, or simply a reissue of the original sheets with a new title-page. To take a modern example, Methuen ordered two sets of electrotype plates of A. A. Milne's *Winnie-the-Pooh*, and had twenty-seven impressions printed from them in the period 1926-41. Although all twenty-seven impressions, deriving from a single setting of type, were part of a single edition, the publishers advertised each one as another edition, so that, when a new set of electros was made in 1942 from a new setting of type, what was then issued as the 'twenty-eighth edition' of *Winnie-the-Pooh* was in fact the first impression of the second edition.[3]

The position of an edition or issue in a series can often be established by comparison with other editions or issues of the same book of which the dates or positions are known. This generally involves detailed textual bibliography (see pp. 336-60), but there may also be typographical clues in altered signature series and press figures, and in the deterioration or altera-tion of blocks and plates.

Printers or publishers were sometimes shy of giving their real names— usually because a book was treasonable, or libellous, or a piracy—and for similar reasons they might give a false place of publication and a false date. Books might also be wrongly dated by accident—roman numerals were often mis-handled—or because of the trade custom of pre-dating: 'The Rule in general observed among Printers,' wrote Nichols concerning eighteenth-century practice, 'is, that when a Book happens not to be ready for publication before November, the date of the ensuing year is

[2] See the bibliography, pp. 392, 401-2, 410-11, for a survey of some of these sources.
[3] Payne, J. R., 'Four children's books by A. A. Milne', *Studies in bibliography*, xxiii, 1970, pp. 127-39.

used.'[4] Confusion is also possible between old and new style dating.[4a] There has always been a proportion of undated books, especially in the machine-press period when cheap reprints were left undated so that they could be sold over periods of years without advertising themselves as old stock.

The most usual problems of identification, indeed, concern imprint information—printers' and publishers' names, places and dates of publication, which are all interconnected—and their solution is best approached by means of a systematic general investigation. The procedure is to date and place the problem book approximately—it is assumed that the investigator has some experience of the sort of books he is working with—and to follow this with a detailed assessment of printed clues, typography, paper, binding, and provenance.

First then printed clues, beginning with anything that the imprint or colophon does reveal. The omission of the names or initials of printer and publisher itself suggests secretiveness, and the practice was often combined with printing a false place of publication. A good many French books of the eighteenth century, printed in a plainly French typographical style, have 'À Londres' or 'À Amsterdam' in their imprints; they were printed in France, but their printers and publishers used this doubtless transparent device to evade the displeasure of the authorities. Similarly, a search should be made for any initials or dates appearing elsewhere in the book. Next the positions, conventions, and typographical style of the signatures, catchwords, pagination, press figures, and imprint dates should be noted, any of which could be strongly characteristic of particular places or periods.[5]

Turning now to typographical evidence, we have seen that the sum of a printer's typographical equipment—all his founts of type in their various stages of wear, his blocks, initials, and plates—was always in practice unique to him, and if the typography of the book under investigation can be matched exactly with the work of a known printer—which is easy if mixed founts and woodcuts are involved—it is virtually certain that he printed it.[5a] Even if this cannot be done, a study of the types will often reveal when they were commonly used, and where. This can also be a powerful tool in the machine-press period—the famous Carter and Pollard investigation depended partly upon the identification of a mixed fount of type[6]— but the widespread use of stereos and electros, which could produce an impression far removed in place and time from the original setting, should

[4] Nichols, J., *Literary anecdotes*, London 1812, iii, p. 249 n.

[4a] See Greg, W. W., *Collected papers*, Oxford 1966, p. 372.

[5] Sayce, R. A., 'Compositorial practices and the localisation of printed books', *The Library*, xxi, 1966, pp. 1–45.   [5a] But see p. 39, n. 36a.

[6] Carter, J. W., and Pollard, H. G., *An enquiry into the nature of certain nineteenth-century pamphlets*, London and New York 1934.

be kept constantly in mind. Type stocks become much more difficult to identify in the period of mechanical composition, when the majority of printers were using closely similar sets of Linotype and Monotype matrixes. On the other hand the numerous different processes used for reproducing illustrations in the machine-press period may be used in dating.

The evidence of the paper is chiefly valuable for placing and dating books of the hand-press period. The watermarks of hand-made paper, or certain combinations of marks, can usually be assigned to their country of origin and approximate period, sometimes (as when individual pairs of moulds can be identified) to within fine limits. There is much evidence to suggest that printers regularly bought paper from particular wholesalers, and that apart from scraps they rarely used paper that was more than about two years old. It could of course happen that a printer used up a substantial batch of an old or unusual paper, but such cases were rare. Occasionally moulds were dated, though there was a tendency for dates to be repeated in later moulds: a French regulation required moulds to be dated in 1742, and French mould-makers continued to date their products '1742' for decades; for similar reasons much English paper made from 1795 to 1800 was dated '1794'.[7] It is much more difficult to date the machine-made papers of the nineteenth and twentieth centuries, which were rarely water-marked and which looked much alike wherever they were made, so that a different batch of paper may identify a new impression, but is unlikely to date or place it. A date of earliest manufacture can sometimes be established by a fibre-analysis carried out at a specialist laboratory.

The evidence of the binding cannot be accorded so much weight as that of the physical make-up of the book itself, since it may have been added long afterwards and in quite a different place. Nevertheless a binding of the hand-press period is more likely than not to be approximately contemporary with the book it covers—say within a decade or two—while, if it appears to be a trade rather than a bespoke binding, it is also quite likely to derive from the same part of the world. It will of course be remembered that a book may have been rebound at any time; and there is also the possibility, though a remote one, that it may have been rebound in a binding taken from another, possibly earlier, book. Edition bindings of the machine-press period are more useful in placing and dating than hand bindings, since they were carried out for the publisher in large batches, usually near the place of printing and often within a few years of publication.

Finally, early marks of ownership may provide useful dates, the owner often being identifiable even if his inscription is undated. They are poor guides to placing, however, since there has always been a brisk international trade in new books.

---

[7] Arrêt du Conseil du 18 Sept. 1741; the Excise Act 1794, 34 Geo. III, c. 20.

FACSIMILES

The identification of a facsimile, usually of a few leaves in a printed book but occasionally of a whole book, is really a special case of the problem of placing and dating. Facsimiles can be hand drawn, with or without the use of some form of mechanical reproduction, or they can involve photographic copying, or they can be printed from type. Mostly they are made without dishonest intent, although some have certainly been intended to deceive, and the ease with which they can be identified varies with the process used.

Surprisingly enough, expert hand-drawn facsimiles are amongst the hardest to spot. There were three nineteenth-century facsimilists called John Harris, of whom the second specialized in supplying missing leaves for early printed books in astonishingly faithful pen facsimiles which can be difficult to tell from the ordinary printed leaves, especially if the rest of the book has been washed and pressed. But no facsimile can resist identification once it is suspected. Examination under a glass will show the hand-drawn letters to have cleaner edges than the printed ones; more important, the paper will almost certainly show some suspicious feature. Even though the facsimilist's paper is of the same period as that of the rest of the book, he is most unlikely to be able to match it precisely in all its characteristics: thickness, texture, colour, chain-lines, watermark, and the propinquity of worm-holes and stains.

A word should be interpolated here about 'made-up' copies. Although it is less common than it used to be, booksellers and collectors sometimes complete an imperfect copy of a valuable book by supplying missing leaves from another, yet more imperfect, copy. In this case, too, any worm-holes and stains in the inserted leaves are sure to be out of line; and although the paper of the inserted leaves will be of the correct thickness, texture, and colour, the chain-line and watermark patterns of the gatherings will be interrupted. (Cancellation, of course, can have a similar effect.)

The other forms of facsimile are easier to identify. Hand-drawn lithographs, anastatic prints, and photolithographs all show the flat, rather lifeless, texture of lithography, and they were seldom printed on early paper. Photo-etched blocks, which became available in the 1870s, give the colour and impression of letterpress printing but they lose definition in the process of reproduction, so that line-block facsimiles combine rough edges with an improbably even colour. Type facsimiles, which have been attempted at various times since the very early days of printing, can be identified immediately if they can be laid beside a copy of the original; and, even if they cannot, they are likely to be given away by anachronistic type and paper.

Bibliographical Description

PURPOSE AND SCOPE

'Bibliography', meaning a list of books described in more or less detail, is an over-used and ambiguous word, for it is applied to anything from an abbreviated check-list of references to a minutely particularized descriptive investigation. The making of book lists, even detailed ones, does not always have much to do with the science of the transmission of documents. But if a group of books is described analytically and in detail the result may be an investigation of their manufacture and distribution which can elucidate the transmission of their texts directly and can also increase our understanding of the transmission of other texts of their period. At the same time an analytically descriptive bibliography of this sort serves as a means of identifying other copies of the books it deals with and of evaluating their status.

A bibliography based on analytical techniques is not the same thing as a catalogue of particular books, however detailed the catalogue may be. Indeed it does not describe particular books but ideal copies of its subjects, following the examination of as many actual copies as possible of each one. (It will be recalled, p. 315, that the basic form of ideal copy is the most perfect state of a work as originally intended by its printer or publisher following the completion of all intentional changes. Books that survive in only one or two copies present an obvious difficulty here; nevertheless the bibliographer's aim will still be to describe ideal copy as far as it can be hypothesized.)

The techniques of description used in analytical bibliography may be considered in five parts. (1) Transcriptions (or reproductions) of the title-page, etc., which both record information and provide identification. (2) A formula which analyses the format and make-up (collation) of the book in a conventional short-hand and, by explaining its construction, says something about its manufacture; added here as further evidence of completeness and identity are notes of the manner of signing, the number of leaves, and the pagination. (3) A technical note, detailing such things as press figures, type, paper, and inserted plates. (4) Details of the contents of the book. (5) Notes of any other information which may throw light on the book's history; and a register of the copies examined.

Although an analytical bibliography will normally contain information under all these five headings, the amount of weight which is attached to each of them will vary. To take simple examples, if the bibliography concerns books which are chiefly of interest for their texts, full details of contents will be needed, but it may be unnecessary to say much about typography or paper; on the other hand, if the subject of the bibliography is the work of a particular printer, the typography and paper of his books will have to be fully described, while details of their contents may be largely omitted.

In deciding what and how much to include, the bibliographer must ask himself repeatedly: 'What is the purpose of the descriptions? Who really needs each item of information? Can anything be abbreviated?' Only thus can he avoid burdensome and expensive superfluity, and escape the ultimate absurdity of mistaking the means of bibliography for its end, of practising bibliography for bibliography's sake.

The conventions of bibliographical description are set out briefly in the following paragraphs. Again they are based on Fredson Bowers's standard *Principles of bibliographical description*, which derives from the fundamental work of Sir Walter Greg, and which must be the vade-mecum of all who engage in analytical bibliography.[1] No one, of course, would claim that these conventions and rules are perfect in every respect; but they serve their purpose and they are the common language of bibliography. The use of private conventions which differ from them can only lead to imprecision and ambiguity. It cannot be emphasized too strongly, therefore, that these conventions—and these conventions only—should be used in bibliographical description.

TRANSCRIPTION AND REPRODUCTION

Bibliographers commonly transcribe a book's title-page in full by the method called quasi-facsimile, and this for two reasons: first because it normally brings together in their original form all the necessary details of author, title, printer, publisher, and place and date of publication; and secondly because it provides a wealth of arbitrary but characteristic typographical detail which will usually serve to distinguish one setting of a title-page from another.

Even quasi-facsimile, however, will not infallibly distinguish one setting from another, since it records only the letters and symbols printed on the page; it does not distinguish between founts of type within the broad boundaries of roman, italic, and gothic, and it does not indicate either the size of the typographical marks or their relative positions on the page. It is perfectly possible (although it rarely happened in practice) for a title-page to have been reset with such fidelity that transcriptions of the original

[1] See also Foxon, D. F., *Thoughts on the history and future of bibliographical description*, Los Angeles 1970.

and reset pages would be identical. Consequently it is essential for the bibliographer, when working on his books, to compare actual copies or photocopies of their title-pages, not just transcriptions. Since, moreover, the use of a collating machine will ensure that the very slightest typographical change will be noticed, and since it is arguable that reproductions can be checked and proof-read as effectively as transcriptions, there is often a case for dispensing with the laborious process of quasi-facsimile for any but short extracts from title-pages, etc.

The amount of material that is to be transcribed, then, must be decided in the light of the requirements of each particular bibliography and of the availability of photographic reproductions. But when transcriptions are made they must be done according to the standard conventions. Happily the rules of quasi-facsimile are easily mastered; what is difficult is to observe them with scrupulous, undeviating accuracy.

The text of the title-page or other subject is copied in full, including all punctuation and such things as long ſ, swash sorts, digraphs, VV for W, and ¶. Line endings are marked by single vertical strokes, but where the original has (for instance) columns of type joined by braces it may be necessary to follow the same arrangement in the transcript (see p. 370). Editorial interpolations are placed in square brackets [ ], and omissions are marked [. . .]; other brackets used are ( ) and ⌈⌉ to transcribe round and square brackets in the original, and ⟨ ⟩ to enclose conjectural reconstructions. If a word has to be divided at the end of a line of the transcription (though this should be avoided as far as possible) it is not given a hyphen unless the original happens to be hyphenated at the same point. The kind of type used (roman, italic, or gothic) is followed; two sizes of type (or capitals and small capitals of a fount) in the same line are distinguished from each other; but if small capitals are used by themselves in a line, they are transcribed as capitals since there is only one size. Words printed in colour are underlined; wrong-fount letters and misprints are noted separately. Descriptions with measurements in mm. are given in square brackets of all rules, frames, printers' flowers, ornaments, and cuts; where two dimensions are given the upright dimension is put first. (The convention of writing ‖ for a line-ending followed by a rule — or ‖‖ for a line-ending plus two rules—might cause confusion, and is not recommended.) Plates are similarly described, together with notes of any captions or signatures, and measurements both of the picture and of the plate-mark.

When the transcription is to be set in type the occurrence of italics, etc., is indicated on the copy in the usual way. Similarly, if the bibliography is prepared in typescript, as a thesis, for instance, or for reproduction by photolithography, it is most convenient to indicate italic by single

MR. WILLIAM
SHAKESPEARES
COMEDIES,
HISTORIES, &
TRAGEDIES.

Published according to the True Originall Copies.

Martin Droeshout sculpsit London.

LONDON
Printed by Isaac Iaggard, and Ed. Blount. 1623.

FIG. 125. Title-page of the Shakespeare first folio, reduced (Univ. Lib. Cam. SSS. 10. 6).

underlining, colour or gothic by underdotting (explaining in each case what the underdotting stands for), small capitals by double underlining, capitals by triple underlining, and ligatures and digraphs by a link over the joined letters. Typewriters can be modified to include vertical strokes, π, χ, etc. instead of less useful symbols such as fractions; but if a modified typewriter is not available these symbols are drawn in by hand. It is not recommended to use the sloped stroke, /, instead of the vertical stroke for line endings, since in early printing it was used as a mark of punctuation.

A few examples will show how the system is used. Here first is a reproduction of a familiar seventeenth-century title-page. In a typeset bibliography the transcription would read:

Mr. VVILLIAM | SHAKESPEARES | COMEDIES, | HISTORIES, & | TRAGEDIES. | Publifhed according to the True Originall Copies. | [copperplate portrait, 188×157 mm., signed '*Martin · Droeshout · fculpsit · London ·*', plate-mark 195×164 mm.] | *LONDON* | Printed by Ifaac Iaggard, and Ed. Blount. 1623.

Here is the same transcription prepared for reproduction from typescript:

MR. VVILLIAM | SHAKESPEARES | COMEDIES, | HISTORIES, & | TRAGEDIES. |
Publifhed according to the True Originall Copies. | [copperplate
portrait, 188 x 157 mm, signed 'Martin • Droeshout • fculpsit • London •',
plate-mark 195 x 164 mm] | LONDON [swash N, D, N] | Printed by Ifaac
Iaggard, and Ed. Blount. 1623.

FIG. 126. Quasi-facsimile transcription in typescript.

Note the indication of two sizes of capitals in the first line, and of the swash italic caps in the penultimate line.

The second example comes from an elaborate folio prayer book of the nineteenth century, set in gothic-revival typography:

[in black and red, within a woodcut compartment, 273×173 mm.]
❧ The Book of | Common Prayer | and Adminiftration of the | Sacraments
& other Rites | & Ceremonies of the Church | according to the Ufe of the |
Church of England; | Together with the Pfalter or Pfalms of Da-|vid, Pointed
as they are to be Sung or Said | in the Churches: And the Form and Manner|
of Making, Ordaining, and Confecrating of | Bifhops, Priefts, and Deacons.|
[woodcut vignette ornament, 33 × 78 mm.] | London: William Pickering. 1844.

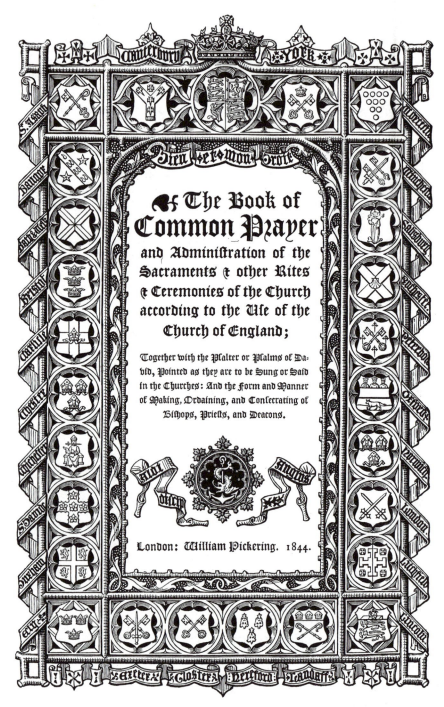

FIG. 127. Title-page of Pickering's folio prayer book, printed by Charles Whittingham, reduced (Trin. Coll. Cam. 299. a. 80. 7).

A typescript version of this transcription would present difficulties because some of the words are both in gothic type and are printed in red; probably the best solution would be to underdot the gothic, and to say in the preliminary note that lines 1, 3, 5, and 7, and the words 𝔏𝔬𝔫𝔡𝔬𝔫: and 1844. in the last line are in red.

Finally, a twentieth-century example which, like the Pickering prayer book, is deliberately anachronistic in its typography:

MECHANICK
EXERCISES

ON THE WHOLE

𝔄𝔯𝔱 𝔬𝔣 𝔓𝔯𝔦𝔫𝔱𝔦𝔫𝔤

(1683–4)

BY

JOSEPH MOXON

Edited by

HERBERT DAVIS & HARRY CARTER

Second Edition

LONDON: OXFORD UNIVERSITY PRESS

1962

FIG. 128. Title-page of Davis and Carter's *Moxon*, reduced.

MECHANICK | EXERCISES | ON THE WHOLE | 𝔄rt of 𝔓rinting | (1683–4) | BY | JOSEPH MOXON | [rule 97 mm.] | Edited by | HERBERT DAVIS & HARRY CARTER | [rule 97 mm.] | Second Edition | LONDON: OXFORD UNIVERSITY PRESS | 1962

The quasi-facsimile method is also used for transcribing imprints, colophons, running titles, and indeed any other printed matter. It can be used, too, for transcribing texts occurring in cuts, plates, and lithographs, but it is recommended that engraved or lithographed title-pages should if possible be reproduced photographically in a published bibliography.

FORMULA

The formula, which includes both the format and the collation or detailed register of signatures, serves the dual purpose of showing how the book was—or ideally should have been—constructed, and of providing a system of reference to its parts.

The imposition, paper size, and folding are determined as far as possible, and the format is then given in the form pot 8°, royal 2° in 6s, medium 18° in 12s and 6s, etc. (see pp. 80–1). This format statement for books of the hand-press period generally indicates not only the size and folding of the gatherings as they are found in the book, but also the sheet size and the imposition used in printing it. Books of the machine-press period, however, were commonly printed in large work-and-turn impositions on double or quad paper, and for them the format statement refers only to the paper size and folding as they appear in the book.

Next comes the collational formula, which is a shorthand note of all the gatherings, individual leaves, and cancels as they occur in the ideal copy. For this purpose it is assumed that the usual 23-letter latin alphabet, or an uninterrupted series of numerals, is used for signing the gatherings. Thus the notation A–Z refers to 23 gatherings signed in alphabetical order from A to Z, less I or J, U or V, and W; similarly with a–z; while 1–10 would indicate 10 gatherings signed with the numerals 1 to 10. But, although signature series set in lower-case type are distinguished from those in capitals, capitals are not distinguished from small capitals; and gothic, roman, and italic founts are not distinguished from each other. Arbitrary symbols (*, ¶, etc.) used as signatures are reproduced. Duplicated signature alphabets, Aa–Zz, Aaa–Zzz, etc., are written 2A–2Z, 3A–3Z, etc.; and if two or more alphabets follow each other in regular sequence, A–Z Aa–Zz for instance, the notation becomes A–2Z. There are then ways of indicating departures from regular series, as will be shown below.

Superior figures are added to the signature notations to show how the gatherings are folded and how many leaves each one contains. A single-sheet folio with two leaves is shown as A^2; a quarto, with four leaves, A^4; an octavo, A^8; and so on. The superior figure indicates that the normal folding for the format has been used, and that pairs of leaves in the gathering are conjugate as usual (in a whole sheet of quarto, for instance, there are two pairs of conjugate leaves, the first and the fourth, and the second and the third). If A^2 is shown in a quarto it means that the gathering is a half-sheet of quarto folded as a conjugate pair; if in an octavo, that it is a quarter sheet folded as a pair. It follows (with one uncommon exception) that *the superior figure must always be even*; the notation A^5 would be meaningless, since it cannot represent an actual folding, but only a gathering which has gained or lost an odd number of leaves. (The exception is the format 18° in 9s which is written A^9, etc., the fifth leaf being a singleton; it is illustrated in the manuals from Smith, 1755,[2] onwards, and was occasionally used for stabbed books in the early nineteenth century.)

Having got so far we can work out the formula for a simple book. Suppose that we have a quarto, printed on foolscap size paper; that it begins with a half sheet, folded as a conjugate pair and signed A; continues with 32 regular whole-sheet gatherings signed B to Kk inclusive, omitting J, U, W, and Jj; and ends with a half-sheet pair signed Ll. The formula is:

foolscap 4°: A^2 B–2K^4 2L^2

Note that the format statement is separated from the collation by a colon, and that this simple formula is not punctuated. The formula will be completed with a statement of signing, described below, which indicates which leaves are signed and which are not.

Not all books, of course, were so regular in construction as this example, and we shall have to speak in a moment of extensions to the system which are used to deal with irregular series, with interpolated or deleted gatherings and leaves, and with cancels. But first a word about reference to the individual parts of the book.

The system of reference is based on the collational formula. Whole gatherings or folds are simply referred to as B^4, L^2, etc., while individual leaves within gatherings take suffix numerals: the four leaves of gathering B^4 are referred to as B1, B2, B3, and B4. (For numerical signatures the suffix numerals have to be written as inferiors, 2_1, 2_2, etc., but for alphabetical signatures this is unnecessary). Conjugate pairs of leaves are written B1.4, B2.3, $2_{1.4}$, $2_{2.3}$, etc., the point indicating conjugacy. When reference is to be made to a page rather than to the whole leaf superior ^{a} and ^{b} are used for the recto and verso respectively; while column references may require

[2] Smith, J., *The printer's grammar*, London 1755, p. 246.

further suffixes, such as $B1^{b2}$ for the second column of type on the verso of leaf B1. (It has been a common bibliographical practice to write plain B1 for the recto of leaf B1 [etc.] and $B1^{v}$ for the verso; there are obvious objections to using the symbol B1 for both the leaf and the page, however, and this form is not recommended.) The pages of books of the machine-press period are referred to by the printed page numbers; the pagination of eighteenth-century books is usually (and of earlier books is occasionally) good enough for this practice if it is preferred.

We can now consider irregular collations, and first unsigned books, for which the gatherings are listed numerically in brackets:

royal 2° in 10s: $[1^2\ 2-8^{10}\ 9^8]$

Much commoner are books in which most but not all the gatherings are signed. Provided that the missing signatures can be safely inferred, they are supplied but are set in italics to show that they are inferences:

foolscap 4°: A^4 B–C^4 D^4 E–G^4 H^2

But if the unsigned sheets or leaves are additional to regular signature series, they are given the symbols π for preliminary gatherings and leaves, and χ for additions elsewhere. Thus (omitting both format statements and statements of signing for the sake of brevity) we can write:

π^2 A–D^4 BUT NOT π^2 B–D^4, which should be A^2 B–D^4
π^2 A–G^8 χ^8 H–K^8 $2\chi1$ L^8

In the second formula, χ^8 and $2\chi1$ are interpolated between gatherings; but if interpolations are made inside gatherings their position and nature are indicated in parentheses:

A–C^4 D^4(D3+$\chi1$) E–G^4 H^4(H1+$\chi1$, 2) I–M^4 N^4(N3+$\chi1.2$)

Here the first interpolation (which comes after the third leaf of D^4) is of a single leaf; the second is of two disjunct leaves; and the third is of a fold of two leaves. References to interpolated leaves are made in the form $D(\chi1)$, $N(\chi2^b)$, etc.

Parenthetical notes are similarly used to indicate leaves which were intentionally cancelled or removed from the gatherings by the printer, here with the minus sign:

A–C^4 D^4(–D3) E–F^4 G^4(–G1.4)

In this case we would write G^4(–G1.4) only if it is certain that it is leaves G1.4 that were removed; if we are not sure (if, for instance, G could have been printed by half-sheet imposition) we would write G^2.

If the cancellandum has been replaced with a cancellans, the same sort of parenthetical note is made with the plus–minus sign:

A–D^4 E^4($\pm$E3) F–H^4 I^4($\pm$I1, 2) K^4($\pm$K2.3) L–M^4 N^4($\pm$N$_1^4$) O–Z^4

Here we have the cancellation and replacement of one leaf, of two disjunct leaves, of a conjugate pair, and of a whole quarto gathering.

Observe that in all these cases when parenthetical notes are used, the signature to which a note applies is separated from the series:

A–F^4 G^4($-$G3) H–Z^4 NOT   A–G^4($-$G3) H–Z^4

If a signature alphabet or other signature series is repeated without the usual doubling, etc., of the symbols, each extra series is given a superior numeral prefix, and commas are used to separate the series from each other:

A–2Z^4, ^{2}A–M^4, ^{3}A–X^4

Duplicated preliminary signatures are distinguished by superior $^\pi$:

$^\pi$A^4 A–K^4
π^2 $^\pi$A–B^4, A–K^4

Obvious mis-signings (such as the series A B C E E F) are corrected in the formula and the fact is noted in the statement of signing; but where signatures are duplicated, they are given superior ^{x}:

A–D^4 ^{x}D^4 E–F^4

Or, if it is obvious that it is the first, not the second, signature D that is the insertion, we may write:

A–C^4 ^{x}D^4 D–F^4

The examples of collational formulae given here will be found to cover most of the situations met with in practice, and any further complications (which will occasionally be found) can be dealt with by logical extensions of the method. Difficulties may be experienced with substitutions in which the substituted leaves differ in form or signature from the originals, and in such cases reference should be made to the full treatment of the formulary in Bowers's *Principles*.

The formula is completed by a statement of signing placed after the collation in square brackets. The dollar sign, which means 'all the signatures', is used with a figure to indicate which leaves are normally signed in the book (up to and including the number given), followed by a note of any departures from this normal practice:

pot 4°: A–Z^4 [\$3 signed (+B4, K4; −A1, L2, P3, Y2, 3; A2 signed 'A3')]

This means that the first three leaves of each gathering are signed, except that B4 and K4 are also signed, that A1, L2, P3, Y2, and Y3 are not signed, and that A2 is wrongly signed A3. It might be taken for granted that the title-page, A1 in this example, is unsigned, but its inclusion in the statement of signing avoids any possible ambiguity.

Although the statement of pagination or foliation (that is, the numbering of the pages or of the leaves, respectively) is not strictly speaking part of the formula, it is added here since the collation and pagination should confirm and thus check each other. It begins with a note of the total number of leaves in a book, excluding inserted plates etc., which will of course be the same as the number of leaves derived from the collation: a book collating A–Z⁴, for instance, should have $23 \times 4 = 92$ leaves. If the book has no printed pagination or foliation, the total number of pages is added in brackets:

> 92 leaves, unnumbered [pp. 1–184]

Otherwise, pagination or foliation is given as it occurs. If every page or leaf were numbered, including the title-page, the statement might read:

> 92 leaves, pp. i–iv, 1–180
> 92 leaves, ff. 1–92

Disturbances in the printed sequence are given as far as possible as they occur, with the addition of the actual number of pages or leaves in brackets:

> 89 leaves, pp. 1–24 26 29 31–182 [= 178]

But misprints which do not upset the sequence are noted in parentheses after the main statement:

> 308 leaves, ff. 1–308 (misprinting 9 as '6', 102 as '201')

Parts of a sequence which are missing, but which can be inferred, are supplied in italics without brackets:

> 32 leaves, pp. *i–ii* iii–vi, *1* 2–45 *46* 47–50 *51–58*

Where the pagination or foliation of unnumbered pages cannot be inferred, however, the total of each unnumbered group of such pages is inserted in italics in brackets:

> 80 leaves, pp. [*2*] *i–ii* iii–xiv, [*4*] 1–16 *17* 18–27 29 31–34 [*24*] 35–108 *109–118*
> [= xvi, 144]
> 40 leaves, pp. [*16*], *1* 2–64
> 48 leaves, pp. [*16*], *1* 2–32 [*32*] 33–48 [= 16, 80]

TECHNICAL NOTES

Included here are details of signature positions, catchwords, and press figures; of the type and paper used; and of any plates or other insets which are not included in the collation.

The positions of the signatures relative to the words in the lines immediately above them are given when it is necessary to identify line-for-line resetting. The word closest to the signature letter is transcribed, with an indication of the actual letter or space beneath which the signature is placed: '*the*' would mean that the signature letter is immediately beneath the h of the word 'the'; and 'the ∧' that it is beneath the space following the word 'the'.

The mention of catchwords may be brief, but it might be noted if they appear regularly (whether on every page, or only at the end of the gathering etc.); whether any catchwords are missing; and whether any catchwords differ from the first words of the following pages, in some form such as

B4ᵃ there] here

meaning that the catchword on B4ᵃ, which ought to be 'there', is printed as 'here'.

A record of press-figures serves both to analyse the press-work of an impression and to differentiate between impressions. Various methods of recording figures for one or other of these purposes have been used,[3] but it is most convenient if both analysis and identification can be dealt with by a single convention, using a form such as:

1: A2ᵇ A7ᵇ, E2ᵇ E7ᵇ, F1ᵇ
2: D1ᵇ D4ᵇ
7: B3ᵇ B6ᵇ

This method gives both the page (for checking identity) and the forme (for analysing the press-work) in which each figure occurs, and follows the work of each press through the book.

The amount of detail to be given about type and paper depends largely upon the purpose for which the bibliography is being made (pp. 321–2). If the investigation is not primarily concerned with production, the note on the type might include the dimensions of a normal type-page less head-line and direction-line, the kind and 20-line measurement of the text type, the number of lines to a normal page, and references to woodcut ornaments etc. :

140 × 78 mm. (B1ᵃ); roman 83; 34 lines; woodcut initials on A4ᵃ, C5ᵃ, E4ᵇ

---

[3] e.g., for identification, by giving the page number followed by the figure (5-1, 20-3, 36-2, etc.); and for analysis by laying out the figures in a grid.

In a bibliography in which production details are important, however, each type used would be separately recorded using the formula explained on p. 14:

A2ᵃ-A4ᵇ: van den Keere's ascendonica roman; body 140; face 138 × 3:4·8

and the details of particular pages would include (in addition to the dimensions of the page and the number of lines) gutter measurements, the number of ems to the measure, and photographic reproductions of woodcuts, ornaments, and flowers. Similarly the amount of detail given about paper may vary considerably. The description of a hand-made paper should include at least a note of the chain-line spacing, of the watermark type if any, and of the uncut sheet-size if an uncut copy is available:

A–E: chain 24–6 mm.; Pro Patria/GR; 42 × 33·5 cm.
F–H: chain 30; no mark; 42 × 33 cm.

More details about hand-made papers can of course be given (see pp. 76–7), even to the extent of identifying individual paper moulds, though it should be remembered that in this case we are describing individual copies of an edition, not ideal copy. It was not uncommon for edition-sheets to be printed on mixed batches of paper, so that particular copies of a gathering were not necessarily or ideally printed on a particular sort of paper. All we can do is to establish the range of papers normally found in the gathering.

Machine-made papers were much more constant in their physical properties, and a description would include leaf (not sheet) size, leaf thickness, watermarks or laid lines if any, surface texture (rough, smooth, or glossy), and colour:

Leaf size 19 × 12·5 cm.; thickness 0·012 mm.; no marks; smooth, white

If a fuller description were necessary the direction and mesh of the machine-wire would be given, together with the results of any chemical tests made on the paper (pp. 226–8).

Plates and other insets printed apart from the body of the book are not included in the collational formula, but are separately described in the technical note. Details should include at least the number and position of each plate, and the process (copperplate engraving, tinted lithograph, half-tone process block, etc.). A fuller description would include the subject of each illustration, and a transcription of any title or signature printed with it; its dimensions and those of the plate mark (if any); and details of the paper used.

CONTENTS

The note of contents accounts for each page in the book, referring to them by signatures (books of the hand-press period) or by page numbers (books of the machine-press period, and also eighteenth-century books if the pagination is adequate). Typical brief notes might read:

A1^a title, A1^b blank, A2^a–A4^b preface, B1^a–Y4^b text, Z1^a–Z4^b index

1 half-title, *2* advertisements, *3* title, *4* imprint, *5* dedication, *6* blank, *7–11* preface, *12* note to the fourth edition, *13–208* ABC for book-collectors

In the second example 'note to the fourth edition' and 'ABC for book-collectors' are in fact quotations from the book being described, but they are not in quasi-facsimile and are therefore not put in quotes. When the contents have to be given in greater detail, however, quasi-facsimile must often be resorted to, the extracts in this form being placed in single quotes:

π1^a half-title 'MEMOIRS | OF THE | LIFE and WRITINGS | OF | M^R· GRAY. | [. . .]'; π1^b blank; π2^a title; π2^b blank; A1^a '[thick and thin rule] | MEMOIRS | OF THE | LIFE and WRITINGS | OF | Mr. GRAY. | [rule] | [. . .]'; A1^a–3E2^b text; on 3E2^b 'THE END OF THE MEMOIRS.'; . . .

A full note of contents would include transcriptions of running titles:

3E3^b–3F4^b: 'CONTENTS of the MEMOIRS.'
a2^b–h2^a: 'ODES.' (no running title on a3^b, b1^a, b4^a, c1^b . . .)

OTHER NOTES

A wide range of additional information may be recorded here. The most important items are: (1) Notes on any features of the structure of the book which call for extended comment, such as peculiarities of printing or gatherings, use of stereotype plates, etc. (2) Full details in sub-paragraphs of variant impressions, issues, and states. (3) Descriptions of any trade or edition bindings that have been identified. (4) Relevant information from external sources (such as printers' and publishers' records, advertisements, and authors' correspondence), including if possible details of edition quantities and prices. (5) A register of the copies examined.

Sample entries from actual bibliographies are reprinted in Appendix B, pp. 368–80, with brief commentaries.

Textual Bibliography

Traditionally the function of textual criticism has been to follow the threads of transmission back from an existing document and to try to restore its text as closely as possible to the form it originally took in the author's manuscript. In textual criticism of the Bible and of the works of classical and medieval authors, two stages are recognized: recension, the establishment of the relationship of the surviving manuscripts to each other (in the form of a *stemma* or family tree), so that their evidence can be used to reconstruct the features of the lost original; and emendation, whereby a knowledge of the processes of transmission—book hands, scribal habits, etc.—is brought to bear on the remaining textual problems, so that the true readings that underlie the corruptions may be deduced.

Textual bibliography is textual criticism adapted to the analogous but not identical problems of editing printed texts. The aim again is to provide the principles and materials for a critical edition which will represent as nearly as possible the author's intentions for his text. In some cases it may be supposed that the author wished to see his manuscript printed exactly as it stood, down to the last detail; but more often it will seem likely that the author expected and approved of the normalization of the spelling, punctuation, etc., which printers ordinarily carried out, in which case the editor will be aiming at a critical version of the printed, not the manuscript, text. By studying the author's manuscript (if it survives) and the various printed versions as material objects, and establishing wherever possible the circumstances of their production, an assessment is made of their relationship to each other. One of them is chosen as the 'copy text' for the edited version; and textual problems are then approached in the light both of an evaluation of the bibliographical and literary merits of each case, and of our general knowledge of the history of book production—and especially of what we know of the habits of compositors.

This assumes, of course, that we are dealing with one basic text, of which the various forms, manuscript and printed, differ from each other in relatively minor and mostly unintentional ways. Some books, however, were revised by their authors to the extent that the different versions could not be combined in a single edited text; Balzac, for example, not only re-wrote his books in proof, but incorporated major textual revisions in each successive edition, and the novels of Richardson, Dickens, and Tolstoy present similar problems. But we are concerned here not with what is at the moment the essentially literary problem of choosing between major versions of a work, but with the technique for arriving at a text of a particular version.

(It is an anomaly of bibliographical scholarship today that, while much effort is expended on the textual bibliography of nineteenth-century books of which the early texts differ from each other only in minor and frequently trivial ways, books of which we have texts in several widely different forms are either avoided by editors or edited in a single version. This may be because the methods evolved for the textual bibliography of Shakespeare, where minor variation is seldom trivial, can be applied to the first class of book but not to the second.)

It would be satisfactory if bibliographical investigation alone could solve the textual problems even of particular versions. Fifty years ago there was a good deal of optimism on this score, and real if modest gains were made, such as the establishment in 1909 of the true textual status of the falsely-dated Shakespeare quartos of 1619; but since then the returns from bibliographical effort have decreased. As Fredson Bowers has said, 'current bibliographical research is moving ahead with astonishing speed, but its general effects tend more to show the specialist what he does not yet know than to open up new territory for exploration by the general scholar. Each fresh bibliographical break-through only discovers more areas for technical investigation before criticism can begin to make use of the newer findings; and thus the day for practical application of bibliographical hypotheses is continually being put off.'[1]

If this seemed true in 1959, it seems even more so today. We now realize in fact that the processes of book production have always been so involved that it is very seldom possible to work out from the evidence in any one book exactly how it was set, proofed, printed, and distributed. To quote another bibliographer, 'wherever full primary evidence has become available it has revealed a geometry of such complexity that even an expert in cybernetics, primed with all the facts, would have little chance of discerning it'.[2] In a few cases—of which Charlton Hinman's work on the Shakespeare Folio is the most eminent—the work of particular compositors can be identified, which assists our detailed assessment of the text. But for the most part we are limited to general evaluations of textual status and to individual deductions based on our knowledge of the printing practices of the past.

So literary criticism is by no means superseded, even in the consideration of problems of corruption in early texts. And when it comes to more recent

[1] Bowers, F. T., *Bibliography and textual criticism*, Oxford 1964, p. 4.
[2] McKenzie, D. F., 'Printers of the mind', *Studies in bibliography*, xxii, 1969, p. 60.

texts, where the editorial problem is likely to be that of revision rather than corruption, a textual editor is nothing if he is not a literary critic. A novel, for example, may exist as an early draft, a serial version, a book version, and a later revision; a play as a pre-production version, an acting version, and a reading version; and all these several versions may have been over-seen by the author.[3] Here the editor must make major critical decisions in preparing a text, for no bibliographical rule of thumb is going to lead him to the right answer every time. Some authors improved their work by revising it, others did the opposite; and the different versions of a text might have served different purposes. Every case is unique, and every one calls for the fresh exercise of an editor's literary judgement. Nevertheless twentieth-century bibliography has penetrated literary criticism and has changed it. Literary judgement alone, without the discipline of textual bibliography, will result in the production of misleading and inaccurate texts as surely as will the mechanical application of bibliographical rules. Textual bibliography is based on the union of literary judgement with bibliographical expertise.

COPY-TEXT[4]

A critical edition of a book will be set from a particular basic text, and the chosen original is called the copy-text. Usually it is fairly easy to see which of the various available texts should be chosen. Let us suppose, for example, that the first edition of a book was set from the author's manuscript, which has survived; that a second edition was set from a copy of the first which had been corrected in a few places by the author; and that the third and last edition was set, during the author's lifetime but without further re-vision by him, from a copy of the second; the three editions thus forming a simple ancestral series deriving from the manuscript.

Now, although the third edition appeared during the author's lifetime, it cannot be supposed to have any authority on that account; he did not revise it, and it is most unlikely that he considered its text in detail or approved of such minor changes of punctuation etc., as had inevitably occurred, chiefly by accident, when it was set up from the second edition. The third edition, then, will not do as copy-text.

The second edition does have some authority, however: final authority as far as certain words in it are concerned, for the author corrected them, showing how he wanted them to stand. Nevertheless it is still unlikely that he considered every minor change that occurred accidentally in setting the

---

[3] See Beaurline, L. A., 'The director, the script, and author's revisions: a critical problem', *Papers in dramatic theory and criticisms*, ed. Knauf, D. M., Iowa 1969, pp. 78-91.

[4] See the bibliography, p. 413.

second edition from the first. Therefore, although we ought to accept and incorporate the changes of sense or wording that he made—which are called 'substantive' alterations—we would again be wrong to copy the minor changes of spelling, capitalization, and punctuation—the 'accidental' alterations—unless there is reason to believe that the author himself ordered them; they have no authority, but are merely the result of the carelessness, or zealousness, of the compositor.

Which brings us back to the first edition and to the manuscript from which it was set. At first glance it might seem that the manuscript will be the obvious choice for copy-text, for it is what the author actually wrote. But does it represent the text as the author wanted it to be read? As far as substantives are concerned (saving later corrections) it certainly does; but this is hardly the case with the accidentals. Most authors even today expect the printer to normalize their spelling and capitalization (and until late in the nineteenth century they expected the punctuation to be normalized as well), relying on the process to dress the text suitably for publication, implicitly endorsing it (with or without further amendment) when correcting proofs. As Rousseau wrote to his publisher Marc-Michel Rey in 1755 about the first batch of author's proofs of *Inégalité*: 'There are innumerable faults in the punctuation. When I said that I wanted the manuscript to be followed exactly, I did not mean this to apply to the punctuation, which is thoroughly defective. Ask the Abbé Yvon to be so good as to put it right in the proofs which are to follow.'[5]

It would normally be wrong, therefore, rigidly to follow the accidentals of the manuscript, which the author would himself have been prepared— or might have preferred—to discard. It could happen, of course, that an author disapproved of the printer's normalization—printers seldom gave authors much choice in the matter[6]—and would have liked to see his manuscript set in type exactly as he wrote it, accidentals and all. If the editor believes this to be the case he will choose the manuscript as the copy-text rather than a printed version. It also follows that if the document being edited was not originally intended to be printed (if it is a collection of

---

[5] 'Les fautes de ponctuation sont innombrables. Quand j'ai désiré qu'on suivit exactement le manuscrit je n'entendois pas parler de la ponctuation qui y est fort vicieuse. Priez M. l'Abbé Yvon de vouloir bien la rétablir dans les épreuves suivantes' (Rousseau, J. J., *Correspondance complète*, ed. Leigh, R. A., iii, Genève and Madison 1966, pp. 85-6.) Similarly in 1692 James Yonge earnestly begged his printer that 'many words misspelt by my Amanuensis, and the several false pointings, and other defects may be rectified' (U.L.C. Add. MS. 7913 f. 1ᵇ).

[6] Authors were sometimes given a choice of style of capitalization and italicization in the eighteenth century, when conventions were changing: 'Before we actually begin to compose, we should be informed, either by the Author, or Master, after what manner our work is to be done; whether the old way, with Capitals to Substantives, and Italic to proper names; or after the more neat practice, all in Roman, and Capitals to Proper names, and Emphatical words' (Smith, J., *The printer's grammar*, London 1755, p. 201); but Smith does not suggest that authors were consulted about punctuation.

letters, for instance, or a diary) the manuscript would be used as copy-text in preference to any earlier printed version, and the accidentals would not be normalized. But in most cases the editor will choose as copy-text an early printed edition, not the manuscript.

This is a satisfactory conclusion, since for many authors the actual writing of the manuscript, with its drafts, re-drafts, erasures, and additions, is a means of composition, not an end; and, although we may on occasion want to follow an author as he brings his work into being, it would be inconvenient to place the apparatus for doing so in the text of a critical edition. A surviving manuscript will of course be of great value to the editor even though it is not used as copy-text, for it will serve as a check upon the accuracy of the printed version, supplying substantives where the compositor has gone wrong, and monitoring the normalization of the accidentals (which is especially important when it is known that the author did not read proofs).

So we are left, finally, with the first edition. Here the accidentals will be largely the result of the process of normalization carried out in the printing house, but they will still be closer both to the text that the author wanted, and to the reading of his manuscript, than the altered accidentals of the second and third editions. The first edition is therefore chosen as copy-text, to be followed in accidentals, and also generally in substantives. But substantive variants will be incorporated from a surviving manuscript or from a later printed text if they are believed, on bibliographical or literary grounds, to have greater authority—that is, to be more likely to be what the author wrote, or (on reflection) re-wrote—than the readings of the first edition.

The normal rule, then, is that the copy-text is that printed edition which is closest in line of descent to the author's manuscript; that it is followed in accidentals; and that it is also followed in substantives unless there is evidence that the author's intentions would be more closely represented by other readings.

In most cases copy-text for a critical edition can be chosen according to these principles, but complex textual situations will give the editor pause. A text much revised by its author in successive editions will certainly be authoritative in each case, yet an editor may decide on critical or historical grounds that the last version is not the best and will therefore edit an earlier version. New readings in later editions of a work may derive from a primary manuscript of equal or higher authority than that used for the first edition, or they may be the author's revisions of his first version, or they may be corruptions. If there are two or more collateral printed texts which were set from manuscript copy, not from other printed editions,[7] the editor

---

[7] The term 'substantive edition' may be used for any edition set from manuscript rather than from

must choose one or other of them as copy-text on the basis of whatever he can discover about their relative status, and follow its accidentals in the usual way, but substantive variants must be chosen from either version according to the editor's estimation of their having been the words the author wrote. But let us look at some examples.

The three early texts of *Hamlet* present a celebrated problem:[8] the 'bad' quarto of 1603 (Q1), the quarto of 1604–5 (Q2), and the folio of 1623 (F). It is believed that Q1 *Hamlet* was set from a manuscript of an incomplete memorial reconstruction of Shakespeare's play as it was acted in the English provinces in 1602–3; and that most of Q2 was set with a degree of probably unavoidable error from Shakespeare's 'foul papers' (a first or other early draft of the play), but that the first act was set from a copy of Q1 corrected by reference to a manuscript (or, if set from manuscript, then with reference to a copy of Q1). F, it is thought, was fairly accurately set from a manuscript (either directly or via a corrected copy of Q2) that had served as the play-house prompt-book, this manuscript being a fair copy made either by an independent scribe or by Shakespeare himself. Q1, moreover, is less than half the length of the other two texts; Q2 contains 200 lines that are not in F; and F contains 85 lines that are not in Q2.

Evidently the choice of copy-text for an edition of *Hamlet* depends on what is believed about the manuscript underlying F. If it was transcribed by someone other than the author, then Q2 is closest to the author's manuscript and will be chosen as copy-text, even though it is manifestly inaccurate in places, is contaminated at the beginning by Q1, and lacks words and lines that are supplied, with more or less authority, by Q1 and F. If on the other hand the manuscript underlying F was copied out by Shakespeare himself, incorporating the kind of verbal revisions that authors commonly make when transcribing their own work, then both Q2 and F have the authority of the author's manuscripts behind them, and the editor might well make F the copy-text as representing the more polished version. Whichever he chooses he will still have to sift out and categorize the numerous errors that disfigure all the early texts of the play, and account for them logically.

When the first edition of a book has been revised by the author and used as copy for a second edition, the copy-text rule is followed as usual, provided that the revision is not extensive (say no more than a word or two in each paragraph) and that there is no particular reason to believe that the author

another printed edition, but I avoid it here because of the possibility of confusion with the 'substantives' of textual variation.

[8] The best summary of *Hamlet* studies up to the mid 1950s is in Greg, W. W., *The Shakespeare first folio*, Oxford 1955, pp. 299–333; for a later approach, see Honigmann, E. A. J., *The stability of Shakespeare's text*, London 1965, *passim*.

interfered with the punctuation: the accidentals are taken from the original edition, the substantives from the revision. But this is uncertain ground. Many authors, especially since the mid nineteenth century, have cared about the details of their punctuation and have bothered to correct it. Dickens was one (see Appendix C (2)); and Hardy, in revising his printed texts for new editions, appears to have changed the normalized accidentals back to the forms of the original manuscript (though without actually collating them), so that an editor would be right to take not only the substantives from the revised editions, but the accidentals as well.[9] The more, of course, that the editor knows about the working habits of his author— or at least of his author's period—the better he can choose his copy-text.

In any case, the more heavily a text has been revised, the more likely it becomes that alterations to the accidentals as well as to the substantives were made by the author, not by the printer, and should therefore be incorporated in the edited text. In extreme cases it will be necessary to abandon one of the versions altogether and produce a critical edition of the other, or even to make a parallel-text edition.

Samuel Richardson's *Pamela* provides an example of this sort of problem. The first edition appeared in 1740-1, but Richardson altered it so extensively in successive editions that the final authorized text (which was published forty years after his death, in 1801) was virtually re-written from end to end; the author's last revision alone involved more than 8,400 changes in the first two volumes, 'ranging from single words to whole pages cut or added. Hardly a paragraph is untouched, hardly a sentence. . . .'[10] Here it would obviously be impossible for an editor to incorporate the first, the intermediate, and the final versions of the novel in a single critical text, and he will have to decide which version he will present.

Similarly there were four distinct stages in the composition of Tenessee Williams's *The glass menagerie*:[11] (1) a short story called 'Portrait of a girl in glass', written before 1943, published 1948; (2) the play in an early version, also written before 1943, of which about one third survives in manuscript; (3) the revised version of the play, longer than (2), which was written *c.* 1943 and published 1945, and was called by Williams the 'reading version'; and (4) the acting version published in 1948 and in a later revision, representing the play as performed and containing over 1,100 verbal changes from (3). Here too an editor will have to choose a particular version;

---

[9] Information from D. F. Foxon (from work in progress by Simon Gatrell). On variation in Hardy's texts, see Kramer, D., 'Two "new" texts of Thomas Hardy's *The Woodlanders*', *Studies in bibliography*, xx, 1967, pp. 135-50.

[10] Eaves, T. C. D., and Kimpel, B. D., 'Richardson's revisions of *Pamela*', *Studies in bibliography*, xx, 1967, pp. 61-88.

[11] Beaurline, L. A., '*The glass menagerie*: from story to play', *Modern drama*, viii, 1965, pp. 142-9.

and it may be added that, should he decide on (3), his evidence will include a 105-page manuscript containing ten different kinds of paper, written on at least six different typewriters, with four different handwritten pencil or ink revisions, and probably representing eight to ten layers of revision.

Alternatively there may be problems of divided authority, as exemplified by the two texts of *Wuthering Heights*.[12] The first edition of 1847 appears to have been set, with a good deal of manifest error, from Emily Brontë's manuscript (which is now lost). In 1850, two years after the author's death, Charlotte Brontë brought out a second edition, which was set from the first but in which the obvious misprints were corrected, the sketchy punctuation was amplified, and certain stylistic changes were made. Here the copy-text will necessarily be the first edition, but the editor will have to decide how far to follow Charlotte in her alterations not only of substantives but also (apart from the misprints) of accidentals, and this will depend in turn upon the likelihood of her having taken them from the original manuscript; for, unless they derived from the manuscript, her emendations have scarcely more authority than those of a modern editor.

THE TRANSMISSION OF THE TEXT[13]

The choice between variant readings, and the emendation of corruptions, will be made by an editor on either bibliographical or on literary grounds, or on both. Literary criticism is not our present concern, but bibliographical criticism is the end towards which our understanding of the processes of book production is eventually directed. In practice the application of the techniques of textual bibliography to individual textual problems involves assessing the probable effect of the production processes—especially composition, correction, and the later stages in handling set type, including plate making—on the transmission of the text from the manuscript to the printed page.

1. *Composition.* The function of the compositor in textual transmission was crucial, for he—and usually he alone—made a complete transcription of the text. He is thus the analogue of the scribe or manuscript copyist and, although the parallel should not be taken too far (for errors made with a pen, which can trace out any shape, may be of a different sort from errors in the manipulation of prefabricated types), many scribal features are found in typeset matter.

It is possible for a compositor to imitate printed copy with great accuracy, but manuscript copy is rarely set in type without being changed in the process. The changes are for the most part either intentional alterations

---

[12] Brontë, E., *Wuthering heights*, eds. Ewbank, I.-S., and Marsden, H., Oxford (in preparation).
[13] See the bibliography, p. 413.

made to improve the detailed presentation of the text, or involuntary errors which may or may not be spotted and corrected later. The amount of compositorial change has varied with period, with place, and with the attitudes and technical accomplishment of both authors and printers; but, although such changes have not always been of equal importance textually, they have nearly always been numerous.

The following discussion of compositorial alteration and error is concerned primarily with the hand-press period, because most variation occurred then. But the situation in the machine-press period differed chiefly in degree, not in kind. Type continued to be hand set for most of the nineteenth century and, although standards of accuracy were higher than they had been and most spelling variation had disappeared, the effects of the compositor's transcription were essentially the same as before. During the present century there has indeed been a growing tendency for the publisher to edit the accidentals in a manuscript before it is sent for setting, but even now this is not always done, and the textual changes occurring in machine composition are otherwise much like those in hand-set work: the keyboard operator, like the hand compositor, transcribes a text from its hand- or type-written form into an assemblage of printable images, and his work is characterized by similar ranges of intentional change and involuntary error.

Compositors, and keyboard operators working with unedited copy, have always acknowledged two duties: one is to set the words of their copy in type as exactly as possible, without addition or omission (or, as we would say, to get the substantives right); the other is to ensure that the typographical 'style' of the result—the spelling, capitalization, punctuation, italicization, and abbreviation, which we call the accidentals—accords with the conventions of the time and place. During the hand-press period the conventions of typographical style were fairly uniform within national printing industries, but the nineteenth century saw the development of 'house styles' of particular printers, which themselves have tended to give way during the present century to the house styles of particular publishers; the house styles have not strayed far from national conventions, however, being chiefly concerned with a handful of spellings (connection—connexion, judgement—judgment, etc.), and such things as capitalization in book titles and the punctuation of abbreviations and quotations.

It is a commonplace that the spelling of English authors in the sixteenth and early seventeenth centuries was very varied.[14] Nevertheless, although there cannot be said to have been a standard orthography during this period, the range of variation that was generally acceptable was limited;

[14] Hill, T. H., 'Spelling and the bibliographer', *The Library*, xviii, 1963, pp. 1–28.

some variant spellings, or groups of variants, were rarely used and were thus in a sense 'wrong', even though they might be as reasonable phonetically as the 'right' spellings. (It must be emphasized that a 'right' spelling was one that was accepted, not necessarily one that later became standard.)

A similar situation prevailed in the printing houses. Compositors considered some spellings to be acceptable and others not, and they regularly brought their author's spellings into line with what they thought was right (unless, as happened occasionally, the author insisted upon the retention of his own spelling). This is not to say that there was a codified or even a standardized printers' orthography—there is no evidence of anything of the kind—but compositors did learn their trade from each other and they did change their jobs, so that it is not surprising to find a greater uniformity of spelling within the printing trade than outside it.

Until the mid seventeenth century variant spelling within limits was a permissible and usual feature of compositors' orthography. Thus in 1600 a particular compositor might feel that he could properly set the word 'do' as 'do' or as 'doe', but that it would be wrong to set 'doo'. However, although either 'do' or 'doe' would seem right to him, he would probably prefer, or be in the habit of setting, one or the other of them. Similarly with other common variants; other things being equal, he would prefer particular forms or groups of forms.

But other things were not always equal. So long as such spelling variants were acceptable in printing, compositors used them as an aid to justification. Thus our man might set 'doe' according to his usual practice and then, finding that his line was a quarter of an em too long for the measure, change 'doe' to 'do' by discarding the e, rather than go to the greater trouble of throwing out spaces and finding thinner ones. Another influence might be the spelling of the manuscript if it differed, within acceptable limits, from his normal preferences.

The compositor of the early hand-press period similarly 'corrected' the capitalization and italicization of the copy, he supplied at least some punctuation (Elizabethan and Jacobean manuscripts were sketchily punctuated, if at all), and he made use of a small and declining number of contractions and abbreviations as a further convenience in justification. The trend was always towards the reduction of the number of variants permitted to the compositor and orthographic variation had virtually disappeared as a feature of English typographical style by 1683, when Moxon wrote: '*it is necessary that a* Compositor *be a good English Schollar at least; and that he know the present traditional* Spelling *of all English Words, and that he have so much Sence and Reason, as to* Point *his Sentences properly: when to begin a Word with a* Capital Letter, *when (to render the Sence of the Author more intelligent to the Reader*) *to* Set *some Words or Sentences in* Italick *or* English [gothic] Letters, *&c.*'[15] Moxon makes it clear, however, that this editing of the accidentals (as we should call it) was to be limited to works in English; copy in other languages was to be followed exactly by English compositors. English typographical style became rather simpler during the eighteenth century, but in general Moxon's instructions held good for the rest of the hand-press period.

It is easier to generalize about compositorial practices in England (where printing was concentrated in London until after the end of the period of spelling variation) than on the continent, where provincial printing was always widespread, and generally involved particular provincial practices. Nevertheless it can be said that German printers, whose spelling was in any case strongly influenced by differences of dialect, had great scope for justification by using recognized spelling variants (such as the vowel forms 'ü' or 'ue', etc., and the suffixes '-n' or '-en') and that they used them for this purpose until the early eighteenth century. The spelling of French, Spanish, and Italian, on the other hand, did not vary to anything like the same extent as did that of English or German in the sixteenth and seventeenth centuries, but the printers of these languages continued the fifteenth-century practice of using conventional contractions (especially 'tildes' over vowels to mark omitted letters) for justification until the mid seventeenth century.[16]

Changes from manuscript copy resulting not from intentional alteration but from involuntary error may be grouped as having derived either from a misunderstanding of the copy by the compositor, or from his having set up in type something other than what he at first intended. Misunderstanding of the manuscript copy was nearly always caused by handwriting so poor that even a compositor—whose profession it was to be familiar with hand-writing of all sorts—could not make it out, or by badly organized corrections and additions to the copy. It is of course necessary, when considering the kind of misreadings a compositor might have made, to be familiar with the form of the script in which the manuscript was probably written. In England, for instance, vernacular manuscripts were generally written up to about 1630 in the English version of gothic cursive called 'secretary', whereas Latin copy was more often written in italic, the still familiar script that was introduced in England in the mid sixteenth century and which later superseded secretary for all purposes. It is also worth remembering that an author's secretary hand was probably no worse written than his italic, and that a compositor of the period, who would have been as familiar

---

[15] Moxon, J., *Mechanick exercises*, eds. Davis and Carter, 2nd ed., Oxford 1962, p. 193.
[16] There is no comprehensive study of compositors' spellings in continental Europe, but see Hellinga, W. Gs., *Copy and print in the Netherlands*, Amsterdam 1962, pp. 100–3; and Beare, R. L. (see p. 40, n. 1).

with the one as with the other, would not have thought that secretary was especially difficult to read. We find it difficult, however; and it has long been recognized that textual students must make themselves thoroughly familiar —if possible as practitioners—with the handwritings of the regions and periods with which they are concerned.[17]

The author's intentions might also have been misunderstood if his manuscript contained obvious lacunae or grammatical errors. The compositor might try to mend them, with the possibility of introducing new errors in the process; but an author's errors were not normally corrected at the compositor's expense, and he might have preferred to leave them alone. Composition, in any case, was a largely automatic process; the compositor took in the sense of each sentence as he went along (he had to in order to point it correctly), but he would be most unlikely to take in the general sense of the chapter, or even the paragraph, that he was setting.

The errors that resulted from the compositor setting in type something other than what he at first intended to set are themselves divisible into those caused by a mental lapse on the part of the compositor, and those deriving from 'foul case', a case that had pieces of type in the wrong boxes. Any number of mental lapses were possible, of course, but only three were really common. In one, the compositor would unconsciously substitute one word for another in the phrase or group of words he had memorized from the copy and was in the process of setting; characteristically the substituted word would have a semantic connection with the original and would be similar to it in shape and rhythm. Secondly, the compositor might omit or repeat part of the copy as the result of going on from the wrong place; it was particularly easy, for instance, where the same word occurred in successive lines of the copy, to set a phrase ending with its first occurrence and then to continue setting from the same word in the next line, omitting everything in between. Thirdly, the compositor might direct his fingers 'involuntarily' into the wrong box of the case, just as a tired typist may set down 'hwen' for 'when'; experiment suggests, however, that individual compositors are liable to their own characteristic errors of this sort, and that simple inversion is only one of a multitude of possibilities.[18]

No doubt it would have been hard to find a case of type in any printing house that had positively no letters in the wrong boxes, but some cases were fouler than others. If a case was carelessly overfilled it was easy for type to spill over from one box to another, usually into the box immediately below. But ordinary distribution could get wrong type into almost any box, either

---

[17] See Appendix A.

[18] Gaskell, P., 'The first two years of the Water Lane Press', *Transactions of the Cambridge Bibliographical Society*, ii, 1954-8, pp. 178-80.

because a compositor made a mistake at the beginning of a word he was distributing and so dropped all its letters successively into wrong boxes, or because he allowed type to spill into the case from the lines balanced on his left hand. Foul case inevitably led to some errors in the stick, for compositors did not read the faces of the letters as they picked them up; experienced men, however, were skilled at gauging the thickness of pieces of type between their fingers, and noticed immediately if they picked up a letter that was even slightly thicker or thinner than it should have been.

It is worth repeating, though, that piecework compositors (but not apprentices) had to correct their own mistakes at their own expense, and that it was far quicker—and therefore more profitable—for them to read and correct each line in the stick as soon as it was set, than to wait and correct them all later when the forme was completed. A serious omission or duplication in a page of prose, for instance, might necessitate the overrunning and rejustification of dozens of lines (see p. 114), whereas if the mistake had been spotted in the stick it could have been set right in a matter of moments.

Let us look, then, at an actual compositor at work, the man employed by Jaggard around 1620 who is known nowadays as 'compositor B' of the Shakespeare First Folio (and whose own name, indeed, may have been John Shakespeare).[19] Compositor B is distinguished from his companions by certain well-established spelling habits: he preferred, amongst other things, to set 'do', 'go', and 'heere', while compositor A (for instance) preferred 'doe', 'goe', and 'here'. Examination of texts set by B show his work to have been marked by a combination of misdirected ingenuity, deliberate tampering, and plain carelessness that makes him an interesting example of how far a compositor could go in the intentional and unintentional alteration of his copy while setting it into type—although it should be understood that B appears to have gone a good deal further than most.

In 1619 B set ten new quarto editions of Shakespearean and pseudo-Shakespearean plays, using earlier printed texts as copy. These plays, many of which bore false dates, were printed by Jaggard for the bookseller Thomas Pavier. Comparison of one of them, *The merchant of Venice*, with his copy (the original edition of 1600) shows clearly the kind of changes that B made. Although he was equipped with approximately the same sort of type and used the same measure and length of page as his predecessor of 1600, B did not set the reprint line for line with the copy, or even page for page, and the reprint is actually four pages longer than the original. What-

---

[19] McKenzie, D. F., 'Compositor B's role in *The merchant of Venice* Q2 (1619)', *Studies in bibliography*, xii, 1959, pp. 75-90. Unpublished work by P. W. M. Blayney suggests that *MV* Q2 was set by two compositors, not one; but the point of the example, the degree to which compositors could alter a text, is unaffected.

ever the reason for this proceeding, it gave B full opportunity to set the book as he wished.

The first question for us, of course, is whether the particular printed copy of the first quarto that B used had first been revised by someone else before he started setting from it. The book does not survive and we cannot be sure of the answer, but the nature of the alterations makes it unlikely that any other reviser was involved: most of the changes were clumsy, otiose, or simply wrong, and it may well be that the few alterations that look like genuine revisions were B's occasional 'successes'. It seems likely, in fact, that B, who quite properly 'rectified' the spelling and punctuation, and used spelling variants for justification, also and less properly took it upon himself to correct what he appears to have considered typographical corruptions, mistakes, and even infelicities in the text. (In this connection it is alarming to learn that this same compositor was also personally responsible for setting more than half of the First Folio, our sole authority for much of Shakespeare.)

To consider first B's legitimate alterations, his imposition of typographical 'style', he regularly changed spellings in accordance with his personal preferences, although he was not entirely consistent in doing so. He set 'do' (his preferred form) on 103 occasions, 'doe' on 11; 'go' (preferred) 41 times, 'goe' 16; 'heere' (preferred) 62 times, 'here' 15. He never set 'doe' except when his copy also read 'doe'; on only one occasion did he set 'goe' when his copy read 'go'; but he set 'here' seven times when the copy gave his normal preference 'heere'. Thus some of B's spelling preferences were stronger than others; his preference for 'do' rather than 'doe' was more commanding than his preference for 'heere' rather than 'here'.

When B followed the usual practice in using spelling changes as an aid to justification, he plainly preferred to contract words for this purpose (269 probable cases) rather than to expand them (96 probable cases). He also made no fewer than 715 changes to the punctuation, of which almost half (347) were additions of commas.

B's illegitimate alterations (illegitimate, at any rate, in our view) included both unintentional mistakes and intentional emendations. It is not always clear, of course, whether a particular alteration was intentional or not. For instance, at III. i. 40 (to use the modern reference system) the copy read 'I fay my daughter is my flefh and my blood', but B omitted the third 'my'. Was this because he considered it tautological? because he was trying to make the line into verse (although it is in a prose section)? because he was influenced by the common phrase 'flesh and blood'? or because he left it out accidentally? We cannot tell.

Most of his 30 omissions, 16 additions, and 13 transpositions, indeed, seem to have been unintentional mistakes rather than attempts at emendation. His substitutions (36 of single words, 4 of phrases) are more difficult to class with certainty, but again many of them appear to have been mistakes. For instance, when he set 'Ile pay it prefently with all my heart' instead of '*I*le pay it inftantly with all my hart' (IV. i. 281), he had probably made an unintentional error. On the other hand, his major substitution of phrases at I. iii. 65–6 ('are you refolu'd, How much he would haue?', instead of 'is hee yet poffeft How much ye would?') was clearly intentional and was very much in B's style, being an unnecessary solution of a non-existent textual difficulty. His largest group of intentional alterations consisted of 27 relatively minor emendations, mostly wrong-headed; typical was his setting of IV. i. 349, where he changed 'an' to 'any' in the phrase 'if it be proued againft an alien', which spoiled the verse without improving the sense. Altogether, in setting the 2,648 lines of the play, B made on average one significant error to every 23 lines.

This example suggests the potential value to an editor of knowing who set what in a printed text but, to be effective, spelling analysis must be more than a matter of spotting two or three characteristic spellings for each supposed compositor and counting their appearances. Although A might characteristically set 'doe', 'goe', and 'here', while B set 'do', 'go', and 'heere', this does not prove that there were not other compositors involved in setting the text alongside A and B whose spelling preferences in these words happened to match those of A or B (or to be a mixture of the two), and whose identifiable spelling habits would have to be sought in other groups of words. It is therefore essential to include *all* the words of a text in a spelling analysis, not merely a selection of them, since the over-all spelling pattern is bound to be a complex mixture of the spelling standards of the period with the individual spelling habits of the author, the copyist (if any), the compositors, and the corrector. Only a complete analysis can hope to separate the various components, and even then it will probably be necessary to compare the result with the spelling of other texts from the same printing house.[20]

There is another way of identifying the work of particular compositors. By correlating the work of compositors (known from spelling tests) with the appearances of particular assemblages of broken or otherwise identifiable types, Professor Hinman has been able to show that, at the time of the printing of the First Folio, each of Jaggard's compositors normally worked from a particular pair of cases, into which he would distribute the matter which he himself had set.[21] Thus in early-seventeenth-century English

[20] See Hill, T. H., 'Spelling and the bibliographer', *The Library*, xviii, 1963, pp. 1–28; and cf. p. 348 n. 19.

[21] Hinman, C., *The printing and proof-reading of the first folio of Shakespeare*, 2 vols., Oxford 1963.

printing particular compositors might use and re-use particular and identifiable fractions of a fount of type.

But these techniques of spelling analysis and of type identification will be of little use after the seventeenth century; spelling variation had virtually disappeared, and there is no evidence that the compositors in eighteenth-century printing houses had their personal cases of type (certainly nineteenth-century compositors did not). Nevertheless the effect of eighteenth- and nineteenth-century compositors on the transmission of texts continued to be of major importance; apart from their liability to error, they had a large measure of control over the punctuation, and as always they differed from each other in their competence and typographical habits. Evidence for identification is rarely available, but in a few cases very full printers' records have survived in which individual stints are accounted for; in others, the printers' copy has survived, marked up to show the compositors' 'takes'.

It used to be thought that the pattern of skeletons[22] in a sixteenth- or seventeenth-century book could yield useful information about its production: that single-skeleton working, for instance, indicated that only one compositor was at work, that the use of more than two skeletons indicated urgency, that the appearance of a new set of skeletons indicated an interruption in the printing arrangements, and so on. Recent investigations of printers' records, however, have shown that skeleton patterns can be extremely unreliable guides, and that they do not necessarily—or even probably—tell us much about the complex patterns of composition and presswork in concurrent production (see pp. 109–10). The most that can be said is that there might be some correlation between particular skeletons and the work of particular compositors; but that even this could change in the course of printing. (Skeleton patterns may of course provide useful evidence of cancellation; see p. 134.)

2. *Proof-correction.* The routines of proof-correction which were probably established by the later sixteenth century were continued with little change until towards the end of the nineteenth century (pp. 110–16). First, the corrector had the copy read aloud to him while he scanned a first proof of each new-set forme in order to correct any substantive errors and to check the compositor's normalization of the accidentals; and later a revise— a proof of the type after correction—might be compared with the marked first proof to see that the corrector's instructions had been carried out (followed by further revises if necessary). Secondly, a clean proof of the sheet—both formes—was generally shown to the author for his approval

---

[22] Properly speaking, the pattern of the *typographical* parts of the skeleton (the headlines, rules, etc.), which could easily become detached from the rest of the skeleton (the chase, furniture, and quoins).

and (if the printer was unlucky) his second thoughts, again followed by revises if the author's corrections and alterations were extensive. Finally, the formes or sheets were read for press immediately before printing was to begin and last corrections were made, possibly stop-press; again there might be a revise.

To deal first with the printer's corrections, copy was ordinarily referred to only for the reading of the first proof, and even then no direct comparison was made between the manuscript and the printed text. The method of having the copy read aloud meant that the corrector was made aware only of substantive variation between copy and first proof; he could not know from this the details of the compositor's normalization of the accidentals, but simply checked that the punctuation etc. was reasonable and the typographical style correct. Unless the corrector took upon himself an editorial function, the correction of the first proof tended to bring the printed text nearer to the manuscript in substantive readings, but to widen the difference between them in accidentals; but even as late as 1899 it was possible to write: 'It is a disputed point how far the reader [i.e. corrector] is justified in going in the way of altering an author's spelling and grammar.'[23]

It was also possible for new substantive errors to be introduced at this stage, because of faults in the verbal transmission of the copy; if the reading-boy misread the copy, or if the corrector misheard or misunderstood the reading-boy, a wrong word might be entered on the proof as a correction whether or not the compositor had got it right in the first place. Mistakes in printed texts which appear to derive from faults of verbal transmission are known[24] and, while they could be the result of dictation in manuscript copying—or conceivably of setting type from dictation (see p. 49)—it is also possible that they were introduced during proof-correction.

The revise, or review, of the first proof was unlikely either to introduce or to eliminate textual variation; the revise was not normally compared with copy, and its purpose was simply to ensure that the corrector's instructions had been properly carried out.

The author's correction of a clean proof could of course result in any amount of change, of accidentals as well as of substantives. It was not uncommon for authors to see proofs, even in the early hand-press period, and by the eighteenth century it was the normal practice. It does not appear, however, that copy was normally returned to the author with the proof until the later nineteenth century, and even when it was the author did not

---

[23] Southward, J., *Modern printing*, ii, London 1899, p. 187.
[24] Three interesting examples are recorded by McKerrow (*Introduction*, pp. 241-3). See also *Encyclopédie*, v, Paris 1755, p. 212, s.v. 'ébarber' in type-founding, where the phrase 'qu'il a séparé le jet de la lettre' appears as 'qu'il a assez paré le jet de la lettre' (communicated by Jacques Rychner).

necessarily compare the two. An author's proof-correction, moreover, might be uneven, some parts of his book receiving more attention than others. Authors might be shown revises of their own corrections by the later eighteenth century, although it seems that then as now they had to ask for them; thus Boswell in 1791: 'I am much pleased with the sheet as now arranged. As I have a little alteration which will only shorten a note a line or so, let me have another *Revise* sent to Sir Joshua Reynolds's in Liecester Square where I dine, & it shall be returned instantly.'[25]

Finally, proofs were usually read and corrected at the press as the run was about to begin. In English printing houses around 1600, indeed, further reading for press might take place after the run was under way, an early sheet being extracted from the heap and read (without reference to copy) while the printing proceeded; the press was then stopped and the type corrected; and copies of the book were subsequently made up with sheets printed from formes in their earlier as well as in their later states. It is not clear how long this practice continued, but by the end of the seventeenth century it was probably more usual to complete the final correction before beginning the run, as it certainly was by the beginning of the machine-press period. The press could still be stopped later for correction in the event of the development of imperfections in type or plates; and stop-press corrections might also be made in order to cancel unwanted readings.[26]

There have been three main changes in the routines of proof-correction since the later nineteenth century. First, it became usual in book as well as in news work (around 1880 in London, see p. 195) to take first proofs in galley before imposition, corrected slips sometimes but not always being sent to the author in advance of page proofs. Secondly, it has become increasingly common for the accidentals of the copy to be professionally edited before setting, the compositor and corrector then being required to follow copy as far as possible in accidentals as well as in substantives. Finally, the reading-boy disappeared in English printing houses around 1900, since when the corrector has made direct ocular comparison of the (probably edited) copy with the first proof. (In many American and a few English houses proof correction by reading aloud has continued, but the accidentals are specified in the reading, and copy and proof are supposed to agree in detail.)

[25] Boswell, J., *Life of Johnson*, eds. Hill, G. B., and Powell, L. F., i, Oxford 1934, facing p. 25.

[26] It may be that Professor Hinman is mistaken (in his great work on the printing and proof-reading of the first folio of Shakespeare) in suggesting that the only correction that the text of the folio received was reading for press, carried out at the beginning of the run without reference to copy. While there is no doubt that many of the folio formes were read and corrected during printing, it also seems likely that all of them had previously been first-proofed (though with varying degrees of accuracy) and corrected in the usual way.

3. *Later stages of production.* The transmission of a text might be affected by variations occurring within the edition after the completion of the main stages of composition and proof correction. They may generally be assigned to one of three categories: first, changes made to type or plates during the printing of an impression; secondly, changes made to type or plates between impressions; and thirdly, changes made in the preparation of sets of duplicate plates, which might then be printed either simultaneously or consecutively. Substantive variants in all these categories will normally—though not invariably—have been made intentionally, and an editor will deal with them in accordance with the theory of copy-text.

We have already come across an example of variation in the first category arising from the stop-press correction of late press-proofs in Jacobean printing; and there are the further possibilities of stop-press correction of type or plates damaged during the run, and of stop-press alteration or cancellation of particular passages (that is, deliberate textual change rather than the correction of errors). As a rule in the hand-press period, and not infrequently afterwards, sheets in both the original and the altered states were used indifferently to make up copies of the book; and if, as did sometimes happen, both the formes of a sheet were altered stop-press during their runs, perhaps more than once, sheets may be found with a variety of different states on either side of them. But, because the order of the sheets in the heap at the press could be altered for various arbitrary reasons during or after each run, the relationship of the variant states in one forme of a sheet to those in the other will not necessarily have any textual significance; what may matter is the order and purpose of the variants within the basic bibliographical unit, the forme.

Variation in this first category has always been common, and the detailed collation of several copies from editions even of nineteenth- and twentieth-century plated books seldom fails to reveal a few—usually minor—variants. In the earlier hand-press period variation was often substantial. Thus the twelve known copies of the first quarto of *King Lear* (1608) show eight variant formes in seven of the ten sheets, encompassing nearly 150 substantive alterations, apparently made during the stop-press correction of late press-proofs.[27] The assembly of the variant sheets into copies was random; no one copy has either corrected or uncorrected formes throughout; and only two pairs of copies are made up in the same way as each other. One of the sheets has variants in both formes but, even though the variants are in this case textually interdependent, one of the copies has them in different, and therefore incompatible, states.

Changes belonging to the second category, alterations made to standing

[27] Greg, W. W., *The variants in the first quarto of 'King Lear'*, London 1940.

type or plates between impressions, are usually self-consistent (although there may also be stop-press corrections in the same text). They should be suspected when there is evidence of re-impression, such as differences in the title-page or press-figures, in the pagination or direction lines, in the paper used, in the relative positions of the pages in the forme, or in the relative positions of lines of type in the page. This sort of variation was rare before the eighteenth century simply because there were then no plates, and books were seldom kept in standing type; but it is frequently encountered when settings were kept for later impressions. For instance, what is probably the very first stereotyped book, the Syriac *Testament* of Luchtmans and Müller (4°, Leyden 1708, etc.), shows a substantial textual variant in the Latin text on D1 recto (p. 25) which was introduced between the first impression (1708, re-issued 1709) and the second impression (1717).[28]

Changes in the third category, those associated with the duplication of plates, may or may not be of textual importance. When a printer had two sets of plates made and printed from them simultaneously—possibly on the same machine—the difference between them could be virtually indistinguishable. On the other hand there could be deliberate and substantive variation between 'duplicate' sets of plates printed at different places or times, or on different sides of the Atlantic. The relationship between the early texts of Henry James's *The portrait of a lady* was of a complexity typical of the period.[29] The author's manuscript was the copy for the serial in *Macmillan's magazine* (1880-1), and a set of English serial parts, slightly revised, was sent to America as copy for serialization in *Atlantic monthly* (1880-1). Another set of the English serial parts, with more and different revisions, went to Clay's in Suffolk as copy for the book edition, which was newly set in Long Primer solid. Stereotype moulds were made straight away from the type pages, and a set of plates was cast and sent to America for printing in one volume (Boston '1882', and later impressions). Next the same type was leaded out to look like Pica (making more and emptier pages) with alterations both deliberate and inadvertant, and used for printing an English three-decker (3 vols., London 1881, and another impression, 3 vols., London 1882). Finally a second set of plates was cast from the original, full-page, moulds, further corrections were made to them in a few places by patching in new metal, and they were used for printing the English one-volume issue (London 1882). There were thus three main

---

[28] Work in progress by the present author. It seems likely that the first impression was printed from type, the second from plates made (apart from the variant pages) before the first impression was machined. (*Novum testamentum Syriacum*, eds. Leusden, J., and Schaaf, C., Lugd. Bat. 1708, 1709; 1717.)

[29] Nowell-Smith, S., 'Texts of *The portrait of a lady* 1881-2: the bibliographical evidence', *Papers of the Bibliographical Society of America*, lxiii, 1969, pp. 304-10.

issues of the first book edition of *The portrait*, two in single volumes and the other looking very different in three volumes, each of which has its own distinguishable textual variants.[30]

Another example: two sets of plates were made for Sinclair Lewis's *Babbit*, one of which was used and gradually revised for the early impressions (Harcourt, Brace, 1922–4); but in 1941–2 these revised plates, being worn out, were discarded and subsequent impressions were printed from the other, *unrevised*, set of plates.[31]

It should be emphasized that until very recently the British and American versions of a book were usually printed from different settings of type, and that there was generally considerable variation between British and American texts, intentional as well as unintentional. The unauthorized American reprints of British books of the period before the American copyright Act of 1891 were always reset; so were most of the authorized reprints, although as in the case of *The portrait of a lady* sets of plates were sometimes sent across the Atlantic; and during the same period the British publishers of American books preferred to reset rather than to import plates or sheets. In the period between the copyright legislation of 1891 and that of 1957 resetting remained the normal practice on both sides of the ocean; in any case British books published in America had to be set there if they were to be copyright, a condition that was not disregarded if substantial American sales could be anticipated.

The unintentional variants introduced into texts as a result of trans-atlantic resetting involved the usual minor errors that creep into all transcripts, but the intentional changes were of quite a different sort, and were often substantial.[32] Leaving aside the gross cuts etc. occasionally made by the publishers of unauthorized reprints (who were answerable to no one), intentional variants occurred either because the copy for one of the editions was in a different stage of revision from that for the other, as often happened before 1891 when unrevised proofs would be hurried across to America in order to forestall piracy; or because the reprint publisher deliberately edited the copy, substituting English spelling for American and vice versa, and changing the text if he thought it would bewilder or offend his customers.

The textual vicissitudes of British nineteenth-century novels in America are notorious. All thirty American editions of Hardy's *The Woodlanders* published up to 1926 derived from advance sheets of the serialization of

[30] All this is of course apart from James's major revision of the text for the New York edition of 1907. The reader may care to consider the question of copy-text for a critical edition.

[31] Bruccoli, M. J., 'Textual variants in Sinclair Lewis's *Babbit*', *Studies in bibliography*, xi, 1958, pp. 263–8.

[32] Bruccoli, M. J., 'Some transatlantic texts: west to east', *Bibliography and textual criticism*, eds. Brack, O. M., and Barnes, W., Chicago 1969, pp. 244–55.

the novel in *Macmillan's magazine*, and none included the important re-visions made by the author for the first and second British book editions of 1887 or his further revisions of 1895 and 1912.[33] The majority of English publishers of American novels have done as badly: the dialect in several of Faulkner's books was normalized for the supposed benefit of English readers, to the detriment of literary quality; while 'as might be expected, the history of Ernest Hemingway's British texts is a chronicle of dashes, deletions, asterisks and stars'.[34] It is needless to lengthen the list: it is easy to find transatlantic reprints that have suffered major, and usually silent, altera-tion, and positively difficult to find one that does not show at least minor change.

Textual variation between copies of an edition can only be discovered by a detailed collation of their texts. A particular copy is chosen as a control, and this control (or a film or photocopy of it) is taken round for comparison with each of the other copies. The collation, without apparatus, of several lengthy texts is an appallingly laborious process, and is one which (like proof-correction) is liable to a good deal of error; fortunately, however, it is no longer necessary to collate unaided, since copies (or photocopies) can now be compared mechanically with a Hinman collating machine, which rapidly shows up all variation between them. Hinman machines are expen-sive, but most major libraries now have one.[34a]

Warner Barnes, in compiling his bibliography of the writings of Elizabeth Barrett Browning, machine-collated an average of six copies of each of his author's eighteen primary editions, which covered the period 1820–63. In ten of them he found possible evidence of concealed, and previously unsuspected, reimpressions; in another four, variant states of the type not indicating reimpression; and in only four out of the eighteen was there no perceptible typographical variation.[35] Most of the variants shown up by the machine were trivial—minor changes in the spacing, dropped letters, etc.—and there was only one substantive change. Since Mrs. Browning's books do not appear to have been unusual in their production, it would seem likely that a thorough examination of similar works by other nineteenth-century authors would show comparable variation.

[33] Weber, C. J., 'American editions of English authors', *Nineteenth-century English books*, Urbana 1952, pp. 42–3.

[34] Bruccoli, M. J., 'Some transatlantic texts', op. cit., pp. 245, 247.

[34a] A less costly but apparently equally efficient collating machine, the Lindstrand Comparator, has recently been marketed in America.

[35] Barnes, W., *A bibliography of Elizabeth Barrett Browning*, Austin 1967. See Appendix B (4); it is not clear that all the variants found by Mr. Barnes resulted from reimpression.

THE TREATMENT OF ACCIDENTALS

In theory an editor should be able to identify the copy-text for his edition, and to deal with accidentals, substantives, variants, and errors, in accordance with the normal procedures outlined in the preceding sections. Many texts can indeed be edited according to the rules, but some cannot, and the editor may find himself in difficulties. There are a great many possible textual complications, each of which will have to be considered individually, but an indication of their nature may be had from a review of some of the problems concerning accidentals.

In a straightforward case, the accidentals will be taken from the copy-text, which will be the first printed edition; the manuscript if it survives, will be consulted but will not be followed in accidentals unless the compositor appears to have misrepresented the author's intentions; and if corrected copy or proofs of a later edition survive from which it is evident that the author revised the accidentals, those revisions will be adopted.

But editors are rarely lucky enough to have the evidence presented so neatly. Usually there is a printed copy-text, but no manuscript, and no evidence as to how the variant accidentals in later editions came to pass. This situation is not necessarily a difficult one (the accidentals are simply taken from the copy-text unless it is quite clear that they are wrong, when the editor has to emend them), but it becomes difficult either if the accidentals are grossly inadequate or defective, or if the editor has cause to suspect that the author has had a hand in revising them for later editions.

Where the accidentals of a printed copy-text are seriously inadequate, it is usually because the author's manuscript was inadequate in this respect and the printer failed to normalize it (for it is unlikely that the printer ignored the accidentals in the manuscript if they were adequate). In a really bad case there is nothing for it but to scrap the lot and start again. 'If the punctuation is persistently erroneous or defective,' wrote Greg, 'an editor may prefer to discard it altogether to make way for one of his own.'[36] This is good sense, and there is no reason why the same should not be done, with due consideration, where the accidentals are grossly defective in one part of the text but not in another, or where different compositors appear to have followed different typographical conventions, for an editor may reasonably aim at consistency in his final version.

Greg was not disposed to compromise about an author's own accidentals, but even so it may be doubted whether it is worth preserving thoroughly bad punctuation just because it is the author's. The case for preferring the printer's normalization to the author's manuscript has already been argued;

[36] Greg, W. W., *Collected papers*, Oxford 1966, p. 385.

and, if it is allowed, there would seem to be little point in sticking to an inadequately punctuated manuscript copy-text. Consider the Shakespearean addition to *Sir Thomas More*, in which spelling and capitalization are wildly inconsistent and punctuation is largely absent:

Linc	Shreiff moor speakes shall we heare shreef more speake
Doll	Letts heare him a keepes a plentyfull shrevaltry, and a made my Brother Arther watchin⟨s⟩ Seriant Safes yeoman lets heare shreeve moore
all	Shreiue moor moor more Shreue moore
moor	⟨even⟩ by the rule yo^u haue among yor sealues Comand still audience
all	⟨S⟩urrey Sury
all	moor moor
Lincolne betts	peace peace scilens peace.
moor	Yo^u that haue voyce and Credyt w^t the [mv] nvmber Comaund them to a stilnes
Lincolne	a plaigue on them they will not hold their peace the deule Cannot rule them
Moor	Then what a rough and ryotous charge haue yo^u to Leade those that the deule Cannot rule good masters heare me speake
Doll	I byth mas will we moor thart a good howskeeper and I thanck thy good worship for my Brother Arthur watchins
all	peace peace [37]

Although a direct transcript such as this tells the specialist much of value about the author's scribal habits, it would hardly help a more general student of literature, let alone an actor. The editor is bound to make sense of it, which means that he must emend the accidentals wholesale and supply punctuation. This is an extreme case, but it is one which has implications for all editing, from printed as well as from manuscript copy. Let us carry out the author's intentions wherever we can, but not to the extent of taking pride in reproducing the manifest inadequacies of his accidentals.

Even more difficult are the cases where the author appears to have revised the accidentals for a later edition, either in preparing printed copy or in correcting proofs, but where detailed evidence of what he did is lacking. Authors are not professional correctors and they do not always read their

[37] There is both a facsimile of the addition and a transcript in *Shakespeare survey*, ii, Cambridge 1949, plates 13-15 and pp. 62-3. The rules indicate changes of speaker, and 'moor' (etc.) means More. Note that the word 'sheriff' appears five times in the first five lines in five different spellings. For an editor's solution to the problem of normalizing *Sir Thomas More*, see Shakespeare, W., *Works*, ed. Sisson, C. J., London [1954].

proofs with consistent care. Some pages are better read than others, some with reference to copy, some without. Johnson's corrected proofs for the first edition of the *Prefaces* to the poets, 1779–81 (most of which are now at the Victoria and Albert Museum, Forster 298), show him skimming the text, tinkering with the accidentals but not revising them systematically, so that particular corrections are made in one place on a page but not in another even on the same page.[38] But in the absence of such evidence it is difficult even to guess at the extent of an author's revision.

Similarly with the problem of distinguishing the author's corrections from those of a publisher or of a friend. Dickens, for instance, rushed away from London in the autumn of 1838, leaving his friend John Forster to correct the proofs of the last few sheets of *Oliver Twist*; then he returned to town on the very last day before publication in order to look over, and if necessary to correct further, the final revised sheets. We know from other evidence that a number of corrections were made in these last sheets, but there is no way of knowing which of them were made by Dickens and which by Forster.[39] Publishers' readers, moreover, often concerned themselves with details of the text, as well as offering broader editorial advice, usually before a manuscript was set in type; and this was additional to the editorial function of the printer's reader (who was of course a different person).[40]

Again therefore the editor must exercise his discretion. While he will follow the accidentals of the copy-text as far as possible, he need not consider them to be immutable. Printed accidentals are unlikely to have had more than the general approval of the author, and if they seem to be both unsatisfactory and in contravention of the author's usual practice, the editor will have to emend them. (Whether he will emend them according to the conventions of the author's period or to those of his own is something else which he will have to decide.)

But the need to emend the accidentals is not altogether a misfortune: it makes the editor think hard about what his author really meant; and that in the end is what bibliography is all about.

---

[38] Fleeman, J. D., 'Some proofs of Johnson's *Prefaces to the poets*', *The Library*, xvii, 1962, pp. 213–30.

[39] Dickens, C., *Oliver Twist*, ed. Tillotson, K., Oxford 1966, appendixes.

[40] Gettmann, R. A., *A Victorian publisher*, Cambridge 1960, ch. 7.

Appendix A

A Note on Elizabethan Handwriting

(reprinted from McKerrow, R. B., *An introduction to bibliography*, Oxford 1928, pp. 341-50)

I T is, I think, generally with the writing of the period between 1500 and 1650 that the literary student finds most difficulty, and until quite recently there has been for this period hardly any help available.[1] The majority of Old English and Medieval MSS. that he is likely to come across, being in the more or less careful and practised hands of professional scribes, are when once the forms of the letters are known, easy enough to decipher with a little practice, or if they are difficult the difficulty is due to the condition of the MS. rather than to the writing itself. Such help as is needed will be found in W. W. Skeat's *Twelve Facsimiles of Old English Manuscripts* and Dr. W. W. Greg's *Facsimiles of Twelve Early English Manuscripts in the Library of Trinity College, Cambridge*, and a student who works through these should have little difficulty with most other literary MSS. up to the fifteenth century. Charters and other documents written in legal hands are another matter. For these the best guide is *English Court Hand* A.D. *1066 to 1500*, by C. Johnson and Hilary Jenkinson, with the invaluable portfolio of facsimiles which accompanies it. The deciphering of legal documents of any period is, it may be remarked, very largely a matter of knowing what the writer is likely to have intended to convey, for common formulae are often so much abbreviated that without a knowledge of them it is impossible to read them correctly. The student who concerns himself with such things must therefore begin by familiarizing himself with the formulae used in other documents of the same kind by reference to works in which these are printed at length.

When we come to the sixteenth century, and especially to the later years of the century, we find a much larger number of literary documents which, not being the work of professional scribes, are in cursive hands of various degrees of informality and carelessness, and some of these are by no means easy to read.[2] The only way in which the student can learn to make them out is by practice, and he should be warned that however much he practises he must not expect to be able

---

[1] I know of no elementary introduction to the subject except Miss M. St. Clare Byrne's very useful article entitled 'Elizabethan Handwriting for Beginners' in *The Review of English studies*, i, 198 ff. Students would be well advised to read this article, to which I am indebted for several points in the pages which follow. [For more recent studies of Elizabethan handwriting see the bibliography, p. 394. P. G.]

[2] For a sketch of the history of handwriting during the Elizabethan period the student may be referred to Sir E. Maunde Thompson's chapter on the subject in *Shakespeare's England*, vol. i. The subject will be fully dealt with in a work on Elizabethan Handwriting which Mr. Hilary Jenkinson has now in preparation [Jenkinson, C. H., *The later court hands in England*, 2 vols., Cambridge 1927. P. G.].

to read every unfamiliar hand at a glance. The most skilled palaeographer may find the first few lines of a new manuscript somewhat puzzling.

The best way of acquiring a sufficient knowledge of the matter for ordinary purposes is, I think, to take some facsimile of a good and clear Elizabethan hand such as Kyd's letter to the Lord Keeper Puckering, which forms the frontispiece of Dr. Boas's edition of Kyd,[3] and having read it through two or three times with the transcript printed in the book, to proceed to *imitate* it, taking first single words and then passages of two or three lines together, writing them over and over again until he has the 'feel' of the letters and working from the transcript can produce something which he is certain that Puckering could have read with ease. The essential thing is that he should be very careful to make all the strokes in the right order and direction, especially in the case of such letters as c, e, f. and p (see the notes on pages [363-6]). When he can produce a fair imitation of any one Elizabethan hand he should proceed to work through a collection of facsimiles such as the series of *English Literary Autographs*, 1550-1650, edited by Dr. W. W. Greg.[4] In a first reading of these he would be wise to begin with the easier pieces, leaving the more difficult and all short scraps (generally somewhat puzzling) until later. Before beginning to read a MS. he should always take a general glance at it and note whether the hand is Italian or English or mixed. The habit of keeping the two styles distinct in his mind may often save him from mistakes.

As has been stated . . . above, there were two forms of handwriting in regular use during the Elizabethan period, the 'English', or 'Secretary', hand, which had developed naturally out of the current hands in use in earlier times in this country, and the imported 'Italian' hand, which from about 1580 was gradually replacing it. About the Italian hand there is no difficulty whatever, except such as may be due to the carelessness of the writer, for the formation of the letters is practically that of the 'copy-book' hand of today. The notes which follow are therefore confined to the current 'English' style.

The following general tendencies may be noted in English hands:

1. The downstrokes are as a rule more nearly vertical than in modern writing.

2. Uprights ending on the line often have a small spur to the left, the pen being carried horizontally along the line first to left and then again to the right so as to form a kind of foot (as in a printed letter).

3. If we call a curve starting downwards on the right then moving from right to left and so upwards to the left 'clockwise', we may describe the sixteenth-century English hand as having a more anti-clockwise tendency than the hand-writing of today. Especially is this the case with tailed letters, such as h, y, x, which are often brought round in such a large left-to-right sweep that a word may seem to be divided into two. In the Italian hand the tails of g and y are generally made clockwise and crossed as at present.

It is quite impossible to describe adequately the formation of a written letter.

[3] I suggest this, not as being an absolutely typical hand, for it is in some respects rather legal, but as including all the normal characteristics of the English hand and as showing, more clearly than most, the way in which the letters were formed.

[4] Part I (Dramatic), issued 1925. To be completed in three parts, containing in all about 100 fac-similes. [110 plates, completed 1932. P.G.]

Fɪɢ. 129. Elizabethan Handwriting. Typical forms of the minuscules.

The following notes must therefore be read in close conjunction with the out-lines of letters here given. These have been chosen from a variety of documents of the period, written in widely differing styles, and are believed to represent the chief forms which will be commonly met with.

A roman letter (a, b, &c.) stands for the letter in the English hand, an italic letter (*a*, *b*, &c.) for a written letter in the customary 'copy-book' hand of today.

a. Often like *a*. Sometimes, however, written more like *u*, the top being after-wards closed by a short horizontal stroke similar to that which closes the top of g (see below). Sometimes, again, the letter is left open at the top, in which case it may resemble *u* or *ir*. There is also a form, especially of initial a, which begins with a large curve brought down to the line and slightly spurred; the whole may then look like a loosely written 2 followed by a minim.[5]

b. Differs from *b* in that the upstroke instead of being looped to form a forward link is simply brought round towards the downstroke. The downstroke is generally looped, and in upright hands often has a small spur to the left on the line.

c. Quite different from *c*. Generally a simple short downstroke, with a thin cross-stroke at the head, which may form a forward link. Not unlike the lower part of an upright *t*.

d. Occasionally as *d*, but more often resembling a *c* through the top point of which is a heavy straight dash, much back-sloped. In such cases there is no forward link. Another common form is written without raising the pen. If this is carried round in a bow to the right the letter may resemble the older form of the Greek θ (ϑ) and may then be similar to a rather large e.

e. The important point to remember is that the lower part of this letter is always made first. It may be considered as an ϵ begun and ended in the centre and formed of two almost similar curves: the upper is often continued forward from the centre to form a link with the next letter. When written without raising the pen so that the lower and upper strokes are connected by a bow on the right it may much resemble a loosely written small d.

f. The tail is written first, as a straight downstroke, then from the top of this a loop is made sloping to the right and ending in a small tick across the downstroke. In some hands this tick is a horizontal dash at the end of the loop, not touching the downstroke: the letter may then be very similar to ft or even ft.

ff is often written with two tails diverging slightly and but one loop (cf. ff in fig. 129).

g. The usual form of this is like a rather angular *y* closed at the top by a cross-stroke. This cross-stroke is sometimes formed by bringing up the tail of the *y*, but more often it is separate.

h. The common form is quite different from modern *h*. It consists of a small loop at the head of a short vertical stroke which is continued in a wide sweep to the left and up again to join the following letter. In many hands the lower curve of the sweep is the heaviest part of the letter. Occasionally the lower curve is made in a clockwise direction and crosses the downstroke; the letter may then be not unlike a rather wide Italian *f*, as in the last form shown.

i. As *i*, but tending to be more upright and angular, as is the case with minims generally. If not linked to the preceding letter it may begin with a long thin upstroke. It may be written with a minim exactly like those of n, so that 'in' and 'm' may be indistinguishable save by the dot.

[5] A 'minim' is the single stroke of which three form an m—like a 'hanger', but in Elizabethan hands generally more angular.

k.   Generally formed like an l crossed by a small *z* or 2, the lower portion of which is continued as a forward link. Sometimes the *z* is continuous with the end of the upstroke, in which case it may degenerate into a small loop which may or may not cross or touch the upright. If it does not, the letter may resemble a modern *b* (not, however, an English b, for this normally has no forward link).

l.   As *l*, but in upright hands the downstroke instead of being curved round to the right is sometimes terminated by a small spur to the left. This also applies to the upright of k.

m, n.   As *m*, *n*, but in many Elizabethan hands the minims are all exactly similar, and there seems less sense of the individuality of the letter than in modern writing; thus mn may be written as five similar and equally spaced minims, with the result that the count sometimes goes wrong and there are one too many or too few.

o.   As *o*, but in careless writing sometimes not closed at the top.

p.   Quite differently written from *p*. It begins with a stroke like a 2. The end of this is continued upwards in a loop until it touches the bow of the 2 and then brought downwards in a straight stroke or anti-clockwise curve. In some hands, not very distinct from y; in others, resembling x, from which, however, it should be distinguishable by the form of the tail.

q.   As *q*, but sometimes ends in an anti-clockwise curve.

r.   There are several forms, perhaps the commonest being one which survived until recently, I believe, in copy-books, but not elsewhere. It can most simply be described as a 2 with the end brought up and looped, the loop being carried forward as a link. Sometimes there is a little cusp in the middle of the lower stroke so that it resembles a *w* with the middle point only slightly indicated. In some forms r might be confused with v, only that the latter has no forward link.

s.   The long ſ is as f but without the tick across the downstroke. ſſ, like ff, often has two tails and but one loop. Occasionally a form in one stroke, beginning with the upper loop, similar to the Italian ſ, is found in conjunction with an English hand.
     Final s is a clockwise loop ending generally in a blob or thickened tail above the letter. The little anti-clockwise loop or curl properly standing for final -es or -is is also found for simple final s. There is also a form resembling a much elongated roman S.

t.   An upright, generally looped, with a cross-bar, very like one modern form of *t*. Occasionally has a spur or foot like *l*.

u.   Generally like *u*, but sometimes consisting of two similar minims and then indistinguishable from n.

v.   Resembles the form of r described above, except that the 2 is simply carried upwards in a curve to the left without being looped. It consequently does not link with a following letter.

w.   A v preceded by a minim or an n with the last stroke brought up in a curve to the left.

x.   This is generally formed by writing a roman v (downward and upward) and continuing the top of the second limb in an anti-clockwise curve crossing the centre of the first limb and returning in an upward sweep to link with the letter following.

y. Like *y*, but the tail usually anti-clockwise and not crossed.

z. Generally much like *z*, nearly always tailed.

&. The forms of this are so various that it seemed useless to attempt to give them; one of the commoner resembles a reversed 3; another is like the -es contraction, i.e. an anti-clockwise curl beginning in a small loop.

Capitals. The forms of these vary so much that it is difficult to say anything useful about them. They frequently resemble, more or less vaguely, the usual black letter printed capitals, and fortunately it is generally possible to guess what they are meant to be. One or two hints may be given: occasionally a capital, especially B, H, M, and P, is very wide, so that it may at first sight appear to be two, or even more, separate letters; certain letters, especially L, are often practically the same as the small letter, only written slightly larger; F is two small f's; a capital I or J carelessly written may resemble *g* or *y* (with clockwise crossed tail); and an unrecognizable letter consisting of several interlacing curves is likely to be either C, E, or G.

Some of the commoner forms of capitals are given in the accompanying figure. A slightly larger selection, together with notes on the formation of the letters, will be found in a short article on 'The Capital Letters in Elizabethan Handwriting' in *The Review of English Studies*, iii. 28–36.

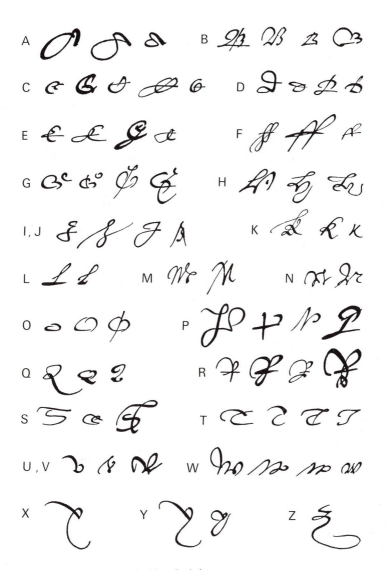

FIG. 130. Elizabethan Handwriting. Capitals.

Appendix B

Four Specimen Bibliographical Descriptions

THE extracts reprinted here, which are from four different bibliographies, are given as examples of how problems of description have been handled by experts. A short commentary is appended to each one. All four authors describe ideal copy, and all use approximately the same descriptive conventions, though with differences of aim and emphasis. The descriptions are all very full and could be much abbreviated if their only purpose were to identify copies of their subjects, but the major purpose of all of them is to elucidate the transmission of the texts they concern and to increase our understanding of the transmission of other texts of their period.

1. Entry 202 (*a*) from Greg, W. W., *A bibliography of the English printed drama to the Restoration*, i, London 1939, pp. 320-1, with corrections from ibid., iv, London 1959, p. 1675.

202 **The Entertainment through London [Dekker's Magnificent Entertainment]**   **2 Apr. 1604**

SR 1604 Apr. 2. *Ent. T. Man jr.: lic. Pasfeild: The magnificent entertainement gyven to King James, Queen Anne his wife, and Henry Friderick the Prince, uppon the day of his Majesties triumphant passage from the Tower through his honorable city and chamber of London, the 15 of March 1603.*

SR 1604 May 14. *See* 200-1.
    It is, of course, uncertain whether Man's book had already been published when this entry was made.

(*a*) THE | MAGNIFICENT | Entertainment: | Giuen to King *Iames*, Queene
1604 *Anne* his wife, | and *Henry Frederick* the Prince, vpon the day | of his Maiesties Tryumphant Paſſage (from | the Tower) through his Honourable Citie | (and Chamber) of *London*, being the | 15. of March. 1603. | *As well by the Engliſh as by the Strangers: VVith* | *the ſpeeches and Songes, deliuered in the ſeue-* | rall Pageants.

             Mart. *Templa Deis, mores populis dedit, otia ferro,*
                Aſtra ſuis, Cœlo ſydera, ſerta Ioui.

Tho. Dekker. | [device 339] | Imprinted at London by T. C. for Tho. Man | the yonger. 1604.   [*Strangers*:]
    RT](AB) *The Kings Entertainment* | *through the Cittie of London.* [*Citie* on B3, 4]
    (CD) *The Kings entertaynment* | *through the City of London.*
                            [*entertainment* on C2^v D1^{v}2^v]
      (E) *The Kinges Entertainement through* | *the Cittie of London.*

(F–H) *The Kings entertainment | through the Citie of London.*
[*entertainement* on G1ᵛ2ᵛ and in H; *City* in H]
(I) *The Kings Entertainment | through the Citie of London.* [note 1]

Collation: 4°, A–I⁴ [C–D fully signed; leaving H2 unsigned], 36 leaves unnumbered. Title, A2 (A1 and A2ᵛ blank). Text headed 'A Deuice (proiected downe, but till now not publisht,) that should haue serued at his Maiesties first accesse to the Citie' with lace ornament and initial, A3 [the heading referring to the first device and speeches only, prepared for James's original entry into London in May 1603]. Note 'To the Reader' on I4 (verso blank) [explaining that 'A great part of' the speeches 'which are in this Booke set downe, were left vnspoken', and including errata].

Catchwords: A–B, *Genius* [Genius] B–C, The [꜒ The] C–D, *The* [The] D–E, Iuft E–F, *Fama.* H–I, And FINIS.

The speeches are some in English and some in Latin, some verse and some prose.

Notes—1. Five different types are used in the RT, and divide the volume into sections as follows: A–B, C–D, E, F–H, I. Lace ornaments and a second initial appear in the text of A–B, two ornaments in that of sheet H. There are notes printed in the margin.
2. Presumably the five sections were the work of as many different presses. The first sheet appears from his initials and device on the title to have been printed by Thomas Creede; H appears from the ornaments used to have been printed either by Humphrey Lownes or by Emma widow of Peter Short whom he married this year; I was probably printed by Edward Allde [cf. (*b*)]. The printers of the other two sections (in which there are no ornaments) have not been identified (*The Library*, Mar. 1937, xvii. 476-8), but C–D probably came from the press of Simon Stafford (J. Crow).
3. On I1 Dekker records that 'If there be any glorie to be won by writing these lynes, I do freelie bestow it (as his due) on Tho. Middleton, in whose braine they were begotten, though they were deliuered heere: Quæ nos non fecimus ipsi, vix ea nostra voco.' The reference is to the preceding speech by Zeale, 'whose personage was put on by W. Bourne, one of the seruants to the young Prince' (i.e. William Birde or Borne) as mentioned in an earlier note on H4. On C1 is a list of 'The Personages (as well Mutes as Speakers) in this [first] Pageant' with the remark: 'Of all which personages, Genius and Thamesis were the only Speakers: Thamesis being presented by one of the children of her Maiesties Reuels: Genius by M. Allin (seruant to the young Prince)', i.e. Edward Alleyn. A Latin oration was delivered before St. Paul's school 'by one of maister Mulcasters Schollers' (H1). On I3ᵛ-4 is an 'Artificum Operariumque in hoc tam celebri apparatu, summa', mentioning by name 'William Friselfield. George Mosse. Iohn Knight. Paul Isacson. Samuell Goodrick. Richard Wood. George Heron' as 'those that gaue the maine direction, and vndertooke for the whole busines', 'Ouer whom, Stephen Harrison Ioyner was appointed chiefe; who was the sole Inuenter of the Architecture'.
4. Most of the speeches, but not the songs, also appear in *The Entertainment through London* [*Harrison's Arches of Triumph*] [206].
5. Copies are known to differ in certain readings in B(i) H I (o, i).

Copies: BM (C. 34. c. 23, —A1)   Dyce (—A1)   Bodl. (—A1)   Wise (—A1)
Boston   Chapin   Congress   Folger   Harvard (+A1)   Hunt   Morgan
Texas

Commentary on Greg's bibliography of the English printed drama

The scope and authority of Greg's great work of bibliographical analysis remain unparalleled. It covers all the editions of dramatic works by English authors down to the year 1700 which were either written before 1643 or printed before 1660 in a chronological series of 836 main entries, together with sections on Latin plays, lost plays, collections, etc., and an invaluable apparatus of supplementary lists and investigations. The descriptions do contain a few imperfections—it is a work of man—but the standard of accuracy is amazingly high. Greg succeeds magnificently, moreover, in illuminating the transmission of sixteenth- and seventeenth-century dramatic texts in general as well as in particular and, although fun has been poked at Professor Bowers for suggesting that a complete reading of these four large volumes 'is essential for an understanding of the whole background of Elizabethan printing of play manuscripts',[6] it is hard to see how any editor of a play of its period can afford to be unfamiliar with its riches.

Entry 202 begins with an extract from the Stationers Register and then gives descriptions of three successive editions of Dekker's play, only the first of which is reprinted here. Greg uses quasi-facsimile transcription throughout for title-pages, running titles, and catchwords, as he was almost bound to do for his own research before the days of xerox, although 'in almost every case a straightforward transcription of the title in roman type (without line endings) and the collation suffices to distinguish editions; only in three cases out of about a thousand is quasi-facsimile transcription necessary to distinguish editions, and in three further cases it fails to do the job'.[7]

Greg's identification of the work of no less than five different presses in the production of this one small book is exemplary. Nowadays a bibliographer would probably identify the type and ornaments in the different sections, and would give details of the paper used.

2. Entry 131 from Appendix I of McKenzie, D. F., *The Cambridge University Press 1696–1712*, Cambridge 1966, i. 273–6.

131 *Title.* [In red and black] C. CRISPI | SALLUSTII | Quae extant; cum NOTIS |

GLAREANI,			CARRIONIS,
RIVII,	}	INTEGRIS	MANUTII,
CIACCONII,			PUTSCHII,
GRUTERI,			DOUSAE.
CASTILIONEI,			URSINI,
C. ET A. POPMAE,	}	SELECTIS	J. FR. GRONOVII,
PALMERII,			VICTORII, &c.

| ACCEDUNT | JULIUS EXSUPERANTIUS, PORCIUS | LATRO: | ET | *FRAGMENTA HISTORICORUM VETT.* | Cum Notis *A. POPMAE.* | [rule] | Recenfuit, NOTAS perpetuas, & INDICES adjecit | *JOSEPHUS WASSE,* | *Coll. Regin.* apud CANTAB. Socius; & Nobiliff. | Marchioni de KENT a Sacris Domefticis. | [rule] | *Praemittitur SALLUSTII VITA, Auctore, V. Cl.* | JOANNE CLERICO. | [rule] | *CANTABRIGIAE,* | Typis ACADEMICIS, | Apud CORNELIUM CROWNFIELD, Celeberrimae Academiae | Typographum. MDCCX.

---

[6] Bowers, F. T., *Principles of bibliographical description*, Princeton 1949, p. 16.

[7] Foxon, D. F., *Thoughts on the history and future of bibliographical description*, Los Angeles 1970, p. 19.

Formula. 4°: πa–d⁴ A–3V⁴ 3X² a–2m⁴ 2n⁴ (2n1+²20–²2r⁴ ²2s²) 20–3n⁴; [\$2 (+\$3 in F–S, a, c–k, y, ²20–²2q, 2q, 2s, 2x, 2z–3c) signed]; 536 leaves, pp. [*8*] [1] II–XV [XVI] XVII–XXIV 1–304 307–532 [*2*]; 1–143 [144] 145–294 285 296–318; 283–304 [*168*].

Paper. (*a*) Large: mixed: i. Fleur-de-lis/PC; ii. -/-; $9\frac{1}{2} \times 7\frac{5}{8}$ in.; (*b*) Small: mixed: i. Coat of Arms with Cross of Lorraine and circles/–; ii. Cross of Lorraine and circles/–; iii. -/-; $8 \times 5\frac{7}{8}$ in.

Types. Dedicatio: Great Primer roman (18 ems × 28 lines). Præfatio: English italic with some roman (23 ems × 35 lines). Vita: Pica roman with some italic (26 ems × 39 lines). Text: English roman (23 ems, number of lines variable). Footnotes to text: Long Primer roman, italic, and Greek (double column, 16 ems each, number of lines variable). Text of Julius Exuperantius De Marii, Lepidi, ac Sertorii Bellis Civilibus, Porcii Latronis Declamatio, and Fragmenta Historicorum Veterum: Pica roman (26 ems, number of lines variable). Footnotes to Julius Exuperantius and Fragmenta: Brevier roman and italic (double column, 20 ems each, number of lines variable). Spicilegium: Long Primer roman and italic (double column, 16 ems each, × 52 lines). Addenda: Long Primer roman, italic, and Greek (double column, 16 ems each, × 50 lines). Index: Long Primer roman, italic, and Greek (double column, 16 ems each, × 51 lines). Errata (on 3n1ᵛ): Pearl roman and italic. Index Auctorum: Brevier roman and italic.

Contents. πa1, title (verso blank); πa2, Dedicatio; πb1, Lectori S.D.; πc4ᵛ, C. Crispi Sallustii Vita; A1, Bellum Catilinarium; 2E2ᵛ, Corollarium de Sallustio; 2E3ᵛ, Bellum Jugurthinum; 3X2, Omissa; a1, Historiarum Fragmenta; o2, Orationes duæ ad C. Cæsarem; o3, Oratio I; q2, Oratio II; s2, Declamatio in M. Tullium Ciceronem; s4ᵛ, blank; t1, Julii Exuperantii De Marii, Lepidi, ac Sertorii Bellis Civilibus; t3ᵛ, Porcii Latronis Declamatio; y1, Fragmenta Historicorum Veterum; ²201, P. Parkesio . . . Salutem; on ²201ᵛ, Addenda ad Notas in Fragmentis; on ²2s2ᵛ, errata; 2n2, Jani Melleri Palmerii Spicilegium; 2q1, Index in Sallustium; on 3n1ᵛ, errata; 3n2, Index Auctorum; on 3n4ᵛ, 'FINIS.'.

Copies. BM 53.c.3; ULC Adv. c.94.150; Q.3.32; CUP.

Production. Minute Book 1. 5. 05; 150 large, 1000 small; composition 8*s*.; presswork 5*s*. 6*d*.; correction 1*s*. 4*d*.; profit 7*s*. 5*d*.; price per sheet £1. 2*s*. 3*d*.

SHEETS	COMPOSITORS	PAID BY		PRESSMEN	PAID BY		CORRECTOR	PAID BY	
a–f	Great	7.	4. 05	Brown	7.	4. 05	Hoppe	7.	4. 05
g	,,	,,		Coldenhoff Ponder	,,		,,	,,	
h	,,	,,		Brown	,,		,, .	,,	
i	Knell	,,		,,	,,		,,	,,	
k	,,	,,		Coldenhoff Ponder	,,		,,	,,	
l	,,	,,		Brown	7.	7. 05	,,	,,	
m–n	,,	,,		,,	,,		,,	17.	9. 05
o–p	Apprentice	11.	8. 05	,,	,,		,,	,,	
q	,,	,,		Coldenhoff	4.	8. 05	,,	,,	
r–u	,,	,,		Brown	7.	7. 05	,,	,,	
x½	,,	,,		Coldenhoff	4.	8. 05	,,	,,	
x½	Knell	30.	9. 05	,,	,,		,,	,,	
y	,,	,,		Brown	7.	7. 05	,,	,,	
z–2d	,,	,,		Coldenhoff	4.	8. 05	,,	,,	
2e	,,	,,		Brown	3.	11. 05	,,	,,	

SHEETS	COMPOSITORS	PAID BY	PRESSMEN	PAID BY	CORRECTOR	PAID BY
2f-2k	Knell Muckeus }	30. 9. 05	Coldenhoff	4. 8. 05	Hoppe	17. 9. 05
2l-2n	,,	,,	,,	3. 11. 05	,,	,,
2o	,,	,,	Brown	,,	,,	,,
2p	,,	,,	Coldenhoff	,,	,,	,,
2q	,,	3. 11. 05	Brown	19. 1. 06	,,	29. 9. 06
2r	Muckeus	26. 1. 06	,,	29. 6. 06	,,	,,
2s-2x½	,,	24. 6. 06	,,	,,	,,	,,
2x½-3f	Pokins, Jun.	,,	,,	,,	,,	,,
3g-3m	Pokins, Sen.	22. 6. 06	,,	,,	,,	,,
3n	Negus	15. 3. 10	Sudworth	8. 4. 10	?	?
A-B	Knell	3. 11. 08	Brown Gathurn }	3. 11. 08	Hoppe	30. 10. 08
C	,,	,,	Ponder	7. 8. 08	,,	,,
D-E	,,	,,	Brown Gathurn }	3. 11. 08	,,	,,
F	Délié	2. 11. 08	,,	,,	,,	,,
G	,,	,,	?	?	,,	,,
H-I	,,	,,	,,	,,	,,	29. 6. 09
K-O	,,	23. 7. 09	Brown Gathurn }	?. 8. 09	,,	,,
P-Q	,,	,,	?	?	,,	,,
R	,,	,,	Sudworth	24. 9. 09	,,	,,
S	,,	,,	?	?	,,	5. 11. 09
T-2A	Negus	10. 9. 09	Sudworth	24. 9. 09	,,	,,
2B-2C	,,	,,	Gathurn	4. 11. 09	,,	,,
2D	,,	,,	Sudworth	24. 9. 09	,,	,,
2E	,,	,,	,,	5. 11. 09	,,	,,
2F-2G	,,	5. 11. 09	,,	,,	,,	,,
2H	,,	,,	Gathurn	4. 11. 09	,,	,,
2I	,,	,,	Sudworth	5. 11. 09	,,	,,
2K-2M	,,	,,	Gathurn	4. 11. 09	,,	,,
2N	,,	15. 3. 10	Sudworth	8. 4. 10	,,	10. 10. 10
2O	,,	,,	Gathurn Peachy }	4. 11. 10	,,	,,
2P-2Q	,,	,,	Sudworth	8. 4. 10	,,	,,
2R	,,	,,	Gathurn Peachy }	4. 11. 10	,,	,,
2S-2U	,,	,,	Sudworth	8. 4. 10	,,	,,
2X	,,	,,	?	?	,,	,,
2Y-3K	,,	,,	Sudworth	8. 4. 10	,,	,,
3L-3M	,,	,,	Gathurn Peachy }	4. 11. 10	,,	,,
3N-3O	,,	,,	Sudworth	8. 4. 10	,,	,,
3P	,,	,,	Gathurn Peachy }	4. 11. 10	,,	,,
3Q-3X $^\pi$a-$^\pi$d	,,	,,	Sudworth	8. 4. 10	,,	,,
^{2}2o-^{2}2q	Muckeus	4. 11. 09	Brown Gathurn }	?. 8. 09	,,	29. 6. 09
^{2}2r-^{2}2s	,,	,,	,,	,,	?	?

Notes. Pokins, Senior, also claimed '2 pages of Mr Waffe's Index, Saluft' (V.06.42). Sudworth was paid an additional 2s. 6d. for working the red of the title page, 2s. for making and cutting the two friskets, and 2s. for sticking titles in red and black (V.10.10).

As the catchwords on 2n1^v and 2o4^v indicate, the original intention was to follow the

Fragmenta Historicorum by the Spicilegium (which begins on 2n2) and the Spicilegium by the Index (which begins on 2q1). The additional matter of the address to P. Parkes and the Addenda, printed off in 1709 as the four and a half sheets ^{2}2o–^{2}2s and paged 283–294 285 296–318, was clearly intended to be bound in between 2n1^v and 2n2 (hence the adoption of ^{2}2o–^{2}2s and pagination commencing with 283). And such is the order in the two large-paper copies in ULC. In small-paper copies, however, the additional matter may be bound in between 2n1^v and 2n2, between 2p4^v and 2q1, or even between x4^v and y1.

The publication of this book was originally undertaken by John Owen (M.28), but on Owen's continued failure to pay his other outstanding debts the university took over the total stock of printed books. Sir Theodore Janssen had supplied Owen with 150 reams of small Genoa paper at 6s. per ream on 19. 10. 04 and a further 150 reams of the same paper together with 100 reams of fine Demy at 11s. per ream on 19. 4. 05 for the present work and for Davies's edition of Cæsar (V.07.8).

In 1709–10 20 large-paper copies were sold, presumably to the trade, at 14s. each and 44 small-paper copies at 9s. each (PA.10). A further 20 large-paper copies were sold the following year to Paul Vaillant at 12s. each (PA.11). The price noted by Rudd for his copy of this edition is 18s. 6d. (TC MS B.7.6). Hearne has several references to this 'large 4to. Ed. of Sallust, full of riff-raff Notes'. On 7 March 1706 he wrote: 'Mr. Wase . . . has a Sallust in ye Press wch has stuck there these two years. He is also for printing a Catalogue of all printed Books in ye Libraries at Cambridge. Wch shows that he is a Man of no fixt Resolution, but is more for carrying on new Projects than finishing what he has in Hand.' On 7 August 1707: 'Mr. Wasse . . . has so swell'd his Salust, which he is publishing with Notes, yt the undertaker is quite weary, who tells me yt his Index will be upwards of 20 sheets.' And on 12 April 1710: 'Mr. Wasse . . . has just publish'd his Edit. of Sallust, with long & tedious & indeed unnecessary Notes, in Quarto. the large Paper is 14s. at ye University Price, & the less 9s.' (*Remarks*, I, 200; II, 31, 372; and III, 243).

Commentary on D. F. McKenzie's bibliography of Cambridge books c. 1700

Here the subject of the bibliography is the output of a particular printing house, and the emphasis is on the details of the manufacture of everything printed at the Cambridge University Press from 1696 to 1712 rather than on the authorship or contents of the books. Basing his study on the very fine Press archives kept intact at Cambridge, Professor McKenzie uses descriptive bibliography to analyse the production details of each item. The heart of the entry given here is the long production schedule which shows exactly who set each sheet of Wasse's *Sallust* during the four years it was in the works, who printed it, and who corrected it. The type used is noted—and there is a fully illustrated catalogue of the Press types elsewhere—and some paper details are given, though not for all the entries. Note, too, how the production schedule and the complex formula complement each other.

It may be doubted whether the full analysis of contents serves much purpose—an abbreviated version would have shown which journeymen were concerned with which parts of the book—and it is arguable that a reproduction of the rather complicated title-page would be preferable to the quasi-facsimile transcription (which in McKenzie's original has intrusive hyphens at the line-endings); there also seems to be some inconsistency in the use of semicolons in the pagination formula. But these are minor matters. This remarkable bibliography is the best account we have of the detailed working arrangements over a considerable period of time of any printing house of the hand-press period.[8]

[8] See also my review in *Journal of the Printing Historical Society*, iii, 1967, pp. 100–3.

3. Entry 53*a* from Todd, W. B., *A bibliography of Edmund Burke*, London 1964, pp. 142–5.

53   REFLECTIONS ON THE REVOLUTION   1790
                            IN FRANCE

53*a. First edition:*

REFLECTIONS | ON THE | REVOLUTION IN FRANCE, | AND ON THE | PROCEEDINGS IN CERTAIN SOCIETIES | IN LONDON | RELATIVE TO THAT EVENT. | IN A | LETTER | INTENDED TO HAVE BEEN SENT TO A GENTLEMAN | *IN PARIS.* | BY THE RIGHT HONOURABLE | *EDMUND BURKE.* | [*short French rule*] | LONDON: | PRINTED FOR J. DOD SLEY, IN PALL-MALL. | M.DCC.XC.

Under the title *Reflections on certain Proceedings of the Revolution Society of the 4th of November* 1789 advertised as 'in the Press, and speedily will be published' 13 February 1790 (*The World*); published 1 November at 5*s* 'sewed', though actually in blue paper wrappers (*Public Advertiser*); a certain number, according to Prior (1824, p. 365), 'elegantly bound' at the direction of George III for distribution among his friends.

Demy 8° (227×142 mm. uncut). [A]² B⁸(−B8+'B8') C–D⁸ E⁸(±E2) F⁸(−F6+'F6') G⁸ H⁸(−H2,3+H2:3) I–Z⁸ 2A². Pp. [i] title, [iii]–iv preface, 1–356 text.

TYPOGRAPHY: Catchwords 41 "obey 87 tures 96 "of 102 —Miserable 197 year. For all copies of the first two impressions the terminal gatherings were set in duplicate and thus may occur in any one of four possible combinations. The distinguishing features are these:

gathering:	[A]²	2A²
point:	p. [iv], ornamental flower	p. 354, press figure
setting	*a* points to right	*x* none
	b points up	*y* *

Though less easily distinguished, the corresponding titles also exhibit differences, notably in the position of 'M' in imprint date (*a*) immediately below 'D' of DODSLEY, (*b*) to the right of 'D.'

FIGURES: 10–X . . . 116 *none* . . . 171–* . . . 354–* *or none*. See page 154.

PAPER: Bluish laid, unwatermarked.

NOTES: An issue of approximately 4000 copies, printed apparently by Henry Hughs.⁹ Occasionally a copy of this or later impression has inserted after text an 8-page catalogue of 'New Publications Printed for J. Debrett', one of the persons authorized to sell the book.

At the time of the preliminary announcement, 13 February, Burke had evidently read printed drafts of material ultimately imposed in sheet I, for this signature at page 113 concludes the description of Marie Antoinette which, on 19 February, Philip Francis dismissed as 'pure foppery.'¹⁰ Faced with this and other deterrents it is not surprising, as Paine remarked on 16 April, that 'Mr. Burke was much at a loss how to go on; that he had revised some of the sheets, six, seven, and one nine times!' and further, according to

---

⁹ J. C. Trewin and E. M. King, *Printer to the House: The Story of Hansard*, London [1952], p. 48. The assignment appears to be correct, though the book also attributes to Hughs (p. 49) Johnson's *Taxation No Tyranny*, a work actually printed by Strahan. See *The Book Collector*, ii (1953), 63.

¹⁰ *Corr.* (1844), iii. 129. Sir Joshua Reynolds is also reported to have read the whole work as it progressed in manuscript (*Prior* (1826), ii. 110); William Windham the earlier part either in MS or proof (*Windham Papers* (1913), i. 93); and Sir Gilbert Elliot a certain portion in April (*Minto*, i. 357–8).

Paine's informant, Debrett, that 'he has stopped the work.'[11] Possibly the stoppage occurred at L, where there appears to be a considerable delay in printing terminating in a new procedure. The interval is marked first by the removal of pressman 6, who after printing inner forme L does no further work either on this or the next edition, secondly by the assignment of three men not previously on the job, 1, 2, and †, each of whom takes one of the succeeding formes (in L, M, N) and together work off seventeen others in the two editions. The new procedure is also observed at M and N, both of which were held in anticipation of a second edition, and from O to Z, all of which, when finally approved, were overprinted to provide copy for that edition. An extension of presswork would of course cause further delay; but this was for awhile of no concern to Burke, who candidly admitted at R (p. 241) that 'various avocations have from time to time called my mind from the subject.' With the oncoming session of Parliament, however, he eventually recognized the need for haste, finished the work by 8 September, as Richard Burke Jr then advised Fitzwilliam, and later on urged his representative at press (William Thomas Swift?) to 'move heaven and earth to get it out' on the scheduled date of issue, 1 November.[12]

The copies issued of each impression are of a ratio not too dissimilar to that already cited in *The Library*, but apparently of a number twice the totals there presumed.[13] Among examined copies of the earlier issues, including those in private collections, the particulars may now be represented as:

Impression	*a*	*b*	*c*	*d*	*e*	*f*
Published November	1	[2?]	[6?]	[8?]	[12?]	16
Copies inspected	22	9	10	10	5	10
Ratio	4	2	2	2	1	2
Approximate issue	4000	2000	2000	2000	1000	2000

Edition *b*, as previously argued in *The Library*, could have been readied immediately after *a*;[14] and the later impressions (as I now believe) at stated intervals thereafter—perhaps every four days—with *d*, however, following closely upon its near-equivalent *c*. Both in timing and in number these estimates accord very well, first with Walpole's report on Monday the 8th that 'seven *thousand* copies have been taken off by the booksellers already —and a new edition is preparing'[15] (i.e., if he had the news the previous Saturday, that sales had half depleted *c* and a new 'edition'—or *d*, the first one so distinguished—was imminent), and again with Burke's own notice of the 29th that 'the demand for this piece has been without example; they are now in the sale of the 12th thousand'[16] (i.e., that the demand had now accounted for half of *f*, the first edition to be revised). For later sales see note to *g*.

[11] Letter to Thomas Christie (in W. E. Woodward), *Tom Paine*, New York 1945, pp. 186–7). Prior (1824, p. 363) reports more than a dozen proofs worked off, M'Cormick (p. 339) that 'he wrote, blotted, rewrote, printed, cancelled, re-printed it so often, that when it appeared at length, it did not contain even one sheet of the original composition.'

[12] M'Cormick, p. 339, note. Much of this author's information seems to come from Swift, then Richard Burke's secretary.

[13] 5th ser., vi (1951), 100-8. For impressions *c-f* twice the number could be printed only by continuous presswork: an extraordinary circumstance which may account for some of the 'overlapping' noted later.

[14] But probably not before first issue since, of the earlier impressions, *a* alone appears to be the one sent to Burke's friends, and seized by his antagonists. Francis and Windham had received their copies by 27 October.

[15] Letter to Mary Berry, *Horace Walpole's Correspondence* (Yale University Press, 1944), xi. 132. On this same day Richard Burke Sr conveyed to Shackleton an identical report. (Osborn MS.)

[16] Letter to Sir Gilbert Elliot, *Minto*, i. 365. Six days earlier the *Gazetteer* affirmed that 'nine thousand copies are already sold; a greater number than was ever known to be disposed of in the same time.'

COPIES: [combination a,x] NYP UC UT (inscribed to Frederick Montagu) Y. [a,y] BP(2, one lacking prelims) H(2, one with Horne Tooke's annotations) N O Y. [b,x] H PM(inscribed 'To Her Grace the Dutchess of Portland From the Author') Y(inscribed 'From the Author'). [b,y] BM CU H(with Sir Philip Francis's annotations) NYP(only copy noted with figure [iii]-1) UV(2).

Commentary on W. B. Todd's bibliography of Burke

This, unlike the first two extracts, comes from an author bibliography, but what an author: the bibliography is concerned with 79 publications in a total of at least 570 editions and impressions over the period 1748-1827. Contents and production details are less important than the publishing history of this complex mass of material, and Professor Todd orders and interprets the tortuous succession of editions and impressions with great skill; to reprint the entry for one impression of one edition is to do the whole work less than justice.

There was only one impression of the first edition of *Reflections*, but there were four of the second edition, nine of the third, and one of the fourth, all of which are identified and evaluated in shorter entries following 53*a*. The transcription of the title-page is supplemented by reproductions of its two settings (which quasi-facsimile cannot distinguish); and a full register of press figures, which do distinguish the impressions, is given in a separate table, not reproduced here. Paper details are brief but sufficient, and no details are given of types used (which would be of little use unless it were important to identify the printers involved). Contents are not listed except in tabular form for the collected editions. There are a few minor points to question: the paragraph immediately following the transcription might have been better placed under NOTES below; the term 'sewed' normally meant 'sewed in wrappers'; the symbol H2:3 in the second line of the formula should read H2.3; and the catchword Miserable has a long f.

4. Entry A5a from Barnes, W., *A bibliography of Elizabeth Barrett Browning*, Austin 1967, pp. 30-5.

A5a: A Drama of Exile 1844

[*within a ruled frame and corner ornaments*] A | DRAMA OF EXILE: | AND | OTHER POEMS. | BY | ELIZABETH BARRETT BARRETT, | AUTHOR OF 'THE SERAPHIM: AND OTHER POEMS.' | VOL. I. [II.] | NEW-YORK: | HENRY G. LANGLEY, | NO. 8, ASTOR-HOUSE. | [*short rule 0·3 cm.*] | M.DCCC.XLV.

Special imprints: Vol. 1 (on p. [ii] at the foot) H. LUDWIG, PRINTER, | Nos. 70 and 72, Vesey-st. Vol. 2 (on p. [ii] as above.)

Collation: Vol. 1 17.7 × 11.3 cm; 1^6 2-11^{12} 12^6; 132 leaves. Vol. 2 17.7 × 11.3 cm; $[13]^2$ 14-24^{12} 25^{10}; 144 leaves.

Pagination: Vol. 1 [i-iii] iv [v] vi-x [xi] xii, [13-15] 16-131 [132-135] 136-162 [163-165] 166-182 [183-185] 186-213 [214] 215-217 [218] 219-220 [221-223] 224-264. Vol. 2 [i-iii] iv, [5-7] 8-63 [64-67] 68-99 [100] 101 [102] 103 [104] 105-126 [127] 128-130 [131] 132-139 [140] 141-145 [146] 147-155 [156] 157-162 [163] 164-169 [170] 171-176 [177] 178-183 [184] 185-194 [195] 196-206 [207] 208 [209] 210-212 [213] 214-222 [223] 224-226

[227] 228-232 [233] 234-240 [241] 242-244 [245] 246-247 [248] 249-257 [258] 259-263 [264] 265 [266] 267-279 [280]. [1] 2-8.

Contents: Vol. 1 [i] title page; [ii] printer's imprint; [iii] 'DEDICATION. | [*wavy rule*] | TO MY FATHER.'; [v] 'PREFACE | TO THE | AMERICAN EDITION.'; [xi] 'CONTENTS.'; [13] fly title 'A DRAMA OF EXILE.'; [14] '𝕻𝖊𝖗𝖘𝖔𝖓𝖘 𝖔𝖋 𝖙𝖍𝖊 𝕯𝖗𝖆𝖒𝖆.'; [15] text; [132] blank; [133] fly title 'SONNETS.'; [134] blank; [135] 'SONNETS. | [*wavy rule*] | THE SOUL'S EXPRESSION.'; 136 'THE SERAPH AND POET.'; 137 'ON A PORTRAIT OF WORDSWORTH, BY | B. R. HAYDON.'; 138 'PAST AND FUTURE.'; 139 'IRREPARABLENESS'; 140 'TEARS.'; 141 'GRIEF.'; 142 'SUBSTITUTION.'; 143 'COMFORT.'; 144 'PERPLEXED MUSIC.'; 145 'WORK.'; 146 'FUTURITY.'; 147 'THE TWO SAYINGS.'; 148 'THE LOOK.'; 149 'THE MEANING OF THE LOOK.'; 150 'A THOUGHT FOR A LONELY DEATH-BED.'; 151 'WORK AND CONTEMPLATION.'; 152 'PAIN AND PLEASURE.'; 153 'AN APPREHENSION.'; 154 'DISCONTENT.'; 155 'PATIENCE TAUGHT BY NATURE.'; 156 'CHEERFULNESS TAUGHT BY REASON.'; 157 'EXAG-GERATION.'; 158 'ADEQUACY.'; 159 'TO GEORGE SAND. | [*rule*] | A DESIRE.'; 160 'TO GEORGE SAND. | [*rule*] | A RECOGNITION.'; 161 'THE PRISONER.'; 162 'INSUFFICIENCY.'; [163] fly title 'THE | ROMAUNT OF THE PAGE.'; [164] blank; [165] text; [183] fly title 'THE | LAY OF THE BROWN ROSARY.'; [184] blank; [185] text; [214] 'THE MOURNFUL MOTHER, | (OF THE DEAD BLIND.)'; [218] 'A VALEDICTION.'; [221] fly title 'LADY GERALDINE'S COURTSHIP. | A ROMANCE OF THE AGE.'; [222] blank; [223] text. 264 'END OF VOL. I.'

Vol. 2 [i] title page; [ii] printer's imprint; [iii] contents; [5] fly title 'A VISION OF POETS.'; [6] twelve line quotation from 'BRITANNIA'S PASTORALS.'; [7] text; [64] blank; 65 fly title 'RHYME OF THE DUCHESS MAY.'; [66] blank; [67] text; [100] 'THE LADY'S YES.'; [102] 'THE POET AND THE BIRD. | A FABLE.'; [104] 'THE LOST BOWER.'; [127] 'A CHILD ASLEEP.'; [131] 'THE CRY OF THE CHILDREN.'; [140] 'CROWNED AND WEDDED.'; [146] 'CROWNED AND BURIED,'; [156] 'TO FLUSH, MY DOG.'; [163] 'THE FOURFOLD ASPECT.'; [170] 'A FLOWER IN A LETTER. | WRITTEN 1839.'; [177] 'THE CRY OF THE HUMAN.'; [184] 'A LAY OF THE EARLY ROSE.'; [195] 'BERTHA IN THE LANE.'; [207] 'THAT DAY. | FOR MUSIC.'; [209] 'LOVED ONCE.'; [213] 'A RHAPSODY OF LIFE'S PROGRESS.'; [223] 'L.E.L.'S LAST QUESTION.'; [227] 'THE HOUSE OF CLOUDS.'; [233] 'CATARINA TO CAMOËNS.'; [241] 'A POR-TRAIT.'; [245] 'SLEEPING AND WATCHING.'; [248] 'WINE OF CYPRUS.'; [258] 'THE ROMANCE OF THE SWAN'S NEST.'; [264] 'LESSONS FROM THE GORSE.'; [266] 'THE DEAD PAN.'; [279] 'END OF THE SECOND VOLUME.'; [280] blank; [1] 2-8 publisher's catalogue of 8 pages advertising 'VALUABLE WORKS | PUBLISHED BY | HENRY G. LANGLEY, | 8 ASTOR HOUSE, NEW YORK.'

Typography and paper: Vol. 1 $1,5* signed below ruled frame toward inner margin of foot. Leaf 1$_3$ signed 1*; leaf 12$_3$ signed 12*. Each page enclosed by a ruled frame with rosettes as corner ornaments. Running titles set within ruled frame above a single rule in rom. caps with the titles of the individual poems as 'THE ROMAUNT OF THE PAGE.' Pagination set in the outer margin of the headline. Text irregular, 22 lines + headline and direction line. Leaf 5$_{5r}$ measures 11.9 (14.5)×8.1 cm. Gutter margins mea-sure, pp. 96-97 = 3.2 cm; 120-121 = 3.0 cm; 216-217 = 3.0 cm. Page 137 has no orna-ment in the lower right hand corner in all copies seen. Page 145 has no period following the word 'SONNETS' in the headlines. White wove paper unwatermarked. Sheets bulk 2.1 cm. Vol. 2 $1,5* signed with the typographical features of Vol. 1. Sigs 19-23 are printed on a heavier, whiter paper than the rest of the book. Leaf 21₅ missigned 20*. Gutter margins measure, pp. 112-113 = 3.2 cm; 136-137 = 3.0 cm; 232-[233] = 3.1 cm. Sheets bulk 2.3 cm.

Notes: Published October 1, 1844 at $1.00; 1500 copies were printed in the edition. In a letter to her sister Elizabeth remarks that her American publisher would use only the finest types and highest quality paper.

Binding: Yellow paper covered boards: Printed paper label on spine: '[*double rule*] | DRAMA | OF | EXILE, | AND | OTHER POEMS. | BY | E. B. BARRETT. | TWO VOLS. | [*short rule*] | VOL. I. [II.] | [*double rule*]' White wove end papers. Single binder's leaf at front and back. Five stab holes at inner margin. All edges trimmed. (CtY)

Binding variants: Claret vertically ribbed (T) cloth. Sides blind stamped with a frame of three rules with floral corner points enclosing a wreath of leaves and an eight pointed floral design. Spine: '[*ornamental design of two bell shaped flowers*] | DRAMA | OF | EXILE | AND | OTHER POEMS | [*short rule*] | BARRETT. | [*short rule*] | VOL. 1 [2] | [*design of two bell shaped flowers as above and two floral ornaments of three parts each*]' All in gilt. Yellow end papers. (CtY)

Green vertically ribbed (T) cloth. Sides blind stamped with a frame of three rules enclosing a lyre. Spine: '[*two stems of flowers surrounding a fan shaped design*] | DRAMA | OF | EXILE | AND | OTHER POEMS | [*short rule*] | BARRETT. | [*short rule*] | VOL. 1 [2] | [*ornamental floral design*]' All in gilt. (MH)

Also in purple diaper cloth with the same stamping. (MB)

Brown vertically ribbed (T) cloth. Sides blind stamped with a frame of three rules. Running around the edge is an ornate design of leaves enclosing a crest with seven plumes. Spine: '[*floral device surrounding a group of seven circles*] | DRAMA | OF | EXILE | AND | OTHER POEMS | [*short rule*] | BARRETT. | [*short rule*] | VOL. 1 [2] | [*bouquet of flowers flanked on each side by two vertical rules and on top and bottom by a group of seven circles with floral ornamentation*]' All in gilt. (TxWB)

Olive green vertically ribbed (T) cloth. Sides blind stamped with a frame of three rules with floral corner points enclosing a center design of two groups of leaves and four flower stems each decorated to a spiral. Spine: '[*ornamental floral design*] | DREAM | OF | EXILE | AND | OTHER POEMS | [*short rule*] | BARRETT. | [*short rule*] | VOL. 1 [2] | [*two floral designs facing each other, flanked on each side by semi-circles of fifteen dots*]' All in gilt. (CtY)

Brown vertically ribbed (T) cloth. Sides blind stamped with a frame of three rules. Running around the edge is an ornate floral design enclosing a centerpiece of leaves and flower petals. Spine: '[*floral design of two large flower heads and intertwining stems*] | DRAMA | OF | EXILE | AND | OTHER POEMS | [*short rule*] | BARRETT. | [*short rule*] | VOL. 1 [2] | [*design of flower heads as above and crown shaped design with floral ornamentation*]' All in gilt. (CtY)

Claret vertically ribbed (T) cloth. Sides blind stamped with a frame of three rules with floral corner points enclosing a hexagon shaped design. Spine: '[*floral ornament of three parts*] | DRAMA | OF | EXILE | AND | OTHER POEMS | [*short rule*] | BARRETT. | [*short rule*] | VOL. 1 [2] | [*ornament as above repeated three times*]' All in gilt. (TxWB)

Impressions

There are at least two impressions of this book with variants in the following apparent order:

A. Vol. 1 Page 65 is numbered correctly. Page 70 has the ornament present in the upper left hand corner. Page 91 is numbered correctly. Page 137 has the ornament present in the upper left hand corner. Page 162 has the ornament present in the upper left hand corner. Page 174 has the ornament present in the upper left hand corner. Line 19, page 180 reads "And see if ye can find him!" Page 210 has the ornament present in the upper left hand corner.

Vol. 2 Page 218 is numbered correctly. Page 223 the title reads ". . . QUESTION." Page 244 is numbered correctly.

B. Vol. 1 Page 65 unnumbered. Page 70 has no ornament in the upper left hand corner. Page 91 is unnumbered. Page 137 has no ornament in the upper left hand corner. Page 162 has no ornament in the upper left hand corner. Page 174 has no ornament in the upper left hand corner. Line 19, page 180 reads "An $_d$ see if ye can find im!" Page 210 has no ornament in the upper left hand corner.

Vol. 2 Page 218 misnumbered 18. Page 223 reads ". . . QUESTIO ." Page 244 misnumbered 2 . Copies containing mixed sheets can occur in 256 possible combinations for Vol. 1; 8 for Vol. 2 and I have never found any two copies alike. Several variations seen are as follows:

Vol. 1 p. 65 numbered correctly; p. 70 ornament absent; p. 91 unnumbered; p. 137 ornament present; p. 162 ornament absent; p. 174 ornament absent; p. 180.19 reads "An $_d$ see if ye can find im!"; p. 210 ornament present. Vol. 2 p. 218 misnumbered 18; p. 22$_3^d$ reads ". . . QUESTIO ."; p. 244 numbered correctly. (TxWB)

Vol. 1 p. 65 numbered correctly; p. 70 ornament present; p. 91 numbered correctly; p. 137 ornament absent; p. 162 ornament present; p. 174 ornament present; p. 180.19 reads "And see if ye can find him!"; p. 210 ornament absent. Vol. 2 p. 218 numbered correctly; p. 223 reads ". . . QUESTION."; p. 244 numbered correctly. (TxWB)

Vol. 1 p. 65 unnumbered; p. 70 ornament present; p. 91 unnumbered; p. 137 ornament present; p. 162 ornament absent; p. 174 ornament absent; p. 180.19 reads "An $_d$ ee if ye can find im!"; p. 210 ornament absent; Vol. 2 p. 218 misnumbered 18; p. 22$_3^{ds}$ reads ". . . QUESTION."; p. 244 numbered correctly. (MB)

Vol. 1 p. 65 numbered correctly; p. 70 ornament present; p. 91 unnumbered; p. 137 ornament absent; p. 162 ornament present; p. 174 ornament present; p. 180.19 reads "And see if ye can find him!"; p. 210 ornament present. Vol. 2 p. 218 numbered correctly; p. 223 reads ". . . QUESTIO ."; p. 244 misnumbered 2 (CSmH)

Copies examined: NN MH MWelC MB CtY DLC TxWB WB L CSmH.

Commentary on Warner Barnes's bibliography of E. B. Browning

The fourth extract, like the third, is from an author bibliography, but Mrs. Browning's literary output was smaller and bibliographically simpler than Burke's. There are forty-five full entries for primary texts, posthumously printed works, forgeries, and collections of letters; with check-lists for reprints, contributions to periodicals, etc. The particular interest of this bibliography lies in the fact that Mr. Barnes machine-collated an average of six copies of each of the first English (and two of the American) editions, and found a variant state or a concealed impression, hitherto unrecognized, in every one of them. Collation on this scale is a laborious but commendable technique for investigating the writings of a poet, in which textual minutiae are liable to matter; and the fact that nearly all the variants found in Mrs. Browning's books turned out to be typographic trivia of no textual importance does not lessen the value of Mr. Barnes's work: nil returns are as important as reports of textual variation. It is possible to question the order of priority in which some of the variants are placed here,[17] but again this does not affect the main outcome, which is that typographic variation of this sort was a normal feature of the printed literature of the period.

Entry A5a, which describes the American edition of *Poems* 1844 (dated 1845 in spite of publication on 1 October 1844) is an example of the full treatment given to the primary editions. Attention is drawn to the *six* binding variants in an edition of only 1,500 copies; and to the diverse mixtures of the sheets containing variants. This mixture indicates that the impressions from which the variants came were at least ill defined; and indeed suggests the possibility that there were not two impressions at all, but only one with press variants or accidental changes. The notation '$1,5* signed' is not altogether clear (*Typography and paper*); and under *Binding* 'stab holes' may mean 'sewing holes' (stab holes go through the side of the section, not through the fold). The register of contents is very long, and in some other entries is even longer, and it is questionable whether quasi-facsimile transcription (which is allowed intrusive hyphens) is really necessary here.

---

[17] See the review in *T.L.S.*, 1969, p. 864.

Appendix C

The Transmission of the Text: Two Examples

1. COMPOSITOR B AND THE MERCHANT OF VENICE Q2[18]

The resetting of *The merchant of Venice* in 1619 by Jaggard's compositor B has already been described (pp. 348–50); here a specimen of his work is illustrated and analysed. It is Portia's speech at what is now called III. ii. 1–24.

> *Portia.* I pray you tarry, paufe a day or two
> 2 Before you hazard, for in choofing wrong
>   *I* loofe your companie; therefore forbeare a while,
> 4 Theres fomething tells me (but it is not loue)
>   *I* would not loofe you, and you know your felfe,
> 6 Hate counfailes not in fuch a quallity;
>   But leaft you fhould not vnderftand me well,
> 8 And yet a mayden hath no tongue, but thought,
>   *I* would detaine you heere fome moneth or two
> 10 before you venture for me. I could teach you
>   how to choofe right, but then I am forfworne,
> 12 So will *I* neuer be, fo may you miffe me,
>   But if you doe, youle make me wifh a finne,
> 14 That *I* had beene forfworne: Befhrow your eyes,
>   They haue ore-lookt me and deuided me,
> 16 One halfe of me is yours, the other halfe yours,
>   Mine owne I would fay: but if mine then yours,
> 18 And fo all yours; ô thefe naughty times
>   puts barres betweene the ovvners and their rights,
> 20 And fo though yours, not yours, (proue it fo)
>   Let Fortune goe to hell for it, not I.
> 22 I fpeake too long, but tis to peize the time,
>   To ech it, and to draw it out in length,
> 24 To ftay you from election.

FIG. 131. *The merchant of Venice* Q1 (London, I. R. for Thomas Heyes, 1600, Greg 172 (*a*); Trin. Coll. Cam. Capell S. 30. 4, E3ᵇ).

---

[18] See McKenzie, D. F., 'Compositor B's role in *The merchant of Venice* Q2 (1619)', *Studies in bibliography*, xii, 1959, pp. 75–90; and cf. p. 348 n. 19.

Por. I pray you tarry, paufe a day or two
2 Before you hazard : for in choofing wrong
I loofe your company, therefore forbeare a while,
4 There's fomething tels me (but it is not loue)
I would not lofe you, and you know your felfe,
6 Hate counfels not in fuch a quality.
But leaft you fhould not vnderftand me well,
8 And yet a maiden hath no tongue, but thought,
I would detaine you heere fome moneth or two
10 Before you venture for me. I could teach you
How to choofe right, but I am then forfworne,
12 So will I neuer-be, fo may you miffe me,
But if you do, you'l make me wifh a finne,
14 That I had bene forfworne. Befhrew your eyes,
They haue ore- lookt me, and diuided me,
16 One halfe of me is yours,the other halfe yours,
Mine owne I would fay ; but if mine then yours,
18 And fo all yours. O thefe naughty times
Puts barres betweene the owners and their rights.
20 And fo though yours, not yours (proue it fo)
Let fortune go to hell for it, not I.
22 I fpeake too long, but tis to peize the time,
To eck it,and to dravv out in length,
24 To ftay you from election.

FIG. 132. *The merchant of Venice* Q2 (London, 'J. Roberts 1600' [Jaggard 1619], Greg 172 (*b*); Trin. Coll. Cam. Capell Q. 11. 5, E4ᵇ).

The copy used by B was Q1, 1600, and in resetting these 24 lines he introduced 39 variants, a slightly higher proportion than his average for the whole play. Two of them were substantive errors, a transposition and an omission:

	Q1	Q2
11	then I am	I am then
23	draw it out	dravv out

The remaining 37 variants were alterations of accidentals. Of greater textual importance than the rest were 11 changes of punctuation, B tending towards heavier stops than his predecessor:

2	hazard,	hazard:
3	companie;	company,
4	Theres	There's
6	quallity;	quality.
14	forfworn:	forfworn.
15	ore-lookt	ore lookt
15	me	me,
17	fay:	fay;

	Q1	Q2
18	yours;	yours.
19	rights,	rights.
20	yours,	yours

This extract happens to have fewer extra commas than B usually added.

Then there were 13 spelling changes, B preferring his usual 'do', 'go', etc.

3	companie	company
4	tells	tels
5	loofe	lofe
6	counfailes	counfels
6	quallity	quality
8	mayden	maiden
13	doe	do
13	youle	you'l
14	beene	bene
14	Befhrow	Befhrew
15	deuided	diuided
21	goe	go
23	ech	eck

It may be that B's 'eck' for 'ech' should be considered a substantive change: although *eche* and *eke* were cognate words of similar meaning, there were differences between them of usage and pronunciation.

Least significant textually of the accidental variants were the abbreviation of the speech heading (*Por.* for *Portia.*), and 12 substitutions of sorts, chiefly in order to correct faults caused by shortages in the Q1 compositor's case:

3, 5, 9, 12, 14	*I*	I
10	before	Before
11	how	*How*
18	ô	O
19	puts	Puts
19	ovvners	owners
21	Fortune	fortune
23	draw	dravv

When the text of this speech was set for the 1623 Shakespeare folio by another of Jaggard's compositors—probably A—the copy was again Q1. On this occasion there was one substantive error (17, 'of' for 'if'), but only 22 alterations of accidentals, most of them unimportant: there were 2 changes of punctuation, 9 of spelling, 10 substitutions of sorts, and the same abbreviation of the speech heading.

2. THE TEXTUAL HISTORY OF DAVID COPPERFIELD[19]

The collation of successive versions of an extract from a nineteenth-century text shows that London compositors of the 1850s followed copy with much greater fidelity than did their seventeenth-century forebears. *David Copperfield* has been chosen for a demonstration not only because of its importance as a novel but also because the evidence concerning its early textual history is almost complete and because its textual development was fairly typical of its period.

As was his usual practice, Dickens wrote a single manuscript draft of *Copperfield* which he amended as he went along, and he sent it part by part to Bradbury & Evans (who both printed and published it) as each number was required. Type was set direct from the manuscript, proofs were corrected in the usual way, and stereo plates were made from the corrected type pages. The first impression, probably printed from type, was issued in eighteen demy-octavo monthly parts and one double part, 1849–50; and further impressions were printed from plates in 1850 and afterwards for issue in single-volume form (Edition I).

TABLE 10

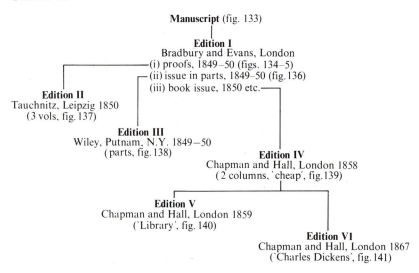

A three-volume edition, meanwhile, had been set for Tauchnitz from corrected proofs sent to Leipzig for the purpose (1850, Edition II); and the book was also set for part-issue in America, possibly from proofs but more likely from the English parts (11 parts published by John Wiley and 9 by G. P. Putnam, New York 1849–50; Edition III); Dickens did not revise the text for either of these editions. There were then three London editions published by Chapman & Hall:

¹⁹ This appendix was compiled with the help of Miss Nina Burgis, who is editing *David Copperfield* for the Clarendon Dickens. The history of the writing and publishing of the novel month by month is detailed in Butt, J., and Tillotson, K., *Dickens at work*, London 1957, ch. 6.

the two-column cheap edition of 1858 (Edition IV) set from an impression of Edition I; and two editions set from the cheap edition, the Library edition of 1859 (Edition V) and the Charles Dickens edition of 1867 (Edition VI). It was claimed by the publishers that the texts of Editions IV and V were 'carefully revised' by the author, and similar revision of Edition VI was implied, but in each case the textual changes were few and trivial and, although Dickens may have revised these texts sporadically, it seems unlikely that he did so with consistent care.[20] Editions IV, V, and VI were frequently reprinted from plates. No later edition has any independent textual authority.

Here a brief extract from chapter 54 (Part XVIII) is followed through all but one of its main textual stages: manuscript copy, author's proof, author's revise, and Editions I to VI; the missing stage is the printer's first proof marked by the corrector. The copy for the whole extract is reproduced, with a transcript, in fig. 133, and the whole text of the extract also appears in figs. 138 and 140. In each of the other six reproductions the extract lacks a line or two at the beginning or end, but in each case the text of the unreproduced portion has been checked for variants and the results are included in the captions.

Collation of the series shows the high degree of compositorial accuracy that was typical of the period. The compositors and correctors who first got the text into type were especially competent. Dickens's manuscript was characteristically difficult to read, yet there were no substantive changes in the extract between copy and author's proof, and the 16 alterations of accidentals were probably intentional (figs. 133, 134). In correcting his first proof Dickens accepted most of these alterations—indeed he may have been unaware of them since he seems not to have read proofs against copy—and he made several corrections himself, both of substantives and of accidentals, which the printer carried out accurately. Later Dickens made further corrections to a revise of the author's proof (fig. 135) which were attended to with equal efficiency. This established the text of Edition I (fig. 136), which was not altered in subsequent impressions.

No substantive changes were made to the text of the extract in Editions II, III, IV, V, or VI, and there were no further changes of accidentals in Editions II or IV (figs. 137, 139; there were of course changes, both of substantives and of accidentals, elsewhere in all these editions). There were four changes in the punctuation of the extract in Edition III (fig. 138), which were not authorized by Dickens; and two changes of punctuation in Edition V (fig. 140) and one in Edition VI (fig. 141) which could have been but probably were not made by Dickens: changes which have some importance in view of the weight which Dickens plainly attached to the pointing of his work.

This small sample—about a third of a page, one-hundredth of a periodical part, one two-thousandth of the whole book—does not indicate the rate of substantive change in the setting and resetting of the novel as a whole. The highest rate of substantive error is found in the original typesetting from the manuscript; in terms of substantive variants per part, the maximum was 114, the minimum 25, and the norm 30-50 or about 1-2 errors per page, of which Dickens found and

---

[20] The cheap, Library and Charles Dickens editions are discussed in the Clarendon edition of *Oliver Twist*, ed. Tillotson, K., Oxford 1966, pp. xxviii-xxx.

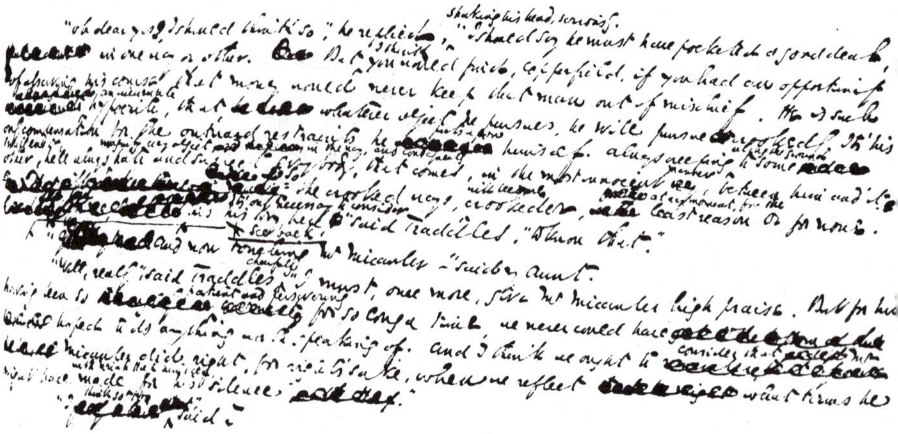

FIG. 133. *David Copperfield*: manuscript copy written by Dickens in purple ink, September 1850 (V & A, 47. A. 26. 161, f. 228). *Transcript*:

[1] "Oh dear yes, I should think so," he replied, shaking his head, seriously. "I should say he must have pocketed a good deal, [2] in one way or other. But I think you would find, Copperfield, if you had an opportunity [3] of observing his course, that money would never keep that man out of mischief. He is such [4] an incarnate hypocrite, that, whatever object he pursues, he will pursue crookedly. It's his [5] only compensation for the outward restraints he puts upon himself. Always creeping along the ground to some [6] small end or other, he'll always magnify every object in the way, and consequently hate and suspect everybody, that comes, in the most innocent manner, between him and it. [7] So the crooked ways, will become crookeder, at any moment, for the least reason or for none. [8] It's only necessary to consider his history here," said Traddles, "to know that."

[9] * *See back.*

[verso] "He's a monster of meanness!" said my Aunt.

"Really I don't know about that," observed Traddles thoughtfully. Many people can be very mean (as far as that goes) when they give their minds to it."

---

[10] "And now touching Mr Micawber—" said my Aunt.

[11] "Well, really," said Traddles, cheerfully "I must, once more, give Mr Micawber high praise. But for his [12] having been so patient and persevering for so long a time, we could never have [13] hoped to do anything worth speaking of. And I think we ought to consider that M^r [14] Micawber did right, for right's sake, when we reflect what terms he [15] might have made with Uriah Heep himself, for his silence."

[16] "I think so too," said I

corrected just over half in proof. About 60 substantive errors were introduced in setting Edition IV from Edition I, or about 1 per 10 pages. In setting Editions V and VI from Edition IV a further 35-40 (different) errors were introduced in each case, so that—with the 60 errors repeated from Edition IV—Editions V and VI each had about 100 substantive errors not in Edition I, or about 1 per 6 pages.

other. But I think you would find, Copperfield, if you had an opportunity of observing his course, that money would never keep that man out of mischief. He is such an incarnate hypocrite, that whatever object he pursues, he will pursue crookedly. It's his only compensation for the outward restraints he puts upon himself. Always creeping along the ground to some small end or other, he always magnify every object in the way and consequently hate and suspect every body that comes, in the most innocent manner, between him and it. So the crooked ways will become crookeder, at any moment, for the least reason, or for none. It's only necessary to consider his history here," said Traddles, "to know that."

"He's a monster of meanness," said my aunt.

"Really I don't know about that," observed Traddles thoughtfully. "Many people can be very mean (as far as that goes) when they give their minds to it."

"And now touching Mr. Micawber," said my aunt.

"Well, really," said Traddles, cheerfully, "I must, once more, give Mr. Micawber high praise. But for his having been so patient and per-severing for so long a time, we never could have hoped to do anything worth speaking of. And I think we ought to consider that Mr. Micawber did right, for right's sake, when we reflect what terms he might have made with Uriah Heep himself, for his silence."

"I think so too," said I.

FIG. 134. *David Copperfield*: author's proof for Edition I, 1850, corrected by Dickens in black ink (V & A, 2421. 48. B. 14A, f. 659). Variants:

manuscript		*author's proof*	
1	dear		[dear,]
1	seriously.		[seriously,] *corrected to full stop*
4	that,	3	that
6	everybody	7	every body
7	ways,	8	ways
7	reason	9	reason,
[v. 1	meanness!]	12	meanness,
[v. 1	Aunt]	12	aunt
[v. 2	Many]	13	"Many
10, 11, 13	Mr	16, 18, 20	Mr.
10	Micawber—"	16	Micawber,"
10	Aunt	16	aunt
11	cheerfully	17	cheerfully,
16	I	23	I.

seriously. "I should say he must have pocketed a good deal, in one way or
other. But, I think you would find, Copperfield, if you had an opportunity of observing his course, that money would never keep that man
out of mischief. He is such an incarnate hypocrite, that whatever object
he pursues, he must pursue crookedly. It's his only compensation for the
outward restraints he puts upon himself. Always creeping along the
ground to some small end or other, he will always magnify every object in
the way; and consequently hate and suspect every body that comes, in
the most innocent manner, between him and it. So, the crooked courses
will become crookeder, at any moment, for the least reason, or for none.
It's only necessary to consider his history here," said Traddles, "to
know that."

"He's a monster of meanness!" said my aunt.

"Really I don't know about that," observed Traddles thoughtfully.
"Many people can be very mean when they give their minds to it."

"And now, touching Mr. Micawber," said my aunt.

"Well, really," said Traddles, cheerfully, "I must, once more, give
Mr. Micawber high praise. But for his having been so patient and persevering for so long a time, we never could have hoped to do anything
worth speaking of. And I think we ought to consider that Mr. Micawber
did right, for right's sake, when we reflect what terms he might have made
with Uriah Heep himself, for his silence."

"I think so too," said I.

Fig. 135. *David Copperfield*: author's revise for Edition I, 1850, corrected by Dickens in blue ink (V & A, 2421. 48. B. 14A, f. 695). No variants other than the corrections marked in the author's first proof.

seriously. "I should say he must have pocketed a good deal, in one way or
other. But, I think you would find, Copperfield, if you had an oppor- 2
tunity of observing his course, that money would never keep that man
out of mischief. He is such an incarnate hypocrite, that whatever object 4
he pursues, he must pursue crookedly. It's his only compensation for the
outward restraints he puts upon himself. Always creeping along the 6
ground to some small end or other, he will always magnify every object in
the way; and consequently will hate and suspect every body that comes, in 8
the most innocent manner, between him and it. So, the crooked courses
will become crookeder, at any moment, for the least reason, or for none. 10
It's only necessary to consider his history here," said Traddles, "to
know that." 12

"He's a monster of meanness!" said my aunt.

"Really I don't know about that," observed Traddles thoughtfully. 14
"Many people can be very mean, when they give their minds to it."

"And now, touching Mr. Micawber," said my aunt. 16

"Well, really," said Traddles, cheerfully, "I must, once more, give
Mr. Micawber high praise. But for his having been so patient and per- 18
severing for so long a time, we never could have hoped to do anything
worth speaking of. And I think we ought to consider that Mr. Micawber 20
did right, for right's sake, when we reflect what terms he might have made
with Uriah Heep himself, for his silence." 22

"I think so too," said I.

Fig. 136. *David Copperfield*: Edition I (first impression), Bradbury & Evans, London 1850 (V & A, Dyce printed books 3053, p. 552). No variants other than the corrections marked in the author's revise.

FIG. 137. *David Copperfield*: Edition II,
Tauchnitz, Leipzig 1850 (Bodleian,
256. f. 3344/3, p. 302). No variation
from Edition I.

"Oh dear, yes, I should think so," he replied, shaking
his head, seriously. "I should say he must have pocketed a 2
good deal, in one way or other. But, I think you would find,
Copperfield, if you had an opportunity of observing his course, 4
that money would never keep that man out of mischief. He is
such an incarnate hypocrite, that whatever object he pursues, he 6
must pursue crookedly. It's his only compensation for the outward restraints he puts upon himself. Always creeping along 8
the ground to some small end or other, he will always magnify
every object in the way; and consequently will hate and 10
suspect every body that comes, in the most innocent manner,
between him and it. So, the crooked courses will become 12
crookeder, at any moment, for the least reason, or for none.
It's only necessary to consider his history here," said Trad- 14
dles, "to know that."

"He's a monster of meanness!" said my aunt. 16

"Really I don't know about that," observed Traddles
thoughtfully. "Many people can be very mean, when they 18
give their minds to it."

"And now, touching Mr. Micawber," said my aunt. 20

"Well, really," said Traddles, cheerfully, "I must, once
more, give Mr. Micawber high praise. But for his having 22
been so patient and persevering for so long a time, we never
could have hoped to do anything worth speaking of. And I 24
think we ought to consider that Mr. Micawber did right, for
right's sake, when we reflect what terms he might have made 26
with Uriah Heep himself, for his silence."

FIG. 138. *David Copperfield*: Edition
II, Putnam, New York 1950 (Bodleian,
arch. A. A. e. 100, pp. 346-7). Variants:

Edition I	Edition III
8 way;	9 way:
8 every body	10 everybody
14 Traddles	16 Traddles,
16 "And	19 "And,
23 so	26 so,

"Oh dear, yes, I should think so," he replied, shaking his head,
seriously. "I should say he must have pocketed a good deal, in one 2
way or other. But, I think you would find, Copperfield, if you had
an opportunity of observing his course, that money would never keep 4
that man out of mischief. He is such an incarnate hypocrite, that
whatever object he pursues, he must pursue crookedly. It's his only 6
compensation for the outward restraints he puts upon himself.
Always creeping along the ground to some small end or other, he 8
will always magnify every object in the way: and consequently will
hate and suspect everybody that comes, in the most innocent man- 10
ner, between him and it. So, the crooked courses will become crookeder, at any moment, for the least reason, or for none. It's only 12
necessary to consider his history here," said Traddles, "to know
that." 14

"He's a monster of meanness!" said my aunt.

"Really I don't know about that," observed Traddles, thought- 16
fully. "Many people can be very mean, when they give their minds
to it." 18

"And, now, touching Mr. Micawber," said my aunt.

"Well, really," said Traddles, cheerfully, "I must, once more, 20
give Mr. Micawber high praise. But for his having been so patient
and persevering for so long a time, we never could have hoped to do 22
anything worth speaking of. And I think we ought to consider that
Mr. Micawber did right, for right's sake, when we reflect what terms 24
he might have made with Uriah Heep himself, for his silence."

"I think so, too," said I. 26

I think you would find, Copperfield, if
you had an opportunity of observing his 2
course, that money would never keep
that man out of mischief. He is such 4
an incarnate hypocrite, that whatever
object he pursues, he must pursue 6
crookedly. It's his only compensation
for the outward restraints he puts upon 8
himself. Always creeping along the
ground to some small end or other, he 10
will always magnify every object in the
way; and consequently will hate and 12
suspect every body that comes, in the
most innocent manner, between him and 14
it. So, the crooked courses will become
crookeder, at any moment, for the least 16
reason, or for none. It's only necessary to consider his history here," said 18
Traddles, "to know that."
    "He's a monster of meanness!" 20
said my aunt.
    "Really I don't know about that," 22
observed Traddles thoughtfully. "Many
people can be very mean, when they 24
give their minds to it."
    "And now, touching Mr. Micawber," 26
said my aunt.
    "Well, really," said Traddles, cheer- 28
fully, "I must, once more, give Mr.
Micawber high praise. But for his 30
having been so patient and persevering
for so long a time, we never could have 32
hoped to do anything worth speaking
of. And I think we ought to consider 34
that Mr. Micawber did right, for right's
sake, when we reflect what terms he 36
might have made with Uriah Heep himself, for his silence." 38
    "I think so too," said I.

FIG. 139. *David Copperfield*: Edition IV, Chapman &
Hall, London 1858 (V & A, 2399. 6. o. 11, p. 458).
No variation from Edition I.

"Oh dear, yes, I should think so," he replied, shaking his head, seriously. "I should say he must have pocketed a good 2 deal, in one way or other. But, I think you would find, Copperfield, if you had an opportunity of observing his course, 4 that money would never keep that man out of mischief. He is such an incarnate hypocrite, that whatever object he pursues, 6 he must pursue crookedly. It's his only compensation for the outward restraints he puts upon himself. Always creeping 8 along the ground to some small end or other, he will always magnify every object in the way; and consequently will hate 10 and suspect every body that comes, in the most innocent manner, between him and it. So, the crooked courses will 12 become crookeder, at any moment, for the least reason or for none. It's only necessary to consider his history here," said 14 Traddles, "to know that."

"He's a monster of meanness!" said my aunt.   16

"Really I don't know about that," observed Traddles, thoughtfully. "Many people can be very mean, when they 18 give their minds to it."

"And now, touching Mr. Micawber," said my aunt.   20

"Well, really," said Traddles, cheerfully, "I must, once more, give Mr. Micawber high praise. But for his having 22 been so patient and persevering for so long a time, we never could have hoped to do anything worth speaking of. And I 24 think we ought to consider that Mr. Micawber did right, for right's sake, when we reflect what terms he might have made 26 with Uriah Heep himself, for his silence."

"I think so too," said I.   28

FIG. 140. *David Copperfield*: Edition V, Chapman & Hall, London 1859 (BM 12603. k. 9, vol. xvi, pp. 356-7). Variants:

Edition IV	*Edition V*
17 reason,	13 reason
23 Traddles	17 Traddles,

"Oh dear, yes, I should think so," he replied, shaking his head, seriously. "I should say he must have pocketed a good deal, in one way or other. But, I think 2 you would find, Copperfield, if you had an opportunity of observing his course, that money would never keep that man out of mischief. He is such an incarnate 4 hypocrite, that whatever object he pursues, he must pursue crookedly. It's his only compensation for the outward restraints he puts upon himself. Always creep- 6 ing along the ground to some small end or other, he will always magnify every object in the way; and consequently will hate and suspect every body that comes, 8 in the most innocent manner, between him and it. So, the crooked courses will become crookeder, at any moment, for the least reason, or for none. It's only 10 necessary to consider his history here," said Traddles, "to know that."

"He's a monster of meanness!" said my aunt. 12

"Really I don't know about that," observed Traddles, thoughtfully. "Many people can be very mean, when they give their minds to it." 14

FIG. 141. *David Copperfield*: Edition VI, Chapman & Hall, London 1867 (V & A, 2401. 6. A. 7, p. 473). Variant:

Edition IV	*Edition VI*
23 Traddles	13 Traddles,

Reference Bibliography

I: GENERAL

An important—but inadequately classified—selective listing of bibliographical scholarship appears annually in the periodical *Studies in bibliography* (see section II): x, 1957, for the years 1949-55; Series B, 1966, for the years 1956-62; and xviii, 1965, onwards for the years 1963-. Still valuable are the sections on 'Book production and distribution' by Graham Pollard in *The Cambridge bibliography of English literature*, 4 vols., Cambridge 1940 (revised in *The new Cambridge bibliography of English literature*, Cambridge 1969-). Bigmore, E. C., and Wyman, C. W. H., *A bibliography of printing*, 3 vols., London 1884-6 (repr. London 1969) is astonishingly comprehensive and still very useful in spite of its age. Berry, W. T., and Poole, H. E., *Annals of printing*, London 1966, contains much interesting material that is not easily available elsewhere, but it is marred by small slips and lack of references.

The great *Dictionary catalog of the history of printing from the John M. Wing Foundation in the Newberry Library* [*Chicago*], 6 vols., Boston, Mass. 1961, is rich in secondary works and easy to use. The *Saint Bride Foundation catalogue of the technical reference library of works on printing and the allied arts*, London 1919, includes more primary sources than the Wing catalogue, but is unclassified; it should be used in connection with the admirable *Catalogue of periodicals relating to printing & allied subjects in the technical library of the Saint Bride Institute*, London 1951.

The basic tools of enumerative bibliography are Goff, F. R., *Incunabula in American libraries*, New York 1964, which can be used as a key to the specialist bibliographies of fifteenth-century printing; Pollard, A. W., and Redgrave, G. R., *A short-title catalogue of books printed in England, Scotland, & Ireland and of English books printed abroad, 1475-1640*, London 1926 (abbreviated STC; now in process of revision); and Wing, D. G., *Short-title catalogue of books printed in England, Scotland, Ireland, Wales, and British America and of English books printed in other countries 1641-1700*, 3 vols., New York 1945 (revised ed. 1973-, abbreviated Wing). See also Sabin, J., *A dictionary of books relating to America*, 29 vols., New York 1868-1936. The 'Term catalogues', ed. E. Arber, 3 vols., 1903-6, cover the period 1668-1709.

The British Museum *General catalogue of printed books to 1955*, 263 vols., London 1965-6 (repr. New York, 27 vols., 1967) is itself an enumerative tool of primary importance, the value of which is enhanced by the series of geographical short-title catalogues of books to 1600 in the British Museum (French books, 1924; Italian books, 1958; German books, 1962; Dutch books, 1965; and Spanish, Spanish-american, and Portuguese books, 1966). Work on the following period has now begun with Goldsmith, V. F., *A short title catalogue of French books 1601-1700 in the library of the British Museum*, Folkestone and London 1969-. Adams, H. M., *Catalogue of books printed on the continent of Europe, 1501-1600, in Cambridge Libraries*, 2 vols., Cambridge 1967, concerns collections of books comparable to that of the British Museum, and includes both an index of printers and collations of each book.

II: PERIODICALS

Two bibliographical journals are especially distinguished for the wide range and rigorous scholarship of their contents; they are *The Library* (London 1889-), being the quarterly transactions of the Bibliographical Society;[1] and the annual *Studies in bibliography* (Charlottesville, Va. 1948-), the papers of the Bibliographical Society of the University of Virginia. At one time rather lighter in weight, but now of comparable importance, is the quarterly *Papers of the Bibliographical Society of America* (New York 1909-).

Transactions of the Cambridge Bibliographical Society (Cambridge 1949-) includes some articles of general interest, as does the *Harvard Library bulletin* (Cambridge, Mass. 1947-); while *The book collector* (London 1952-), although not primarily bibliographical in approach, contains many scholarly articles of bibliographical interest.

Two foreign journals of more than local importance, both of which include English summaries, are *Het boek* (The Hague 1912-69) and *Den gulden passer* (Antwerp 1923-). The *Gutenberg Jahrbuch* (Mainz 1926-) includes articles in English but not summaries of those in other languages; its contents are of uneven quality.

Printing and graphic arts (Lunenburg, Vt. 1953-65) and *The black art* (London 1962-5) both specialize, rather patchily, in printing history; but *The black art* has now been replaced by the distinguished *Journal of the Printing Historical Society* (London 1965-).

III: BOOK PRODUCTION: THE HAND-PRESS PERIOD

I. HAND-PRINTING TECHNOLOGY

a. General

The best contemporary evidence of early printing-house practice (apart from what is deducible from the product itself) is to be found in the early printers' manuals, and in the printers' business records which have survived to the present day. Gaskell, P., Barber, G., and Warrilow, G., 'An annotated list of printers' manuals to 1850', *Journal of the Printing Historical Society*, iv, 1968, pp. 11–32, and addenda (1972), describes 69 manuals in English, French, German, Spanish, and Dutch. Incomparably the most valuable manual is Moxon, J., *Mechanick exercises*, London 1683 (eds. Davis, H., and Carter, H., 2nd ed., Oxford 1962). Mention may also be made here of the illustrated articles (referred to individually below) in *Encyclopédie*, Paris 1751-, and *Encyclopédie méthodique*, Paris 1784-.

The most important study of an early printer's business records is D. F. McKenzie's distinguished *The Cambridge University Press 1696-1712*, 2 vols., Cambridge 1966; and the records of other English printers of the eighteenth

---

[1] The volume numbers of *The Library* (which incorporated *The transactions of the Bibliographical Society* in 1920) are arranged in five numbered Series; but, since volume number and date suffice for reference, the confusing series numbers are omitted in the present work.

century are examined in McKenzie, D. F., and Ross, J. C., *A ledger of Charles Ackers*, Oxford 1968; Hernlund, P., 'William Strahan's ledgers', *Studies in bibliography*, xx, 1967, pp. 89-111, and xxii, 1969, pp. 179-95; and in works in progress on the Bowyer ledgers by K. I. Maslen and on the archives of the Société Typographique de Neuchâtel by Jacques Rychner. For earlier periods see Frobenius, H., *Rechnungsbuch der Froben & Episcopius*, ed. Wackernagel, H., Basel 1881; and Voet, L., *The golden compasses*, 2 vols., Amsterdam 1969- (vol. ii consulted by the present author in manuscript), which is based on the richest of all the early printers' archives, the Plantinian collection at Antwerp, and is chiefly concerned with sixteenth- and early-seventeenth-century practice.

Many printers' inventories have survived; there is no good general collection, but Gray, G. J., and Palmer, W. M., *Abstracts from the wills and testamentary documents of printers, binders, and stationers of Cambridge, from 1504 to 1699*, London 1915, is valuable for the sixteenth century.

The following general surveys of early American printing are particularly recommended: Wroth, L. C., *The colonial printer*, Portland (Me.) 1938 (repr. Charlottesville 1964); and Silver, R. G., *The American printer 1787-1825*, Charlottesville 1967.

b. Composition, imposition, correction

Reference should be made in the first place to the early manuals (III. 1. *a* above). The following studies deal with individual aspects of the subject.

English handwriting: Wright, C. E., *English vernacular hands from the twelfth to the fifteenth centuries*, Oxford 1960; Greg, W. W., *English literary autographs, 1550-1650*, Oxford 1925-32, and *Dramatic documents from the Elizabethan playhouses*, 2 vols., Oxford 1931 (the most valuable collections, but not easy to get hold of); Dawson, G. E., and Kennedy-Skipton, L., *Elizabethan handwriting 1500-1650*, London 1968, is an excellent manual.

Copy, typesetting, correction: Simpson, P., *Proof-reading in the sixteenth, seventeenth and eighteenth centuries*, Oxford 1935 (repr. 1970); Hellinga, W. Gs., *Copy and print in the Netherlands*, Amsterdam 1962; Foxon, D. F., 'The varieties of early proof', *The Library*, xxv, 1970, pp. 151-4. On setting by formes, see Bond, W. H., 'Casting off copy by Elizabethan printers', *Papers of the Bibliographical Society of America*, xlii, 1948, pp. 281-91; and Hinman, C., *The printing and proof-reading of the first folio of Shakespeare*, 2 vols., Oxford 1963.

Signatures, etc.: Sayce, R. A., 'Compositorial practices and the localisation of printed books, 1530-1800', *The Library*, xxi, 1966, pp. 1-45.

Compositors' output: McKenzie, D. F., *The Cambridge University Press 1696-1712*, 2 vols., Cambridge 1966, ch. 5; Barnes, W. C., McCann, J. W., and Duguid, A., *A collation of facts relative to fast typesetting*, New York 1887.

Imposition: The following four early manuals between them cover nearly all the impositions of the hand-press period: Wolffger, G., *Neu-auffgesetztes Format-büchlein*, Graz 1673 (repr. Prague 1925); Moxon, J., *Mechanick exercises*,

London 1683 (repr. Oxford 1962); Fertel, M. D., *La science pratique de l'impri-merie*, Saint-Omer 1723; and Smith, J., *The printer's grammar*, London 1755 (repr. London 1965). French impositions are also illustrated in *Encyclopédie*, planches vii, Paris 1769. The largest collection (153 impositions) is in Savage, W., *A dictionary of the art of printing*, London 1841 (repr. London 1966).

See also Povey, K., 'On the diagnosis of half-sheet imposition', *The Library*, xi, 1956, pp. 268-72; Cook, D. F., 'Inverted imposition', *The Library*, xii, 1957, pp. 193-6 (with a valuable list of books in inverted impositions); Povey, K., 'Twenty-fours with three signatures', *Studies in bibliography*, ix, 1957, pp. 215-16; Foxon, D. F., 'Some notes on agenda format', *The Library*, viii, 1953, pp. 163-73 (deals with long 24°, and other foldings for tall, narrow books).

c. Presswork

The classic account is Moxon, J., *Mechanick exercises*, London 1683 (repr. Oxford 1962), which may usefully be compared with Plantin, C., *La première, et la second partie des dialogues François*, Anvers 1567 (repr. in Nash, R., *Calligraphy & printing in the sixteenth-century dialogue attributed to Christopher Plantin*, Antwerp 1964); *Encyclopédie*, viii, 'Neufchastel' 1765 s.v. 'Imprimerie', and planches vii, Paris 1769; and Savage, W., *Practical hints on decorative printing*, London 1822.

See also Povey, K., 'Variant formes in Elizabethan printing', *The Library*, x, 1955, pp. 41-8 (which includes Le Roy's very important account of sixteenth-century techniques, and Ashley's near-contemporary adaptation); Povey, K., 'Working to rule, 1600-1800: a study of pressmen's practice', *The Library*, xx, 1965, pp. 13-54 (on priority of formes); Foxon, D. F., 'On printing "at one pull", and distinguishing impressions by point-holes', *The Library*, xi, 1956, pp. 284-5.

The wooden hand-press: The English version is best described in Stower, C., *The printer's grammar*, London 1808 (repr. London 1965); Moxon describes a Dutch press; and the French version is well illustrated in *Encyclopédie*, planches vii, Paris 1769. There is a collection of early illustrations of presses in Enschedé, J. W., 'Houten handpersen in de zestiende eeuw', *Tijdschrift voor boek- en biblioteekswesen*, iv, 1906, pp. 196-215; while Gaskell, P., 'A census of wooden presses', *Journal of the Printing Historical Society*, vi, 1970, pp. 1-32, describes and illustrates surviving presses.

Ink: Bloy, C. H., *A history of printing ink, balls and rollers, 1440-1850*, London 1967.

Recurrent printing: Bowers, F. T., 'Notes on standing type in Elizabethan printing', *Papers of the Bibliographical Society of America*, xl, 1946, pp. 205-24; Todd, W. B., 'Recurrent printing', *Studies in bibliography*, xii, 1959, pp. 189-98.

Press figures: Povey, K., 'A century of press figures', *The Library*, xiv, 1959, pp. 251-73 (which includes references to earlier papers); Tanselle, G. T., 'Press figures in America', *Studies in bibliography*, xix, 1966, pp. 123-60.

Cancels: Chapman, R. W., *Cancels*, London and New York 1930.

Two colours: The basic accounts are in Moxon, J., *Mechanick exercises*, London 1683 (repr. Oxford 1962), pp. 299-302; and Fertel, M. D., *La science pratique de l'imprimerie*, Saint-Omer 1723, pp. 277-83. See also Savage, W., *Practical hints on decorative printing*, London 1822.

Music printing: King, A. H., *Four hundred years of music printing*, London 1964; Vervliet, H. D. L., *Sixteenth-century printing types of the Low Countries*, Amsterdam 1968, ch. 6; Poole, H. E., 'New music types', *Journal of the Printing Historical Society*, i, 1965, pp. 21-38, and ii, 1966, pp. 23-44.

Pressmen's output: McKenzie, D. F., *The Cambridge University Press 1696-1712*, 2 vols., Cambridge 1966, ch. 5.

d. Patterns of production

The basic sources are the early printers' business records (see III. 1. *a* above), which include statistics of edition quantities; and an invaluable commentary is McKenzie, D. F., 'Printers of the mind', *Studies in bibliography*, xxii, 1969, pp. 1-75. For a detailed investigation of compositors' work routines in the early seventeenth century, see Hinman, C., *The printing and proof-reading of the first folio of Shakespeare*, 2 vols., Oxford 1963. See also de Roover, R., 'The business organisation of the Plantin press in the setting of sixteenth-century Antwerp', *De gulden passer*, xxxiv, 1956, pp. 104-20 (reprinted, see p. 165; good on productive capacity); Maslen, K. I. D., 'The printing of the votes of the House of Commons 1730-1781', *The Library*, xxv, 1970, pp. 120-35; and Todd, W. B., 'Concurrent printing: an analysis of Dodsley's Collection of poems by several hands', *Papers of the Bibliographical Society of America*, xlvi, 1952, pp. 45-57.

2. TYPE

For a useful survey of typographical studies up to the mid 1960s, see the footnotes to Tanselle, G. T., 'The identification of type-faces in bibliographical description', *Papers of the Bibliographical Society of America*, lx, 1966, pp. 185-202. There is no general guide to the whole history of printing type in the hand-press period that adequately incorporates recent work on the subject, for Updike, D. B., *Printing types, their history forms and use*, 3rd ed., Oxford 1963, is seriously out of date; but the history of type up to about 1600 is superbly treated in Carter, H., *A view of early typography*, Oxford 1969.

The best early accounts of type-founding technique are in Moxon, J., *Mechanick exercises*, London 1683 (repr. Oxford 1962); and *Encyclopédie*, ii, Paris 1751, s.v. 'Caractères d'imprimerie', and planches ii, Paris 1763.

The development of type design in the sixteenth and seventeenth centuries can be studied in *Type specimen facsimiles*, ed. Dreyfus, J. G., London 1963 (to be extended to cover the eighteenth century); Vervliet, H. D. L., *Sixteenth-century printing types of the Low Countries*, Amsterdam 1968; Morison, S., *John Fell*, Oxford 1967 (to be used with some caution); and in the type specimens of the Vatican Press 1628 (ed. Vervliet, H. D. L., Amsterdam 1967), Claude Lamesle 1742 (ed. Johnson, A. F., 1965), and Delacolonge 1773 (ed. Carter, H., Amsterdam

1969), the two eighteenth-century specimens showing mostly earlier types. The pioneering essays by A. F. Johnson collected as *Type designs*, 3rd ed., London 1966, are stimulating but out-dated. Early type specimens are catalogued in Audin, M., *Les livrets typographiques des fonderies françaises créés avant 1800*, Paris 1934 (repr. Amsterdam 1964); and Berry, W. T., and Johnson, A. F., *Catalogue of specimens of printing types by English and Scottish printers and founders 1665-1830*, Oxford 1935.

    T. B. Reed's *A history of the old English letter foundries*, rev. Johnson, A. F., London 1952, is still valuable, and deals with Scottish as well as English founders; see also Mores, E. R., *A dissertation upon English typographical founders and founderies* (*1788*), eds. Carter, H., and Ricks, C., Oxford 1961. For France see 'Aperçu sur la fonderie typographique parisienne au XVIIIe siècle', *The Library*, xxiv, 1969, pp. 200-18. Early American type is dealt with in Wroth, L. C., *The colonial printer*, 2nd ed., Portland 1938 (repr. Charlottesville 1964); and Silver, R. G., *Typefounding in America, 1787-1825*, Charlottesville 1965.

    There is no good general book about gothic types, but see again Vervliet, H. D. L., *Sixteenth-century printing types of the Low Countries*, Amsterdam 1968; and (on gothic script types) Carter, H., and Vervliet, H. D. L., *Civilité types*, Oxford 1966. The development of Greek typography is covered definitively in Scholderer, V., *Greek printing types 1465-1927*, London 1927. See also the references under 'Music printing' in III. 1. *c* above.

    Mosley, J., 'English vernacular', *Motif*, xi, 1963-4, pp. 3-53, is an important discussion of the relationship between typographic and inscriptional lettering, and is supplemented by the same author's 'Trajan revived', *Alphabet*, i, 1964, pp. 17-48.

    Type sizes are discussed in Gaskell, P., 'Type sizes in the eighteenth century', *Studies in bibliography*, v, 1952-3, pp. 147-51 (and see the references to Table 1, p. 15). For the lay of the case, see Gaskell, P., 'The lay of the case', *Studies in bibliography*, xxii, 1969, pp. 125-42.

3. PAPER

Although E. J. Labarre's *Dictionary and encyclopaedia of paper and paper-making*, Oxford 1952 (repr. Amsterdam 1969; *Supplement*, Amsterdam 1967) is a comprehensive guide to modern paper technology and terminology, it is unreliable on early paper-making. Dard Hunter's *Papermaking, the history and technique of an ancient craft*, 2nd ed., New York 1947 (repr. London 1957) contains a mass of information, discursively treated. Much the best accounts of paper-making in the hand-press period are the illustrated articles by Goussier in *Encyclopédie*, xi, 'Neufchastel' 1765, and planches v, Paris 1767; and by Desmarest in *Encyclopédie méthodique: arts et métiers mécaniques*, v, Paris 1788. A short but satisfactory survey of the whole history of paper-making, with good illustrations, is *Papermaking: art and craft*, Washington 1968 (a Library of Congress exhibition catalogue).

    The history of paper-making in Britain is authoritatively treated in Coleman, D. C., *The British paper industry 1495-1860*, Oxford 1958; and individual English mills are described in Shorter, A., *Paper mills in England 1495-1800*, Hilversum 1957. On the taxation of paper see Jarvis, R. C., 'The paper-makers and the excise in the eighteenth century', *The Library*, xiv, 1959, pp. 100–16. Balston, T., *James Whatman father & son*, London 1957, is a good study of the foremost paper-making firm of its period, supplemented by the same author's *William Balston paper-maker 1759–1849*, London 1954.

Briquet's great collection of watermarks is now available in a new edition (Briquet, C. M., *Les Filigranes*, ed. Stevenson, A. H., 4 vols., Amsterdam 1968), and is essential for most aspects of paper history up to 1600; unfortunately it does not cover English or Iberian paper. Watermarks of the later hand-press period are illustrated (less adequately than by Briquet) in Churchill, W. A., *Watermarks in paper in Holland, England, France, etc., in the XVII and XVIII centuries*, Amsterdam 1935 (repr. Amsterdam 1967); and Heawood, E., *Watermarks mainly in the 17th and 18th centuries*, Hilversum 1950 (repr. Amsterdam 1970).

Recent bibliographical studies of paper include several important articles by A. H. Stevenson, of which 'Watermarks are twins', *Studies in bibliography*, iv, 1951–2, pp. 57–91, is outstanding. The same author's *The problem of the Missale speciale*, London 1968, uses paper and typographical evidence in a remarkable bibliographical detective story.

For paper sizes see Graham Pollard's pioneering 'Notes on the size of the sheet', *The Library*, xxii, 1941–2, pp. 105–37; and the tables in Gaskell, P., 'Notes on eighteenth-century British paper', *The Library*, xii, 1957, pp. 34–42 (superseded on trade history by R. C. Jarvis's paper, mentioned above). Double moulds are considered in Povey, K., and Foster, I. J. C., 'Turned chain lines', *The Library*, v, 1950–1, pp. 184–200. R. W. Chapman's 'An inventory of paper, 1674', *The Library*, vii, 1926–7, pp. 402–8, describes an actual paper stock of the seventeenth century, complete with marks and sizes.

4. BINDING

There is no general work on trade binding in the hand-press period. Pollard, H. G., 'Changes in the style of bookbinding, 1550–1830', *The Library*, xi, 1956, pp. 71–94, is not intended to be comprehensive, but contains much illuminating observation. For American binding in the Colonial period, see Lehmann-Haupt, H., *Bookbinding in America*, New York 1941 (repr. 1967), pp. 8–47. Sadleir, M., *The evolution of publishers' binding styles 1770–1900*, London and New York 1930, contains useful facts about later developments, but is misleading about the extent of edition binding in the eighteenth century. Individual British binders are listed in Howe, E., *A list of London bookbinders 1648–1815*, London 1950; Pollard, H. G. (ed.), *The earliest directory of the book trade, by John Pendred (1785)*, London 1955; and in the dictionaries of printers, booksellers, and binders referred to in III. 6. *b* below.

For binding technique, Middleton, B. C., *A history of English craft bookbinding technique*, New York and London 1963, is an essential source; the best early account is the article 'Relieure' [*sic*] in *Encyclopédie*, xiv, 'Neufchastel' 1765, and planches viii, Paris 1771. There are useful notes on early techniques in Zaehnsdorf, J. W., *The art of bookbinding*, 2nd ed., London 1890 (repr. Farnborough 1967); and in Cockerell, D., *Bookbinding, and the care of books*, 4th ed., London 1925.

The numerous monographs on particular binders or groups of bindings are nearly all concerned with the finest bespoke work, and have little to say about ordinary trade binding; an exception is H. M. Nixon's admirable *Broxbourne Library: styles and designs of bookbindings from the twelfth to the twentieth century*, London 1956, which does not ignore the relationship between bespoke and trade binding. It includes important notes on early printed covers, which are also treated in Jackson, W. A., 'Printed wrappers of the fifteenth to the eighteenth centuries', *Harvard Library bulletin*, vi, 1952, pp. 313-21. See also Nixon, H. M., 'The memorandum book of James Coghlan: the stock of an 18th-century printer and binder', *Journal of the Printing Historical Society*, vi, 1970, pp. 33-52. A short guide to the history of bespoke bindings, with a select bibliography, is Harthan, J. P., *Bookbindings*, 2nd ed., London 1961.

5. DECORATION AND ILLUSTRATION

A convenient modern introduction to the techniques of the early processes, both relief and intaglio, is Hind, A. M., *The processes and schools of engraving*, 4th ed., London 1952; much stronger on the development of style is W. M. Ivins's admirable *Prints and visual communication*, New York 1969, and the same author's *Notes on prints*, New York 1967. Some of the early accounts of technique are still important, notably Faithorne, W., *The art of graveing and etching*, London 1662 (Wing F294; intaglio); Papillon, J. M., *Traité historique et pratique de la gravure en bois*, 3 vols., Paris 1766 (relief); *Encyclopédie*, vii, Paris 1757, and planches v, Paris 1767, s.v. 'Gravure en bois, gravure en taille-douce' (relief and intaglio); ibid. viii, 'Neufchastel' 1765, and planches vii, Paris 1769, s.v. 'Imprimerie en taille-douce' (intaglio); and Savage, W., *Practical hints on decorative printing*, London 1822 (relief, including colour).

A workmanlike account of the methods of modern woodcut and copperplate illustrators is included in Curwen, H., *Processes of graphic reproduction in printing*, new ed., London 1947. The standard work on colour prints is Burch, R. M., *Colour printing and colour printers*, 2nd ed., London 1910.

There are numerous treatises on the art of book illustration, surveyed in David Bland's N.B.L. pamphlet, *A bibliography of book illustration*, London 1955. The same author's *A history of book illustration*, London 1958, is a somewhat unselective guide.

6. THE BOOK TRADE TO 1800

a. General

The European book trade at the beginning of the hand-press period is well surveyed in Hirsch, R., *Printing, selling and reading 1450-1550*, Wiesbaden 1967; and in Febvre, L., and Martin, H. J., *L'apparition du livre*, Paris 1958 (up to about 1600, with special reference to France). But most histories of the trade are national in approach.

The standard work on the trade in England is Plant, M., *The English book trade*, 2nd ed., London 1965, but it is of uneven quality, and takes little account of scholarship since the date of the first edition, 1939. Clair, C., *A history of printing in Britain*, London 1965, is more up to date, but is a cursory treatment of a large subject. Much better are Bennett, H. S., *English books & readers 1475 to 1557*, Cambridge 1952; *English books & readers 1558 to 1603*, Cambridge 1965; and *English books & readers 1603 to 1640*, Cambridge 1970, which are readable and authoritative. There is no similar modern survey of the later hand-press period, but Nichols, J., *Literary anecdotes*, 9 vols., London 1812-15 (index in vol. vii), and *Illustrations* (a sequel to the *Anecdotes*), 8 vols., London 1817-58, are indispensable sources for the eighteenth century; and Timperley, C. H., *A dictionary of printers and printing*, London 1839 (which is well indexed) is still surprisingly useful.

For the book trade in pre-Revolutionary America, see Wroth, L. C., *The colonial printer*, 2nd ed., Portland 1938 (repr. Charlottesville 1964). The story is carried on in Silver, R. G., *The American printer 1787-1825*, Charlottesville 1967.

Mellottée, P., *Histoire économique de l'imprimerie*, vol. i (all that was published), Paris 1905, is a more general account of the French book trade to 1789 than its title would suggest. Pottinger, D. T., *The French book trade in the ancien régime 1500-1791*, Cambridge, Mass. 1958, contains much information badly organized. A remarkable specialist study is Martin, H. J., *Livre, pouvoirs et société à Paris au XVIIe siècle (1598-1701)*, 2 vols., Genève 1969. The collection by Bollème, G., and others, called *Livre et société dans la France du XVIIIe siècle*, Paris 1965, is good in parts.

b. Personnel

The basic works of reference are the biographical dictionaries published by the Bibliographical Society: Duff, E. G., *A century of the English book trade* [1457-1557], London 1905; McKerrow, R. B., *A dictionary of printers and booksellers in England, Scotland and Ireland, and of foreign printers of English books 1557-1640*, London 1910; Plomer, H. R., *A dictionary of the booksellers and printers who were at work in England, Scotland and Ireland from 1641 to 1667*, London 1907; Plomer, H. R., *A dictionary of the printers and booksellers who were at work in England, Scotland and Ireland from 1668 to 1725*, London 1922; Plomer, H. R., Bushnell, G. H., and Dix, E. R. McC., *A dictionary of the printers and booksellers who were at work in England, Scotland and Ireland from 1726 to 1775*, London 1932.

Pendred, J., *The earliest directory of the book trade (1785)*, ed. Pollard, H. G., London 1955, is a valuable contemporary list; see also Howe, E., *A list of London bookbinders 1648-1815*, London 1950; McKenzie, D. F., *Stationers' Company apprentices 1605-1640*, Charlottesville, Va. 1961; and, for the French book trade, Lottin, A. M., *Catalogue chronologique des libraires et des libraires-imprimeurs de Paris*, Paris 1789 (repr. Amsterdam 1969). Chauvet, P., *Les ouvriers du livre en France des origines à la révolution de 1789*, Paris 1959, is a more general secondary work.

The standard work on the English gild is Blagden, C., *The Stationers' Company, a history, 1403-1959*, London 1960. For chapel organization in the sixteenth century, see Voet, L., 'The printers' chapel in the Plantinian house', *The Library*, xvi, 1961, pp. 1-14. Moxon gives a full account of the English chapel in the seventeenth century; and continental chapels of this period are investigated in

Blades, W., *An account of the German morality play entitled Depositio cornuti typographici*, London 1885 (repr. London 1962).

c. *Business organization*

See primarily the studies of early printers' business records mentioned in III. 1. *a*. Additional papers on the Plantinian house include de Roover, F. E., 'Cost accounting in the sixteenth century', *The accounting review*, xii, 1937, pp. 226-37 (an important technical study, repr. in *Studies in costing*, ed. Solomons, D., London 1952, pp. 53-71); and de Roover, R., 'The business organisation of the Plantin press in the setting of sixteenth-century Antwerp', *De gulden passer*, xxxiv, 1956, pp. 104-20 (reprinted, see p. 165). Philip, I. G., *William Blackstone and the reform of the Oxford University Press in the eighteenth century*, Oxford 1957, an admirable monograph, includes details of Samuel Richardson's practice. See also Sale, W. M., *Samuel Richardson: master printer*, Ithaca 1950; and Cochrane, J. A., *Dr. Johnson's printer: the life of William Strahan*, London 1964.

d. *Publishing and bookselling*

Perhaps Pollard, H. G., and Ehrman, A., *The distribution of books by catalogue to 1800*, privately printed Cambridge 1965, is the best approach to a general history of the book trade in the hand-press period that has yet been written; certainly it is a brilliant and extensive treatment of its subject, and it is unfortunate that it is not generally available. Handover, P. M., *Printing in London*, London 1960, is good on London publishing in the hand-press period.

The records of the English Stationers' Company in the later sixteenth and early seventeenth centuries have been thoroughly investigated. E. Arber's basic *A transcript of the registers of the Company of Stationers of London 1554-1640*, 5 vols., London and Birmingham 1875-94, is calendared and supplemented by Greg, W. W., *A companion to Arber*, Oxford 1967. Greg's outstanding studies of this period also include *Records of the court of the Stationers' Company 1576-1602* (with Boswell, E.), London 1930, continued by Jackson, W. A., *Records of the court of the Stationers' Company 1602-1640*, London 1957; *Some aspects and problems of London publishing between 1550 and 1650*, Oxford 1956; *Licensers for the press, &c. to 1640*, Oxford 1962 (a biographical index); and *Collected papers*, ed. Maxwell, J. C., Oxford 1966. The transcript of the Stationers' Company Register was continued for the years 1640-1708 in four Roxburghe Club volumes, privately printed 1913-14, which are now being indexed by W. P. Williams. For the 'Term catalogues' see Section I.

For the later development of the Stationers' Company, see Blagden's standard history (III. 6. *b* above). Blagden, C., and Hodgson, N., *The notebook of Thomas Bennet and Henry Clements*, Oxford 1956, includes a lucid study of the congers and of the foreign trade; see also Blagden, C., 'The memorandum book of Henry Rhodes, 1695-1720', *The book collector*, 1954, pp. 28-38, 103-16; both studies include information about prices. The early number books are investigated in Wiles, R. M., *Serial publication in England before 1750*, Cambridge 1957.

Booksellers' stocks of the sixteenth and seventeenth centuries can be studied in their wills; important published collections are Gray, G. J., and Palmer, W. M., *Abstracts from the wills and testamentary documents of printers, binders, and stationers of Cambridge, from 1504 to 1699*, London 1915; and *The Bannatyne miscellany*, vol. ii, Edinburgh 1836, pp. 185-296 (Edinburgh printers' and booksellers' wills, 1567-1717, full of detail). Several sixteenth-century booksellers' account books have been described. The most extensive of them is Madan, F., 'Day-book of John Dorne, bookseller in Oxford, A.D. 1520', *Oxford Historical Society, Collectanea*, i, Oxford 1885, pp. 71-177, and ii, Oxford 1890, pp. 453-80; see also Kronenberg, M. E., 'Fragment of a bookseller's list, probably Antwerp, about 1533-35', *Transactions of the Cambridge Bibliographical Society*, ii, 1958, pp. 14-37; and Oliver, L. M., 'A bookseller's account book, 1545', *Harvard library bulletin*, xvi, 1968, pp. 139-55, and footnote references on p. 139. For eighteenth-century publishing and bookselling, see Knight, C., *Shadows of the old booksellers*, London 1865 (repr. London 1927); and Parks, S., 'Booksellers' trade sales', *The Library*, xxiv, 1969, pp. 241-3.

e. *Authorship, copyright, and censorship*

The most valuable guides up to the early seventeenth century are Greg's studies (detailed in III. 6. *d*) and H. S. Bennett's more general surveys (III. 6. *a*). For the later seventeenth and eighteenth centuries, see Johnson, J., and Gibson, S., *Print and privilege at Oxford to the year 1700*, Oxford 1946 (repr. 1966); Hanson, L. W., *Government and the press 1695-1763*, Oxford 1936 (repr. 1967); Collins, A. S., *Authorship in the days of Johnson*, London 1927; and Nichols's *Literary anecdotes* (III. 6. *a* above).

IV: BOOK PRODUCTION: THE MACHINE-PRESS PERIOD

1. GENERAL

There is not yet any adequate general history of book production since 1800, although Silver, R. G., *The American printer 1787-1825*, Charlottesville 1967, is good on the transitional period, and Lehmann-Haupt, H., *The book in America*, 2nd ed., New York 1952, contains valuable material. A simple account of the working of a large London printing house in the 1840s appears in Dodd, G., *Days at the factories. Series 1*, London 1843, pp. 326-60; and there is a description of the working of each department in what was probably the most advanced American printing business of the 1850s in Abbott, J., *The Harper establishment*, New York 1855 (repr. Hamden, Conn. 1956). (See also the 1851 account of the state printing house in Vienna mentioned in IV. 10 below.) Technological developments are surveyed in Southward, J., *Progress in printing and the graphic arts during the Victorian era*, London 1897. The situation at the turn of the century was admirably described in Southward, J., *Modern printing*, 4 vols., London 1899-1900; and De Vinne, T. L., *The practice of typography*, 4 vols., New York 1900-4. Ordinary methods of the first half of the present century are described simply in Whetton, H., *Practical printing and binding*, London 1946, and later editions.

Charles Manby Smith's *The working man's way in the world*, London 1853 (repr. London 1967), is a vivid account of what it was like to be a journeyman compositor in England and France from the 1820s to the 1840s (but see Nowell-Smith, S., 'Charles Manby Smith', *Journal of the Printing Historical Society*, vii, 1971, pp. 1-28, who questions Smith's reliability); Scurfield, G., *A stickful of nonpareil*, privately printed Cambridge 1956, describes working conditions at the Cambridge University Press around 1900. There are poignant glimpses of mid-nineteenth-century conditions in the evidence given to a number of government commissions, notably in the 5th report of the Children's Employment Commission (1866); see IV. 10 below.

The early printers' manuals are again valuable evidence of what was supposed to happen. The best of the English ones were Stower, C., *The printer's grammar*, London 1808 (repr. London 1965); Hansard, T. C., *Typographia*, London 1825 (repr. London 1967); Savage, W., *A dictionary of the art of printing*, London 1841 (repr. London 1966); Gould, J., *The letterpress printer*, Middlesbrough 1876 (and later editions); and Southward, J., *Practical printing*, London 1882 (and later editions, esp. the 4th ed., London 1892). The earlier American manuals were abridged from Stower and Hansard, but Grattan, E., *The printer's companion*, Philadelphia 1846, was largely original and referred to American practices; see also MacKellar, T., *The American printer*, Philadelphia 1866 (and later editions). The standard French manual for the nineteenth century was Fournier, H., *Traité de la typographie*, Paris 1825 (and later editions up to 1919); for Germany see Hasper, W., *Handbuch der Buchdruckerkunst*, Carlsruhe und Baden 1835. Particular British technological developments up to the mid nineteenth century may be followed in *Patents for inventions: abridgments of specifications relating to printing*, London 1859 (and supplement; repr. London 1969).

2. SURVIVAL AND CHANGE

a. Hand composition

The companionship system in England and America is described in the manuals listed in IV. 1 above, and in Scurfield's retrospective view of the Cambridge University Press in 1900 (also in IV. 1). The manuals also include large collections of imposition schemes, the most useful of which is in Savage, W., *A dictionary of the art of printing*, London 1841 (repr. London 1966). Nineteenth-century wages and working conditions are documented in Howe, E., *The London compositor*, London 1947. See also p. 195 n. 18.

b. Iron hand-presses

The introduction of the Stanhope press is described in Hart, H., *Charles Earl Stanhope and the Oxford University Press*, ed. Mosley, J., London 1966. For the Columbian, see Moran, J., 'The Columbian press', *Journal of the Printing Historical Society*, v, 1969, pp. 1-23; and for the Albion, Stone, R., 'The Albion press', *Journal of the Printing Historical Society*, ii, 1966, pp. 58-73, and iii, 1967, pp. 97-9. American developments are described in Green, R., *The iron hand press in America*, Rowayton 1948; and Silver, R. G., *The American printer 1787-1825*, Charlottesville 1967.

3. PLATES

Three early works investigate the beginnings of stereotyping, in each case with some national bias; they are, for Holland, Westreenen van Tiellandt, W. H. J. van, *Verslag der naspooringen omtrent . . . der stereotypische drukwijze* (with parallel text in French), 's Gravenhage 1833; for Britain, Hodgson, T., *Essay on the origin and progress of stereotype printing*, Newcastle 1820; and for France, Camus, A. G., *Histoire et procédés du polytypage et de la stéréotypie*, Paris an X [1801]. A plate deriving from Müller's work is illustrated in the *Catalogue* of the 'Printing and the mind of man' exhibition, London 1963 (plate 8). The Ged process is investigated in Carter, J. W., 'William Ged and the invention of stereotype', *The Library*, xv, 1960, pp. 161–92; ibid. xvi, 1961, pp. 143–5; ibid. xviii, 1963, pp. 308–9.

Of several early accounts of the plaster-mould process, the best is included in Hansard's manual (IV. 1 above); the flexible-mould process is well described and illustrated in Southward's manual. Stereotyping at the Clowes works around 1840 is described in Dodd, G., *Days at the factories: series 1*, London 1843, pp. 342–6.

Savage, W., *A dictionary of the art of printing*, London 1841 (repr. London 1966), includes an important article on the beginnings of electrotyping s.v. 'galvanism'. The process as applied to plate-making is described in chapter 10 of Abbott, J., *The Harper establishment*, New York 1855 (repr. Hamden, Conn. 1956) and, more fully, in Southward's manual of 1882 (IV. 1 above).

4. TYPE

a. *1800–1875*

The outstanding account of type manufacture in the period is the account of the Marr foundry in parts viii and ix of Henry Mayhew's short-lived periodical *The shops and companies of London and the trades and manufactories of Great Britain*, London 1865, pp. 241–71. Figgins, J., *Type founding and printing during the nineteenth century, a short review*, London 1900, is also useful, especially on standard sizes. The technological developments of the earlier nineteenth century are discussed in *Patents for inventions* (see IV. 1 above); Johnson, J. R., 'On certain improvements in the manufacture of printing types', *Journal of the Society of Arts*, xxi, 1873, pp. 330–8 (with a discussion of the ethics of the electrotyping of matrices); and Legros, L. A., and Grant, J. C., *Typographical printing surfaces*, London 1916. There are also valuable notes on nineteenth-century developments in Reed, T. B., *A history of the old English letter foundries*, rev. Johnson, A. F., London 1952, although the arrangement by founders makes them hard to find.

There is no satisfactory general account of nineteenth-century type design. Johnson, A. F., *Type designs: their history and development*, 3rd ed., London 1966, contains good chapters on early modern-face, early display types, and the old-face revival. See also Mosley, J., 'English vernacular', *Motif*, xi, 1963–4, pp. 3–55; and Gray, N., *XIXth century ornamented types and title pages*, London 1938. Individual founts must usually be sought in founders' specimen books, few of which have yet been reprinted (an exception is *Vincent Figgins type specimens 1801 and 1815*, ed. Wolpe, B., London 1967). A number of early-nineteenth-century specimens are listed in Berry, W. T., and Johnson, A. F., *Catalogue of specimens of printing types by English and Scottish printers and founders 1665-1830*, London 1935; and Audin, M., *Les livrets typographiques des fonderies françaises créées avant 1800*, Paris 1934 (repr. Amsterdam 1964).

America was the leader in the production of wood letter, and Kelly, R. R., *American wood type 1828-1900*, New York 1969, is an admirably illustrated treatment of the subject, including discussion of manufacturing techniques.

b. Since 1875

Legros and Grant (see previous section) is again the main authority for the technological developments of the period, and also comments on the stylistic development of commercial type up to 1916. The only worth-while general survey of type- and book-design in the machine-press period is the collection of long essays edited by K. Day as *Book typography 1815-1965 in Europe and the United States of America*, London 1966; the essays, by various authors on the typography of the major book-producing countries, are of varying quality, but the general standard is high. The collection contains little about modernist trends in twentieth-century typography, for which see John Lewis's short but stimulating *Typography/ basic principles*, 2nd ed., London 1967.

Developments since Morris are treated in Ruari McLean's admirable *Modern book design, from William Morris to the present day*, [2nd ed.], London 1958. The Monotype revival is chronicled, with some justified self-satisfaction, in 'The pioneer days of "Monotype" composing machines' and 'Fifty years of type cutting', *The Monotype recorder*, xxxix, 1950, nos. 1 and 2. The central years of the revival are covered with idiosyncratic scholarship by Stanley Morison in *A tally of types cut for machine composition and introduced at the University Press, Cambridge, 1922-1932*, privately printed Cambridge 1953. The Linotype companies do not share Monotype's flair for publicity, but *Linotype matrix 18*, London 1954, included the useful 'L & M's first fifty years of experience, enterprise, and technical development'. For a current guide see Jaspert, W. P., Berry, W. T., and Johnson, A. F., *The encyclopaedia of type faces*, 4th ed., London 1970.

See also the section on mechanical composition, IV. 9 below.

5. PAPER

Contemporary accounts of nineteenth-century paper manufacture include Tomlinson, C., *Cyclopaedia of useful arts*, ii, London 1854, pp. 364-74; Herring, P., *Paper and paper-making*, London 1855, and later editions; and anon., *The art of paper making*, 2nd ed., London 1876. The most important early manual is Hofmann, C., *A practical treatise on the manufacture of paper*, Philadelphia 1873. For paper-making in the twentieth century, see Clapperton, R. H., and Henderson, W., *Modern paper-making*, London 1929, and later editions; Technical Section of the British Paper and Board Makers' Association, *Paper making*, London 1949, and later editions; and, for America, Witham, G. S., *Modern pulp and paper making*, New York 1942, and later editions.

The Library of Congress exhibition catalogue *Papermaking, art and craft*, Washington D.C. 1968, surveys later as well as earlier paper history; but Hunter,

D., *Papermaking*, 2nd ed., New York 1947 (repr. London 1957), is patchy on machine-made paper. Balston, T., *William Balston paper maker 1759-1849*, London 1954, shows how Whatman's successor continued to make hand-made paper in the nineteenth century.

For the early development of paper-making machinery, see *Patents for inventions: abridgments of the specifications relating to the manufacture of paper, pasteboard, and paper mâché*, London 1858; and R. H. Clapperton's fascinating *The paper-making machine, its invention, evolution and development*, Oxford 1967, which is superbly illustrated but awkwardly arranged.

The best general history of the industry in the nineteenth century is still Spicer, A. D., *The paper trade*, London 1907, although part of it is now superseded by Coleman, D. C., *The British paper industry*, Oxford 1958. For the American trade, see Weeks, L. H., *A history of paper-manufacturing in the United States, 1690-1916*, New York 1916.

Labarre, E. J., *Dictionary and encyclopaedia of paper and papermaking*, 2nd ed., Oxford 1952 (repr. Amsterdam 1969, with *Supplement* by E. G. Loeber, Amsterdam 1967), explains the technical terms (and includes paper vocabularies in six languages besides English).

The only important survey of the characteristics of nineteenth-century printing papers that has yet been carried out is reported in the fifth pamphlet in the W. J. Barrow Research Laboratory's series *Permanence/Durability of the book*: 'Strength and other characteristics of book paper 1800-1899', Richmond, Va. 1967, the results of the thorough testing of the (mostly American) paper in 500 nineteenth-century books.

6. BINDING

There are good accounts of large binderies in the early cloth period in Dodd, G., *Days at the factories, series 1*, London 1843, pp. 362-84; Tomlinson, C., *Cyclopaedia of useful arts*, i, London 1854, pp. 152-62; and Abbott, J., *The Harper establishment*, New York 1855 (repr. Hamden, Conn. 1956), pp. 123-55. An excellent short survey of early techniques and of changes up to the 1930s is Leighton, D., *Modern bookbinding, a survey and a prospect*, London 1935; and techniques, especially of mechanization, are the chief concern of Rogers, J. W., 'The rise of American edition binding', in *Bookbinding in America*, ed. Lehmann-Haupt, H., New York 1967. Still the prime authority on the evolution of nineteenth-century English binding styles is Carter, J. W., *Publishers' cloth 1820-1900*, New York and London 1938.

For the forerunners of publishers' cloth, see Leighton, D., 'Canvas and book-cloth', *The Library*, iii, 1948-9, pp. 39-49. Cloth binding variants are dealt with in Carter, J. W., *Binding variants in English publishing*, London and New York 1932; and in the same author's *More binding variants*, London 1938. Much miscellaneous information about nineteenth-century binding styles is to be found in Sadleir, M., *The evolution of publishers' binding styles 1770-1900*, London and New York 1930; and in his *XIX century fiction, a bibliographical record*, 2 vols., London and Los Angeles 1951. Michael Sadleir also surveys the history of 'Yellow-backs' in *New paths in book collecting*, ed. Carter, J. W., London 1934, pp. 125–61. The design of ornate gift-book covers is investigated in Pantazzi, S., 'Four designers of English publishers' bindings, 1850–1880, and their signatures', *Papers of the Bibliographical Society of America*, lv, 1961, pp. 88–99. The history of dust-jackets is sketched in Rosner, C., *The growth of the book-jacket*, London 1954; Tanselle, G. T., 'Book jackets, blurbs and bibliographers', *The Library*, xxvi, 1971, pp. 91–134, is a good recent survey.

The nomenclature and designation of the colours and patterns of binding cloths are discussed in two papers by G. T. Tanselle: 'A system of color identification for bibliographical description', *Studies in bibliography*, xx, 1967, pp. 203–34, which is likely to remain the standard work on the subject; and 'The bibliographical description of patterns', *Studies in bibliography*, xxiii, 1970, pp. 71–102, from which the present scheme of classification has been developed. The colour standards recommended by Mr. Tanselle and referred to here are the U.S. National Bureau of Standards' *The ISCC–NBS method of designating colors and a dictionary of color names* (National Bureau of Standards circular 553), Washington D.C. 1965, and its associated *Centroid color charts* (Standard sample no. 2106).

7. PRINTING MACHINES

The development of early-nineteenth-century machinery, including printing machinery, was rarely well documented. The patent specifications are the most detailed source of information as far as they go, but not all inventions were patented; while in the United States the earlier specifications were lost by fire in 1837. For British patents see *Patents for inventions: abridgments of specifications relating to printing*, London 1859 (and supplement; repr. London 1969), although it is usually necessary to consult the complete printed specifications as well in order to see the drawings.

The outstanding early surveys are Monet, A. L., *Les machines et appareils typographiques en France et à l'étranger suivi des procédés d'impression*, Paris 1878; and Wilson, F. J. F., and Grey, D., *A practical treatise upon modern printing machinery and letterpress printing*, London 1888, meticulous and well-illustrated accounts of the machines used in France and Britain during the third quarter of the century, with instructions for operating them. Some of the later manuals also give instructions and imposition schemes for machine printing. Recommended are Gould, J., *The letterpress printer*, London 1876 (and later editions); the various editions of J. Southward's *Practical printing* (from 1882); and vol. iii of his *Modern printing*, London 1899; MacKellar, T., *The American printer*, Philadelphia 1873; and De Vinne, T. L., *The practice of typography*, *Modern methods of book composition*, New York 1904.

The comprehensive modern work is Moran, J., *Printing presses*, London 1973; see also Neipp, L., *Les machines à imprimer depuis Gutenberg*, privately printed Paris 1951. Green, R., 'Early American power printing presses', *Studies in bibliography*, iv, 1951, pp. 143–53, is good though short, and the same author's *The history of the platen jobber*, privately printed Chicago 1953, is the only book on its subject. There are important notes and a few illustrations in the exhibition *Catalogue* for 'Printing and the mind of man', London 1963, pp. 75–81. For news machinery see Southward, J., *Progress in printing*, London 1897, pp. 32–43;

E e

Howe, E., *Newspaper printing in the nineteenth century*, privately printed London 1943; and Isaacs, G. A., *The story of the newspaper printing press*, London 1931.

8. PROCESSES OF REPRODUCTION

The development of lithography and photographic reproduction was rich in patents, many of which are usefully summarized in *Patents for inventions: abridgments of specifications relating to printing*, London 1859 (and supplement; repr. London 1969). Fielding, T. H., *The art of engraving*, London 1841, is an account of the traditional methods of preparing copperplates, together with sections on lithography, photography, etc. [Wood, Sir H. T.], *Modern methods of illustrating books*, London 1887, is a full survey of the processes used in the 1870s and 1880s; while Singer, H. W., and Strang, W., *Etching, engraving and the other methods of printing pictures*, London 1897, is more historical than Wood and includes a useful selection of examples. The minor processes of reproduction are described and illustrated in Harris, E. M., 'Experimental graphic processes in England 1800–1859', *Journal of the Printing Historical Society*, iv, 1968, pp. 33–86, v, 1969, pp. 41–80, and vi, 1970, pp. 53–89. A simple modern textbook is Curwen, H., *Processes of graphic reproduction in printing*, London 1934 (and later editions). McLean, R., *Victorian book design & colour printing*, 2nd ed., London 1972, includes admirable descriptions of the development of colour woodcut and chromolithography.

A jolly account of the trade by a nineteenth-century specialist in wood-engraving and colour-printing is Evans, E., *Reminiscences* (ed. R. McLean), Oxford 1967. Bain, I., 'Thomas Ross & Son, copper- and steel-plate printers since 1833', *Journal of the Printing Historical Society*, ii, 1966, pp. 4–22, describes intaglio printing in the late nineteenth and early twentieth century. Lithography to 1850 has been thoroughly covered by Michael Twyman in a book and two articles: *Lithography 1800–1850*, Oxford 1970; 'The tinted lithograph', *Journal of the Printing Historical Society*, i, 1965, pp. 39–56; and 'The lithographic hand press 1796–1850', ibid. iii, 1967, pp. 3–50.

For the photographic processes it is necessary to consult both the leading histories of photography: Eder, J. F., *History of photography* (trs. E. Epstean), New York 1945, which is full but chauvinistic (Eder seeks to prove that the world owes photography to Germany); and Gernsheim, H. and A., *The history of photography . . . up to 1914*, 2nd ed., London 1970, which is sketchy on the photomechanical processes. See also ch. 32 of Legros, L. A., and Grant, J. C., *Typographical printing-surfaces*, London 1916.

On the development of style in book illustration see the two works by W. M. Ivins mentioned in III. 5 above. Two perceptive investigations of the relationship between authors and illustrators in the nineteenth century are Stevens, J., 'Woodcuts dropped into the text', *Studies in bibliography*, xx, 1967, pp. 113–34; and Harvey, J. R., *Victorian novelists and their illustrators*, London 1970.

9. MECHANICAL COMPOSITION

One book towers above the rest in authority and scope: Legros, L. A., and Grant, J. C., *Typographical printing surfaces*, London 1916, deals comprehensively with the development of all sorts of composing machinery, both cold-metal and hot-, and is fully illustrated; it includes important discussions of the design and production of founts of type, of units and dimensions, and of keyboard layouts. There are useful notes on early mechanical composition in the exhibition *Catalogue*, 'Printing and the mind of man', London 1963, pp. 85-8; but the best modern survey is Moran, J., *The composition of reading matter*, London 1965. See also the section on type since 1875, IV. 4. *b* above.

10. PRINTING-HOUSE ORGANIZATION

In the absence, so far, of any detailed studies of printing-house organization in the machine-press period, we have to turn again to the few contemporary accounts of printing offices and to the printers' manuals of the later nineteenth century. Two simple accounts are Dodd, G., *Days at the factories*, series *1*, London 1843, pp. 326-60; and Abbott, J., *The Harper establishment*, New York 1855 (repr. Hamden, Conn. 1956); also of interest is the official *Geschichte der Kaiserlich-Königliche Hof- und 'Staatsdruckerei* [of Vienna], Wien 1851, which includes detailed statistics of an enormous printing factory presented in German, English, Italian, and French (see especially pp. 195 and 232-61).

British methods in the last three decades of the century are best described by J. Southward, in *A dictionary of typography*, London 1871, 1875; *Practical printing*, London 1882, 1884, 1887, 1892, 1900, 1911 (from 1892 with A. Powell); *Progress in printing*, London 1897; and *Modern printing*, 4 vols., London 1899-1900 — a remarkable and authoritative series of publications. Gould, J., *The letterpress printer*, London 1876 (and later editions) is best on small businesses. For American methods see MacKellar, T., *The American printer*, Philadelphia 1866 (and later editions); and De Vinne, T. L., *The practice of typography*, 4 vols., New York 1900-4.

Investigation of conditions in the English printing trade must begin with the reports of parliamentary inquiries, notably 'Children's employment Commission (1843), 2nd report of the Commissioners', *Parliamentary papers 1843*, xiii, pp. 133-6, and xiv, pp. 238-51; 'Children's employment Commission (1862), 5th report of the Commissioners', *Parliamentary papers 1866*, xxiv, pp. v-viii, 1-52; and 'Report by Dr. Edward Smith on the sanitary circumstances of printers in London' in '6th report of the medical officer of the Privy Council', *Reports 1864*, xxviii, pp. 383-415. Printers' memoirs include C. M. Smith's somewhat fanciful *The working man's way in the world*, London 1857 (repr. London 1967); [Wilson, J. F.], *A few personal recollections by an old printer*, London 1896; and *A stickful of nonpareil*, a 'composite' memoir assembled by G. Scurfield and privately printed, Cambridge 1956.

Howe, E., *The London compositor*, London 1947, reprints many nineteenth-century documents; see also Howe, E., and Waite, H. E., *The London Society of Compositors*, London 1948. For trade organization in the English provinces, see Musson, A. E., *The Typographical Association*, Oxford 1954; for America, Baker, E. F., *Printers and technology*, New York 1957; and for France, Chauvet, P., *Les ouvriers du livre en France de 1789 à la constitution de la Fédération du Livre*, Paris 1956. Plant, M., *The English book trade*, 2nd ed., London 1965, is at its best on nineteenth-century trade conditions.

Recent bibliographical studies which touch on particular aspects of printing-house organization include Steele, O. L., 'Half-sheet imposition of eight-leaf quires in formes of thirty-two and sixty-four pages', *Studies in bibliography*, xv, 1962, pp. 274–8; Bruccoli, M. J., 'A mirror for bibliographers: duplicate plates in modern printing', *The papers of the Bibliographical Society of America*, liv, 1960, pp. 83–8; Bruccoli, M. J., and Rheault, C. A., Jr., 'Imposition figures and plate gangs in *The Rescue*', *Studies in bibliography*, xiv, 1961, pp. 258–62; and Wyllie, J. C., 'The forms of twentieth-century cancels', *The papers of the Bibliographical Society of America*, xlvii, 1953, pp. 95–112. See also the important textual introductions to the Centenary Edition of the *Works* of Nathaniel Hawthorne, for example F. T. Bowers's introductions to *The house of the seven gables*, Columbus 1965; and *The marble faun*, Columbus 1968.

11. THE BOOK TRADE IN BRITAIN AND AMERICA SINCE 1800

Although it does not have much to say about recent studies, Plant, M., *The English book trade*, 2nd ed., London 1965, has useful references to early sources; Lehmann-Haupt, H., *The book in America*, 2nd ed., New York 1952, is rather fuller, and includes authoritative surveys by L. C. Wroth and R. G. Silver. G. T. Tanselle's 'The historiography of American literary publishing', *Studies in bibliography*, xviii, 1965, pp. 3–39, assembles references to research materials. Altick, R. D., *The English common reader, a social history of the mass reading public 1800–1900*, Chicago 1957, includes valuable chapters on the book trade and a collection of best-seller edition quantities. For the later part of the period, Unwin, S., *The truth about publishing*, London 1926 (7th ed., London 1960) is a lively if idiosyncratic account of the trade from the inside.

There were several nineteenth-century authors' manuals; a particularly informative one is [Saunders, F.], *The author's printing and publishing assistant*, 2nd ed., London 1839. General surveys of the relationship between publishers and authors begin with A. S. Collins's continuation of his earlier study (III. 6. *e* above), *The profession of letters*, London 1928, a period also covered in Besterman, T., *The publishing firm of Cadell & Davis*, Oxford 1938. R. A. Gettman's entertaining study of the Bentley papers, *A Victorian publisher*, Cambridge 1960, is good on author–publisher agreements, but is disappointingly short of statistics. A chronological collection of *Letters to Macmillan* (ed. Nowell-Smith, S.), London 1967, illustrates authors' attitudes from the mid nineteenth to the mid twentieth century.

Outstanding amongst accounts of the dealings of individual authors with their publishers is Michael Sadleir's work on Trollope; the most convenient survey is still 'Anthony Trollope and his publishers', *The Library*, v, 1924–5, pp. 215–42. See also W. J. B. Owen, 'Costs, sales and profits of Longman's editions of Wordsworth', *The Library*, xii, 1957, pp. 93–107; Butt, J., and Tillotson, K., *Dickens at work*, London 1957; Tillotson, K., '*Oliver Twist* in three volumes', *The Library*, xviii, 1963, pp. 113–32. There is also much to be gleaned from the biographies of particular authors, e.g. Haight, G. S., *George Eliot, a biography*, Oxford 1968.

Particular forms of nineteenth-century publishing are investigated in Lauterbach, C. E. and E. S., 'The nineteenth century three-volume novel', *Papers of the Bibliographical Society of America*, li, 1957, pp. 263–302; Pollard, H. G., 'Serial fiction', and Sadleir, M., 'Yellow backs', both in *New paths in book collecting*, London 1934 (pp. 245–77 and 125–61); and Johannsen, A., *The house of Beadle and Adams and its dime and nickel novels*, Norman, Okla. [1950]. Michael Sadleir's catalogue *XIX century fiction*, 2 vols., London 1951, is especially valuable for its notes on cheap series. The N.B.L. exhibition catalogue *Victorian fiction* (ed. Carter, J.), Cambridge 1947, offers good summary descriptions of the major forms. For part publication see Dickson, S. A., *The Arents collection of books in parts*, New York 1957 (supplement 1964), a comprehensive catalogue.

For miscellaneous information about edition quantities, see the studies of author–publisher relationships detailed above; for a discussion of large and mid-century editions, see Altick, R. D., 'English publishing and the mass audience in 1852', *Studies in bibliography*, vi, 1953, pp. 3–24. The history of retail price maintenance in the English book trade can be followed in Lackington, J., *Memoirs*, London [1791]–1794; Barnes, J. J., *Free trade in books*, Oxford 1964; Kingsford, R. J. L., *The Publishers Association*, Cambridge 1970; and Barker, R. E., and Davies, G. R. (editors), *Books are different*, London 1966, an account of the case brought before the Restrictive Practices Court in 1962.

A large body of evidence concerning nineteenth-century attitudes to copyright is attached to the report of the Copyright Commission on 1876–8, *Parliamentary papers 1878*, xxiv, pp. 163 ff. Nowell-Smith, S., *International copyright and the publisher in the reign of Queen Victoria*, Oxford 1968, is informative and readable.

V: BIBLIOGRAPHICAL APPLICATIONS

I. GENERAL

R. B. McKerrow's *An introduction to bibliography for literary students*, Oxford 1928, the predecessor of the present work, is a classic of scholarship. Lucid and interesting from end to end, it is particularly rich in examples drawn from McKerrow's experience as an editor of sixteenth- and seventeenth-century texts, although as a history of book production it has been largely superseded by the researches which it helped to inspire. For earlier periods see Ivy, G. S., 'The bibliography of the manuscript book', in Wormald, F., and Wright, C. E., *The English library before 1700*, London 1958, pp. 32–65; and Haebler, K., *The study of incunabula*, New York 1933 (repr. New York 1967), which is still the best survey, though badly translated.

Two names are pre-eminent in twentieth-century bibliographical scholarship: those of Sir Walter Greg and Professor Fredson Bowers. Greg, who was both the clearest and the most original thinker in the history of the subject, made a collection of his penetrating and stylish papers for a collection which in the event appeared posthumously: Greg, W. W., *Collected papers*, ed. Maxwell, J. C., Oxford 1966. For Greg's period see *The Bibliographical Society 1892–1942: studies in retrospect*, London 1945; F. P. Wilson's important article from this collection has been reprinted, revised by Helen Gardner, as *Shakespeare and the new bibliography*, Oxford 1970. Bowers, a scholar of great range and insight, has been chiefly concerned with developing and consolidating Greg's innovations both as a bibliographical theoretician and as an editor. His major work, *Principles of bibliographical description*, Princeton 1949, contains a wealth of bibliographical wisdom and is much more than a mere textbook; his widely scattered papers—often pugnacious, always stimulating—have not yet been collected, but some of them are referred to below.

The theoretical basis of mid-twentieth-century bibliography is now being re-examined by another generation of scholars. Two revaluations of outstanding importance are McKenzie, D. F., 'Printers of the mind: some notes on bibliographical theories and printing-house practices', *Studies in bibliography*, xxii, 1969, pp. 1–75; and Foxon, D. F., *Thoughts on the history and future of bibliographical description*, Los Angeles 1970. Though less concerned with bibliographical theory, E. A. J. Honigmann's review of Shakespearean textual studies, *The stability of Shakespeare's text*, London 1965, also questions conventional beliefs.

J. W. Carter's *Taste & technique in book collecting*, Cambridge 1948 (repr. with additions London 1970), is an elegant account of a pursuit that has always had a considerable effect upon bibliographical studies; and the same author's *ABC for book-collectors*, 5th ed., London 1972, contains much miscellaneous information which bibliographers will find useful.

2. IDENTIFICATION AND DESCRIPTION

The key book here, of course, is Bowers, F. T., *Principles of bibliographical description*, Princeton 1949 (and later impressions), the one comprehensive and authoritative treatment of the subject. Sayce, R. A., 'Compositorial practices and the localisation of printed books, 1530–1800', *The Library*, xxi, 1966, pp. 1–45, is a useful summary of what to look for in unidentified books of the hand-press period; a well-known classic of identification is Carter, J. W., and Pollard, H. G., *An enquiry into the nature of certain nineteenth-century pamphlets*, London and New York 1934.

Specialized techniques of investigation are used with dazzling skill in Hinman, C., *The printing and proof-reading of the first folio of Shakespeare*, 2 vols., Oxford 1963, where individual cases of type are identified and followed through their careers; and in Stevenson, A., *The problem of the Missale speciale*, London 1967, where evidence of both type and paper is used to solve an old problem of identification.

Greg's classic paper on description is 'A formulary of collation' (1934), *Collected papers*, Oxford 1966, pp. 298–313. More recently G. T. Tanselle has explored some of the problems of description which were not fully developed by Bowers, in a series of diligent (if occasionally uneven) papers which are notable not least for their valuable apparatus of references; they are 'The identification of type faces in bibliographical description', *Papers of the Bibliographical Society of America*, lx, 1966, pp. 185–202; 'The recording of press figures', *The Library*, xxi, 1966, pp. 318–25; 'A system of color identification for bibliographical description', *Studies in bibliography*, xx, 1967, pp. 203–34; 'Tolerances in bibliographical description', *The Library*, xxiii, 1968, pp. 1–12; 'The use of type damage as evidence in bibliographical description', *The Library*, xxiii, 1968, pp. 328-51; 'The bibliographical description of patterns', *Studies in bibliography*, xxiii, 1970, pp. 71-102; and 'The bibliographical description of paper', *Studies in bibliography*, xxiv, 1971, pp. 27-67.

A number of sample bibliographical descriptions are included in Bowers's *Principles*; and others are collected in Appendix B, pp. 368-80.

3. TEXTUAL BIBLIOGRAPHY

An excellent short introduction to traditional textual criticism is Reynolds, L. D., and Wilson, N. G., *Scribes and scholars, a guide to the transmission of Greek and Latin literature*, Oxford 1968; it includes a simple account of the stemmatic theory of recension, a subject that is dealt with at greater length by Greg in *The calculus of variants*, Oxford 1927 (a rather difficult book, concerned primarily with the transmission of manuscript, not printed, texts).

R. B. McKerrow's *Prolegomena for the Oxford Shakespeare, a study in editorial method*, Oxford 1939 (repr. 1969), remains an admirable introduction to the textual bibliography of the Elizabethan-Jacobean period, although it was outdated in 1950-1 on the theory of copy-text by Greg's classic paper 'The rationale of copy-text', *Collected papers*, Oxford 1966, pp. 374-91. Bowers developed Greg's theme in 'Current theories of copy text' (1950), repr. in Brack, O. M., Jr., and Barnes, W., *Bibliography and textual criticism*, Chicago 1969, pp. 59-72, a well-chosen collection which includes J. Thorpe's important 'The Aesthetics of textual criticism', pp. 102-38. Bowers has expounded his theories of textual bibliography at greater length in *Textual and literary criticism*, Cambridge 1959; and *Bibliography and textual criticism*, Oxford 1964. Bowers's most important recent paper is 'Old wine in new bottles: problems of machine printing', in Robson, J. M., *Editing nineteenth-century texts*, Toronto 1967, pp. 9-36; the same collection includes B. Weinberg's thought-provoking 'Editing Balzac', pp. 60-76; and J. M. Robson's 'Principles and methods in the collected works of John Stuart Mill', pp. 96-122, together with a valuable selective bibliography of papers on nineteenth-century editorial problems, pp. 123-32. Gottesman, R., and Bennett, S., *Art and error*, London 1970, is yet another collection of theoretical papers, duplicating some of those in the earlier collections. An important study of modern textual problems, as yet uncollected, is Beaurline, L. A., 'The director, the script, and author's revisions: a critical problem', *Papers in dramatic theory and criticism*, ed. Knauf, D. M., Iowa 1969, pp. 78-91.

Composition: McKerrow, R. B., 'The Elizabethan printer and dramatic manuscripts', *The Library*, xii, 1931, pp. 253-75; Hill, T. H., 'Spelling and the bibliographer', *The Library*, xviii, 1963, pp. 1-28; McKenzie, D. F., 'Compositor B's role in *The merchant of Venice* Q2 (1619)', *Studies in bibliography*, xii, 1959, pp. 75-90; Hinman, C., *The printing and proof-reading of the first folio of Shakespeare*, 2 vols., Oxford 1963; Bowers, F. T., 'Textual introduction' to the Centenary Edition of Hawthorne, N., *The marble faun*, Columbus 1968, pp. xlv-cxxxiii.

Index

The following abbreviations are used:

h.p.p.   hand-press period
m.p.p.   machine-press period

References are to page numbers and to figure numbers.